Dr **William Horbury** is a Reader in

Jewish and Early Christian Studies in

the University of Cambridge, and a

Fellow of the British Academy.

JEWS AND CHRISTIANS
IN
CONTACT AND CONTROVERSY

JEWS AND CHRISTIANS
IN
CONTACT AND CONTROVERSY

William Horbury

T&T CLARK
EDINBURGH

T&T CLARK LTD
59 GEORGE STREET
EDINBURGH EH2 2LQ
SCOTLAND

First published 1998

ISBN 0 567 08590 2

British Library Cataloguing-in-Publication Data
A catalogue record for this book is available from the British Library

Typeset by Fakenham Photosetting Limited, Fakenham, Norfolk
Printed and bound in Great Britain by Bookcraft Ltd, Avon

CONTENTS

ABBREVIATIONS

AGJU	Arbeiten zur Geschichte des antiken Judentums und des Urchristentums
ANRW	Aufstieg und Niedergang der römischen Welt
BAR	British Archaeological Reports
BJRL	*Bulletin of the John Rylands Library*
CCL	Corpus Christianorum, Series Latina
CSEL	Corpus Scriptorum Ecclesiasticorum Latinorum
EH	Encyclopaedia Hebraica
EJ	Encyclopaedia Judaica [to distinguish the two works bearing this title, references include a date]
ET	*Expository Times*
ETL	Ephemerides Theologicae Lovanienses
GCS	Die griechischen christlichen Schriftsteller
HTR	*Harvard Theological Review*
HUCA	*Hebrew Union College Annual*
ICC	International Critical Commentary
JAOS	*Journal of the American Oriental Society*
JE	Jewish Encyclopaedia
JEH	*Journal of Ecclesiastical History*
JJS	*Journal of Jewish Studies*
JQR	*Jewish Quarterly Review*
JRS	*Journal of Roman Studies*
JSNT	*Journal for the Study of the New Testatment*
JSS	*Journal of Semitic Studies*
JTS	*Journal of Theological Studies*
MGWJ	*Monatsschrift für die Geschichte und Wissenschaft des Judentums*
NAK	*Nederlands Archief voor Kerkgeschiedenis*
NT	*Novum Testamentum*
NTS	*New Testament Studies*
PAAJR	*Proceedings of the American Academy for Jewish Research*
PEQ	*Palestine Exploration Quarterly*
PG	J. P. Migne, *Patrologia Graeca*
PL	J. P. Migne, *Patrologia Latina*
RAC	Reallexikon für Antike und Christentum
REJ	*Revue des études juives*
RHPR	*Revue d'histoire et de philosophie religieuses*
RHR	*Revue de l'histoire des religions*

RIDA	*Revue international des droits de l'Antiquité*
RQ	*Revue de Qumran*
SC	Sources chrétiennes
SVT	Supplements to *Vetus Testamentum*
TSAJ	Texte und Studien zum Antiken Judentum
TU	Texte und Untersuchungen zur Geschichte der altchristlichen Literatur
TWAT	Theologisches Wörterbuch zum Alten Testament
TWNT	Theologisches Wörterbuch zum Neuen Testament
VC	*Vigiliae Christianae*
VT	*Vetus Testamentum*
WUNT	Wissenchaftliche Untersuchungen zum Neuen Testament
ZKG	*Zeitschrift für Kirchengeschichte*
ZTK	*Zeitschrift für Theologie und Kirche*
ZWT	*Zeitschrift für wissenschaftliche Theologie*

INTRODUCTION

Jewish–Christian contact and controversy were central in Christian origins, and of great moment in later Christian and Jewish history. Gallio cared for none of these things, but his successors in Roman and Byzantine and later administration had to notice them. These matters remain central to an historical understanding of Christianity, and of significance also, in the writer's opinion, for an understanding of Judaism both before and after Christianity arose.

The twelve chapters of this book are formed by twelve of my essays on Jewish–Christian contact and controversy. They deal with the interconnected subjects of polemic and biblical interpretation. Nine chapters are concerned with the ancient world, beginning with post-exilic Jewish writings and the New Testament and going on to later pagan, Jewish and Christian controversy; the last three chapters concentrate on mediaeval and early modern Jewish polemic. These studies were first published individually from 1982 onwards, with the exception of chapter 6, from 1972. A long-standing debate over the historical significance of polemic, both Jewish and Christian, has been intensively renewed in recent years; on the other hand, the abundant primary sources, both Jewish and Christian, remain in large part under-explored.

The book as a whole illustrates some interrelated themes and arguments.

(i) I have tried to show that the Jewish community of the Second Temple period had stronger elements of order and cohesion than is usually allowed, and that these influenced the theory and practice, both Jewish and Christian, which governed Christian separation from the majority Jewish community (see chapters 1–2). Biblically derived ideals of national order and unity emerge especially in Jewish messianism, and chapter 4 includes an argument that second-century Christians continued to mirror a strong contemporary Jewish messianism.

(ii) Against the influential view that the Jewish and Christian communities were largely insulated from one another, I have urged that some debated Christian sources reflect intra-communal polemic, and not simply internal needs (see chapters 3–4, 6–7, and 9). I have also argued that similarly debated rabbinic texts preserve adverse comments on Jesus and his followers (see chapters 2 and 8), and that pagan anti-Christian writing includes genuine reflections of further Jewish narrative polemic on the figure of Jesus (chapter 5).

(iii) Christians and Jews in the ancient world, despite their divergence, can be said to have shared a common Bible and a common biblically-oriented culture. I have argued for this disputed position in chapter 8, considering among other things the dependence of Christians on Jews in the biblical sphere, and the biblical basis of Jewish–Christian controversy.

(iv) An attempt has been made throughout to reassess or introduce primary sources for polemic, including well-known and less-known New Testament and patristic texts (see especially chapters 3–7 and 9), and unpublished or little known mediaeval and early modern Jewish writings (see chapters 10–12).

To present the chapters in order: chapters 1–9 are on the ancient world, down to the time of the later Roman empire. Chapters 1–2 deal with exclusion and the Benediction of the *Minim*, with reference to the Jewish community before and after the destruction of the temple, and the emergence of the Christian body. Then 3–7 treat aspects of Jewish and Christian polemic in antiquity, from the New Testament onwards. The links between polemic and biblical study, and the special biblical culture shared by Jews and Christians, are important especially but not only in chapter 8, on biblical interpretation. Chapter 9 takes up the claim that Christian sources can preserve some genuine perception of contemporary Judaism, with special reference to a subject also central in chapter 2 – the synagogue and Jewish prayer. Lastly, chapters 10–12, on mediaeval and early modern polemic, tackle some of the bibliographical problems which arise in this less cultivated field; but they return to the link between polemic and biblical exegesis, and chapter 12 considers, with special reference to Italy, how biblically-based Jewish polemic against Christianity developed in the early modern context of rational apologetic for revealed religion.

The remainder of this introduction consists of some comment on current discussion of these themes and subjects. It is arranged with reference once more to the successive chapters, considered in order under five main headings: (i) Jewish unity and the Benediction of the *Minim*; (ii) Jewish and Christian polemic in antiquity; (iii) Jews and Christians on the Bible; (iv) early Christians on Jewish prayer; and (v) mediaeval and early modern Jewish polemic. The aim of the comments is to integrate each chapter with current work, and at the same time to offer a measure of general introduction to the subject. The bibliography gives further details of works cited by author's name and short title. It also provides an inadequate indication of my continuing debt to my teachers E. Bammel* and C. F. D. Moule, acknowledged here with gratitude and affection.

---

*Ernst Bammel died on 5 December 1996.

I. Jewish Unity and the Benediction of the *Minim*

In chapters 1–2, on excommunication and the Benediction 'of the *Minim*', it is argued that the far-flung Jewish community of the Second Temple period retained enough cohesion for norms to be preserved concerning offences demanding exclusion; the atmosphere of zeal evident in Philo, Josephus and the New Testament would have sharpened awareness of these norms, and the Eighteen Benedictions themselves form a document of corporate zeal, not without overtones of mission and messianism. The Twelfth Benediction is to be interpreted within this context; it was a focus of the communal cursing of Christians reported by Justin Martyr and later on by Jerome, and was one of a number of measures related to the exclusion of Christians from Jewish communities, and to the polemic against Christianity and its founder which is reflected in a number of rabbinic texts. These measures are considered again in chapter 4, on Barnabas and Justin, and the associated polemic is further illuminated by Christian and pagan reaction to it or adoption of it, as illustrated in chapters 3, 5 and 6. Norms developed in the Second Temple period are important again in chapter 8, 'Jews and Christians on the Bible', in connection with the canon. Lively debate has surrounded the two questions of Jewish unity and of communal repression treated in the first two chapters.

(a) Unity in ancient Judaism

First, diversity rather than unity in the Jewish practice and belief of the Second Temple period has been repeatedly discerned and stressed in the last thirty years.[1] Thus L. H. Schiffman holds that divergent views and groups proliferated and were tolerated while the temple stood, but that afterwards Jewish unity was strongly emphasized, as rabbinic tradition from the tannaitic period suggests, in what was in effect a reconstituted community; some views which had hitherto been current were now left to the Christians, whose rise contributed to the 'shift from sectarianism to consensus'.[2] This position has strong antecedents in earlier study, notably in Wilhelm Bousset's brilliant but one-sided sketch of the ancient Jewish community as a loosely united 'church' embracing a

---

[1]See for example Nickelsburg, with Kraft, 'The Modern Study of Early Judaism', or the editors and many contributors in Neusner & Frerichs, *Judaisms and Their Messiahs*.

[2]Schiffman, 'Perspectives', 147–8, reprinted with slight revision as *Who Was*, 53; *Reclaiming the Dead Sea Scrolls*, 404.

great range of unsystematized opinion, chaos with a keynote of disharmony.[3] In recent years, however, such views have been questioned especially in the work of E. P. Sanders. In *Paul and Palestinian Judaism* he was able to bring many different ancient Jewish writings, rabbinic and non-rabbinic, under the aegis of 'covenantal nomism' – and indeed this label for obedience to commandment under the presupposition of grace could arguably be applied to some works from which he withholds it, including the Ezra-apocalypse and the writings of Paul.[4] Then, in the second volume of the studies he edited on *Self-Definition* some contributions, notably those by F. Dexinger and E. E. Urbach, brought out the limits of communal tolerance and the pressures making for unity. Finally, his monumental *Judaism: Practice and Belief* recognizes Judaism as 'dynamic and diverse', but shows the prevalence of a common Judaism which embraces the particular emphases of the different schools of thought.

Herein Sanders recalls a number of predecessors. Thus J. H. A. Hart, borrowing a phrase from Solomon Schechter, had discerned in the Second Temple and early rabbinic period a generally-shared or 'catholic Judaism' unified above all by the festivals and the common hope. With reference to Philo, Josephus, the apocalypses and rabbinic writings, Hart wrote that 'it is easy to lay stress upon the superficial differences of the different branches of ... ancient Jewish literature'; and he urged that the gospels, Paul, and Hebrews too should be read as examples of *Jewish* literature, as 'witnesses to the Judaism from which the Christian church was to separate itself'.[5]

In 1927–30 G. F. Moore showed in expounding (to quote his title) 'Judaism in the first centuries of the Christian era, the age of the tannaim' how much in rabbinic and pre-rabbinic literature could be drawn into a common pattern; by contrast with Bousset, he gave rabbinic sources pre-eminence, and he often succeeded in showing that they continued and illuminated an approach already discernible in literature of the Second Temple period. His claim that the Judaism thus discerned was 'normative' begged questions, however, notably because he seemed to undervalue the dramatic development of the prophetic tradition in the apocalypses, and to play down its seeming contrast with the rabbinic moderation.[6] In the nineteen-forties

---

[3]Bousset, *Religion*, 469–75, 523–4.
[4]Horbury, 'Paul and Judaism'.
[5]Hart, *Hope*, 19, 23–5; this point is stressed again by Boccaccini, *Portraits*, xxvi.
[6]See Davies, *Paul and Rabbinic Judaism*, 9–10; Neusner, *Judaism: The Evidence of the Mishnah*, 5–14, quoting and discussing F. C. Porter's criticism of Moore.

W. D. Davies shared this criticism of Moore, but emphasized the social bonds of the world-wide Jewish community, drawing espe-cially on Wilfred Knox.[7] In critical reflection on Bousset's work, N. A. Dahl brought out with force and detail the importance of a national and corporate ethos in the Jewish sources of the Second-Temple period, thereby justly modifying Bousset's perception of a loosely-knit 'church' marked by chaotic individualism.[8]

After the Second World War, however, this modification towards a recognition of unity was in some places overshadowed by reaction against G. F. Moore. Thus E. R. Goodenough, in his work on Philo and then on Jewish symbols, argued for a mystical Greek-speaking Judaism which was concurrent but hardly reconcilable with the Torah-centred way of life represented in Moore's rabbinic sources.[9] Morton Smith, from a different point of view, showed the impor-tance of parties in ancient Judaism during the whole post-exilic period.[10] More recently Jacob Neusner, summing up his large-scale studies of Judaism as attested in the Mishnah, urged that the task of the historian of religion is not to range widely like Moore over teachings current in different social settings, but to investigate the religion of a coherent social group, as may be attempted in the case of the Mishnah. Neusner would insist that other writings which clearly speak to a distinctive social setting, including the New Testament and the Dead Sea Scrolls, comparably reflect their own distinct 'Judaisms'; on the other hand Philo and Josephus, the mainstays of Sanders's reconstruction, in Neusner's view speak only for individuals.[11] In this way Neusner's work, sharply contrasting

---

[7]Davies, *Paul and Rabbinic Judaism*, 5–10.

[8]Dahl, *Volk Gottes*, especially 51–143, 226–8, 267–9.

[9]Goodenough's reaction against Moore is brought out in the review of the first four volumes of Goodenough, *Jewish Symbols in the Greco-Roman Period* by H. StJ. Hart, *JTS* N.S. vii (1956), 92–7. The importance of the Mosaic law in both Diaspora Greek and rabbinical Hebrew sources speaks against an opposition of 'Judaisms' in the form suggested by Goodenough (compare Horbury, 'Jewish Dimension', 46–7).

[10]See his *Palestinian Parties and Politics*. Josephus was probably not wrong, however, in maintaining both the importance of parties and a genuine measure of *homonoia* among Jews (*Ap.* ii 179); the context of his assertions is illuminated by B. Reicke's observation that party strife developed specifically at and through the festivals and common meals which were also foci of unity (Reicke, *Diakonie*, concentrating on the Christian agape, but bringing out corresponding Jewish phenomena, e.g. 198–9, 331–2).

[11]See Neusner, *Judaism: The Evidence of the Mishnah*, 12–14, and in Chilton & Neusner, *Judaism in the New Testament*, 19–57 (including criticism of Sanders). Recognition of these special 'Judaisms', however, need not exclude recognition of the broader Judaism, showing continuity as well as variation between times and places, which Philo and Josephus presuppose; the contacts of these authors with one another and with other ancient Jewish literature in Greek and Hebrew (often illustrated in Sanders's work) suggest that they are not unrepresentative.

with that of Sanders, has helped to maintain the widespread current emphasis on diversity in Judaism noted at the start.

The present writer, following those who recognize the prevalence of common traditions, has drawn attention especially to the Pentateuchally based constitutional ideal of a holy nation governed within the covenant by high priest and king.[12] In chapters 1, 2 and 4 it is urged that there was a good measure of common practice and tenet, in particular on the question of norms and exclusion, which was closely connected with the influential concept of covenant.[13] The means by which norms could have been enforced are envisaged as the authority of the high priest, his advisers, the council, and also the king, until the death of Agrippa II;[14] but also effectual in this period and later (see the closing pages of chapter 4) were the inter-communal network of office-holders and teachers, mentioned in Acts and Justin, and the constituency of the more zealous in each place, described especially in Susanna, III Maccabees, Philo and Acts. Their authority could bring about discipline and punishment, including beating such as that undergone by Paul (II Cor. xi 24, cf. Mark xiii 9 and parallels, Acts xxii 19), exclusion from the assembly, such as is mentioned in the gospels (e.g. Luke vi 22, John ix 22) and sometimes also execution, as in the case of the apostates in III Maccabees vii 12–15, or James son of Zebedee, under Agrippa I, and James the Lord's brother, under the Sadducaic high priest Ananus (see Acts xii 1–3; Josephus, *Ant.* xx 199–203).

This claim makes for a considerably less tolerant picture of ancient Judaism than that outlined by Sanders and (from a different point of view) by Schiffman, but it perhaps does more justice to the importance of zeal and messianism in the Second Temple period, underlined by Martin Hengel,[15] and to the light which the New Testament writings (as J. H. A. Hart perceived) and the separation of the Christians shed on Jewish as well as Christian loyalties. It also suggests a greater measure of continuity between the periods before and after the destruction of the temple in 70 than emerges when the

---

[12]See, as well as chapter 1, Horbury, 'Aaronic Priesthood', 'Jewish Dimension', and 'Constitutional Aspects'.

[13]Note the references to scriptural books 'of the covenant', Ecclus. xxiv 23, I Macc. i 57; cf. II Cor. iii 14, and the early Christian use of 'covenantal' (ἐνδιάθηκος) for 'canonical', for example in Origen on the twenty-two biblical books 'as the Hebrews hand down', quoted by Eusebius, *H. E.* vi 25, 1.

[14]See especially Josephus, the gospels and the Acts, discussed in the light of interpretations by E. Bammel, F. Millar, M. Goodman and E. P. Sanders by Horbury, 'Caiaphas', 43–5.

[15]Compare the criticisms of Sanders by Hengel and Deines, 'Common Judaism', 53–5.

main stress is laid on a shift from sectarianism to consensus. Thus, the urgent prayer for ingathering and redemption which is central to the Amidah itself, as the present Tenth to Fourteenth Benedictions show, and to which the Benediction of the *Minim* belongs, comes in essence from the Second-Temple period (compare Ecclus. xxxvi 1–17, II Macc. i 27–9, and see chapter 2, part II); the attention given to it at the time of Gamaliel II represents not a contrast with the period before 66, but the continuation of an emphasis on national unity and hope which was already central in the Second Temple period itself, and which Paul and other New Testament writers themselves reflect.[16]

The ban and exclusion, it is argued here, comparably belonged to general rather than simply sectarian practice in the Second Temple period, based on widely attested exegesis of the Pentateuch, Joshua and Judges. This point has been taken up in Pauline interpretation,[17] but seems not to have been been discussed in further study of Jewish identity as attested in rabbinic evidence. Apostasy and heresy, however, are considered by L. H. Schiffman and Sacha Stern, both emphasizing that the apostate (and the *min*) is treated like a non-Jew – a point brought out especially clearly by Stern – but retains Jewish status.[18] Stern follows Schiffman in underlining the latter point, but the reservation expressed with regard to Schiffman here in chapter 1, n. 31 perhaps applies also to him: the treatment of the apostate with the enmity recommended in rabbinic precept can render Jewish status in practice nugatory, for the apostate is excluded from joining in the communal service of God and from being treated by members of the Jewish community as a neighbour.[19] Moreover, the rabbinic evidence for connection of the ban with a death-penalty for offences against the covenant, such as that committed by Achan (see chapter 1, parts IV–V), suggests both rabbinic continuity with the Pentateuchal interpretation of the Second Temple period, and an aspect of exclusion under which it was viewed in the Targums and rabbinic literature as much graver and more absolute than a regular disciplinary measure – a point which perhaps deserves further

[16]The Amidah, with its blessing on proselytes and curse on apostates, is among the documents which suggest that early Christian proselytism had Jewish counterparts; see chapter 2, part III, and Carleton Paget, 'Proselytism', 86.

[17]Rosner, *Paul, Scripture & Ethics*, 61–93; Barclay, 'Paul among Diaspora Jews', 117, and *Mediterranean Diaspora*, 394.

[18]Schiffman, *Who Was*, 41–53, largely corresponding to his 'Perspectives', 139–49; Stern, *Identity*, 105–112.

[19]This point is made, with special reference to the rabbinic conviction that heresy excludes from the community, by Alexander, 'Parting', 5.

review in consideration of the apostate's status in early rabbinic writings.

(b) The Benediction of the Minim

Secondly, the interpretation of the Twelfth Benediction offered here has evoked considerable discussion. One element in the writer's argument which it seems worthwhile to emphasize afresh is the coherence of the curse on heretics with its context in the Amidah, and the importance of recognizing that context as a prayer for communal messianic redemption, informed, as already noted, by zeal for a purified and united people. Thus in part II of 'Benediction' it was suggested, following a talmudic explanation taken up by I. Loeb and I. Elbogen, that, precisely because the central section of the Amidah prays for judgement and redemption, it was relatively easy to unite in it a formula directed against heretics with one directed against oppressive rulers; both classes of evil-doer will be judged at the time of visitation, as might be suggested by the prophecy of redemption in Isaiah i 24–8, a passage which is echoed in the Eleventh Benediction and expects divine vengeance both on unjust rulers and on those who forsake the Lord (one might further compare in this respect Wisd. iii 8–9).[20] This suggestion on the link between heretics and oppressors has been questioned as speculative,[21] but it begins from what was regarded in the rabbinic period as the theme of this section of the Prayer (Jerusalem Talmud, Ber. ii 4, paralleled in Babylonian Talmud, Meg. 17b). That this rabbinic understanding genuinely identified the theme is borne out by comparison of the Amidah with the prayers of Ecclesiasticus xxxvi 1–17 and II Maccabees i 27–9, already noted, and by the contact between the Prayer and the vocabulary of the Jewish revolt coinage.[22] The theme of redemption is prominent also in 'the substance of the Eighteen Benedictions', the shortened substitute Prayer known as Habinenu.[23] It may be added that ancient Jewish recognition of this theme of redemption in the Amidah would have cohered well with rabbinic preference for recital of the morning

---

[20]Elbogen, *Gottesdienst*, 34–5, 516, E.T. 30, 394.

[21]Alexander, 'Parting', 8.

[22]On the central section of the Amidah as a prayer for redemption see Heinemann, *Prayer in the Talmud*, 34–5. The importance of the Prayer for the ethos of the revolts is discussed by the present writer, *The Jewish Revolts under Trajan and Hadrian*, forthcoming.

[23]Jerusalem Talmud, Ber. iv 3, 8a, and Babylonian Talmud, Ber. 29a, both expounding Mishnah, Ber. iv 3 'R. Akiba said, If his Prayer is fluent, he prays Eighteen; if not, the substance of Eighteen'.

Amidah immediately after the benediction Ge'ullah, on the redemption from Egypt (e.g. Babylonian Talmud, Ber. 9b), and with the notion – discerned in rabbinic sources in the light of the Targums by G. Glazov – that the Amidah should be regarded as inspired, prophetic prayer like that of Moses in his song at the Red Sea.[24] Moreover, such prayer for communal redemption presupposes an atmosphere, breathed equally by Jews and early Christians, in which rigour against heretics and sinners seems only fitting.

On the relation of the Benediction to Christianity, chapter 9, below, on early Christians on synagogue prayer, includes notice of two criticisms, with a response which can now be summarized with some additions. First, it is urged by critics (exemplified by P. W. van der Horst) that those envisaged in the imprecation at the time of Justin Martyr can at most have been Jewish members of the church, and not, as argued here and as Justin seems to assume, the Christian body as a whole; Christians in general, in van der Horst's view, will not have been cursed in the Amidah until the time of the Christian empire, in the fourth century. Not all commentators concur with this criticism, as regards the time of Justin himself. Thus L. H. Schiffman argues that, although Jewish Christians only will have been envisaged under a curse on *minim* at the end of the first century, perhaps by 150 – and certainly later – gentile Christians also will have been cursed under the name *noṣerim*; and J. T. Sanders and S. G. Wilson similarly hold that by Justin's time all Christians were probably included in the curse.[25] In any case, however, the criticism sponsored by van der Horst does less than justice to the early image of the church (for example in Celsus, as noted here in chapter 5) as a minority faction breaking off from the majority community of the Jews – an image further commended as applicable by the fact that the majority, like the Christian minority, included gentiles as well as Jews (compare Tertullian on the *populus amplus* constituted by 'the Jews and their proselytes', as cited in chapter 7, below). This point already applies to the Jewish community and the Christian movement in the time of Paul, and it still seems probable to the present writer that, as soon as Christians were condemned under one of the headings incorporated in the Amidah, the whole Christian body was in view. As argued in chapter 2, before the outbreak of war in 66 existing curses on 'separatists' or 'the wicked' were probably already used with special reference to the sect of the Nazarenes (Acts xxiv 5), where the situation seemed to

[24]Glazov, 'Invocation', 181, also quoting Wisd. x 20–21.
[25]J. T. Sanders, *Schismatics*, 53; Wilson, *Related Strangers*, 179–83.

warrant it. Similarly, the test-measure of a curse directed against Christ was probably also already in use (see I Cor. xii 3, Acts xxvi 11); within the Christian community, the curse on those who do *not* love the Lord (I Cor. xvi 22) will have performed an opposed but analogous purgation.[26] In the later years of the century the Amidah and the Benediction 'of the *minim*' in particular were discussed under Gamaliel II; the Benediction could still apply to heretics other than Christians, but the Christian body will have been no less prominently in view than was the case before 66, and the Benediction will therefore have impinged on Christians together with the exclusions and other disciplinary measures and propaganda reflected in the New Testament, Barnabas, Justin Martyr, and rabbinic literature.

A second criticism of 'Benediction' concerns the shortage of clear evidence, Jerome excepted, that Christians in the eastern Roman provinces after Constantine understood the benediction as applying to Christians in general. T. C. G. Thornton has argued that Jerome's claims concerning Jewish malediction of all Christians were invented, for in other writings both Jerome and Epiphanius (as cited here) think that cursing applies only to some Jewish Christians; moreover, the imperial authorities would have repressed any such general cursing of Christians, and, if it existed, other complaints about it would be expected. Thus, if one were to extend Thornton's argument to include western evidence, one might note that Ambrose protested against the proposed restoration of the Callinicum synagogue without specifying any such feature of Jewish prayer. In reply it should be stressed that the authorities were in any event reluctant to act against Jews, as the Callinicum incident itself shows. Moreover, in this case Ambrose, with much rhetorical force, simply assumes general agreement that the Jews are enemies of Christ; he makes no claim about the meaning of *minaei*, but no such relatively learned and debatable points need be expected from him, for he can win his argument better with doubtless well-worn invective on the synagogue like 'the place of the Jews' perfidy, ... the temple of impiety; ... the place of perfidy, the house of impiety, the refuge of madness, condemned by God himself' ('locus Iudaeorum perfidiae ... . templum impietatis; ... perfidiae locus, impietatis domus, amentiae receptaculum, quod deus damnavit ipse': *Ep.* xl 10 & 14). Finally, as noted in 'Benediction' (Thornton does not comment on this) and again in 'Early Christians on Synagogue Prayer and Imprecation', there is in fact other evidence that the Benediction of

[26]C. Spicq, *Agape* (3 vols., Paris, 1958, 1959, 1959), iii, 81–5.

the *Minim* became known among Christians in the east; for Babylonian Jewish tradition, as represented in Hebrew in the ninth-century treatise *Pirqoi ben Baboi*, holds that the Amidah was prohibited in Christian Palestine. Despite the tendency of this source to emphasize the disruption of custom among Palestinian Jews caused by persecution, it is likely that it reflects official steps taken with regard to the Benediction of the *Minim*, probably under Justinian.[27]

(c) The separation of Christians from Jews

Lastly, the questions of Jewish unity and the Benediction of the *Minim* have both been taken up in continuing discussion of the separation of the Christian body from the Jewish community. Not surprisingly, at least two authors who survey this complex development independently speak of plural 'Partings of the Ways' (J. D. G. Dunn) or 'Trennungsprozesse' (B. Wander). The former concentrates on Christian attitudes to Judaism, the latter on the placing of tendencies and situations reflected in the New Testament within the context of Roman and Jewish history. One further strand in this discussion is the analysis of Jewish identity, considered by M. Casey with a view to such questions as when and if Christians were perceived as non-Jewish.[28] The following outline is intended only to show how the present writer would envisage the parts played in the process of separation from the community by Jewish unity, the Benediction and Jewish–Christian polemic.

Impulses towards separation came from both inside and outside the Christian body. From within, the teaching of Jesus had a separative tendency because of its implied claim to authority, which

[27]To the literature on Ben Baboi and Justinian in Mann, 'Changes' and Veltri, 'Novelle', cited in chapters 2 and 9 respectively, add the (not always correctly reprinted) quotation of the relevant passage in Ben Baboi from L. Ginzberg, *Ginze Schechter*, ii (New York, 1929), 551–2, with translation and discussion, by P. Kahle, *The Cairo Geniza* (2nd edn, Oxford, 1959), 40–41, representing argument from this and other texts for Justinian's Novella of 553 (regulating synagogal bible-reading) as a prime factor in the origins of piyyut (reserve towards this view on piyyut is expressed in the comment on Ben Baboi by J. Heinemann in Elbogen and Heinemann, *Jewish Liturgy*, 223–4); the discussion of an analogous passage in Ben Baboi on another Palestinian custom, in the general context of Babylonian criticism of Palestinian usage, by Gil, *Palestine, 634–1099*, 503–5 (allowing for validity in the tradition concerning persecution, despite Babylonian exaggeration of its impact on the Jews of Palestine); and the brief discussion of Justinian's Novella in Krauss & Horbury, *Controversy*, 62.
[28]Casey, *From Jewish Prophet to Gentile God*, 11–22 (literature), including an attempt to measure degrees of assimilation; an independent but comparable approach to the assessment of assimilation is taken by Barclay, *Mediterranean Diaspora*, 92–102, without comment on Casey.

is best understood as messianic;[29] before his arrest his followers already formed a recognizably distinct Jewish group. Jesus looked, however, not for the foundation of a sect but for the renewal of Israel, and this attitude remained that of his followers, including Paul.[30] The impetus towards separation inherent in a new movement need not imply that specific members or leaders are deliberately seeking separation. Recognition of Jesus as messiah indeed defined Christians sharply as a group with separate meetings and a distinct allegiance (compare the separative curse in I Cor. xvi 22). They rapidly developed a corresponding sense of themselves as essential Israel, perceptible in such titles as 'the saints' and 'the church of God', and somewhat comparable with the self-awareness of the Qumran community; their gentile adherents had been made subject to the messiah of Israel (Rom. xv 12). This ecclesiastical yet deeply Israelite outlook is vividly reflected in the Pauline corpus. Nevertheless, Paul himself writes to defend the terms on which he accepted gentiles, rather than deliberately to separate Christians from the community of Israel.[31] Comparably, the Fourth Gospel reflects exclusion from the Jewish assembly, but also Christian resentment and disappointment at this measure. A Christian sense of accepted separation from the Jewish community seems first clearly detectable in writings from about the end of the first century onwards, notably the Epistle of Barnabas; the polemical claim that Israel has been dismissed from divine election and replaced by the church is likewise most clearly asserted from this period onward (by contrast with the

[29]On this aspect of the teaching see Sanders, *Historical Figure*, 236–7 (urging that, although in Sanders's view Jesus did not infringe the law, his assumption of authority implicitly reduced the importance of the law's demands); Hengel, *Charismatic Leader*, especially 2, 67–71, 87–8.

[30]On Paul and Israel see Moule, *Birth*, 48–50; Watson, *Paul, Judaism and the Gentiles* seems to me right in affirming the importance attached by Jews to communal norms, but mistaken in depicting Paul as endeavouring to separate Christians from the Jewish community (see below). For the outlook ascribed here to Jesus and primitive Christians, including Paul, see Horbury, 'The Twelve and the Phylarchs', 'Constitutional Aspects', and 'Land, Sanctuary, and Worship'.

[31]Watson, *Paul, Judaism and the Gentiles*, interpreting Paul as a separatist (see the preceding note), upholds F. C. Baur's insistence on reading Romans in its historical context, and opposes a 'Lutheran approach' to Paul. Historical interpretation on the lines sketched in the text seems to the present writer to meet Baur's point better than does the argument for a deliberately separatist Paul, not least because of the positive significance of Israel in Romans. Lest Baur be thought to be without honour in his own country, note the advocacy of a consistently historical theology by Köpf, 'Baur'. The rhetorical function of Paul's arguments on the law is underlined by Vos, 'Legem statuimus', in a brief treatment (also reviewing Acts and Justin Martyr on this subject) which broadly resembles Watson's, but presupposes defence of gentile mission as Paul's overriding aim.

stress in earlier polemic on *warning* that God may cast Israel out).[32]

External impulses towards separation therefore impinged on Christians from the majority Jewish community long before the Christians themselves were ready to envisage separate existence. Polemic accompanied 'the sect of the Nazarenes' from the beginning; the charges of magic and deceit originated during Jesus' ministry, and a similar form of anti-Pauline polemic is discussed in chapter 3, below. Paul's own autobiographical remarks attest Jewish measures of discipline and forcible suppression, as noted above. This early and continuing Jewish hostility is most readily explained by the incompatibility of Christian messianic obedience with the zeal, norms and solidarity of the Jewish majority.[33] Separation did not turn on Christian adoption of specially high Christology (a view represented by G. Lindeskog) or on Christian attitudes to Torah and gentilic tendencies (a view represented by L. H. Schiffman and M. Casey);[34] these will have been contributory factors, but more fundamental, both for Christians and for non-Christian Jews, was the special loyalty of the Christian group to Jesus as messiah.[35] The application of the formidable Benediction of the *Minim* to Christians would not of itself have sufficed to bring about separation, but it was consistent with earlier measures, as noted above, and will have contributed to the ultimate Christian acceptance of separate

[32]Krauss & Horbury, *Controversy*, i, 16–17.

[33]Dunn, *Partings* is sensitive to unity as well as diversity in Judaism, but he does not bring out the importance, for the question of separation, of the biblically-derived ideals of Jewish unity and the zeal which they kindled. Bauckham, 'Parting' takes further Dunn's own recognition of the importance of the temple, and well puts it into the context of 'common Judaism'. For the present writer, the *differentia* of Christian opinion on this subject was not so much the self-identification of the community as a new temple (highlighted by Bauckham, ibid., 146–8), as the challenge to the authority of the high-priest and the priesthood – including their position as authorized biblical interpreters – implied by adherence to Jesus as messianic king.

[34]Lindeskog, *Problem*, 122–3, 136; Schiffman, *Who Was*, 6–7; Casey, *From Jewish Prophet to Gentile God*, 31–2 (he holds that the high Johannine Christology *followed* from the exclusion of Christians after 70). Christian attitudes to purity belong to one of the two clusters of questions picked out by Wander as leading to separation; the other cluster surrounds the justice or injustice of the crucifixion.

[35]This position has been represented in different ways by D. Daube in his preface to J. Jocz, *The Jewish People and Jesus Christ* (London, 1949), ix–x; W. D. Davies, 'The Differences between Judaism and Christianity. Torah and Dogma: a Comment', reprinted from *HTR* lxi (1968) in his *The Gospel and the Land*, 390–404 (403–4); and G. Kretschmar, 'Die Kirche aus Juden und Heiden', 16–22. Moule, *Birth*, 57–64 is close to this position, with the proviso that Torah-loyalty might have lessened the relative importance of the authority of Jesus in the eyes of some Judaistic Christians; even for them, however, adherence to the name of Jesus seems likely to have been divisive.

existence. This acceptance seemed to be belied by the continuing participation of Christians in the biblically-formed Jewish culture, but it is illustrated by the *adversus Iudaeos* literature and the mutual polemic of Jews and Christians.

II Jewish and Christian Polemic in Antiquity

The four following chapters (3–6) are mainly concerned with this polemic. The period of Christian origins is represented in chapter 3. Here the Apostle's self-defence in I Thessalonians ii 3 is judged to be a rebuttal of the charge of false prophecy, which will have been used in invective by non-Christian Jews, as I Thessalonians ii 16 suggests, and probably also by Christians who differed from him. Then there follows in chapter 4 a study of apologetic and polemic in the Epistle of Barnabas and the writings of Justin Martyr, from about fifty and a hundred years respectively after Paul. By this time these later authors can envisage the Christians as definitely distinct from the Jewish community. Their writings reflect, it is argued, some Christian attitudes to the Jews and the Jewish scriptures; it is also possible to discern in the Christian sources some Jewish attitudes to the Christian body, and Jewish institutional measures which impinged on Christians (here a return is made to subjects treated in chapter 2).

At this point comment is restricted to Paul (chapter 3) and the Epistle of Barnabas (chapter 4); the treatment of Justin Martyr in chapter 4 is considered below under the heading *Adversus Iudaeos texts*.

(a) Paul and the charge of false prophecy

In chapter 3, interpretation of I Thessalonians ii 3 as rebuttal in the context of Jewish pressure starts from the Septuagintal background of Paul's language. Its approach is therefore akin to that subsequently followed with regard to many other Pauline passages (this one is not treated) by R. B. Hays, *Echoes of Scripture in the Letters of Paul*. It aims not to dismiss the important contacts of the passage with Greek philosophical self-presentation, brought out with special reference to Dio Chrysostom by E. von Dobschütz and A. J. Malherbe, but to show that language which may seem simply to recall this Greek *topos* is also and especially appropriate to the Jewish post-biblical development of the biblical passages on true and false prophecy. Hence it is thought to be of some moment that the ancient Pauline commentators, who were familiar with the self-defence characteristic of philosophers, did not pick out philosophers as the imagined rivals, but mainly judged that either Jewish false prophets or Christian false apostles were in view. The aim of the piece therefore seems not to be fully grasped when R. Jewett takes it as restricting Paul's background in this passage to Old Testament discussion of prophecy.[36] In fact, the specifically post-biblical Jewish *development* of the relevant Old Testament texts, from the LXX onwards, forms the principal subject, and Paul's debt to this development in particular is thought to cohere with the likelihood that Jewish charges are being rebutted, as I Thessalonians ii 16 'forbidding us to speak to gentiles' suggests.

Subsequent study, however, has continued to combine an emphasis on the Greek background of this chapter with the view that Jewish opposition was not envisaged in it.[37] On the other hand, the interpretation of I Thessalonians ii 16 as a reference to Jewish opposition has been convincingly stated and reasserted, and the importance of sometimes strongly ethnic Jewish assumptions in Paul's writing in I Thessalonians has been underlined.[38] The present writer has urged that such assumptions prevail in Paul's future expectations, which would have remained strongly Jerusalem-centred but (here recalling the opposition expressed in I Thessalonians) would have involved the exclusion of Jewish opponents, as strongly hinted in Galatians iv 29–30.[39]

If, however, Paul's Thessalonians were to have moved in a mainly Greek and gentilic mental world, as is widely supposed, could they have recognized an allusion to false prophecy in ii 3? My main contention in this chapter would be satisfied in any case if it could be allowed that Paul himself had false prophecy in mind, whether he was understood or no. In fact, however, I think it likely that the addressees also were sufficiently tinged with Jewish ideas, and sufficiently affected by the Jewish community, to pick up such an

[36]Jewett, *Correspondence*, 150.

[37]Schoon-Janssen, *Umstrittene 'Apologien'*, 39–65 urges (without a special treatment of ii 3) that the conventional language of this passage need not reflect opposition, and that Jewish hostility in particular can be ruled out, for no biblical proof-texts are quoted – but both arguments are called into question by the Septuagintal vocabulary of ii 3. Again without discussion of this verse J. T. Sanders, *Schismatics*, 205 judges that the Thessalonian correspondence gives no information on Jewish–Christian relations in Greece, but he does not consider I Thess. ii 16 in this context.

[38]On ii 16, see Sanders, *Paul, the Law, and the Jewish People*, 190–2, partly following E. Bammel, 'Judenverfolgung und Naherwartung', *ZTK* lvi (1959), 294–315; and Schlueter, *Filling up the Measure*, 184–95. On Jewish assumptions in I Thessalonians, see the comments on the dismissive 'gentiles who know not God' (I Thess. iv 5) in Barclay, 'Paul among Diaspora Jews', 107 and *Mediterranean Diaspora*, 388, and on I Thess. iv 13–v 10 in Barclay, *Mediterranean Diaspora*, 390.

[39]Horbury, 'Land, Sanctuary, and Worship', 219–22.

allusion. They could clearly have done so, if Acts xvii 1–9 could be relied on when it mentions synagogue-centred preaching at Thessalonica, and trouble there instigated by Jews.[40] Both points touch prominent themes in Acts, but seem less questionable than is commonly thought.[41] Nevertheless, even if Acts is wholly set aside, it remains probable from I Thessalonians that even gentiles without any contact with Judaism would have experienced a scriptural and Jewish form of catechesis under Paul (as appears, for example, from the references to prophecy noted at the end of the chapter).[42] Moreover, the denunciation of the Jews in ii 14–16 (see Schlueter's study) presupposes hearers who know the influence of the Jewish community, and are aware of the actions of Jews and Christians in Judaea. Paul could accordingly have assumed that the brimstone whiff of a charge of false prophecy would not have escaped his addressees.

Within the present volume Paul's rebuttal in I Thessalonians is important as, if rightly interpreted here, an addition – perhaps from about the year 50 – to the early evidence for anti-Christian polemic in the form of Pentateuchally based charges of false teaching. It can be ranked chronologically with hints from the gospels of Pentateuchally based charges against Jesus of magic and false prophecy (Mark iii 22 and parallels, Matt. xxvii 63–4, John vii 12, 47), noted here in chapters 2 and 5 and further discussed by G. N. Stanton.[43]

---

[40]Recent studies of the treatment of the Jews in Acts, notably that of W. Stegemann, are reviewed by Wilson, *Related Strangers*, 56–71 (add Oster, 'Supposed Anachronism'); the history of the *Tendenzkritik* of Acts in this connection is surveyed by Merkel, 'Israel im lukanischen Werk', 372–82.

[41]Both are viewed as unhistorical by Best, *Thessalonians*, 4–7 and (in a full and suggestive source-critical study) by Taylor, *Les Actes des deux apôtres*, 264–79; but I Thess. i 9, 'you turned to God from idols', need not be incompatible with the view of Acts xvii 4 that the gentile converts had been 'godfearers' before Paul arrived (here I would differ from Taylor, *Les Actes*, 270), for their baptism would have marked their definitive 'turning' after a period of synagogue attendance, as in other circumstances circumcision might have done. Again, Moule, *Birth*, 158 notes that I Thess. ii 14, on persecution by gentile συμφυλέται, need not rule out the circumstantial account of Jews as instigators of repression in Acts xvii 5 (discussed in the light of ancient urban strife by Reicke, *Diakonie*, 311–14). There is a case for extending to these points, despite their contact with favourite themes of the source, Taylor's observation that the informative report preserved here cannot be reduced to a mere literary scheme (Taylor, *Les Actes*, 265). Merkel, 'Israel im lukanischen Werk', 393–4, similarly finds that Acts on Paul's diaspora mission and the Jews is not wholly schematized or unhistorical.

[42]Eduard Meyer, who saw I Thess. i 9 as one of the very few divergences between the Epistle and Acts, stressed this point in his argument that, nevertheless, the two sources are not far apart here (E. Meyer, *Ursprung und Anfänge des Christentums*, iii (Stuttgart & Berlin, 1923), 86).

[43]Stanton, *A Gospel for a New People*, 169–79, 232–55; 'Early Objections to the Resurrection of Jesus', 83–5.

(b) The Epistle of Barnabas

The polemic reflected in Barnabas, by contrast, is largely Christian, and it is at the same time apologetic, a response (it is argued here) to the attraction and the propaganda of the majority Jewish community, in which hopes for a rebuilt temple are alive. The writer, afraid of assimilation, 'lest we be shipwrecked as if proselytes to their law' (iii 6), justifies Christian divergence from contemporary Jewish fasting custom, and follows and expounds a theory according to which only Christians understand the scriptures, for the seemingly literal sense of the ritual laws was never divinely intended. The Christian polemic of the period before Barnabas, as reflected in the New Testament, verges on but never fully adopts such a theory.[44] In all this, however, the epistle remains, for example in its anti-Roman hopes for the future, deeply indebted to Jewish culture and public opinion. This dependence is still paramount in Justin, probably fifty years later, not least, once again, in the Christian share in a zealot-like messianism looking to the overthrow of Rome, and in Christian efforts to cope with Jewish employment of revised versions of the Septuagint; but Justin also reflects Jewish propaganda and counter-measures, and the discussion of these in chapter 2 in connection with rabbinic texts on Christianity and *minim* is amplified here by an attempt, noted above, to envisage means of enforcement and links between diaspora and homeland. The treatment of Justin's *Dialogue* in these two papers is considered further below in connection with debate on the historical significance of works written *adversus Iudaeos*.

(c) Polemic against the figure of Christ (second to fourth centuries)

Chapters 5 and 6, on Christ as brigand and on Tertullian's sketch of Jewish allegations, deal with polemic against the figure of Christ in the second, third and early fourth centuries. Both pagan and Christian sources preserve forthright critical remarks on the life, death and burial of Christ which are probably ultimately Jewish in

[44]See the sketch of New Testament polemic in Krauss & Horbury, *Controversy*, 14–17; on Barnabas's theory of scripture, Hvalvik, *Struggle*. Carleton Paget, *Barnabas*, 105–7, arguing that a source representing a different theory is also discernible, urges that ii 6, on 'the new law of our lord Jesus Christ which is without the yoke of necessity', does not fit the view of Barnabas (as reconstructed here), acccording to which the republication of the law after the tablets had been broken was the law which Christians only can understand; for 'necessity' regularly appears elsewhere in the context of the abrogation of the ritual law. It seems likely that a source is indeed used here, as Carleton Paget argues, and is understood in a new way – a way which, however, is not impossibly awkward, for on Barnabas's theory the objectionable 'necessity' still rests on the uncomprehending Jews.

origin; they are sometimes ascribed to Jews, and they have points in common with the rabbinic texts on Christianity discussed in chapter 2, but they correspond most closely to themes and narratives of the Toldoth Jeshu. This work is mainly early mediaeval in its surviving forms, but preserves much from the ancient period.[45] Thus at the beginning of the fourth century a pagan anti-Christian writer, probably Sossianus Hierocles, as quoted by Lactantius, presents Christ as driven out by the Jews and gathering nine hundred followers to commit acts of brigandage. This narrative fragment recalls comparable narrative polemic attributed by Celsus to his Jewish source, and paralleled in the Toldoth Jeshu. Similarly, Tertullian takes up the *topos* of Jewish confusion at the Second Coming (now further studied in connection with Cyril of Jerusalem by O. Irshai[46]) to present Christ's return as an answer to Jewish denials of his resurrection; these are adumbrated in the gospels, but occur in the developed form given by Tertullian only in the Toldoth Jeshu – a point which coheres with further evidence for Tertullian's contact with Jews, underlined especially by W. H. C. Frend, minimized by H. Tränkle and others, but explored further in more recent discussion.[47]

The pagan invective against Christians as criminals with which the polemic against the figure of Christ was integrated, as noted at the beginning of chapter 5, has been further illuminated by the late C. P. Bammel.[48] She argues that Fronto was the main source of this invective in its Latin form, as it is reflected in Minucius Felix, who refers to him, and in Tertullian (here she develops earlier recognition that Fronto's argument was known to the Christian writers); his speech against the Christians would have been impelled, she suggests, by the charges of immorality and cannibalism which Justin Martyr takes seriously in his First and Second Apologies, and Fronto would have modelled himself on Cato the Censor's denunciation of the Bacchanals in 186 B.C. In the present context it is noteworthy that Fronto's hostility to Christianity coheres with the hostility to Jews attested in his comment on Hadrian's grievous losses in suppressing the revolt of Bar-Kokhba (Fronto, *Parth.*, 2), and

---

[45]See Krauss & Horbury, *Controversy*, 11–13.

[46]Irshai, 'Cyril', 97–104.

[47]Barnes, 'Tertullian Revisited', 330 judges that Tertullian's awareness of contemporary Jews was underestimated in the first edition of Barnes, *Tertullian*, although it reflects detached and unsympathetic observation rather than friendship; see further Aziza, *Tertullien* (reviewed by W. H. C. Frend in *JTS* N.S. xxx (1979), 318–20), and chapter 9, below, on Tertullian on Jewish prayer.

[48]C. P. Bammel, 'Die erste lateinische Rede gegen die Christen'.

probably also reflected in Minucius Felix's imagined pagan inter-
locutor, on the Jews as the only others who worship the Christians'
'one God' – but the Jews have been 'taken captive with their god' (x
4, 'cum deo suo capti', quoted in 'Pseudo-Cyprian', below). A
similar hostility both to Christians and to the people from whom
they derive emerges at about the same time in Celsus, who nevertheless freely deploys Jewish criticisms in his attack on Christianity.
Fronto thus probably offers one further reflection of the view that
Christians are primarily linked with the Jews, which has been noted
already in connection with the Benediction of the *Minim*.

The polemic of Jewish origin discussed in these papers has points
of contact, as already noted, with the polemic expressed in some
rabbinic passages. In chapter 2 an important text from the Babylonian Talmud (Sanhedrin 43a) on Jesus as magician, false prophet
and deceiver was discussed in the light of J. Maier, *Jesus von
Nazareth in der talmudischen Ueberlieferung*. Maier completed his
treatment of rabbinic material on Christianity with *Jüdische Auseinandersetzung mit dem Christentum in der Antike*. The two works
form a genuinely substantial contribution, far outdoing such still
useful older handbooks as those by Strack or Travers Herford in
their thorough synoptic presentation of the material within its
various rabbinic contexts, their critical study of the development of
the traditions, and their wealth of bibliographical information; but
what is won in the way of a sympathetic critical understanding of
the development and function of these passages within rabbinic
literature and inner-Jewish halakhic controversy is countervailed, it
seems to the present writer, by loss of the context provided by the
direct and indirect contacts of Jews with Christians and pagans.
Thus Maier holds that the Christian community made no impression
on Jews in Judaea and Galilee until the Byzantine period; only then,
in a process which was given further impetus by the Arab conquest,
were figures and stories which had had nothing to do with Christianity given a Christian application. The western diaspora, in which
Christianity had greater influence on Jews, was largely separate in its
development. The insulation thus envisaged is implausible in view of
the New Testament material on the churches of Judaea (see for
example I Thess. ii 14), the information gathered by Eusebius in his
History on the Christian past in the Holy Land,[49] and the Jewish
links between homeland and diaspora discussed above; and this
general view of the Jewish community as insulated leads the author
to keenly-argued but implausible critical conclusions. Thus, in Sanh.

---

[49]On reports relating to the beginning of the third century see Irshai, 'Narcissus'.

43a, the tally between the Pentateuchally based charges of magic, false prophecy and deception and those found in Justin and the gospels, and between the presentation on death by hanging as a rightly-imposed penalty here and in Celsus, where Jesus is the son of Pantera, is explained by the suggestion that the traditions found in Sanh. 43a and in Celsus both originally referred to an otherwise unknown second-century magician, Ben Pandera, who was later on mistakenly identified with Jesus; similarly, two anecdotes in the Tosefta (Hullin 22–3; 24) on the rejection of healing or teaching in the name of ben Pantera refer respectively to this magician, and to another otherwise unknown figure called Jeshua ben Pantiri. It is more natural to take these rabbinic passages as reflecting the polemic against Jesus which is also found in passages ascribed by Celsus to his Jewish source, and in the Toldoth Jeshu, and which in an earlier form is already reflected in the New Testament. Accordingly, a number of authors have rightly continued to explore rabbinic material with the working hypothesis that Christianity may indeed be in view, as noted in chapter 8, below; see also the bibliography, below, under Alexander, Hirshman, Irshai and Visotzky, and S. G. Wilson's treatment of 'Jewish allusions to Jesus and Christians'.[50]

(d) Adversus Iudaeos texts

In chapter 7 an effort is made to reconstruct the setting and objectives of a probably third-century Latin writing entitled *adversus Iudaeos*, handed down among the works of Cyprian of Carthage but of unknown authorship. It has been considered an inner-Christian argument against Jewish Christians, in an informative study by D. van Damme, but in the present writer's view its appeal is far better suited to non-Christian Jews, above all when the author exhorts to baptism.[51] It is a sermon often reminiscent of Melito of Sardis, in which Israel's rejection of Christ and consequent punishment – see R. Kampling's careful study of the quotation here of the Matthaean 'his blood be on us' – is the prelude to a call to repentance and baptismal washing; the preacher's lofty enthusiasm imagines Jewish levites, priests and high pontiffs now assisting a child who offers sacrifice, Christ himself. This flight of fancy reflects not only the biblically moulded Christian image of the Jews, but also the importance of the priesthood and the sanctuary in contemporary Jewish thought and symbolism. The sermon as a whole is fully in

[50]Wilson, *Related Strangers*, 183–93.
[51]Van Damme's view was similarly rejected by Kampling, *Blut*, 17–27.

accord with what is known through inscriptions and archaeological remains of western Jewish communities in Africa and Italy, and with the Christian addresses and responses to Jews from these communities – responses which still include an imagined scene of general Jewish baptism – in Tertullian, Cyprian, and Novatian.

Here, therefore, a work entitled *adversus Iudaeos* is judged to be in truth concerned with the non-Christian Jewish community, which the Christian writer still feels to be enjoying greater prestige than the church. The Epistle of Barnabas was interpreted similarly in chapter 4, above, and in chapters 2 and 4 Justin Martyr's *Dialogue* was treated as a source for Jewish polemic and disciplinary measures directed against Christianity. These approaches to a literature which has regularly been judged to reflect inner-Christian needs rather than Christian–Jewish relations bring the present volume into a long-standing discussion which has been vigorously renewed.

As the present writer has noted elsewhere,[52] A. Harnack (1883 and onwards) influentially expounded the view that most *adversus Iudaeos* literature reflects the inner-Christian needs for self-definition and catechesis, and the external pressure of a pagan rather than a Jewish environment (Harnack allowed for certain exceptions to this rule); he also observed that those New Testament writers who exalt the status of Christ likewise lay emphasis on the conquest of Judaism. J. Juster, on the other hand, in his great work on the Jews in the Roman Empire (1914), gave monumental expression to the view – in which of course he had predecessors, as noted below – that Jews and their objections are genuinely envisaged in writings *adversus Iudaeos*. Each position has been taken up and developed. Followers of Harnack (especially influential in Germany and the USA) have included A. C. MacGiffert; G. F. Moore, 'Christian Writers'; H. Tränkle; D. Rokeah; R. R. Ruether; and the author of the fullest recent survey of this literature, H. Schreckenberg. Ruether in particular developed the point, which has evoked separate discussion, that anti-Judaism could be understood as a consequence of the exaltation of Christ.[53] Juster's position, on the other hand, is

---

[52]See chapter 8, below, and Krauss & Horbury, *Controversy*, i, 13–14. For works by authors named in the remainder of this paragraph see the bibliography.

[53]Ruether, *Faith and Fratricide*, further discussed in her 'Tradition in the Church Fathers: the Exegesis of Christian Anti-Judaism', with comments by J. D. Adams; Gager, *Origins*, 19–34; Langmuir, 'The Faith of Christians and Hostility to Jews' (showing that a high doctrine of Christ has been compatible with varying attitudes to Jews); Taylor, *Anti-Judaism*, 129–31, 149–51 (urging that Ruether is mistaken in maintaining that, although the Christian representation of Jewish arguments is insubstantial, a real Christian–Jewish polemic took place).

represented, broadly speaking, in general works on the subject by authors including Samuel Krauss, Lukyn Williams (too independent to be called Juster's follower, but taking a similar view), James Parkes, M. Simon, B. Blumenkranz, O. Skarsaune, and F. Blanchetière, and in studies of particular church fathers by R. L. Wilken (Cyril of Alexandria and Chrysostom); H. Bietenhard, N. R. M. de Lange, and G. Sgherri (Origen); C. Aziza (Tertullian); and J. Neusner (Aphrahat). Inevitably, some authors scarcely fit this rough division. Thus S. Krauss in his articles on individual church fathers, J. Bergmann on the first and second centuries, L. Lucas on the fourth, and M. Freimann in his study of the Christian dialogues took differing but broadly 'Justerian' positions before Juster's influential book of 1914; Freimann for example developed the view that, although the sayings attributed by Christians to Jewish spokesmen might seem out of touch with rabbinic Judaism, they were probably not unrepresentative of diaspora Jewish thought. On the other hand, some authors follow Harnack in allowing instances or periods in which *adversus Iudaeos* literature reflects contact with Jews, although in the main it solely answers inner-Christian needs. Thus for D. Rokeah there is contact in the early period, but not later on; or for J. Neusner, *Constantine*, Jews and Christians begin to take note of one another's views in the new situation of the Constantinian age, but have kept their interests separate before. More generally, Ruether (see the previous footnote) envisages genuine Christian–Jewish controversy despite her stress on the insubstantial character of Christian portraits of Judaism, and Schreckenberg holds that the Christian dialogues are for the most part *Scheinpolemik*, but allows that occasionally they may reflect genuine contemporary Jewish arguments.[54] Nevertheless, so long as such qualifications are borne in mind, it can be said that modern study has continued to exhibit a division between students of the literature for whom its *Sitz im Leben* within the church is decisive, and those prepared to envisage Christian–Jewish contact as part of its setting.

This division is central in the subject matter of recent books by M. S. Taylor and J. M. Lieu. In *Anti-Judaism and Early Christian Identity: a Critique of the Scholarly Consensus* Miriam Taylor criticizes Marcel Simon, whose interpretation of anti-Jewish texts she calls the 'conflict theory', for it presupposes Jewish–Christian rivalry. This theory can suggest several different motives for anti-Judaism. She classifies these, as found in the work of Simon and others, and examines arguments which use them, with reference to

[54]Schreckenberg, *1–11 Jh.*, 16, 26–7.

the period 150–312.[55] The 'conflict theory' as a whole fails, in her
view, because the church fathers are concerned to attack a symbolic
Judaism, not the opinions of contemporary Jews; the two explanations cannot stand together, and only the former succeeds in
explaining the persistence of Christian hostility to Jews after Jews
had ceased to be a threat. For the purposes of this critique Miriam
Taylor somewhat misleadingly singles out Simon and takes him to
represent 'the current scholarly consensus'. This procedure reflects a
severely restricted survey of study since 1945. Thus Simon is
considered without reference to the debt to Juster which he
acknowledges, or to the importance of his contemporary Bernhard
Blumenkranz, whose approach is closely similar; moreover, the
claim of consensus takes no account of the different view of the
adversus Iudaeos literature adopted by Tränkle and Schreckenberg,
as noted above. Nevertheless, Miriam Taylor's analysis of Simon
and others enables her to identify several types of argument which
are indeed widespread. One such, followed here in respect of
Barnabas, Justin and Pseudo-Cyprian, she calls argument for 'reactive anti-Judaism', a Christian reaction thought to stem from the
church's need to affirm itself over against the larger and more
powerful Jewish community.[56]

    She criticizes the application of this explanation to the Paschal
Homily of Melito of Sardis, noting with reference to Theophilus of
Antioch that a prosperous Jewish community seems not necessarily
to evoke the strident Christian rebukes heard in Melito, and on the
other hand that Melito is taking up an existing Christian tradition of
anti-Jewish invective. She does not examine the somewhat comparable pseudo-Cyprianic *Adversus Iudaeos*, which also includes emotional address to Israel, and falls within her chosen period; but
similar criticism could clearly be levelled at the 'reactive' explanation
of its argument given summarily by Blumenkranz and developed in
the paper reprinted here. This point is underlined by the fact that, in
contrast with Taylor's impression of consensus, only Blumenkranz
and Kampling, among several authors noted here who have written
on this text since 1945, have been willing to see it as genuinely
concerned with the contemporary Jewish community. Its coherence
with other anti-Jewish polemic and the prominence of its summons
to baptism, features for which argument is offered here against

----

[55]For fuller description and discussion of Taylor's work see Blanchetière, *Aux sources*,
169–83 and Carleton Paget, 'Anti-Judaism and Early Christian Identity: a Response to a
Recent Work'.
    [56]Taylor, *Anti-Judaism*, 52–74.

various contrary assertions in the literature, could still be consistent with Taylor's preferred interpretation of such polemic as an attack on symbolic Judaism. Thus the strong emotion of the writer is comprehensible, like Melito's emotion as discussed by Taylor, simply in the context of such an attack; it need not point to the contemporary Jewish strength with which it is connected in this paper.

An interpretation of the pseudo-Cyprianic sermon solely on the lines indicated by Taylor could be questioned, however, in connection with the sermon's repeated call to repentance and baptism, which is rooted in Christian tradition but inevitably evokes, both for author and recipients, the contemporary Jewish community.[57] Such questioning of a solely 'symbolic' interpretation is further implied by the present writer's concluding observation that the stereotyped Christian view of the Jewish community – in this case as a body of hierarchs and learned teachers, representing the ancient biblical law and worship – has much in common with Jewish self-presentation, as reflected in the Jewish symbols and inscriptions met in the catacombs, the Ostia synagogue and elsewhere.[58] (Comparably, Melito's emphasis on Jewish responsibility for the death of Christ, and his rebuttal of the defence that it was foreordained (*Pasch.* 73), both probably correspond to Jewish claims; Celsus ascribes to his Jewish source the claims that 'we punished this fellow who cheated you [Christians]' (Origen, *contra Celsum* ii 4), together with the remark that the death was in any case foreordained (Origen, *contra Celsum* ii 20).[59]) Points of this kind, specific to a particular work, should then be viewed together with two more general arguments not discussed by Taylor: there is evidence for Jewish anti-Christian polemic and Christian knowledge of it, as noted in the two preceding chapters, and there is evidence for Christian respect for and contact with Jews in biblical study, as the following chapter shows. Against this background the interpretation of anti-Jewish polemic as concerned simply with symbolic Judaism seems insufficient.[60]

An interplay between stereotypic views and more genuine perception

---

[57]This point is made in response to Taylor, with regard to the comparable address to Israel in Melito, by Lieu, *Image and Reality*, 213–15 and n. 72.

[58]This epigraphic material is now collected with commentary by Noy, *Western Europe.*

[59]These passages are discussed, with other comparable material from Justin, Aristides, Origen, Commodian and Sanh. 43a, by Horbury, 'The Trial of Jesus in Jewish Tradition', 113–14.

[60]The approaches represented by Simon and Taylor are both criticized as allowing too little for the continual changes in Christian self-perception, especially those involved in the establishment of a Christian empire, by Stroumsa, 'From Anti-Judaism to Antisemitism?', 16–18.

by Christians is in fact envisaged in Judith Lieu, *Image and Reality*, on second-century Christian writings from Asia Minor. This book takes up considerations of the kind just noted, which the author has herself emphasized in earlier work, and it includes sympathetic critical response to Miriam Taylor, as seen already with regard to Melito. For Lieu, the Christian image of Jews – more varied, and more varied in its degree of importance to Christians, than is often recognized – is indeed and inevitably part of the Christian self-image; but it can also offer clues to the imperfectly attested contemporary Jewish reality. *Image and Reality* is therefore a discussion of Judaism, as well as its Christian image, and in the broader setting of Jewish and early Christian studies it stands out for its examination of Christian writing of several different kinds from a single region and century, against the background of epigraphic and other archaeologically-derived information about the Asian Jews. In this regard it converges with S. G. Wilson's *Related Strangers* (1995), a study of Jewish–Christian relations in the period 70–170, on the basis of many of the same sources. In the present context it may be noted that in treating Justin's *Dialogue* Lieu and Wilson both find, like the present writer, genuine reflection of anti-Christian propaganda and disciplinary measures, and of Jewish as well as Christian messianism.[61] Lieu also agrees in finding hints of Jewish institutions and organization, notably in her remarks on the synagogue; but she affirms local rather than more widely concerted organization, whereas the present writer thinks, as noted above, that on the basis of Justin's evidence there is a case for envisaging intercommunal co-operation, including links between diaspora and homeland (see chapter 4).[62]

III Jews and Christians on the Bible

Chapter 8, on Jews and Christians on the Bible in the fourth and fifth centuries, was first published in 1992. It offers an argument for genuine Jewish–Christian contact and debate in the field of exegesis, presented on the following lines. Exegesis was closely bound up with polemic and apologetic, and Jewish as well as patristic sources suggest Jewish–Christian exegetical argument in this context; moreover, the Christians, recognizing their biblical inheritance as Jewish,

---

[61]Wilson, *Related Strangers*, 179–83, 258–84; Lieu, *Image and Reality*, 101–50. Justin on messianism is considered also in the present writer's 'Messianism among Jews and Christians in the Second Century'.

[62]See Lieu, *Image and Reality*, 127–30, 138–40 (without specific comment on 'Barnabas and Justin').

wanted to share the Jewish Bible in the canonical form recognized by Jews. The Jewish scriptures continued to be viewed in each community as an independent body of authoritative writings, despite their close links with the New Testament and ecclesiastical tradition in the church, and with Mishnah, Talmud and rabbinic tradition in the Jewish community. Jewish–Christian contact on this subject was facilitated by the familiarity of Jews as well as Christians with the languages of Christian biblical interpretation – Greek, Aramaic (including Syriac) and Latin. Jews and Christians made common use of some biblical versions, notably but not only the LXX and its revisions, and Christians drew on Jewish exegetical help, personal as well as literary. The exegesis of Jews and Christians diverged over differences of tenet and custom rather than hermeneutical method; recognition of a biblical canon was a fundamental common presupposition, and both communities shared a biblical culture focused on what can properly be called a common Bible. This paper presupposes and develops some observations in an earlier survey of patristic Old Testament interpretation (not reprinted here), in which attention is also given to the period before 325 and to the exegesis of the Jewish scriptures in various settings in church literature and life.[63] There slightly fuller attention could be given to the possible contacts suggested by art and liturgical poetry, briefly indicated here in part 3. The mention of epigraphic evidence in part 3 recalls its significance in the preceding chapter.

(a) Christian–Jewish exegetical contacts

The question of exegetical contacts between Christians and Jews has been discussed again by G. Stemberger, with special reference to overlaps between patristic and rabbinic interpretation.[64] In his concise and informative study Stemberger accepts that Jews and Christians had a common Bible, but he emphasizes – without seeking to exaggerate – the disproportion of Jewish and Christian exegesis, the difference between Jewish and Christian biblical texts, and the difficulty of demonstrating contact between Christians and their Jewish contemporaries. The present writer, finding more community and convergence between Jews and Christians on the Bible, takes a somewhat different general view of both sides. As far as the Christians are concerned, the paper reprinted here gives more

[63]Horbury, 'Old Testament Interpretation in the Writings of the Church Fathers'.
[64]Stemberger, 'Exegetical Contacts between Christians and Jews in the Roman Empire'; compare the present writer's 'Old Testament Interpretation', 770–76, as well as 'Jews and Christians on the Bible'.

weight to Christian respect for 'the scriptures' (I Cor. xv 3–4) and Jewish biblical knowledge; Stemberger does not discuss the implications in this regard of Christian concern for the canon, or of the biblical focus of inter-communal Jewish and Christian polemic. Similarly, on the Jewish side, the present writer gives a less marked pre-eminence than Stemberger to the Hebrew Bible and classical rabbinic literature, and envisages Jewish biblical versions and exegesis in Greek and Aramaic as also important for Jews. Thus the contrast between the lack of Jewish midrashim on the prophets and the wealth of Christian comment on these books, a phenomenon which for Stemberger is a notable instance of disproportion between Jewish and Christian exegesis, would be less striking if the strongly interpretative Targum on the Prophets were mentioned; comparably, the difference between Jewish and Christian biblical texts is qualified if one reckons with the value, for Jews as well as Christians, of biblical versions in Greek and Aramaic. Stemberger cautiously affirms Christian contact with contemporary Jews in the cases of Justin Martyr, Origen and Jerome, but notes that the undoubted overlaps with Jewish exegesis in the works of writers like Eusebius, Theodore of Mopsuestia or Aphrahat fall short of proving such contact; the present writer fully agrees that Christians drank in much Jewish exegesis from other channels too, but does not view the documented instances of contact as wholly exceptional. They were indeed in some cases confessions of dependence on Jewish knowledge, and therefore unwelcome to Christian zeal or ecclesiastical authority, as the opposition to Jerome attests; but they were also manifestations of a widely-attested stream of Christian respect for the Jews as custodians and interpreters of the biblical books.[65]

(b) The Septuagint as a Jewish and a Christian book-collection

At least three individual points of significance in assessment of ancient Jewish–Christian exegetical contact have been considered with some fulness in work issued since chapter 8 was written. First, the use and status of the Septuagint (LXX) among Jews and Christians have been intensively discussed. To begin with a question of use, how far were early Christians who used Greek in fact familiar with the Jewish scriptures? O. Skarsaune has urged that an initial period of great familiarity, reflected in the New Testament, was followed by a stage when testimony-books were far better known to gentile Christians than the biblical books themselves; this

---

[65]See chapter 8, Part 2, and the summary at the end of Part 3.

stage is reflected in Justin Martyr (here Skarsaune draws from the rich mine of his *Proof from Prophecy*), when Justin treats quotations evidently taken from testimony-books as if they were the true text of the LXX, yet also quotes the same passages from the LXX text, and makes occasional attempts to broaden his scope by considering continuous passages.[66] His recourse to the LXX text itself as well as to testimony-collections marks the beginning of a third stage, leading through Irenaeus to Origen, in which Christians endeavour to acquire again a real familiarity with the Jewish scriptures as a whole.[67]

Skarsaune's reconstruction might indicate a period between the New Testament and Justin when Jews concentrated on the scriptures themselves, but Christians on anthologies of excerpts. In approaching the Bible Jews and Christians would then have been dissociated to an extent which exceeds the contrast between Christian veneration for the LXX in forms familiar in the church, and Jewish concern for a corrected text. One might suspect that a position on the way to that envisaged by Skarsaune is already reflected when the Alexandrian Jew Apollos, 'strong in the scriptures', is remarkable in the church for his biblical knowledge as well as his eloquence, and is correspondingly strong in putting the Christian case to Jews (Acts xviii 24–8).

Yet the case for dissociation should not be pushed too far. Testimony-books belonged to the widespread ancient genre of collections of excerpts, and their Jewish as well as their Christian use is indicated by the Qumran 'Testimonia' (4Q 175); this Qumran evidence also underlines the point that such collections are often supplements to, rather than substitutes for, consultation of the scriptures themselves. Christian writing accordingly seems to presuppose moral testimonies, such as could have been common to Christians and Jews (for example in connection with the Two Ways[68]), as well as Christological testimonies developed in a specially Christian way. Varying degrees of familiarity with the scriptures are in any case to be expected among Jews, as among Christians; thus it is clear from the commendation of Ben Sira's biblical exposition in the grandson's preface to Ecclesiasticus that

---

[66]An instance of this is his quotation of Ps. xcvi (LXX xcv) both with and without the testimony that the Lord reigns 'from the tree', discussed in chapter 4, above.

[67]Skarsaune, 'From Books to Testimonies' (not considered by the present writer when chapter 8 was first written).

[68]Brock, 'The Two Ways', noting for example Christian and Targumic quotations of Deut. xxx 15, 19 fused with Jer. xxi 8.

not all Jews in Egypt were equally familiar with 'the law, the prophets and the other ancestral books'. On the other hand, it should not be assumed that gentile Christians were necessarily ignorant of the Bible; many of them will have been, as envisaged in Acts, already within the penumbra of the synagogue. Skarsaune, then, well draws attention to the importance of testimony-books in any description of early Christian exegesis; but this importance is not simply a Christian peculiarity, and, especially given some variation in Jewish biblical knowledge, need not be considered a sign of sharp divergence between Jews and Christians on the Bible.

To turn now to questions of status as well as use, the LXX has been studied under its aspect as a specifically Christian book-collection by M. Hengel, with special reference to the problem of the canon and with characteristic observation of detail and creative conjecture.[69] He judges that, as a collection of books including works like Wisdom which are approved but outside the Hebrew canon, it is Christian rather than Jewish. It would then of course have contributed mainly to demarcation rather than convergence, to use the terms employed in chapter 8.

Hengel suggests that the early and intensive Christian copying of Septuagintal books which is made apparent by Egyptian papyrus-finds sharpened dissatisfaction with the LXX among Jews; as regards the Christian side, he notes the markedly Christian character of the LXX as it has come down to us (for example when New Testament canticles are included in the book of Odes), and he tentatively advances the hypothesis that the combination of the books of the Hebrew canon with acceptable adjuncts like Wisdom in a single collection among Christians derives from late first-century Roman ecclesiastical usage, itself reflecting the contemporary usage of the Roman Jews.[70] I Clement shows Roman Christian use of the LXX collection of books at this period, whereas the New Testament is notoriously lacking in clear attestations of the books peculiar to the LXX; and Hengel points out further that the influence of the Roman Christian congregation would help to explain why Christian esteem for the Wisdom of Solomon and its congeners is attested above all in the west and in Alexandria. The first-century Roman development suggested by Hengel was particularly momentous, in his view, because it is unlikely that pre-Christian Jews accepted a

---

[69]Hengel, with Deines, 'Die Septuaginta als "christliche Schriftensammlung", ihre Vorgeschichte und das Problem ihres Kanons'.

[70]Hengel, 'Die Septuaginta als "christliche Schriftensammlung"', especially 203–9, 270–84.

canon including the books peculiar to the LXX, and in any case they had no central authority to decide canonical questions. (Here Hengel emphatically endorses the rejection of theories of an 'Alexandrian canon').[71] The specifically Roman Jewish use of these books – together with but not on a level with the law and the prophets – would thus have led, via the Roman Christian congregation, to the Septuagintal collection as it ultimately circulated in the church – an essentially 'Christian collection of scriptures', as his title suggests.

With this fascinating Roman hypothesis Hengel illuminates an internal ecclesiastical factor in the Christian reception of the LXX which will certainly have been important. Was this factor, however, so pivotal in the overall history of the LXX collection of books as he suggests? One can agree that there was no pre-Christian Alexandrian *canon* without denying the possible pre-Christian currency of something like the LXX *collection*. Among the Christians, the currency of this collection did not prevent recognition that some items in it were canonical, others not, and there is no reason to suppose that Jews at an earlier date could not have drawn corresponding distinctions.[72] Despite the assumed lack of central authority among Jews in such questions, they are likely to have compared congregational usages, as Christians later did; and the fact that a fixed number of biblical books is assumed in Josephus and II Esdras, and probably also in Jubilees, shows that general consideration had been given to canonical questions by the time of the rise of Christianity.[73] This point is indeed one of the indications of the currency of certain Jewish norms during the Second Temple period, on the lines discussed above. It seems very probable that, as Hengel says, the Roman Jews read the peculiarly Septuagintal books as well as the law and the prophets, without setting them on the same level. It also seems likely, however, that many other Jewish communities at the time of the rise of Christianity followed the same practice. Hence, while affirming Hengel's perception that Roman Jewish practice will have affected a particularly influential Christian community, one might add the qualifying consideration that the use made of the Septuagintal collection of books among the Roman

[71]Hengel, ibid., 183–7.

[72]Compare D. Barthélemy, 'L'état de la bible juive', 41–2; he argues that the LXX reflects the practice of Greek-speaking Jewish circles who had not yet accepted the canon advocated by the Pharisees, whereas I would suppose that the short canon was widely accepted by the time of Christian origins, but that many read other approved books with it.

[73]See chapter 8, part 2, and Horbury, 'The Christian Use and the Jewish Origins of the Wisdom of Solomon', 183–7.

Jews probably represented more widespread pre-Christian Jewish usage.

Correspondingly, the impact of the Jewish Septuagintal collection is likely to have been felt by Christians in other places as well as Rome. Hengel recognizes this point as far as the traces of individual books are concerned. Thus, he affirms the likelihood that Paul presupposes Wisdom, and the Fourth Gospel, Ecclesiasticus; and he allows that the Christian adoption of marginal Septuagintal works like III–IV Maccabees and the Psalms of Solomon may represent eastern rather than Roman influence.[74] To considerations arising from the traces of the influence of the books peculiar to the LXX may be added the likelihood already noticed that other Jewish communities read from book-collections comparable with that of the Jews of Rome. (Hengel is not so very far from this supposition when he suggests that among Jews in many places at the time of Christian origins a 'core canon' was accompanied by a penumbra of other esteemed writings, but he lays emphasis on the variations to be expected.)[75] Hengel's attractive indication of a specifically Christian factor in Christian reception of the LXX might then be complemented by a second qualifying point, from the background of the studies collected here: Jewish usage with regard to the biblical books is likely for a long while to have been at least as important a consideration for Christians as the internal influence of the Christian Roman congregation.

Hengel's study, concentrated as it is on the Christian treatment of the sacred books, inevitably highlights the possibility of Christian innovation and of divergence between Christian and Jewish bible-reading. The present writer would sometimes attribute greater strength than Hengel to the conservative Christian instinct of continuing in the Jewish biblical inheritance. Thus, to take a small but not insignificant example, when Wisdom is named in the Muratorian fragment after the principal New Testament books, Hengel takes up the long-standing opinion that this placing reflects a Christian endeavour to associate the well-loved Wisdom of Solomon with the New Testament books, and he adds the suggestion that such an endeavour is well-suited to Christian Rome about the end of the second century.[76] More probably, however, the mention of Wisdom at this point in the fragment simply reflects the view that Wisdom is one of the non-canonical but acceptable Old Testament

---

[74]Hengel, 'Die Septuaginta als "christliche Schriftensammlung"', 268–9, 281.
[75]Hengel, ibid., 269–70.
[76]Hengel, ibid., 231–2.

books, which in other Christian sources too are named after the canonical books of the Old and New Testaments.[77] This association and separation of canonical and approved non-canonical writings in the listing of biblical books itself probably reflects Jewish practice, as is suggested by the convergence between rabbinic passages on 'outside books' and Origen's report of a Jewish book-list with the Maccabees 'outside'.[78] Hengel does not discuss this particular aspect of Origen's list, but he allows for the association yet distinction of canonical and approved books among the Roman Jews at the time of Domitian, and envisages that the threefold Christian distinction between canonical, approved and prohibited books arose in the second century against a background which included argument with Jews.[79]

Correspondingly, therefore, Hengel's hypothesis itself allows for some functioning of the LXX collection as a 'common bible' of Jews and Christians, at least in Rome and for a time. The present writer would be inclined to enlarge the sphere of this 'common Bible', not least because the evident Christian wish to possess the scriptures reverenced by Jews would have hindered Christian adoption of a strikingly non-Jewish collection. Against the background of a Jewish distinction between canonical and 'outside' books it can be argued that the Septuagintal combination of the books of the Hebrew canon with approved extra-canonical adjuncts will not have contradicted the insistence on the Hebrew canon evident in Josephus and II Esdras, and is likely to have been widely established in Jewish usage. In his survey of Christian debate on the canon Hengel indeed recognizes the strong Christian desire to possess the scriptures of the Jews which is emphasized in part 2 of 'Jews and Christians on the Bible'.[80]

In sum, Hengel's work properly directs attention to the Christian treatment of the LXX collection, and to the largely though not entirely Christian character of its surviving attestation in manuscripts. His Roman hypothesis identifies an important internal Christian influence on ecclesiastical reception of the LXX book-collection. It seems likely, however, that such a collection was more widely current among Jews than his hypothesis would allow. His valuable reminders of the Christian transmission to which the LXX

---

[77]Horbury, 'The Wisdom of Solomon in the Muratorian Fragment', 152–6.

[78]Eusebius, H. E. vi 25, 1, cited above; see chapter 8, part 2, and Horbury, 'The Christian Use and the Jewish Origins of the Wisdom of Solomon', 185–6, with notes 17–18.

[79]Hengel, 'Die Septuaginta als "christliche Schriftensammlung"', 280–1, 225–6, respectively.

[80]Hengel, 'Die Septuaginta als "christliche Schriftensammlung"', 270.

is chiefly owed should be complemented by appreciation of the great strength of Jewish influence on early Christians in this matter, and of the probably pre-Christian currency of the collection. The LXX then emerges as a Jewish as well as a Christian collection, and a link as well as a barrier between Jews and Christians.

On the status of the LXX, a striking counterpart to Hengel's study of its Christian use is formed by G. Veltri's argument for the abidingly high place of the LXX Pentateuch among Jews after the rise of Christianity. He urges that the LXX Pentateuch was accorded continuing esteem in rabbinical texts (see especially Meg. 9a–b and parallels) as an alternative form of the Torah, on the lines sketched earlier in Philo.[81] He establishes this point, but seems less successful in his associated argument that there was no Jewish opposition to the LXX until the time of Justinian.[82] Early Christians had the impression that Jews were ready to reject LXX renderings, and Jewish revisions of the LXX were current still earlier. Rabbinic tradition correspondingly includes criticism as well as praise of the LXX. Although the criticism appears in the tractate Sopherim, which was edited relatively late, it need not reflect simply the Byzantine situation, as Veltri suggests. Veltri's work is important, however, as discouraging any simplistic assumption that Christians were all for the LXX, Jews all against it. More probably, Christian use of the LXX added to existing Jewish reservations over its value as a translation, as noted by Hengel with special reference to intensive Christian copying; the Christian tension between veneration for the LXX and recognition of its shortcomings was peculiarly painful because of the value of Septuagintal proof-texts for Christianity, but it will have reflected a similar tension between veneration and criticism among Jews. In both attitudes the Christians followed Jewish biblical culture.

(c) Jerome and Christian recourse to Jewish tradition

Secondly, Jerome is viewed in chapter 8 as representing a widespread Christian instinct of respect for the Hebrew text and the Jewish canon. In his particular philological method, however, he has recently been assessed as a thorough innovator. A. Kamesar has argued that the priority which Jerome gave to the Hebrew text and rabbinic interpretation, in conjunction with the Jewish or Jewish-

---

[81]Veltri, *Eine Tora für den König Talmai*; 'Der griechische Targum Aquilas'; 'Die Novelle 146'.

[82]See the present writer's review in *Bulletin of Judaeo-Greek Studies* 16 (Summer, 1995), 20–21.

inspired revisions of the LXX by Aquila, Symmachus and Theodotion, was an essentially new method, worked out in the tradition of Greek and Latin philology. The importance of the philological impulse for Jerome has been independently stressed by C. Markschies.[83] In Kamesar's view, Jerome was not even anticipated by Origen, who despite his work on the Hebrew text and traditions and the Jewish revisions of the LXX remained fundamentally LXX-centred. For this reason Jerome was right in describing his own Hebrew Questions on Genesis, in which his new philological method is employed, as a hitherto unheard-of work.[84]

The special question of the originality of Jerome's philological approach to scripture is of course distinct from, as well as connected with, the larger question of his location within a Christian tradition of respect for Jewish biblical knowledge. As far as assessment of Jerome's method is concerned, Kamesar's view of Origen is debatable,[85] and the purposes of the Hebrew Questions continue to be discussed; C. T. R. Hayward shows that their novelty probably lay not specially in their presentation of a method followed in Jerome's rendering of the Hebrew text, but more particularly in their collection of Jewish interpretative traditions.[86] S. Kamin argued (against the tendency continued by both Kamesar and Markschies) that the importance of philological motives for Jerome has been overrated; his theological motives should be taken seriously, notably when he supposes that a Christian might do better as a translator of the Hebrew than the pre-Christian Seventy, from whom the historical fulfilment of the prophecies they heard was still veiled.[87] However this particular motive should be ranked, her general indication of the importance of Christian convictions should be heeded. Nevertheless, the view of Jerome as an innovator in a larger sense has prima facie support not only from his own commendation

[83]Markschies, 'Hieronymus und die "Hebraica Veritas"'; the importance earlier ascribed to philological motivation by D. Barthélemy and P. Benoit is noted by Kamin, 'Hebraica Veritas', n. 7.

[84]Kamesar, Jerome, Greek Scholarship, and the Hebrew Bible, especially 76–81, 174–5, 189–94; the description of the forthcoming Hebrew Questions as 'opus novum et tam Graecis quam Latinis usque ad id locorum inauditum' appeared in Jerome's preface to his version of Eusebius on Hebrew names.

[85]This point is noted in the review by J. N. B. Carleton Paget in Bulletin of Judaeo-Greek Studies 13 (Winter, 1993), 18–21.

[86]Hayward, Jerome's Hebrew Questions on Genesis, 7–14.

[87]Kamin, 'Hebraica Veritas', with special reference to Jerome's Prologue to the Pentateuch, 'illi interpretati sunt ante adventum Christi et quod nesciebant dubiis protulere sententiis, nos autem post passionem et resurrectionem eius non tam prophetiam quam historiam scribimus; aliter enim audita, aliter visa narrantur' (also discussed by Markschies, 'Hieronymus und die "Hebraica Veritas"', 162–3).

of his literary undertakings (a context in which claims to offer something new are only to be expected), but also from the opposition on behalf of the LXX which he continually rebutted in varying ways.[88] His rebuttals include, however, at least one argument worthy of respect: Jerome's claim that he had many Christian predecessors in appealing to Hebrew tradition (*Apology against Rufinus*, i 13, ii 34).[89] Similarly, the priority which he gave to the Hebrew canon, although it is sometimes regarded as an innovation, represented a widespread and long-standing Christian view;[90] it was particularly influential in the eastern empire, it was – like esteem for Aquila, Symmachus and Theodotion – a point common to Jerome and Rufinus, and it reflects Jewish opinion, as noted already.[91] Due credit can therefore be given both to Jerome's claim to offer something new in the Hebrew Questions, and to his belief – justified with regard both to exegesis and to the canon – that he stood in a long Christian tradition of appealing to Hebrew biblical knowledge. In this tradition, cultivated philological learning was not far from that less educated Christian instinct of respect for the Jews which ecclesiastical authority often sought to quell, as in Chrysostom's sermons in the east or the canons of the council of Elvira in the west.[92]

(d) Jews and Christians in the pagan literary environment

Thirdly, the importance of the pagan literary environment shared by Jews and Christians, emphasized in part 1 of 'Jews and Christians on the Bible', has been further explored in connection with Jewish–Christian contact in exegesis. The widespread current concern with early Christian writers as representatives of Greek and Roman literary convention has already been noted in study of Jerome. A. Kamesar has directed this concern towards patristic comment on

[88]These are analysed by Markschies, 'Hieronymus und die "Hebraica Veritas"', in his argument that Jerome's impulse towards the Hebrew was primarily philological rather than theological.

[89]See Horbury, 'Old Testament Interpretation', 770–76.

[90]That Jerome's remarks on the canon should be viewed against the background of Christian canon-discussion is noted by Hengel, 'Die Septuaginta als "christliche Schriftensammlung"', 227.

[91]Chapter 8, Part 2; the association of acceptable 'outside books' with the Hebrew canon is ascribed to Christian adoption of Jewish usage in Horbury, 'The Wisdom of Solomon in the Muratorian Fragment' and 'The Christian Use and Jewish Origins of the Wisdom of Solomon', 185–94.

[92]The importance of this instinct in forming the ecclesiastical situation envisaged in writings *adversus Iudaeos* is justly underlined, with reference to Ignatius of Antioch, Chrysostom and Agobard, by Skarsaune, 'Philo-Semitism'.

Jewish traditions, moving from the questions whether and how Jewish tradition was known (compare the discussion of Stemberger, above) to the question of how it was assessed. Kamesar urges that the varying Christian views of narrative haggadah – Jewish expansion and elaboration of the biblical text in narrative form – were determined less by specifically Christian attitudes than by approaches grounded in the teaching of Greek and Roman grammarians; and he suggests that Josephus, similarly, formulated his positive estimate of Jewish historical traditions against this philological background.[93] The recognition of the importance of the Greek philological tradition which is clearly due need not rule out allowance (as indicated by Kamin) for the concurrent or overriding influence of specifically Christian or Jewish tenets in particular cases.

Judgements on the relation of Jews in particular to the pagan literary environment in the later Roman empire are bound up with the question how far Jews entered into Latin as opposed to Greek literary culture. This question is correspondingly central in assessment of the Jewish share in biblical interpretation in Latin in antiquity. Did Jews produce a Latin Jewish literature to set beside their rich literary inheritance in Greek? This question is sharpened by the striking importance of Greek, as opposed to Latin, in Jewish inscriptions from western Europe. An affirmative answer on Jewish Latin writing was nevertheless favoured in chapter 8, part 3. The subject has been reconsidered by L. V. Rutgers, who upholds the attribution of the *Collatio Legum* and the *Epistula Annae ad Senecam* to Jewish authors.[94] Some Jewish use of the Old Latin and Jewish participation in Latin-based exegetical discussion could then be envisaged without difficulty.

IV Early Christians on Jewish Prayer

Chapter 9 returns to the theme of Christian participation in Jewish culture. Were Christians in a position to receive some impression of Jewish prayer practice? Some New Testament and patristic passages which appear to reflect knowledge of the synagogue and synagogue prayer and imprecation are considered. Students of the history of Jewish prayer customarily draw on Christian sources, but there remains material which seems not to have been fully exploited;

---

[93]Kamesar, 'The Evaluation of the Narrative Aggada in Greek and Latin Patristic Literature' and 'The Narrative Aggada as Seen from the Graeco-Latin Perspective'.
[94]Rutgers, *Late Ancient Rome*, 210–59.

moreover, the predominantly polemical tone of Christian reference raises the questions about its historical value which were considered above in connection with *adversus Iudaeos* literature.

The approach followed here is not wholly dissimilar from that adopted by Lieu, *Image and Reality*, but the focus of interest is on the hints concerning the customs of the Jewish community rather than the total image to which the hints belong. It is argued that Christian literature, although it inevitably represents a polemical and distorted view of contemporary Jews, preserves valuable information on some debated aspects of the history of Jewish common prayer, including the rise of the synagogue, the significance of the ark, and the development of public prayer and its associated gestures. In the last section, as noted already, the Benediction 'of the *Minim*' is reconsidered.

New Testament investigation on these lines is now represented by D. K. Falk's study of Acts on the prayers of the Jerusalem church in the light of information on Jewish prayer from other sources; he shows that Acts on this subject corresponds to what is known of Jewish prayer before the destruction of Jerusalem.[95] In the study of Jewish prayer, work of this kind on New Testament and patristic writings can perhaps stand beside the line of inquiry which has found adoption of Jewish prayer in Christian sources, notably in the prayers of I Clement, the Didache and the Apostolic Constitutions. This line has been followed recently in G. Glazov's argument that the recitation of Ps. li 17 – in petition for the opening of the lips – before the Tefillah lies behind its appearance in Christian morning prayer, even though he judges that its Jewish use will not have been fixed until the third century.[96] An argument such as this, whatever its force, depends in any case on two presuppositions which receive some confirmation from the study of explicit patristic references to Jewish prayer: on the Christian side, some continuing awareness of synagogue usage, and on the Jewish side, a certain regularity in such usage, in the homeland and beyond.

V Mediaeval and Early Modern Jewish Polemic

The remaining three chapters deal with mediaeval and early modern Jewish polemic. The greater degree of concentration on bibliographical questions encountered in this section reflects the fact that much

---

[95]Falk, 'Jewish Prayer Literature and the Jerusalem Church in Acts'.
[96]Glazov, 'The invocation of Ps. 51:17'.

mediaeval Jewish anti-Christian polemic remains unpublished, partly by reason of external and internal censorship in the past.[97] Nevertheless, in the sixteenth, seventeenth and eighteenth centuries some Hebrew polemical works were quoted or published by Christian students of Hebrew manuscripts, and Jews themselves printed such works in havens like Constantinople and Leghorn. The unpublished work from a Basle MS. considered in chapter 10 as 'The Basle Nizzahon' shares some of its material with a work well known through seventeenth-century Christian publication under the title Nizzahon Vetus.

Nizzaḥon, 'Confutation' or 'Victory', was a popular mediaeval title for polemical writings. Theodor Hackspan (1644) edited the work of this title by Lipmann Mühlhausen, who had experienced anti-Jewish measures in Prague at the end of the fourteenth century, and J. C. Wagenseil (1681) edited and translated the older and anonymous writing known as Nizzaḥon yashan, 'Nizzahon Vetus', which had been extensively quoted by Sebastian Munster in the sixteenth century. Both works belong to the fundamentally biblical polemic of Germany and northern France, based on proof-texts and in subject-matter closely recalling the early Christian and mediaeval writings adversus Iudaeos, and full of lively references to oral debate; philosophical polemic was not unknown in these northern regions, but is more typical of Provence, Spain and Italy.[98] The biblical orientation of these writings extended to criticism of a series of New Testament texts as well as rebuttal of Christian interpretation of texts from the Hebrew scriptures. The re-edition of Nizzahon Vetus with translation and commentary by David Berger forms a valuable introduction to the Franco-German biblical genre of polemical literature, which is also represented in several of the writings surveyed more recently by Hanne Trautner-Kromann.[99] Just as the ancient adversus Iudaeos texts are linked with biblical exegesis, so these mediaeval writings are closely linked with the efflorescence of Jewish biblical interpretation in northern France and the Rhineland, from Rashi in the eleventh century onwards; Jewish biblical commentaries from this setting include much polemic, and this aspect of them did not escape such contemporary Christian

[97]For a survey of authors and works, with literature, see Krauss & Horbury, Controversy, i, 201–61.
[98]Lasker, 'Jewish Philosophical Polemics in Ashkenaz'.
[99]See Berger, Debate, reviewed in JTS N.S. xxxiv (1983), 329–37; Berger, 'Mission to the Jews and Jewish-Christian Contacts'; Trautner-Kromann, Shield and Sword, especially 90–116.

students of Jewish exegesis as Andrew of St Victor or, later on, Nicholas de Lyra.[100]

In the paper reprinted as chapter 10 a Basle MS. bearing this title *Nizzaḥon* is identified as a copy of an unpublished mediaeval polemic known hitherto only in a shorter form from a Rome MS. Once again it is predominantly concerned with biblical proof-texts, including criticism of New Testament texts, and stems from northern France or Germany. Its material overlaps with that of Nizzahon Vetus, but it has much of its own to offer. A summary of its opening section suggests that it is concerned not just to answer Christian claims, but also to build up a Jewish hope in which the rise and future fall of Christianity are prophetically foretold as a prelude to the messianic restoration of Israel. Herein it recalls the treatment of Christianity in Maimonides' *Code*, but it also forms an analogue to the early Christian expectations of the future baptism of the Jews, discussed above in connection with pseudo-Cyprian.

The unpublished handwritten catalogue of the Basle Hebrew MSS. by J. Prijs, not known to me when I was working on this study, has now been printed in a shortened but supplemented edition.[101] Prijs did not of course follow the erroneous marginal note, identifying this as Lipmann Mühlhausen's work, which was taken up in the *List of Photocopies* (see chapter 9, section I, below). He identifies the hand of the Latin description discussed in section II as that of Johann Buxtorf the younger (who was mentioned there as a possible author, although preference was given to his son). Prijs holds that much material in the work is of the twelfth century or earlier, although later editorial work is also likely. The background of polemic in this period includes not only intensive Christian Hebrew study, but also the ritual murder charges which began in the mid-twelfth century with William of Norwich, and seem to be hinted at in the Hebrew polemic, as well as intensive devotion to the humanity of Jesus – a point which the tradition-based polemic against Jesus in the Hebrew work would have touched acutely (see chapter 9, part V).[102]

Contemporary background and oral debate is also reflected in Ibn

---

[100]See Kamin, *Jews and Christians*; Krauss & Horbury, *Controversy*, i, 79–88 (literature).

[101]*Die Handschriften der Universität Basel: Die hebräischen Handschriften. Katalog auf Grund der Beschreibungen von Joseph Prijs redigiert von Bernhard und David Prijs. Mit einem Anhang von Stephen G. Burnett und einem Beitrag von Thomas Willi.* (Basel, 1994). For the MS. discussed here see no. 42, pp. 54–5.

[102]On this background see Trautner-Kromann, *Shield and Sword*, 111–14 (on partly parallel passages in Nizzahon Vetus); Krauss & Horbury, *Controversy*, i, 73–80 and A. Sapir Abulafia, *Christians and Jews*, 134–5.

Shaprut's *Touchstone*, a Hebrew defence of Judaism and critique of Christianity from fourteenth-century Spain, discussed in chapter 11.[103] This large-scale composition is philosophical and theological as well as biblical in its themes, following the southern mode; it is based on the twelfth-century work of the probably Spanish polemist Jacob b. Reuben, which has a philosophical preface to a mainly biblical treatment, incorporating a criticism of the New Testament.[104] The *Touchstone*, two centuries later, represents a response to mission, repression and polemic in Aragon, Navarre and Castile, including Christian argument from and against the haggadoth of the Talmud, as led towards the end of the fourteenth century by cardinal Pedro de Luna (later the antipope Benedict XIII). Christian writings from earlier in the century by master Alphonsus of Valladolid (formerly Abner of Burgos) remained extremely influential at this point.[105] The criticisms of Christianity in the *Touchstone* incorporate a Hebrew rendering of Matthew, edited by George Howard.[106]

The *Touchstone* attests the continuing importance of the biblical argument in a setting where the philosophical and theological discussion of articles of faith is a primary interest, and where attacks on the Talmud, the Toldoth Jeshu and Jewish prayer urgently need rebuttal. In this situation Ibn Shaprut still followed Jacob b. Reuben in combining a defence of Jewish interpretation of the Hebrew scriptures, focused on individual proof-texts, with an attack on the Christian New Testament; and in refuting Alphonsus's refutation of Jacob b. Reuben he had to extend his treatment of proof-texts as well as other portions of his work.

The paper reprinted as chapter 11 is an attempt to elucidate the textual problem of the *Touchstone*, which is mainly known in versions containing fifteen and sixteen books, respectively. Alexander Marx held that only one of the many MSS. – a copy in which no less than seventeen books appear – represented the work in the author's final revision. Here it is urged that this seventeen-book copy is in fact a conflation of the two better-attested versions containing

[103]Discussion and literature in Krauss & Horbury, *Controversy*, i, 167–8, 241–2.

[104]On his work, composed in Gascony or in Huesca in Aragon, depending on identification of a variously transmitted place-name in his foreword, see Krauss & Horbury, *Controversy*, i, 216–17, and R. Schmitz (general introduction, assuming composition in Gascony) and C. del Valle (arguing for Huesca) in del Valle (ed.), *Polémica Judeo-Cristiana*, 49–58, 59–65.

[105]On Alphonsus/Abner see Sainz de la Maza, *Alfonso*; Krauss & Horbury, *Controversy*, i, 94 (literature); and C. del Valle, 'El libro de las Batallas de Dios, de Abner de Burgos'.

[106]Howard, *Hebrew Gospel of Matthew* (1995), forming the second edition of his *The Gospel of Matthew according to a Primitive Hebrew Text* (Macon, 1987). For discussion see the following footnote.

fifteen and sixteen books, and that, as M. Steinschneider thought, these two versions respectively represent the work before and after its last major revision by the author. This revision seems in fact to be the last stage in a long process of composition and revision, which itself reflects the pressure of an unremitting argumentative barrage from the other side.

Ibn Shaprut's Hebrew text of Matthew has been discussed elsewhere by the present writer.[107] Its interesting contacts with old Christian gospel texts such as the Old Syriac, the Old Latin and the Diatessaron are most naturally explained not from the assumption that the Hebrew text is older still, but from the continuing influence of these early text forms among mediaeval Christians.

Lastly, the employment in the early modern period of the biblically focused polemic inherited from the mediaeval and ancient worlds is considered in chapter 12. Italy in the seventeenth and eighteenth centuries rivals Holland as the setting in which Jewish polemical literature probably reached its climax. This phenomenon is studied here through Judah Briel, chief rabbi of Mantua at the end of the sevententh century, and author of apologetic and polemic in Italian and Hebrew. His Italian rebuttal of influential anti-Jewish writing is matched by his Hebrew criticisms of the New Testament; here he follows the polemical tradition already noticed in Jacob b. Reuben, the Basle Nizzahon, and Shem Tob ibn Shaprut. In an attempt to place his biblical yet rational apologetic in its contemporary setting it is suggested that, with due care, some analogies can be drawn between the influence of the rational and mystical streams in north Italian Judaism and in the contemporary Italian church. Briel's opposition to Sabbatianism, discussed in connection with his general reserve towards mysticism, has been further illuminated by Elisheva Carlebach.[108] I have argued that Briel's dismissal of argument from miracle is in touch – especially through his plagiarism of his fellow-apologist Isaac Cardoso – with contemporary rationalizing treatments of Greek and Roman miracle stories, and with the broader debate on 'evidences' for revealed religion; but that it is biblically rooted in the Pentateuchal treatment of miracle and false prophecy which had earlier shaped rabbinic reports on Jesus as well as the anti-Pauline polemic discussed above.

The material reprinted with minor changes below first appeared as follows: chapter 1, in VT xxxv (Leiden: E. J. Brill, 1985), 13–38; chapter 2, in JTS N.S. xxxiii (Oxford: Oxford University Press,

[107]Horbury, 'The Hebrew Text of Matthew in Shem Tob Ibn Shaprut's *Eben Bohan*'.
[108]Carlebach, *The Pursuit of Heresy*.

1982), 19–61; chapter 3, in *JTS* N.S. xxxiii (1982), 492–508; chapter 4, in J. D. G. Dunn (ed.), *Jews and Christians: The Parting of the Ways, A.D. 70–135* (Tübingen: J. C. B. Mohr (Paul Siebeck), 1992), 315–45; chapter 5, in E. Bammel & C. F. D. Moule (edd.), *Jesus and the Politics of His Day* (Cambridge: Cambridge University Press, 1984), 183–95; chapter 6, in *JTS* N.S. xxiii (1972), 455–9; chapter 7, in E. A. Livingstone (ed.), *Studia Patristica* xviii, 3: Papers of the 1983 Oxford Patristics Conference (Kalamazoo & Leuven: Cistercian Publications, 1989), 291–317; chapter 8, in J. van Oort & U. Wickert (edd.), *Christliche Exegese zwischen Nicaea und Chalcedon* (Kampen: Kok Pharos, 1992), 72–103; chapter 10, in *JTS* N.S. xxxiv (1983), 497–514; chapter 11, in *Sefarad* xliii (Madrid: Instituto de Filogía del CSIC, 1983) [issued 1986], 221–37; chapter 12, in *Jewish Studies Quarterly* i (Tübingen: J. C. B. Mohr (Paul Siebeck), 1993–4), 171–92. Chapter 9 is to appear in G. N. Stanton & G. Stroumsa (edd.), *Tolerance and Intolerance in Ancient Judaism and Christianity* (Cambridge: Cambridge University Press, 1998). I would like to thank the respective publishers for permission to reproduce the material here.

It remains to express my warmest thanks to Dr J. N. B. Carleton Paget, who suggested this collection and has commented on the introduction; to Mr D. W. Chapman, for making the indices; to Dr M. N. A. Bockmuehl, for his comments on the introduction; and to my wife, for patience and encouragement with regard to the literary offspring united here.

1

EXTIRPATION AND EXCOMMUNICATION

I

Excommunication is a disciplinary measure which implies a considerable degree of organization and cohesion in the body concerned. The employment of such a measure in post-exilic Jewry would be an important datum for discussion of communal order and self-consciousness in the period. Excommunication, however, has not figured prominently in recent inquiries as to how far the community then either possessed or enforced norms of belief or conduct.[1]

The failure of the subject to win attention doubtless owes much to the paucity of evidence. In post-exilic Jewry, even after Isa. lxvi 5 and Ezra x 8, excommunication is notoriously hard to document; it is disputable whether Pentateuchal sources reflect any practice comparable with that envisaged in Ezra x. Various forms of excommunication are found in the Qumran sect,· and among the Essenes, the early Christians, and the 'Associates' of the Mishnah; but in each case it can be asked whether the custom does not reflect the exclusiveness of a close-knit minority group, rather than the practice of post-exilic Jewry as a whole.

The synagogue ban, which was clearly in use during the Talmudic period, although it is first fully described in later sources,[2] is accordingly sometimes derived from sectarian usage rather than from general Jewish practice.[3] Doubt is thereby cast on the possibility, which has regularly been entertained, that the synagogue ban stands in some continuity with whatever measures of exclusion were known in post-exilic public and common usage.[4] The pre-rabbinic evidence thus attains some fulness solely in sectarian contexts, and the relevance of the rabbinic ban is disputed.

---

[1]Discussion and literature in F. Dexinger, 'Limits of Tolerance in Judaism: The Samaritan Example', in E. P. Sanders, A. I. Baumgarten and A. Mendelson (eds), *Jewish and Christian Self-Definition* 2 (London, 1981), 88–114, and R. Murray, 'Jews, Hebrews and Christians: Some Needed Distinctions', *Novum Testamentum* 24 (1982), 194–208. See also pp. 3–8, above.

[2]S. Krauss, *Synagogale Altertümer* (Berlin and Vienna, 1922), 188 and n. 3.

[3]D. J. Silver, 'Heresy', *Encyclopedia Judaica* 8 (Jerusalem, 1971), cols. 358–62 (361); C.-H. Hunzinger, 'Bann II', *Theologische Realenzyklopädie* 5 (Berlin, 1980), 161–7 (161 f.).

[4]Examples are D. Hoffmann, *Das Buch Leviticus übersetzt und erklärt* 2 (Berlin, 1906), 407–9; K. E. Kirk, *The Vision of God* (London, 1931), 148 f.; W. Doskocil, *Der Bann in der Urkirche* (Munich, 1958), 14–25; G. J. Blidstein, 'Atimia: a Greek Parallel to Ezra x 8 and to post-biblical Exclusion from the Community', *VT* xxiv (1974), 357–60.

The doubts arising from this paucity of evidence are sharpened by more general considerations. Principal among these is the view that, in the Second Temple period, halakhic diversity was so great, and communal organization was so loose, that expulsions could not have been effectively agreed upon or enforced.[5] Hunzinger roundly denies, with this presupposition, that any measures of exclusion from the general Jewish community were known before A.D. 70.[6] The very discussion of expulsion in connection with the synagogue ban has been criticized by Maier as betraying an inappropriate estimate of the Jewish community as a body straightforwardly comparable with the Christian church; and he correspondingly views as misleading the description of exclusion from Jewish fellowship as excommunication.[7]

These more general considerations themselves, however, seem to neglect the widespread emphasis on communal order and unity in Jewish documents of the Second Temple period. J. Wellhausen exhibited the Pentateuchal and later evidence for priestly government of a Jewish polity which was, at once, both civil and ecclesiastical.[8] The association of this hierocratic constitution with a sense of national solidarity is exemplified by the legend on Hasmonaean coins, *hakkōhēn haggādôl wᵉheber hayᵉhûdîm*, and by corresponding Greek allusions to the high priest's prayer for the *systema* of the Jews (2 Macc. xv 12) and his office as common kinsman and ruler of the whole body (Philo, *Spec. leg.* iii 131).[9] Where a constitution which Josephus could term theocracy (*Ap.* ii 165) is thus linked with a consciousness of Jewish unity, the use of measures to effect exclusion from the general body would not be surprising. Further, the common descent from a community so ordered, shared by the Jewry of the rabbinic period and the nascent Christian church, suggests that the application of an ecclesiastical word to a Jewish practice, if made with due care, is not illegitimate.

[5]D. R. A. Hare, *The Theme of Jewish Persecution of Christians in the Gospel according to St. Matthew* (Cambridge, 1967), 50 f.; G. Forkman, *The Limits of the Religious Community* (Lund, 1972), 102 f.; Hunzinger, 161 f.; J. Maier, *Jüdische Auseinandersetzung mit dem Christentum in der Antike* (Darmstadt, 1982), 131.

[6]Pp. 161 f.

[7]Maier, 131, endorsing Billerbeck's view that, because the *mᵉnuddeh* could appear in the temple (M. Middoth II 2), the ban was not meant as an exclusion (Strack-Billerbeck [as in n. 30, below], iv. 1, 330); but, even in its milder versions, it was in practice a form of expulsion, as noted by Forkman, 102.

[8]*Die Pharisäer und die Sadduzäer* (Greifswald, 1874), 35 f.; *Prolegomena zur Geschichte Israels* (6th edn, Berlin, 1905), 143–5.

[9]The legends are reproduced in E. Schürer, G. Vermes, F. Millar and M. Black, *The History of the Jewish People in the Age of Jesus Christ* 1 (Edinburgh, 1973), 603–5.

This response to the broader considerations which make for doubt concerning the availability of excommunication can be complemented by appeal to the Qumran and New Testament evidence on the measure itself. Here, as in other constitutional matters, Qumran may reflect older or more widespread Jewish practice. That this is the case is suggested by the fact that the New Testament mentions exclusion not only from the church, but also from the synagogue (Luke vi 22; John ix 22, xii 42, xvi 2). Moreover, as early as I Cor. v, the procedure of Christian excommunication is assumed without discussion; and it is likely, therefore, that existing synagogue custom is presupposed. On such a basis the editors of the revised Schürer, against the opinion recently predominant, perpetuate Schürer's own view that, by the early first century A.D., expulsion from the synagogue could take place, with or without a reinforcing anathema.[10]

There is therefore ground, despite the sectarian reference of much of the evidence, for asking once more whether excommunication can be traced in the post-exilic and pre-rabbinic community as a whole. G. Forkman, in the fullest recent study, has no special examination of this question, although he concurs in passing (cf. n. 5, above) with the view that the practice is unlikely to have been current in the general body at the end of the Second Temple period. On the other hand, in a survey of Old Testament passages which might have been regarded as normative in the writings he considers, he accepts Ezra x 8 and Neh. xiii 3 as evidence for formal expulsion (Forkman, 20 f.). His inquiry into historical usage is deliberately restricted, however, to the Qumran community, rabbinic Judaism and the primitive church (cf. Forkman, 35, n. 1). The present brief study of general pre-rabbinic practice is itself limited to two aspects. First, what direct evidence for excommunication from the whole body of Jews is extant, what rulings are presupposed in it, and how, if at all, is it linked with the sectarian and rabbinic evidence? Under this aspect falls a query concerning development: was there, as Forkman's judgements imply, a marked change in practice not only between the destruction of the temple and the talmudic period, but also between the beginning and the end of the Second Temple period? The second aspect is posed by the ambiguity of the Pentateuchal penalty of 'cutting off' (*hikkārēt*, often *kārēt*, in the Mishnah[11]), commonly termed 'extirpation'. An old controversy over its meaning is continued in recent study. J. Morgenstern, W. Zimmerli and A. C. J. Phillips have interpreted extirpation, in different ways, as an early

---

[10]Vol. 2 (Edinburgh, 1979), 432.
[11]M. H. Segal, *A Grammar of Mishnaic Hebrew* (Oxford, 1927), 58.

form of excommunication,[12] M. Tsevat and M. Weinfeld understand it, with the rabbis, as premature death.[13] How, if at all, was it connected, after the exile, with the practice of excommunication?

II

The responses offered to these questions can perhaps be clarified, if the rulings here thought to have been influential are first picked out. The practical measure of exclusion from the general body was principally associated, it is suggested here, with the laws concerning two overlapping subjects: admission to the temple congregation, and loyalty to the covenant. Both subjects had an almost painful significance in the mentality of the whole Second Temple period. In the case of the temple congregation, admission or exclusion was itself the point at issue; in the case of the covenant, it will be argued, exclusion was a surrogate for, or preliminary to, the death penalty. The implications of the relevant laws seem not to have been fully considered in study of the ban.

Admission to the temple congregation was regulated by Deut. xxiii 2–9 (1–8); defective Jews, and certain non-Jews, are here excluded. To summarize statements supported more fully in the following section, it may be said that the exclusion of the uncircumcised, the unclean and the alien was emphasized after the exile both in hope and in practice. In the prophets and psalms, however, admission also hung on moral requirements; the probably pre-exilic 'entrance-*tôrōt*' are paralleled in later prophecy by the exclusion of rebellious sinners from the land where the reunited congregation worship (Ezek. xx 38–40), and the aliens debarred from the temple are taken to be uncircumcised in heart as well as flesh (Ezek. xliv 6–9). Hence it is not surprising that Philo and Josephus take Deut. xxiii to exclude Jews who are defective not only in body or descent, but also in ethical obedience, and that the same Deuteronomic regulations seem to be presupposed in some of the sparse evidence for exclusion in practice.

In the case of the covenant, it is suggested, the curses of the law bring exclusion into view as one of a group of penalties comprising

---

[12]J. Morgenstern, 'The Book of the Covenant, Part III – The Huqqim', *HUCA* 8–9 (1931–2), 1–150 (33–58); W. Zimmerli, 'Die Eigenart der prophetischen Rede des Ezechiel', *ZAW* 66 (1954), 1–26, and *Ezechiel* (Neukirchen-Vluyn, 1969), 305–7; A. C. J. Phillips, *Ancient Israel's Criminal Law* (Oxford, 1970), 28–32, 183–5.

[13]M. Tsevat, 'Studies in the Book of Samuel', *HUCA* 32 (1961), 195–216; M. Weinfeld, *Deuteronomy and the Deuteronomic School* (Oxford, 1972), 241–3; similarly, G. J. Wenham, *The Book of Leviticus* (Grand Rapids and London, 1979), 125, 241 f., 285 f.

curse, exclusion and death. The curses bring divinely-ordained exclusion from the land and destruction on the covenant-breakers (Lev. xxvi 14–39; Deut. xxvii 11–26, xxviii 15–68, xxix 10–30; dispersion, Lev. xxvi 33, Deut. xxvii 25; separation for evil, Deut. xxix 21). The death-penalty for idolatry, the most fundamental breach of covenant, can be inflicted not only by heaven (Num. xxv 9; Deut. iv 3), but also by men (Exod. xxii 19 [20]; Num; xxv 4–8; Deut. xiii 7–19 [6–18], xvii 2–7). Likewise, when the whole congregation enter afresh into a covenant, they guard it by the same measures of a curse (Neh. x 29) and the threat of excommunication (Ezra x 3, 8) or death (Asa's covenant, as narrated in II Chron. xv 12 f.). The abiding vigour of this covenantal line of thought emerges, in a sectarian group, when breach of 'the new covenant in the land of Damascus', is visited with the excommunication threatened in Ezek. xiii 9, and, in the general body of Jews, when Mattathias maintains the covenant by slaying the Jew who comes to sacrifice at Modin (CD xix 34 f.; I Macc. ii 23–7). That exclusion, in this covenantal context, could be a preparation or substitution for death at the hands of men, is suggested by other passages from the evidence for practice discussed below.

It is in this same covenantal context that excommunication was linked, so it is argued here, both with *kārēt* and with *ḥērem*. In the Second Temple period the verb *krt* appears to have been associated above all with divinely-ordained death, sometimes inflicted by human beings (section IV, below). *kārēt* was the punishment for 'breaking my covenant' by neglecting or obscuring its outward sign of circumcision, so important throughout the period (Gen. xvii 14; Jub. xv 14, 26, 34), and for sabbath-breaking and the eating of blood, comparably grave breaches of Jewish loyalty. Hence 'extirpation' in this period seems likely to have meant not excommunication itself, but the death which follows breach of covenant, the penalty which excommunication precedes or replaces.

ḥērem, on the other hand, was to be identified with a measure effecting exclusion, as one standard name for the synagogue ban. This development has recently been viewed as a total disjunction from biblical usage.[14] It seems, however, to have two antecedents, in the employment of *ḥrm* in covenantal contexts. First, the verb refers to the death-penalty (usually inflicted by human beings) for covenant-breaking, above all by idolatry (Exod. xxii 19 (20), Deut. xiii 16–18 (15–17), cited above; idolatry or theft, Josh. vii 11–15,

---

[14]Forkman, 22; Hunzinger, 165; N. Lohfink, *ḥrm*, TWAT 3 (Stuttgart, 1981), cols. 192–213 (201).

discussed by Lohfink, cols. 197 f.). Once again, exclusion might later be thought to prepare or substitute for this execution (see the following section). Secondly, during the post-exilic period, ḥērem comes to describe a communal vow, guarded by curse and exclusion or death. These vows closely resemble the congregational covenants noted above. The antecedents of the usage appear in Num. xxi 2 f., where Israel vow to devote Hormah; in Judg. xxi 5–11, breach of oath by non-attendance at the assembly is punished by ḥērem in the sense of execution, just as, in Ezra x 8, non-attendance is more mildly requited by separation, and the ḥērem of the transgressor's property; and the mutual binding of the group by an anathema first emerges clearly at 1 Enoch vi 3–7 (the angelic ḥērem at Hermon).[15] This developed usage continues to be influential (Acts xxiii 12–14; Midrash Tanhuma, Wayyešeb ii [Warsaw, 1875, 1 f. 45a] on Gen. xxxvii 3 [Joseph's brethren join in a ḥērem not to tell Jacob their plot]). When these two covenantal usages are viewed together, ḥrm is seen to have referred, in this period, to the death-penalty for breach of the divine covenant, the covenantal curse which those who vow invoke, and the penalty which breach of promise incurs – 'devotion' to death modified, in Ezra x, to 'devotion' of property and excommunication. Here, as Septuagintal usage discussed below confirms, a line can be traced between post-exilic ḥērem and the synagogue ban, and its course runs through covenantal contexts.

It was noted in the previous section that measures of exclusion from the whole Jewish community lack unambiguous Pentateuchal sanction. This point weighs to a considerable degree, though not decisively, against the view that such measures were in use in the Second Temple period. It is all the more significant that, as can now be said, there is a case for deriving them from two Pentateuchal contexts, the laws on admission to the temple congregation and the penalties for breach of covenant. Both contexts, moreover, represent subjects which were of acute concern throughout the period, precisely because of the zealous corporate loyalty within which the operation of such measures can best be envisaged.[16] Connections

---

[15]J. T. Milik, The Books of Enoch (Oxford, 1976), 150–2, 318–19. The development in the meaning of ḥrm is underlined by the contrast between Numbers and Enoch in word-play on a place-name formed with ḥrm; Hormah is linked with the annihilation of enemies, but Hermon with the angel's mutual anathema.

[16]For the lasting significance of the covenant among Jews in general, despite the relative rarity of brît in rabbinic texts, see the post-exilic narratives of covenantal assemblies, and I Macc. ii 23–7, noticed above, and Ecclus xvii 12, xxiv 23, xxxvi 1–17; Ps. Sol. ix 16–19, with the comments of E. P. Sanders, Paul and Palestinian Judaism (London, 1977), 329–31, 389; these passages make it hard to accept that (as argued by Phillips, 183–5) covenantal thought was ineffective after the exile.

between these Pentateuchal laws and some of the evidence for exclusion in practice have been noticed, and this evidence itself will now be reviewed.

III

Among the sparse narrative evidence for expulsion from the whole community, Ezra x 8 (*yibbādēl*, I Esdras ix 4 ἀλλοτριωθήσεται) is influential because it attributes the measure to Ezra; but it is by no means isolated in early post-exilic sources. *bdl* also refers to exclusion from the congregation at Neh. xiii 3 (*wayyabdîlû*, LXX 2 Esdras xxiii 3 ἐχωρίσθησαν) and Isa. lvi 3 (*habdēl yabdîlanî yhwh*, LXX ἀφοριεῖ με).[17] These two passages enforce and rebut, respectively, the rules for entry into the assembly (*qāhāl*, ἐκκλησία) at Deut. xxiii 2–9 (1–8). *bdl*, 'to separate', is used in a bad sense in these three instances; but it occurs more often, in the sources of this period, with a favourable reference to the covenantal separation (Ezra x 3–5), secured by a curse and an oath (Neh. x 29 f.), which the post-exilic community desired (Ezra vi 21; Neh. ix 2, x 28, with other passages taken to suggest a 'marked separatism' by J. Blenkinsopp[18]). This ethos probably later influenced the similar covenantal separatism of the Pharisees and the Qumran sectaries, but it was part of the common inheritance of the whole Jewish community, as noted above (so Wellhausen, *Pharisäer*, 76 f.). Exclusion, as in Ezra and Nehemiah, is a natural accompaniment of this separatism, and might be expected to recur.

It is likely, then, that Deut. xxix 20 *weʰibdîlô yhwh leʰrāʿāh* (LXX, verse 21, διαστελεῖ) would have recalled to post-exilic readers or hearers the practice of exclusion from the temple congregation, as prescribed in Deut. xxiii; but that this exclusion could have the larger implication of separation 'from Israel' is especially clear from Neh. xiii 3. In Ezra this treatment is applied not to a foreigner, as in Neh. xiii, or to a defective Jew, in the manner rebutted in Isa. lvi, but to a Jew who absents himself from the covenant of separation (Ezra x 3, 11): he himself 'will be separated from the congregation of the captivity' (x 8), in what Deuteronomy calls a separation 'for evil'. In Ezra x the influence of Deut. xxiii converges with that of the second set of laws considered in the previous section, the covenantal

---

[17]Despite the divine subject this verse need not be distinguished (as by Forkman, 20) from the two previously-quoted passages, because human enforcement of a divinely-ordained exclusion is in view.

[18]'Interpretation and the Tendency to Sectarianism: An Aspect of Second Temple History', in Sanders, Baumgarten and Mendelson, *Self-Definition* 2, 1–26 (5).

penalties; *bdl* significantly occurs in the curses of the law (Deut. xxix 20), and the absentee suffers a milder form of the fate of the men of Jabesh-Gilead, as noted above (Judg. xxi 11).

Expulsion is probably, but not certainly, mentioned in the Aramaic passage Ezra vii 11–26, presented in the book of Ezra as the text of Ezra's letter of authorization from Artaxerxes. Its final words (Ezra vii 26) are a list of four punishments: death, or 'uprooting', or confiscation of property and imprisonment. The second punishment, *šršw* (Qere *šršy*), is interpreted in the Greek versions as 'beating' (LXX) or, more generally, 'penalty' (I Esdras viii 24), with other variations;[19] the Vulgate *exilium*, however, is comparable with the rabbinic explanation of the word as a penalty (*hardāpāh*) applied to the banned (M.K. 16a, in the name of Rab Judah (third-century Babylonia)), and it is not impossible that the Vulgate represents a Jewish interpretation of Jerome's time. *hardāpāh* was itself variously interpreted, during the amoraic period (M.K. 16a, with Geonic reading, in Levy [cf. n. 39, below], 1, 491 f., and Billerbeck, IV. 1 [cf. n. 29, below], 301, 303) and in the Middle Ages (Rashi and Maimonides, quoted by E. Ben Yehuda, *Thesaurus totius Hebraitatis*, 3 [Jerusalem and Berlin, 1913], 1185a, n. 1); but in all these interpretations it was viewed as an intensification of the ban, whether by imprisonment or acceleration of the process (amoraic opinions in M.K. 16a), or by other means. Three comparable amoraic citations of proof-texts for the ban (M.K. 16a, 17a) represent tannaitic or (in one case) pre-rabbinic exegesis (see section V, below), and these possibilities should not be ruled out in the case of the citation of Ezra vii 26. The variety of the Greek renderings does not necessarily imply, therefore, that there was no pre-rabbinic tradition of interpretation. To pass to contextual considerations, it is noteworthy that the punishment is differentiated from death, and immediately precedes confiscation of property, as does separation from the congregation in Ezra x 8. Hence, exile or excommunication are the senses preferred by Batten and Rudolph, as just cited. 'Exile' would be more appropriate if the punishment were to be envisaged as inflicted directly by the Persians (so Batten, p. 308), 'excommunication' if it were Ezra's own disposal, as might be suggested by Ezra x 8 (so Rudolph, on the latter verse). Although, as M.K 16a confirms, an explanation on these lines is probable, the case for it depends to a considerable degree on context and on the unambiguous Ezra x 8. In

---

[19]The Greek texts are quoted by L. W. Batten, *A Critical and Exegetical Commentary on the Books of Ezra and Nehemiah* (Edinburgh, 1913), 316; my English renderings follow W. Rudolph, *Esra und Nehemia samt 3. Esra* (Tübingen, 1949), 74; see also Blidstein, 'Atimia'.

the present study, therefore, this likely interpretation of a difficult word in Ezra vii 26 is noted, but no argument for the practice of excommunication in the post-exilic period is rested upon it.

Those who attempt to enforce an excommunication – whether they represent the whole community, or a particular group, is unclear – are described in Isa. lxvi 5 *m^enaddêkem* (LXX τοῖς ... ὕμᾶς ... βδελυσσομένοις). *niddāh* provides one of the rabbinic terms for the ban, *niddûy*. Such exclusion would probably have been viewed as the complement of the favourably-regarded separation already noted, which is recommended within Israel in Num. xvi 21, 26 (*hibbād^elû, sûrû*; LXX ἀποσχίσθητε, in both verses); cf. Isa. lii 11 (*sûrû*, Targum *'itpār^ašû*; *hibbārû*, LXX ἀφορίσθητε), on separation from aliens.

The ideas behind such early post-exilic exclusions, and the formulae of excommunication which could have been employed, are further illuminated by the doom on the false prophets in Ezek. xiii 9: 'they will not be in the council of my people' (*sôd*, Zimmerli ad loc.: 'Gemeinde'; LXX παιδεία) 'and they will not be written in the writing of the house of Israel, and they will not enter the land'. Inclusion in 'the writing of the house of Israel' was of both present and ultimate importance in post-exilic Jerusalem (Ezra ii 62; Isa. iv 3 [dated by R. E. Clements in the Persian period[20]]); exclusion from it is part of a curse in Ps. lxix 29, and these words were later incorporated into the curse on *minim* in the Twelfth Benediction of the Amidah.[21]

Finally, a trace of the technical vocabulary for exclusion from the temple congregation perhaps survives in II Chron. xxvi 21 *nigzar* (LXX ἀπεσχίσθη, cf. LXX Num. xvi 21, 26, quoted above). This exclusion ensues on Uzziah's leprosy, but the disease is itself a divine punishment, as in the case of Miriam, on which the Chronicler's account is modelled,[22] and which was interpreted in the tannaitic period as a divine decree of *niddûy*.[23]

Exclusions in practice are described in two Greek post-biblical narratives. The apostate Jews of Shechem, according to Josephus (*Ant.* xi 340, 346 f., discussed in this connection by Morgenstern [cf. n. 12], 54), used to receive fugitives from Jerusalem, who had been accused of eating what is common or of sabbath-breaking or some

---

[20]*Isaiah 1–39* (Grand Rapids and London, 1980), 53 f.

[21]The biblical and rabbinic background of this section of the Amidah is discussed by W. Horbury, 'The Benediction of the *Minim* and Early Jewish–Christian Controversy', *JTS* xxxiii N.S. (1982), 19–61 (38–44) (pp. 86–93, below).

[22]H. G. M. Williamson, *1 and 2 Chronicles* (Grand Rapids and London, 1982), 340, on xxvi 20.

[23]Sifre Num. 104, on xii 9, in S. Koleditzky (ed.), *Sifre* (Jerusalem, 1948), f.28b.

other such sin, but who would say that they had been unjustly expelled (ἐκβεβλῆσθαι). This verb is one of the Septuagintal renderings (Exod. xii 33, Ps. xliv [xliii] 2) of šillaḥ, the usual Qumran term for 'expel from the community', which is used in the Hebrew Bible of Adam's expulsion from Eden (Gen. iii 23 f. wayᵉšallᵉḥēhû ... wayᵉgāreš, LXX ἐξαπέστειλεν ... καὶ ἐξέβαλεν. The Greek verb recurs in the Johannine writings for expulsion both from synagogue and church (John ix 34 f., 3 John 10). The offences mentioned by Josephus are of the kind noted in the discussion of kārēt in the previous section as tantamount to breach of the covenant; Josephus implies that the fugitives are ἀποστάται, like those to whom they flee. His story, probably drawn from a source of uncertain date,[24] is a Jewish example of the narratives intended to discredit a city's first inhabitants (cf. Ant. xviii 37 f., on the earliest residents of Tiberias, and Augustine on Roman origins, Civ. Dei iv 4). It can be used, with caution, as a witness to the practice of the first century B.C., and it may be taken to represent what Josephus himself regarded as established usage (cf. Ant. iv 309 f., discussed below).

Secondly, in 3 Maccabees some Alexandrian Jews lapse, under pressure, to the Mysteries; in what is doubtless an idealized description of a short and easy way with apostates, their more steadfast fellow-Jews are said to have shunned them (ἐβδελύσσοντο, ii 33), until, in better times, they obtained permission to destroy (ὅπως ... ἐξολοθρεύσωσιν) the law-breakers, and punished them with death (vii 12–15). The Greek verbs are among the Septuagintal renderings, first (ii 33) of niddāh (Isa. lxvi 5), and second (vii 12) of ḥrm, šmd, and krt. This Alexandrian passage, probably of the first century A.D., was noted in the present connection by D. von Dobschütz.[25]

The post-exilic biblical references to exclusion from the general Jewish body are therefore continued by one Palestinian and one Alexandrian witness. The chain of pre-rabbinic evidence is concluded by the New Testament passages on expulsion from synagogue already

---

[24]Dexinger (as in n. 1, above), 96 f., views Ant. xi 340–5 as a separate unit of source-material, later than the preceding Jaddua story (which he dates, with Büchler, to the time of Caesar's Jewish edicts). The story of the fugitives in paragraphs 346 f., considered here, seems likely to belong to the same source as the defamation of Shechem in paragraph 340. Its explanatory character, and the concluding summary (347), suit the criteria for detection of sources suggested by H. G. M. Williamson, 'The Historical Value of Josephus' Jewish Antiquities xi. 297–301', JTS N.S. xxviii (1977), 49–66, even though specific reference to a 'cause' is lacking. The account used here by Josephus could then be tentatively ascribed, following Dexinger, to the second part of the 1st century B.C.

[25]Paulus und die jüdische Thorapolizei (Erlangen, 1968), 24 f., 62 f.; his title doubtless somewhat exaggerates disciplinary organization, but it catches the mood of Philo, Spec. leg. ii 253.

mentioned. How far does this evidence bear out the view, advanced in the previous section, that such measures belonged to generally recognized practice, with its basis in the laws of temple and covenant?

Three aspects of the evidence deserve attention in this connection: the weight of the biblical passages; the terminological links between Hebrew and Greek passages, on the one hand, and the sectarian and rabbinic sources for excommunication, on the other; and the links between the evidence just reviewed, and the biblical rulings already noted in the previous section.

First, it should be noted that the post-exilic biblical passages are weighty in a dual capacity; they witness to influential thought and practice, but by the Maccabaean period the books to which they belong are themselves generally revered as authoritative. The practice of excommunication is mentioned in Isaiah, and clearly described in Ezra and Nehemiah; the community of the returned exiles strongly influenced later Judaism, precisely in the covenantal separatism with which such a practice agrees, and the writings wherein excommunication is described came to be numbered among the sacred books. In these circumstances, which receive surprisingly little attention in discussion of exclusion, the continuance of the practice in the general Jewish body would be expected.

Secondly, terminological links among the Hebrew and Greek passages cited, and between them and the sectarian and rabbinic evidence, are frequent enough to suggest a practice which, though changing, was continuous and general. Such links, some of them already noted in the review above, appear between *bdl* in Ezra, Nehemiah and Isa. lvi, and in 1QS vii 1, where it refers to the more severe form of Qumran excommunication; between *niddāh* in Isa. lxvi, and rabbinic *niddûy*; between ἀφορίζω in Isa. lvi 3 and Luke vi 22; between βδελύσσω in Isa. lxvi and in III Maccabees; and between ἐκβάλλω in Josephus here, and in Josephus on Essene excommunication (*B.J.* ii 143 f.), the Fourth Gospel on expulsion from the synagogue, and 3 John on expulsion from the church (note the possible correspondence with Qumran *šillaḥ*).

It would not be unreasonable to conjecture, from the last set of correspondences, that *šillaḥ* and ἐκβάλλω were current usage for expulsion from synagogue at the beginning of the Christian era. However that may be, it is striking that (allowance being made for the uncertainty of Hebrew-Greek equivalence) two other correspondences extend over the whole Second Temple period (*bdl*/ἀφορίζω, in Ezra and Nehemiah, Trito-Isaiah, the Manual of Discipline, and Luke; *niddāh*/βδελύσσω, in Trito-Isaiah, III Maccabees, and the Mishnah).

Palestinian sources predominate, but the Greek-speaking diaspora is represented in III Maccabees (Alexandria), and possibly reflected in III John (Asia Minor).

The words just noted are only traces of a richer vocabulary, as is suggested by such probably technical terms as the Chronicler's *gzr*, the Septuagintal ἀποσχίζω, and the special adjective ἀποσυνάγωγος found in the Fourth Gospel. This feature itself speaks for familiarity with measures of exclusion. At the same time the degree of consistency, noted in the foregoing paragraph as maintained throughout the period, strongly suggests that a few important terms had extended currencies in connection with a continuously recognized discipline, among the general body of Jews.

Thirdly, the links with Pentateuchal rulings, suggested in the previous section, also imply that this discipline would have received general recognition. Yet, were the laws of temple and covenant acknowledged throughout the period to carry this implication?

The admission-regulations of Deut. xxiii 2–9 (1–8) were linked in rabbinic exegesis with xxiii 1 (xxii 30), and correspondingly understood, as by Targum Pseudo-Jonathan, as marriage laws. Were they also taken, in the Second Temple period, to imply exclusion from the congregation? An affirmative answer was clear in the earlier post-exilic evidence reviewed, at Neh. xiii and Isa lvi; but it is also spelt out by Josephus, when he paraphrases Deut. xxiii 2 (1) as a command to 'drive out' (ἐλαύνειν) the eunuch (*Ant.* iv 290), and Philo on the passage has the same presupposition (*Spec. leg.* i 324–45). The implication is also clear in the exclusion of foreigners from the Second Temple enclosure (Josephus, *B.J.* v 194), a practice which had a prominent place in future hope (Isa. lii 1; Joel iii 17; Zech. xiv 21; Ps. Sol. xvii 31) and in the preoccupations of the zealous (Acts xxi 28; Josephus, *Ant.* xix 332–4).[26]

Did the scope of the Deuteronomic regulations, however, go beyond physique and descent? Moral requirements for admission are stated in the 'entrance-*tôrōt*' (Ps. xv, xxiv 3–5, and [ascribed by Clements, ad loc., to the exile] Isa. xxxiii 14–17); they are comparably prominent in the royal promise to destroy sinners from the city of the Lord, Ps. ci. Despite changes of interpretation in the Second Temple period (in LXX, Isa. xxxiii 14–17 state the qualifications for a prophet), such passages could still be applied to their original context

---

[26]Allusions to Deut. xxiii in the Temple Scroll and 4Q Florilegium are discussed together with Josephus by J. M. Baumgarten, 'Exclusions from the Temple: Proselytes and Agrippa I', *JJS* 33 (1982) (= G. Vermes and J. Neusner [ed.]., *Essays in honour of Yigael Yadin*), 215–25.

of admission (so Targum Isa. xxxiii 14–17). The influence of these moral requirements was noted above in Ezekiel, where grave sinners are excluded from the future congregation (xx 38–40); and it can be seen impinging directly on the Deuteronomic admission rules in the post-exilic Ezek. xliv 6–9, where the aliens are uncircumcised in heart, and their admission breaks the covenant (for dating, see Zimmerli, ad loc.). Hence it is not surprising that in Ezra x, as noted at the beginning of this section, the Jew who absents himself from covenantal assembly is requited by being excluded, as if he were a gentile.

It is against this biblical background that Josephus and Philo take Deut. xxiii to exclude not only aliens and defective Jews, but also gravely-offending Jewish sinners. Both apply xxiii 2(1) not (only) to the born eunuch, but to the voluntary effeminate; the survival of his biblical association with idolatry emerges from the renderings 'initiate' and 'mysteries' in LXX Deut. xxiii 17, III Kgdms xv 12, and from Rom. i 27. It is not a long step, therefore, when Philo goes on to allegorize the admission-laws of Deut. xxiii 2–9 (1–8) as the banishment of atheists and polytheists from the congregation (Philo, *Spec. leg.* i 324–45; Josephus, *Ant.* iv 290 f.). The importance of Deut. xxiii for Philo's doctrine of the Jewish community has been emphasized by N. A. Dahl,[27] but it seems not to have been recognized in study of the ban. The point of significance in the present context is that Deuteronomic admission laws, which are clearly linked with the post-exilic exclusions of Jews reviewed above, continued throughout the Second Temple period to be understood as implying exclusion, and as relevant not only to non-Jews and defective Jews, but also to grave offenders within the community.[28]

The second set of laws with which the exclusions reviewed in this section have been linked are the covenantal penalties, notably the prescription of execution for apostasy (Deut. xiii and xvii, with other passages cited in section II, above). The convergence of covenantal thought with the Deuteronomic admission rules has just been recognized in Ezek. xliv 6–9, and in the exclusion at Ezra x 8. Here, as already noted, the measure seems to be a milder version of a covenantal death-penalty. It was suggested in section II that excommunication was regularly understood as a surrogate or preparation for this penalty, and the evidence will now be summarized.

The expulsions mentioned by Josephus in his anti-Shechemite

---

[27]*Das Volk Gottes* (Oslo, 1941), 109, and n. 171 (stressing that, although exclusion is not explicitly commanded, Philo assumes that it is implied).

[28]The *m⁽nuddeh* found in the temple (Middoth II 2; cf. n. 7, above) must be presumed guilty of a less grave offence (possibilities are discussed by Forkman, 95, 98); Philo and Josephus name offences comparable with idolatry.

narrative, and the ban in 3 Maccabees, seem to be best interpreted as surrogate and preparation, respectively. In each case the offence amounts to apostasy. Josephus interprets the death penalty for apostasy in Deut. xiii when he paraphrases Deut. xxix as a covenantal assembly like those of Ezra, Nehemiah and the Chronicler. Moses makes the ἐκκλησία swear to guard the law, and to penalize those of their blood who attempt to destroy it by annihilating the guilty individual or city (Deut. xiii 7–19 [6–18]); 'but if they should be powerless to exact the punishment, they would at least demonstrate that these things were not done according to their own will' (*Ant.* iv 309 f.). Expulsion or separation, as in *Ant.* xi and 3 Maccabees, would be the clearest such demonstration.

To bear out this interpretation of Josephus, there is evidence both for exclusion as the substitute for a death-penalty, and for exclusion as the due treatment of apostates. The LXX and Paul are relevant in both respects. *ḥrm* is rendered in the LXX, in about half its occurrences (including the penalty on the idolater in Exod. xxii 19 (20)), by words meaning 'destroy'; but in the other half (including Deut. xii 16 [15]) by ἀνάθεμα and cognates (Lohfink, col. 195). The possibility here noted by Lohfink, that cursing, as in the Megara tablet (1st–2nd century A.D.), is already intended, finds support in Pauline usage (Rom. ix 3; I Cor. xii 3, xvi 22; Gal. i 8 f.). At Rom. ix 3 the curse clearly implies exclusion. Even on this understanding, Deut. xiii 9 f., 15a in the LXX still clearly refer to death, as Philo emphasizes (*Spec. leg.* i 55, 316); but a foothold is inserted into the text for the addition, or substitution, of a curse. That such an interpretative practice was Palestinian as well as Alexandrian may be suggested, with due caution, on the basis of passages in which Targum Pseudo-Jonathan adds a reference to the ban as the means of death.[29] Thus Deut. vii 2 *haḥᵃrēm taḥᵃrîm 'ōtām* becomes in Pseudo-Jonathan 'you shall make an end of them with the Lord's *šammᵉtā''*.

The view that this Septuagintal rendering is associated with the use of a curse of exclusion as well as, or instead of, the death penalty is strengthened by the Pauline use of another interpretative translation which is common to both LXX and Targum. 'The evil', *hārā'*, which 'you shall put away', *ûbî'artā*, in the Deuteronomic formula which concludes the prescription of the death penalty at Deut. xiii 6 (5), xvii 7 and elsewhere, is interpreted as 'the evil *man*' sometimes in the LXX, and regularly in Targums Onkelos and Pseudo-Jonathan, and in

---

[29]Billerbeck notes several examples, in H. L. Strack and P. Billerbeck, *Kommentar zum Neuen Testament aus Talmud und Midrasch* IV. 1 (Munich, 1928), 296.

Sifre.[30] St Paul does the same, but uses the quotation (I Cor. v 13, probably from Deut. xvii 7) to support an admonition not to mix with sinners, immediately following a sentence of excommunication (I Cor. v 5). This application of the words, in a passage which seems, as already noted, to reflect established rather than new procedure, is itself likely to be traditional.

Thus far, then, one well-marked interpretative rendering in the LXX and Targum, and the Pauline use of another, viewed together with Josephus's interpretation of Deut. xiii as requiring execution or a surrogate, can all be said to make sense if exclusion did sometimes replace, or prepare for, the covenantal death-penalty. Two sources speak more directly of such a substitution. First, a period of exclusion is expressly made to replace a death-penalty in the Damascus Document. The 'ward' in which the gatherer of sticks on the sabbath was initially guarded (Num. xv 34) is interpreted as seven reformative years for the sabbath-breaker, perhaps in a sectarian guard-room; but (despite the sentence of stoning in Num. xv 35 f.) 'he shall not be put to death' (CD xii 4–6). Secondly, Philo, although he has just praised Phinehas's zealous execution of the death-penalty upon the apostate Zimri, simply says that Moses 'banishes' (ἐλαύνει) the diviners listed in Deut. xviii 10 f. (*Spec. leg.* i 60); but they are sentenced to death in Lev. xx 6, 27.

Lastly, the exclusion of apostates – who have, strictly speaking, incurred the death-penalty – is attested in the Targums and early rabbinic sources. They may not eat the passover (Exod. xii 43 in Targums Onkelos and Pseudo-Jonathan), or receive the help due to an enemy, according to Exod. xxiii 5 (Tos. B.M. ii 33), or offer an oblation with the children of Israel (Lev. i 2 in Targum Pseudo-Jonathan and Sifra).[31] These prohibitions are consonant with the curse upon them in the Twelfth Benediction of the Amidah. The

---

[30]Billerbeck collects the passages in Strack–Billerbeck, *Kommentar* III (Munich, 1926), 362.

[31]Sifra, *Nedabah*, ii 3, on Lev. i 2 (S. Koleditzky [ed.], *Sifra* [Jerusalem, 1961], f. 2a); paradoxically interpreted (with a parallel, Hull. 5a) as implying that the apostate must still be considered a Jew (for a non-Jew would be allowed to offer) by L. Schiffman, 'At the Crossroads: Tannaitic Perspectives on the Jewish–Christian Schism', in Sanders, Baumgarten and Mendelson, *Self-Definition* 2, 115–56 (146). Schiffman unduly softens the negative force of the passage into the expression of 'a legal disability' (p. 146); he does not mention the other passages cited here (which, like *Sifra*, debar the apostate from privileges accorded to every Israelite), the comparable interpretation of Ps. cxxxix 21 f. as an injunction to hate *minim*, apostates and traitors (Aboth de-Rabbi Nathan, First Recension, xvi), or the Geonic opinions noted by Baumgarten (as in n. 26, above), 223, to the effect that apostates can forfeit Jewish status (by contrast with the later mediaeval view). The explicit reference to the covenant in Sifra here is stressed by Sanders, *Paul and Palestinian Judaism*, 84.

covenantal basis of the procedure is still recognized; 'apostates ... do not accept the covenant' (Sifra, loc. cit.)

The expulsion of apostates from Jerusalem in Josephus' anti-Shechemite source, and the ban on the lapsed Jews in 3 Maccabees, can now, therefore, be viewed within a continuum of Jewish practice. The substitution of exclusion for execution, which this practice often involves, is at least once attested as an express reinterpretation of a widely-esteemed covenantal death-penalty (contrast CD xii 4–6 with Ezek. xx 12–24; Jub. ii 25–7, 18–13; and Philo, *Spec. leg.* ii 250 f.). More importantly, the rabbinic procedure of curse and exclusion, applied to apostates, is that which best explains one Septuagintal and targumic interpretation, the Pauline use of another, and Josephus' own view of Deut. xiii as calling for execution or a surrogate corporate demonstration. Summary execution itself might still sometimes be sought by the zealous, as has appeared from III Maccabees and elsewhere (I Macc. ii 23–7; Acts xxiii 12–15; Philo, *Spec. leg.* i 56 f., 316; cf. M. Sanh. ix 6). Nevertheless, as Josephus's paraphrase of Deuteronomy suggests, and the other evidence just mentioned confirms, the substitution of (curse and) exclusion was normal practice towards the end of the Second Temple period; and this upholding of the covenant by excommunication is in full accord with the ethos and practice attested, at the beginning of the period, in Ezra x 8.

The consideration of three important aspects of the chain of direct evidence for excommunication from the general body has now led to conclusions which can be summarized. First, the description of the practice in books which became universally authoritative, and its appropriateness to the influential covenantal separatism of the post-exilic community, together make its continuance probable in the community as a whole. Secondly, the terminology of the passages has links with sectarian and rabbinic sources on exclusion, shows traces of a richer vocabulary connected with this subject, and has a degree of consistency throughout the period which suggests that a few important terms were continuously current; these features indicate continuous awareness of this discipline among Jews in general. Thirdly, the practice, as described in this evidence, is linked with two sets of Pentateuchal laws: on admission to the congregation, and on the penalties for breach of the covenant. These converge in their scope, represent subjects which were continuously important, and were both taken, throughout the period, to imply, in different ways, the exclusion of grave offenders. Exclusion was the direct consequence of the admission laws, but, in the case of the covenant penalties, it was a surrogate or preparation for execution. The discipline suggested by a synoptic view of the LXX and Targums, Josephus, the New

Testament and early rabbinic sources, against this background of covenantal law, is consistent, in ethos and practice, with the post-exilic evidence from the beginning of the period.

These points combine to suggest that the direct evidence for excommunication from the whole community, sparse though it is, represents a custom continuously recognized by Jews in general. The sects did not originate it, but derived it from existing usage, within the common post-exilic inheritance of intense corporate loyalty to the covenant. It was suggested in section II, above, that *kārēt* and *ḥērem* were connected in different ways with excommunication, in this same context of covenantal thought and practice. The arguments can now be briefly reviewed.

IV

The dissociation of extirpation from excommunication goes back at least to John Selden. As part of his argument that excommunication was of human rather than divine origin, he urged, from Jewish sources, that it has no Mosaic authority.[32] The rabbis (he noted) derived the synagogue ban from the curse upon Meroz (Judg. v 23, quoted by Raba [4th century] in M.K. 16a); for the Karaite Elijah ben Moses (Elijah Bashyatsi, 15th century) the practice was authorized by Ezra x 8:[33] and the common Christian interpretation of Pentateuchal 'cutting off' as excommunication was ruled out by the rabbinic understanding of the word, more recently revived by Tsevat (cf. n. 13), to mean premature death.

Selden's large conspectus instructively holds *kārēt* together with rabbinic interpretation of *ḥērem*. The two penalties then appear, against the general trend of his argument, to share a common reference to the covenantal death-penalty, whether inflicted by heaven (*kārēt*) or men (*ḥērem*, in the light of Judg. v 23, xxi 11). Is *kārēt* sufficiently described, for the Second Temple period, as the divinely inflicted penalty of premature death?

Such a description needs modification, first, by recognition of the covenantal reference of *kārēt*. As noted in section II, this penalty guards circumcision, sabbath, and abstinence from blood (Gen. xvii 14; Exod. xxxi 14 f.; Lev. xvii 14). All these observances, circumcision

---

[32]*De Synedriis & Praefecturis Juridicis Veterum Ebraeorum* (Frankfurt, 1696), 55–70, 83–107 (parts of book i, chs. 6 and 7).

[33]Elijah Bashyatsi, *'Adderet 'Eliyyahu*, Seder ʿinyan tᵉpillah, ii 7 (Odessa, 1870, repr. Israel, 1966, 188a).

especially, were viewed in the period as covenantal signs (Gen. xvii 14 [cf. Jub. xv 14, 26, 34]; Exod. xxxi 13, 16 f., with Ezek. xx 12–24; Gen. ix [linked with Jub. vi 10–14 with the Noachic covenant, Gen. ix 9]). Other badges of Jewish loyalty protected by *kārēt* are observance of Passover and the Day of atonement (Exod. xii 15, 19; Num. ix 13), and prohibition of approach to the holy in uncleanness (Lev. xxii 3) and sacrifice to Molech (Lev. xviii 21) – identified by the LXX as idolatry, and by Preshiṭta and Targum Pseudo-Jonathan as intercourse with a gentile woman.[34] The continued association of the word with the penalty for breach of covenant emerges from Targum Pseudo-Jonathan on Num. xv 31, a verse which includes the emphatic *hikkārēt tikkārēt*: 'because he has despised the ancient word which the Lord commanded on Sinai, and has made vain the covenant of circumcision, that soul is cut off in this world; that man shall be cut off in the world to come'.

Secondly, its currency in the period to mean divinely-inflicted death is amply borne out by biblical, Septuagintal, and Qumranic evidence.[35] The premature death, which Tsevat viewed as the regular interpretation on the basis of I Sam. ii 33, is clearly implied at CD iii 6 f., xx 26, where *krt* is used of the wilderness deaths of Num. xiv 30–35; Deut. ii 14. On the other hand, the verb occasionally refers to the human execution of a divinely-ordained death-penalty (Josh. xi 21, I Kings xi 16, both in Deuteronomic style; probably pre-exilic examples, 1 Sam. xxviii 9, Ps. ci 8). This variation foreshadows the fluidity with which, at the end of the period, thought could move between the humanly-inflicted and the divinely-inflicted death-penalty of the law (Sib. Or. iii 259–61 (the disobedient may escape men's judgement, but will, nevertheless, justly perish); Heb. ii 2 (undifferentiated recompense), with Heb. ii 16 f., xii 25 (divinely-inflicted wilderness deaths), and Heb. x 28 (the humanly-inflicted penalty for apostasy, Deut. xiii 8 (9), xvii 6; Philo, *Spec. leg.* ii 253 [God will never free the perjurer from guilt, even if he escape human punishment; but that, the guilty man will never do, for he is under the eyes of thousands of zealots for the laws]).

---

[34]The versions are discussed by Z. Frankel, *Vorstudien zu der Septuaginta* (Leipzig, 1841, repr. Farnborough, 1972), 184, and id., *Ueber den Einfluss der palästinischen Exegese auf die alexandrinische Hermeneutik* (Leipzig, 1851, repr. Farnborough, 1972), 154 f.; he notes that an exegesis on the lines of Peshiṭta and Targum Pseudo-Jonathan is rejected in M. Megillah iv 9.

[35]See G. F. Hasel, *krt*, *TWAT* 4 (Stuttgart, 1982), cols. 355–67; *kārēt* seems also to be viewed as a death-penalty in the Peshiṭta section-heading before Lev. xx 1, *g'zar dinā' d'mawtā' dab'kul dārîn*, to which attention was drawn by J. Perles, *Meletemata Peschittoniana* (Bratislava, 1859), 23.

Thirdly, the circle from which the offender is cut off, in the legal formulae of the Pentateuch typically his kindred, is in probably exilic or post-exilic passages specified as the land (e.g. Ezek. xiv 13, 17, 19; xxxvii 9–11, 22, 28 f., 34, 38) or the city (Ezek. xiv 21; Zech. xiv 2). At Lev. xviii 26–9 the regular Pentateuchal formula is linked with this thought of ejection from the land.[36] Hence derives a less well-marked but visible association between *krt* and the curses of the law. The plagues which effect cutting-off from the land and Jerusalem in Ezek. xiv are the same, with a slight variation of order, as those which light upon the disobedient in the curse of Lev. xxvi 21–7.[37] Dispossession is central in the curses (Lev. xxvi 33 f.; Deut. xxviii 25). Although *krt* has no more than a subordinate part in the curse of Leviticus (xxvi 22), and does not occur in the Deuteronomic parallel (where *šmd*, sometimes synonymous with *krt*, as in Deut. xii 29, is repeatedly used in Deut. xxviii 20–63), its association with the curses of the law would have been encouraged by the specific link between *krt*, dispossession and the divine curse in Ps. xxxvii 22 (the blessed inherit the land, but the accursed will be cut off). This view seems to be borne out by the Manual of Discipline, where *krt* is added to the threat of separation in Deut. xxix 19, to form the climax of a covenant-curse: 'all the curses of this covenant shall stick to him, and God shall separate him for evil, and he shall be cut off from all the children of light' (1QS ii 14). Here, admittedly in prophecy rather than law, is the sequence of curse, expulsion and death which, it has been suggested, was sometimes found in practice. At the same time, the connection with the curse is another aspect of the covenantal reference of *krt*.

In sum, the Mishnaic usage of *krt* does illuminate the biblical, as Tsevat maintained; but covenantal associations of the word, on which he did not dwell, give an important clue to its significance in the Second Temple period. It typically denoted the divinely-inflicted death-penalty of the law. This emerges vividly from Acts iii 22–3, where the *kārēt*-passage Lev. xxiii 29 is quoted in this sense, as the sequel to Deut. xviii 15, 18 on the duty of hearing the prophet who will be raised up; the quotation of Leviticus replaces '*I* will require' in the Deuteronomic continuation, Deut. xviii 19, a verse which refers to punishment at the hands of heaven, according to Mishnah,

---

[36]The Septuagintal interpretation, wherein verse 28 is final (so *RV, RSV*) rather than consecutive (so *NEB*), and *kārēt* is thereby closely linked with ejection, is here followed; the alternatives are set out by J. R. Porter, *Leviticus* (Cambridge, 1976), 149.

[37]The correspondence with Ezekiel is noted by Hoffmann, *Leviticus* 2, 368 (on xxvi 16 f., with acknowledgement to Wessely).

Sanh. xi 5.[38] On the other hand, the occasional references to *krt* to a humanly-inflicted penalty prepared for the fluidity with which thought moves, on this subject, between divine and human causation; and the links with the curse and with dispossession meant that the idea of exclusion was not far away.

Did *kārēt*, then, after the exile, straightforwardly refer to excommunication, as was argued with reference to P by Morgenstern and Phillips (n. 12, above)? It is hard to accept that the meaning of the word *krt* was thus transformed, in view of the usages just noted, the continuance of covenantal thought which they illustrate, and the vigour of the associated recognition that apostasy deserves death; Josephus's version of the protest of Reuben, Gad and the half tribe of Manasseh, that 'all who are of Abraham's race, but embark on new-fangled customs, perversions of established practice, deserve to be destroyed (ἐξώλεις εἶναι)' (addition to Josh. xxii 22 f., 29, in Josephus, *Ant.* v 113), should be compared with the passages on summary execution cited at the end of section III, above. It seems more likely, from the study of exclusions in that section, that excommunication did sometimes take the place of the death-penalty, in accordance with the practice for which Morgenstern, Zimmerli and Phillips all argue; but that this practice would have been viewed not as *kārēt* itself, but as the surrogate or preparation for that 'vengeance of the covenant' (Lev. xxvi 25, viewed as the judgement awaiting apostates in CD xix 13 f.) with which 'cutting off' was often associated. Extirpation, as the covenantal death penalty for which exclusion could prepare or substitute, was thus distinct from, yet linked with, excommunication.

V

The association of *ḥrm* with the covenantal penalty inflicted by human beings has already been illustrated (section II, above) with reference to the death-penalty for idolatry (Exod. xxii 19 [20], Deut. xiii 16–18 [15–17]; Josh. vii 11–15), and the covenantal curse and penalty in a communal vow (Judg. xxi 5–11, cf. Ezra x 8; I Enoch vi 3–7; Acts xxiii 12–14; Midrash Tanhuma, *Wayyešeb*, on Gen. xxxvii 3). These covenantal usages prepare, it was suggested, for the use of *ḥērem* to refer (as in Midrash Tanhuma) to the synagogue ban. The Septuagintal renderings of *ḥrm* with ἀνάθεμα and cognates, viewed together with Pauline usage (section III, above), continue the

---

[38]The conjunction of the quotations from Deuteronomy and Leviticus in Acts iii 22 f. is therefore unlikely to be fortuitous, as was supposed by C. H. Dodd, *According to the Scriptures* (London, 1952), 54.

association of *ḥērem* with a curse. It can now be noted that the rabbinic explanations to which Selden drew attention, and other rabbinic and targumic references to the ban, reflect awareness of these aspects of the biblical *ḥērem*. In these passages the ban appears to have been understood, in a way for which the LXX prepares, as a covenantal curse, effecting exclusion, and expected to issue in death. It could then be viewed, by contrast with the emphasis in recent study on its novelty and sectarian derivation (notes 3, 5 and 14, above), as a continuation and development of the post-exilic practice outlined in section III, above.

Rabbinic explanations, drawn from three biblical contexts, may be held to bear this out. First, Raba's proof for *šammᵉtā'* and *ḥērem* from Judg. v 23, quoted by Selden, continues a tannaitic identification of the curse upon Meroz with the *niddûy* (baraita at Shebuʿot 36a). It coheres with an explanation which circulated in the name of Akiba, identifying *ḥērem* and oath (*šᵉbûʿāh*) with one another on the basis of the transgression of the men of Jabesh-Gilead in Judg. xxi 5–11 (quotation from a Midrash Yelammedenu, in Nahmanides on Lev. xxvii 29, reproduced by Hoffman, ii, p. 407, on Lev. xxvii 28 f.; combined with proofs from Josh. vii, in Midrash Tanhuma, *Wayyešeb* ii [Warsaw, 1875, 1, f. 45a–b]). In these two explanations contemporary practice is interpreted by the use of *ḥrm* for the death penalty for breach of oath in Judg. xxi 11, taken as describing the fate implied by the curse of Judg. v 23.

Raba also explains a number of practices from the judgement of Dathan, Abiram and the company of Korah (Num. xvi 12–16, in M.K. 16a). The connection of this forensic passage with the ban seems likely, once again, to be traditional. The LXX, as noted in section III, above, emphasizes the separation commanded by Moses (verse 21) with a double ἀποσχίσθητε (verses 21, 26). In Targum Pseudo-Jonathan, on verse 26, Moses states that the sinners have deserved *niddûy* and the 'devotion' of their property; *gmr* Paʿel, used here in the sentence of devotion, often represents *ḥrm* Hiphʿil in the Targums (as noted by Billerbeck, IV. 1, p. 296). The end of these men is thus preceded by the measure threatened in Ezra x 8 (a passage also invoked by Raba in M.K. 16a), and so assimilated to the end of Achan; separation by *niddûy*, and destruction of property by *ḥērem*, are preliminary to the death-penalty, in this case inflicted at the hand of heaven.

Lastly, the third-century Palestinian Resh Laqish, according to M.K. 17a (seven lines up), confirms the penetration of the *šammᵉtā'* into all two hundred and forty-eight members of the body from Josh. vi 17 'the city shall be *ḥērem*'; for *ḥērem* by *gematria*, amounts to 248. This explanation of the ban from the *ḥērem* upon Jericho has antecedents in the baraita from Sheb. 36a cited above, where the curse of Josh. vi 26 is quoted to show that the formula *'ārûr* involves the oath (*šᵉbûʿāh*, identified elsewhere, as just noted, with *ḥērem*), and in the Qumran interpretation of this verse as a malediction on the sect's enemies (4Q 175 [Florilegium], lines 21–30). 'The *ḥērem* of Joshua son of Nun' was prominent in a mediaeval ban-formula (Bialoblocki [n. 40, below], cols. 417–18). It was probably not without recollection of his own experience of the ban that Spinoza emphasized, taking Josh. vi 16 as his example, that Mosaic excommunications were pronounced by national rather than ecclesiastical officers (*Tractatus Theologico-Politicus* xviii; ed. A. G. Wernham [Oxford, 1965], p. 190).

It is in accord with this interpretation of Josh. vi that the judgement of Achan, on which the condemned man's confession before execution is modelled in M. Sanh. VI 2, is recounted in Tanhuma (*Wayyešeb* ii (Warsaw, 1875, vol. 1, f. 45b) to illustrate the saying on *ḥērem* attributed to Akiba. What appears to be an assimilation of the end of sinners, viewed as under the ban, to Achan's punishment has already been noted (Pseudo-Jonathan on Num. xvi 26). The tannaitic association of Joshua's ban with contemporary practice permits the observation, speculative though it must be, that features of the Septuagintal and targumic versions of two *ḥērem*-passages could be explained from the same association. In the LXX, Josh. vii 12 'until you put away (ἐξάρητε, MT *tašmîdû*) the anathema from you (ἐξ ὑμῶν)', becomes strikingly close to the formula of Deut. xvii 7, etc., quoted at I Cor. v 13 'you shall put away (ἐξάρατε, plural for the singular of LXX Deut. xvii 7) the evil man from you (ἐξ ὑμῶν αὐτῶν)'. It is not impossible that the LXX translator viewed Achan's removal as the paradigm of the expulsion or death, or both, commanded in Deuteronomy. Secondly, the individual idolater, according to Exod. xxii 20 (19), 'shall be devoted (*yoḥ°rām*)'; but in Targum Pseudo-Jonathan 'he shall be slain with the sword, and his property shall be devoted' (*gmr* Itpaʿal), so that, as in the same Targum on Num. xvi 26, the sentence gains a degree of resemblance to Achan's punishment. In any case, whatever the strength of these two more speculative suggestions, it is clear that, from the tannaitic period onwards, the ban could be explained from the ban and curse upon Jericho, which issued in the city's destruction and the judgement of Achan.

In two of these explanations, then, the ban is interpreted from a curse (Judg. v 23), or a ban and a curse (Josh. vi 17, 26), issuing in a covenantal death-penalty; in the third, it is a separation, followed by a divinely-inflicted death (Num. xvi 26–35). In each case, the biblical context was already associated with contemporary discipline in the tannaitic period; and the LXX, read in conjunction with the Palestinian Targum, indicates at least once that the association was pre-rabbinic. These explanations, which all exhibit a long-standing view of the ban as a preliminary to death, can now be linked with passages, noted by Billerbeck and others, which attest an equation of the ban with death. This equation appears, among other places, in the early third-century explanation of *šammᵉtā'* as *šām mîtā'* (M.K. 16a, in the name of Rab); in the understanding of the ban, in Targum Pseudo-Jonathan, as a death-dealing weapon in the conquest of Canaan (section III, and n. 29, above); and in the probable derivation of *šammᵉtā'* from *šmd*, 'destroy' (cf. Josh. vii 12 (13), just noted), which also supplies the tannaitic words for 'apostate' and 'apostatize'.[39]

This equation of the ban with death has rightly been picked out as a key to the development whereby *ḥērem* can to be applied to excommunication.[40] Such an understanding of the ban would have received impetus not only from the explanations just noted, but also from the Pentateuchal laws wherein *ḥrm* implies death, Exod. xxii 20 (19), discussed above, and Lev. xxvii 29, which ends with the explicit *môt yûmāt*. It can now be seen, however, to belong to a larger context of thought, in which the covenantal associations of *ḥērem* continued to be noticed, so that the ban was seen as preparation or surrogate for the penalty at the hands of men (Josh. vi 17, 26; Judg. xxi 11) or heaven (Num. xvi 26–35). This understanding of the ban fits well with the early rabbinic treatment of apostates, noted in section III, above: curse (incorporated, in a general form, into the Twelfth Benediction), accompanied by exclusion from the normal privileges of Israelites. At the same time, both practice and understanding accord, as argued in section III, with those which prevailed, within the covenantal loyalty of the general Jewish body, from the post-exilic period onwards.

This study has concentrated on the treatment of grave offences, amounting to apostasy. That perspective by no means covers the range of the offences punished by the developed synagogue ban, in its differing degrees of severity. The viewpoint adopted here does, however, allow a thread to emerge which links, so it has been

---

[39] J. Levy, *Neuhebräisches und chaldäisches Wörterbuch über die Talmudim und Midraschim* 4 (2nd edn, Berlin and Vienna, 1924), 583.

[40] I. J. Peritz, 'Synagogue', *Encyclopaedia Biblica* 4 (1907), cols. 4832–40 (4834 f.); S. Bialoblocki, 'Cherem', *Encyclopaedia Judaica* 5 (Berlin, 1930), cols. 411–22 (412).

argued, the post-exilic community with the general Jewish body of the Roman period, both before the First Revolt and after the Second. Failure to uphold certain covenantal observances and beliefs has throughout incurred, according to biblical, pre-rabbinic and rabbinic evidence, a penalty which in theory and sometimes in practice is capital, but which is represented or prepared for by excommunication. Examination of the observances and beliefs concerned belongs to the discussion of norms in ancient Judaism. The argument presented here has been concerned, rather, with the significant point of practice. The evidence for excommunication from the general Jewish body in the pre-rabbinic period is not plentiful, but it is enough to suggest the existence of a recognized custom. Groups such as the Qumran community and the 'Associates' of the Mishnah would have been likely, from their limited and exclusive character, to implement the custom more frequently than the general body. Nevertheless, the evidence reviewed in section III, from references to exclusion, their vocabulary, and their background in biblical law, suggests that the custom was familiar to non-sectarian Jews. Its traces deserve notice as a sign of organization and cohesion in pre-rabbinic Jewry, and of the forces making for continuity amid the developments of the Second Temple period.[41]

[41]The writer gratefully acknowledges comments made in discussion by Prof. D. J. Lane and Dr H. G. M. Williamson, and a series of helpful observations by Dr G. I. Davies, who kindly read a draft typescript.

2

THE BENEDICTION OF THE *MINIM* AND EARLY JEWISH–CHRISTIAN CONTROVERSY

Trypho and his companions are told seven times in Justin's *Dialogue* (xvi, xciii, xcv, xcvi, cviii, cxxiii, cxxxiii) that 'you', the Jews, curse believers in Christ; at xvi and xcvi it is noted that this happens 'in your synagogues'. Four further passages lack the use of καταρᾶσθαι common to this group, but are related in subject-matter. We pray for you, says Justin, that coming to a better mind with us you may not blaspheme Christ Jesus (xxxv); there is no hope for those who keep the law but do not believe in Christ, 'especially those who in the synagogues anathematized and anathematize (καταναθεματίζειν) this Christ' (xlvii); the Jews' high priests and teachers have caused Christ's name to be defiled throughout the world and blasphemed – filthy garments which they have put upon all Christians (cxvii); Jews should not mock the king of Israel, obeying Pharisee teachers – 'such things as your rulers of synagogue teach, after the prayer' (cxxxvii). These remarks are in turn connected with claims that Jews have systematically circulated accounts of Christ as a deceiver whose disciples stole his body (xvii, cviii), and have been forbidden to converse with Christians (xxxviii, cxii).[1]

Modern students since Graetz, inheriting a time-honoured correlation of Christian with Jewish evidence, commonly take Justin's complaints of cursing to refer to the Twelfth Benediction of the Tefillah. According to a baraitha at Ber. 28b–29a this benediction, there and elsewhere termed 'of the heretics', *birkath ha-minim*, was 'ordered' by Samuel the Small at the request of Gamaliel II in Jamnia. This 'ordering', set towards the end of the first century by the names of those involved, is described by the verb *tiqqen*, 'fix, settle, ordain'. It will primarily have affected subject-matter, for the wording of the Eighteen Benedictions as a whole varied widely until well after this period. In its extant Hebrew forms, however, this benediction is regularly an imprecation, in many surviving texts it prays, according to its title, that the *minim* may perish, and in a

---

[1] J. C. T. Otto, *S. Justini Philosophi et Martyris Opera*, ii (Jena, 1843), 56–8, 60, 118, 124, 152, 320–2, 326, 372, 388, 410–12, 440, 448–50; A. Harnack, *Judentum und Juden-christentum in Justins Dialog mit Trypho* (TU 39, Leipzig, 1913), 78–81. On the topics treated below see also pp. 8–14, above.

number of witnesses from the Cairo Geniza and elsewhere *noṣerim*, Christians, are also specified. The first Geniza form to be published (1898) runs: 'For apostates let there be no hope, and the kingdom of insolence mayest thou uproot speedily in our days; and let the Christians (*noṣerim*) and the heretics (*minim*) perish in a moment, let them be blotted out of the book of life and let them not be written with the righteous. Blessed art thou, O Lord, who humblest the insolent.'[2]

Justin's evidence is commonly linked also with New Testament and patristic allusions to Jewish hostility, especially John ix. 22, xii. 42, xvi. 2 on exclusion from synagogue, and Epiphanius and Jerome on the cursing of 'Nazoraeans' in synagogue. On this basis it has been widely held, especially since Samuel Krauss's study of Justin (1893), that a reference to Christians, whether named or understood among the 'heretics', was regularly incorporated in the Eighteen Benedictions from the end of the first century, played an important part in the separation of church and synagogue, and is vividly attested in Justin. Influential exponents of this view include Ismar Elbogen, A. von Harnack, Marcel Simon, W. D. Davies and W. H. C. Frend.[3]

Yet it has been noted that Justin writes with an insouciance which, although it confirms his integrity, often betrays him into trivial mistakes.[4] Graetz, followed by Israel Abrahams and others, held that he erred in supposing the curses to apply to Christians in general, whereas only those of Jewish descent are envisaged in the prayer.[5] Schlatter (1898) was perhaps significantly silent on Justin when he concluded, discussing Krauss, that 'Nazoraeans' represented the rendering of *minim* in Greek synagogue prayer; he set the Hebrew forms of the benediction in the context of rabbinic measures

---

[2]H. L. Strack, *Jesus, die Häretiker und die Christen nach den ältesten jüdischen Angaben* (Leipzig, 1910), lxiv–lxvi, 30 f.; S. Kanter, *Rabban Gamaliel II: the Legal Traditions* (Chico, 1980), 9 f., 285. For Hebrew texts of the Twelfth Benediction see also n. 67 below.

[3]S. Krauss, 'The Jews in the Works of the Church Fathers', *Jewish Quarterly Review* v (1893), 122–57 (123–34); I. Elbogen, *Der jüdische Gottesdienst in seiner geschichtlichen Entwicklung* (3rd edn, Frankfurt a.M., 1931, repr. Hildesheim, 1962), 36–9; Harnack, *Trypho*, 80, 91; M. Simon, *Verus Israel* (2nd edn., Paris, 1964) 234–6; W. D. Davies, *The Setting of the Sermon on the Mount* (Cambridge, 1964), 275–9; W. H. C. Frend, *Martyrdom and Persecution in the Early Church* (Oxford, 1965), 179.

[4]H. Chadwick, 'Justin Martyr's Defence of Christianity', *Bulletin of the John Rylands Library* xlvii (1965), 275–97 (276).

[5]H. Graetz, *Geschichte der Juden*, iv (2nd edn. Leipzig, 1866), 105 f., 434 f. (n. 11); I Abrahams, *A Companion to the Authorized Daily Prayer Book* (3rd edn, London, 1932), lxiv f., and *Studies in Pharisaism and the Gospels*, Second Series (Cambridge, 1924), 59–62, 69–71.

against Christian Jews in Palestine.[6] Schürer distinguished Justin's complaints of cursing from the singular report of mockery *after* the prayer (and therefore presumably not part of the Eighteen Benedictions); and he warned against the assumption that the Geniza text-form was already current at the end of the first century.[7] Gustav Hoennicke accordingly emphasized that Justin cannot be shown to refer to the Eighteen Benedictions in particular.[8] Marmorstein accumulated evidence from Hebrew liturgical texts for a mention of Christians in the twelfth benediction, but questioned Justin's accuracy in general and doubted, like Hoennicke, whether Christians were cursed in the Eighteen Benedictions in Gamaliel II's time.[9] That this benediction was a means towards the division of church and synagogue was questioned by Aptowitzer on the quite different ground that they were already divided well before the end of the first century.[10] Herein he diverged from the influential drift of opinion exemplified by Marmorstein, which tended to emphasize Justin's doubtful accuracy and the solely inner-Jewish relevance of the benediction within a larger view of Pharisaic–rabbinic Judaism as for the most part indifferent to nascent Christianity, in the spirit of Gamaliel I's speech at Acts v 38.

Most of these questions were carefully considered by J. Jocz, who concluded that the benediction was newly created, soon after A.D. 70, with special reference to Hebrew Christians. Jocz accepted that the measure was wholly internal to Judaism, but otherwise gave credit to Justin's evidence, holding the benediction to be one of a number of signs of resistance to a lively Christian movement within the synagogue. In a study of prayer-formulations K. G. Kuhn, without discussing Justin, took a similar view of the historical background and attempted to isolate the words added at Jamnia.[11]

Recently the purpose of the benediction and the value of the early

---

[6]A. Schlatter, 'Die Kirche Jerusalems vom J. 70 bis 130', in id., *Synagoge und Kirche bis zum Barkochba-Aufstand* (Stuttgart, 1966), 108–10.

[7]E. Schürer, *Geschichte des jüdischen Volkes im Zeitalter Jesu Christi* (4th edn, Leipzig, 1901, repr. Hildesheim, 1964), vol. ii, 543 f.

[8]G. Hoennicke, *Das Judenchristentum im ersten und zweiten Jahrhundert* (Berlin, 1908), 387 f.

[9]A. Marmorstein, 'The Attitude of the Jews towards Early Christianity', *The Expositor*, xlix (1923), 383–9, and 'The Amidah of the Public Fast Days', *Jewish Quarterly Review* N.S. xv (1925), 409–18.

[10]V. Aptowitzer, 'Bemerkungen zur Liturgie und Geschichte der Liturgie', *Monatsschrift für Geschichte und Wissenschaft des Judentums*, lxxiv (1930), 104–26 (108–10, 112–15).

[11]J. Jocz, *The Jewish People and Jesus Christ* (London, 1949), 51–7; K. G. Kuhn, *Achtzehngebet und Vaterunser und der Reim* (Tübingen, 1950), 18–21.

Christian evidence have been discussed again, sometimes with surprisingly little reference to earlier questionings. P. Schäfer, followed up to a point by G. Stemberger,[12] concentrates on the benediction itself within the setting of rabbinic literature. From the texts of the prayer he argues that it was directed against 'the kingdom of insolence' as much as against heretics; Christians may or may not have been included among the latter in the Jamnian period, but in any case the benediction cannot have been primarily intended to separate Christians from Jews; it was meant to be what its wording suggests, a prayer for liberation from political oppression and for the annihilation of heretics (the purposes are named here in Schäfer's order). Stemberger, without broaching the question of an anti-Roman intention, underlines the sparseness of evidence for Christians in post-70 Palestine and the questionableness of the assumption that they were envisaged in the Jamnian ordinance; he notes, however, the close parallel between the institutional developments of Judaism and Christianity at this period. R. Kimelman, in a more detailed examination of this historical context, stresses once again (to quote his title) 'the lack of evidence for an anti-Christian Jewish prayer in late antiquity'.[13] With Graetz and his many successors he concludes that only Jews, whether sectarian or Christian, are envisaged in the benediction; and he adds, taking further the type of criticism offered by Hoennicke, that there is no unambiguous evidence for the cursing of Christians during statutory Jewish prayers, whereas many patristic complaints make it clear that Christians were sometimes welcomed in synagogues; consequently the benediction is no watershed in Jewish–Christian separation, which results from a long process rather than any single edict.

The contributions of these articles include Schäfer's renewed consideration of the relation of Jewish views of Rome to the benediction, Stemberger's emphasis on the analogies between the developments of Judaism and Christianity after 70, and Kimelman's distinction between tannaitic, Palestinian, and Babylonian material in his fresh discussion of *minim* and *noṣerim*. Nevertheless, their

---

[12]P. Schäfer, 'Die sogenannte Synode von Jabne', repr. from *Judaica* xxxi (1975) in Schäfer, *Studien zur Geschichte und Theologie des rabbinischen Judentums* (Leiden, 1978), 45–55; G. Stemberger, 'Die sogenannte "Synode von Jabne" und das frühe Christentum', *Kairos* xix (1977), 14–21.

[13]R. Kimelman, '*Birkat Ha-Minim* and the Lack of Evidence for an Anti-Christian Jewish Prayer in Late Antiquity', in E. P. Sanders, A. I. Baumgarten, and Alan Mendelson (edd.), *Jewish and Christian Self-Definition*, ii (London, 1981), 226–44.

predominant tone of cautious warning, however apt in view of the obvious danger of linking unrelated pieces of evidence, serves to underline some unanswered questions. First, what is the value of the early Christian evidence? The negative view that John and Justin do not refer to the Eighteen Benedictions in particular is arguable, but leaves the circumstances of their complaints unillumined. This point is implied in Prof. Barnabas Lindar's insistence, in a comment on Schäfer, that Justin's evidence must not be overlooked.[14] Secondly, recent studies confirm that the early rabbinic attitude to Rome, like that of early Christians, was a complex of favourable as well as unfavourable views.[15] How dominant is an anti-Roman curse within a benediction known as 'of the *minim*'? These questions bring forward a point stressed by C. K. Barrett, the need to set the benediction within a broader historical context.[16] It is suggested here that, as many since Graetz have indicated, the beginnings of Jewish–Christian controversy provide the larger context within which both the Christian and the Jewish evidence are best understood. More particularly it is argued that the benediction as reformulated under Gamaliel II was primarily anti-heretical rather than anti-Roman in intention, that members of 'the sect of the Nazarenes' (Acts xxiv 5) were prominent among those envisaged in its condemnatory clauses, and that its impact was felt not only within the Jewish community but among the circle of Gentile sympathizers. These claims involve a return to three areas, not all discussed in recent study. The early complaints of cursing are viewed together with other allegations about the synagogue and in connection with the later Christian discussion of the benediction itself, which forms the foundation of modern study; the understanding of the benediction in Jewish liturgy and tradition is considered; and the interaction of Judaism and nascent Christianity is briefly recalled.

[14]B. Lindars, 'The Persecution of Chrisitans in John 15: 18–16: 4a', in W. Horbury and Brian McNeil (edd.), *Suffering and Martyrdom in the New Testament: Studies presented to G. M. Styler* (Cambridge, 1981), 48–69 (49 n. 6). For recent positive evaluations of Justin's evidence, see L. W. Barnard, *Justin Martyr* (Cambridge, 1967), 44 f.; F. Blanchetière, 'Aux sources de l'anti-judaïsme chrétien', *Revue d'histoire et de philosophie religieuse* liii (1973), 354–98 (385 ff.). This subject is not discussed by B. Z. Bokser, 'Justin Martyr and the Jews', *Jewish Quarterly Review* N.S. lxiv (1973), 97–122, 204–11, or P. Sigal, 'An Inquiry into Aspects of Judaism in Justin's Dialogue with Trypho', *Abr Nahrain* xviii (1978–9), 74–100.

[15]N. R. M. de Lange, 'Jewish Attitudes to the Roman Empire', in P. D. A. Garnsey and C. R. Whittaker (edd.), *Imperialism in the Ancient World* (Cambridge, 1978), 255–81; G. Stemberger, 'Die Beurteilung Roms in der rabbinischen Literatur', in H. Temporini and W. Haase (edd.), *Aufstieg und Niedergang der römischen Welt*, ii. 19. 2 (Berlin, 1979), 338–96.

[16]C. K. Barrett, *The Gospel of John and Judaism* (E.T. London, 1975), 47 f.

I

For this question, said Krauss, how much blood has been spilt – and how much more ink.[17] Justin's complaints continue those of the New Testament, and open a well-known series of patristic and later comments on Jewish allegations and imprecations. They are traced here as far as the seventeenth-century discussion of the benediction, whence modern study of the subject arises. The object is twofold: to bring out the views of the origin and purpose of the benediction which emerged, from the Middle Ages onwards, in a period of intense apologetic and polemic preoccupation with it, and to identify those patristic comments which have a specificity entitling them to serious consideration.

Justin himself, among eleven relevant passages of the *Dialogue*, speaks four times with greater precision: twice of the cursing of Christians in the synagogue (xvi, xcvi), once of the anathematization of Christ in the synagogues (xlvii), once of the mockery of Christ taught by *archisynagogi* after the prayer (cxxxvii). Schürer, rightly cautious as he was concerning the original form of the benediction of the *minim*, held that actual anathematization in the synagogues was indicated by c. xvi; and Harnack counted the cursing of Christians during prayer, and the mockery of Christ after prayer, among the reliable detailed information in the *Dialogue*.[18] These statements of Justin are consistent with his further allegations of a negative account of Christ and a prohibition of converse with Christians, for both of which some corresponding inner-Jewish evidence is found (pp. 102–8, below). The *Dialogue* comes from between 155 and 160.[19]

Origen's claim that Christ is still anathematized by the Jews (*in Ps. xxxvii (xxxvi) hom.* ii. 8, *P.G.* xii 1387) is suspiciously general, and may simply echo *Dial.* xlvii; in recent study it has been both rejected and accepted as evidence for an anti-Christian curse in the Eighteen Benedictions.[20] Tertullian, however, knows more exactly that 'the Jews call us *Nazareni*' (*Marc.* iv. 8. 1), and that they contemptuously term the Lord 'quaestuariae filius ... quem ...

---

[17]S. Krauss, 'Zur Literatur der Siddurim: christliche Polemik', in A. Marx and H. Meyer (edd.), *Festschrift für Aron Freimann* (Berlin, 1935), 125–40 (137).

[18]Harnack, *Trypho*, 91; E. Schürer, G. Vermes, F. Millar, and M. Black, *The History of the Jewish People in the Age of Jesus Christ*, ii (Edinburgh, 1979), 432.

[19]A. Harnack, *Die Chronologie der altchristlichen Literatur bis Eusebius*, i (Leipzig, 1897), 281.

[20]N. R. M. de Lange, *Origen and the Jews* (Cambridge, 1976), 86, sees a probable reference; to the contrary, Kimelman, 236 f.

hortulanus detraxit' (*de spec.* xxx). Post-biblical Hebrew sources again give corresponding information,[21] and the first statement could conceivably allude to a form of the benediction, perhaps in Greek or Latin, mentioning Nazarenes. The question is raised, however, whether in Jewish usage this term, or its rarely attested equivalent *noṣerim*, refers to Christians in general or a Jewish–Christian sect.[22]

This question is prominent in debate on the relevant passages of Epiphanius and Jerome. Epiphanius says of the Jewish–Christian 'Nazoraeans': 'the sons of the Jews ... standing up at morning and midday and about evening, three times a day when they complete (*or,* are completing) their prayers in the synagogues curse and anathematize them, saying three times a day "God curse the Nazoraeans." '[23] In four closely similar passages Jerome affirms that: 'three times each day in all the synagogues under the name of Nazarenes they anathematize the Christian denomination (*vocabulum*)'.[24] Here, however, he thinks that Christians in general are meant. In *ep.* cxii. 13 to Augustine, on the other hand, he is speaking of the Ebionites when he says that: 'through all the synagogues of the east among the Jews there is a sect, named "of the *Minaei*", and until now it is condemned by the Pharisees; they are commonly called *Nazaraei*,' and want to be Jews as well as Christians, but succeed in being neither.[25]

Graetz held that Epiphanius, a born Jew, knew of the benediction and rightly understood it to refer to the Jewish–Christian Nazarene sect.[26] Kimelman similarly takes Epiphanius and Jerome, when writing to Augustine, as accurate witnesses to the benediction in a form mentioning Nazarenes and referring thereby to Jewish–Christian sectarians; in the other four passages Jerome succumbed to his anti-Jewish tendency.[27] The importance of literary relationships between the passages had, however, been indicated by Alfred

---

[21]S. Krauss, *Das Leben Jesu nach jüdischen Quellen* (Berlin, 1902), 3; Horbury, 'Tertullian on the Jews in the Light of *de spec.* xxx. 13', *J.T.S.* N.S. xxiii (1972), 455–9 (pp. 176–9, below).

[22]C. Aziza, *Tertullien et le judaïsme* (Nice, 1977), 36 f.

[23]*Panarion*, xxix. 9, printed in Strack, lxvi and A. F. J. Klijn and G. J. Reinink, *Patristic Evidence for Jewish-Christian Sects* (Supplements to *Novum Testamentum* xxxvi: Leiden, 1973), 172–5 (where the double rendering of *paides* as 'children' and 'people' is misleading).

[24]*In Esaiam*, ii, on v. 18 f.; cf. xiii, on xlix. 7, and xiv, on lii. 4–6; *in Amos*, i, on i. 11 f.; texts at Strack, lxvi and Klijn–Reinink, 218–25.

[25]Klijn–Reinink, 200 f.

[26]Graetz, iv (2nd edn, 1866), 434 f.

[27]Kimelman, 238.

Schmidtke.[28] He believed that the notice on cursing, like other information about Nazarenes, came to Epiphanius and Jerome from a common source, probably Apollinarius of Laodicea's lost commentary of Isaiah. The source rightly referred to the benediction as a curse on Christians in general, but Epiphanius wrongly applied what he read to the sect of the Nazoraeans, which he is unlikely to have known personally. Jerome, arguing against Augustine that observance of the Mosaic law is incompatible with Christian orthodoxy, gladly took over the remarks on the Nazarenes in Epiphanius, who himself makes short work of them because he regards their views as so indefensible. In the four passages from the commentaries on Amos and Isaiah, however, Jerome drew directly on the source also read by Epiphanius, and understood it rightly.

Schmidtke's argument, based on more instances than this, will not be discussed here. Even if his indication of Apollinarius should be mistaken or insufficient in this case, it would still point to the source-critical question; and he convincingly demonstrates Epiphanius' lack of personal knowledge of his 'Nazoraeans', his compensating readiness as a compiler, and Jerome's debt to him. Schmidtke also notes, however, that Jerome has one piece of information not found in Epiphanius, the mention of *Minaei*. His connection of this word with synagogues and condemnation suggests direct or indirect knowledge of congregational condemnation of the *minim*. It may be concluded that a synagogal curse on 'Nazarenes' was known to Epiphanius, whose contacts with the converted Jew, Joseph of Tiberias, and other Jews may rank beside his reading as possible sources in this case.[29] Jerome also knew it, through Epiphanius and some other source or sources (whence he derived the name *Minaei*), perhaps including Apollinarius on Isaiah, a book which he expressly mentions. The names in the curse were interpreted in each passage according to the exigencies of the moment. Epiphanius the heresiologist, probably identifying the secret believers in Christ among the Jews described by Joseph with the particular heresy of the 'Nazoraeans', links the curse with this sect, and is followed by Jerome in his refutation of Christian law-observance. Elsewhere Jerome gives 'Nazarenes' in the formula the general sense which it may have borne in his source, and which in any case he knew from Tertullian and Acts. Both Fathers, then, are witnesses, probably at second hand, to a synagogal curse mentioning

---

[28] A. Schmidtke, *Neue Fragmente und Untersuchungen zu den judenchristlichen Evangelien* (TU 37. 1, Leipzig, 1911), 64 f., 71–5, 105–8, 249–51. Schmidtke's source-criticism is not discussed by Klijn–Reinink, 46, 52, but they similarly hold Epiphanius to have no first-hand knowledge of Nazoraean belief.

[29] *Panarion*, xxx. 9, discussed by Schmidtke, 252 f.

Nazarenes (and, as Jerome knows, *minim*); but their views of its scope carry much less weight than their attestation of its use and wording.

The value of the patristic passages noted thus far may now be provisionally estimated. Although Jewish hostility is a standard presupposition of the authors, their particular allegations are strikingly various and specific. Justin mentions cursing in the synagogues and the teaching of their 'rulers', together with a ban on converse and a negative account of Christ; Tertullian knows the name *Nazareni* and precisely-formulated allegations about Christ, Epiphanius the words of a curse uttered thrice daily, Jerome the threefold utterance and the names *Minaei* and *Nazaraei*. These specific reports would claim serious consideration even if no inner-Jewish corroboration had survived. In fact, however, Jewish sources retain not only various formulations of a benediction 'of the *minim*', which remain to be discussed, but also material corresponding to the allegations about Christ.

This confirmation of a distinct but related category of patristic evidence gives the reports of cursing a further claim to credit. They may be taken to indicate that, from the second century onwards, an imprecation on Christians was pronounced in synagogue. Justin's references to the cursing and mockery of *Christ* allude to a separate practice; this was probably a requirement that synagogue members of suspect loyalty should vindicate themselves by cursing Christ, such as Bar Cocheba is said by Justin to have imposed on Christian Jews, and is envisaged by J. D. M. Derrett as the background of I Cor. xii 3.[30] By the second half of the fourth century the imprecation against Christians mentioned 'Nazarenes' and *Minaei*, and was pronounced thrice daily.

For the scope of the imprecation, as distinct from its wording, Epiphanius and Jerome are of much less authority than Justin, whose numerous, bitter, and consistent references have an air of immediacy. He believes that it applies to all Christians, but, describing them for his own purposes as those who believe in Christ, fails to reproduce the name by which they were cursed. 'Galilaean' or 'Nazarene' are both possible. The former is applied to Christ in the adverse Jewish statement summarized at *Dial.* cviii, and to Christians (in all probability) by Justin's slightly earlier contemporary Epictetus, who may well have adopted a Jewish usage.[31] 'Nazarene', however, is more

---

[30]J. D. M. Derrett, 'Cursing Jesus (1 Cor. xii 3): The Jews as Religious "Persecutors"', *New Testament Studies* xxi (1975), 544–54; see also n. 135, below.

[31]P. de Labriolle, *La réaction païenne* (Paris, 1934), 49 n.

likely; it became the more widespread term, appears in Epiphanius and Jerome in this context, and at the end of the second century is regarded by Tertullian as the regular Jewish name.

In this case, however, as already noted, the reference of the word, and thereby Justin's view of the scope of the imprecation, is brought into question. Talmudic attestation of the corresponding Hebrew *noṣerim* is so sparse that Krauss held the Geniza text of the benediction of the *minim* to be the best evidence for Jewish usage of the word in the rabbinic period.[32] Kimelman argues that in two passages of the Babylonian Talmud, Gittin 57a (where the word occurs by a probable emendation) and Taanith 27b (R. Johanan, third-century Palestine),[33] it refers to Judaeo-Christians, and that this meaning is also intended in the benediction.[34] These occurrences, however, even if rightly referred to Judaeo-Christians in particular,[35] do not necessarily imply that the word was restricted to this application. In its frequent post-Talmudic occurrences it is regularly used for Christians in general; the same is true of the cognates in Syriac (from the Old Syriac Gospels onward) and Arabic.[36] In the western diaspora of the second century the word need not have been restricted to Jewish Christians, and Tertullian's view that *Nazareni* was used for all Christians can be accepted. If then, as is likely, the imprecation known to Justin mentioned Nazarenes, credit can still be given to his complaint that Christians in general were being cursed.

The view that all Christians are intended in the synagogue imprecation, as patristic evidence can now be seen to suggest, finds some support in the acceptance by outsiders of the self-definition of the Christian community of Jews and gentiles as one body. 'The Church' (Eph. iii 10, etc.; cf. I Cor. x 32) is viewed in Jewish and pagan sources from the beginning of the second century as a single, if faction-ridden, 'tribe' (Josephus, *Ant.* xviii. 64),[37] 'faction' (beginning

---

[32]Krauss, *Leben Jesu*, 254.

[33]Strack, lxxviii, 39.

[34]Kimelman, 240–4, suggesting that the earlier vocalization was *naṣrim*.

[35]Taanith 27b need not imply that the Christians concerned fast on Sunday; other interpretations are cited by Kimelman, loc. cit.

[36]H. H. Schaeder in *TWNT* iv (1942), 880.

[37]J. Maier, *Jesus von Nazareth in der talmudischen Überlieferung* (Darmstadt, 1978), 44, views this sentence as probably authentic; cf., on the whole passage, E. Bammel, 'Zum Testimonium Flavianum', in O. Betz, K. Haacker, and M. Hengel (edd.), *Josephus-Studien* (Göttingen, 1974), 9–22. According to Maier Christianity is viewed here, as in the Twelfth Benediction, as one among many divergences from Judaism; this somewhat presses the implications of *phylos*, which is notable, rather, as an early Jewish allusion to the mixed Christian community as a single body.

from Christ's *stasis* against Jewry, Celsus in Origen, *c. Celsum* iii. 1,
5; viii. 14), or 'race' (*genus tertium* in pagan usage according to
Tertullian, *Scorp.* x. 10).[38] The setting of an imprecation on all
Christians in the Judaism of this period is considered in Part III
below, when these conclusions from the church fathers studied on
their own are taken up after discussion of the benediction within its
contextual prayer.

The next phase of evidence on an anti-Christian imprecation
initiates debate on the purpose of the benediction itself. The synagogue prayers are not mentioned in Justinian's novella of 553, no
doubt because it deals with a specific question on biblical versions,
and accordingly restricts its rulings on Jewish worship to biblical
lection and exposition.[39] A passage in Pirqoi ben Baboi on the
prohibition of the Tefillah in Palestine is explained by Mann,
however, as referring to an early seventh-century ordinance of
Heraclius, otherwise unknown, made with this benediction in view.[40]
In this case the benediction would have been regarded as a politically
relevant curse on the Christian empire. A pastoral interest, on the
other hand, appears when Agobard of Lyons, in the early ninth
century, quotes Jerome on the daily synagogue malediction against
Christians, but adds that many of the Jews themselves attest it.[41] This
claim is supported by Agobard's detailed reports of other material
attributed to Jewish informants. These find correspondence in
Hebrew sources and include, as in the case of Justin and Tertullian,
specific statements about Christ.[42] He is probably referring to the
benediction,[43] and viewing it primarily as one more piece of evidence
for the Jewish denial of the Christian faith in his diocese.

Non-Jewish suspicions that the benediction prays for the downfall
of the gentiles are reflected in Midrash Panim Aherim on Est. iii 8,

---

[38]For comment, with parallels, on *scorp.* x. 10, see A. Harnack, *The Mission and Expansion
of Christianity in the First Three Centuries* (E.T. 2nd edn, London, 1908), 266–78.

[39]J. Juster, *Les juifs dans l'empire romain*, i (Paris, 1914), 369–77; A. Sharf, *Byzantine
Jewry* (London, 1971), 24 f.

[40]J. Mann, 'Changes in the Divine Service of the Synagogue due to Religious Persecution',
Hebrew Union College Annual iv (1927), 241–310 (252–4, 277 f.).

[41]*De insolentia Iudaeorum*, iv, reprinted from *P.L.* civ. 73 at Strack, lxvi; cf. A. Lukyn
Williams, *Adversus Judaeos* (Cambridge, 1935), 353 n. 3.

[42]B. Blumenkranz, *Les auteurs chrétiens latins du moyen âge sur les juifs et le judaïsme*
(Paris, 1963), 161 (Agobard refers to the benediction), 164 f. (his Jewish knowledge).

[43]Ch. Merchavia, *The Church versus Talmudic and Midrashic Literature (500–1248)*
(Hebrew: Jerusalem, 1970), 82 f., holds that he simply depends on Jerome; the benediction
made no explicit reference to Christians, for the texts with *noṣerim* had no influence in
Christian Europe. The contrary is suggested by the extent of Agobard's contemporary Jewish
information, and the eleventh-century European Jewish application of this benediction to
Christianity (p. 95, below).

quoted in Yalkut ad loc.[44] Krauss, who drew attention to the passage, notes that whereas in other midrashic versions of Haman's speech the Jews are accused of cursing the gentiles, here only is the charge connected with the benediction.[45] Haman complains that once a week the Jews celebrate what they call sabbath, and they open the synagogues, read words which one cannot hear, and say 'Hear, O Israel ...'. 'After that they stand up for prayer, and say in their Prayer "who humblest the insolent", and they say that we are the insolent; and after that they say "who lovest righteousness and judgement", and they expect that the Holy One, blessed be he, will execute judgement upon us; and after that they take the scroll of the law and curse us craftily, and they say "Let thine enemies be subdued unto thee".' The midrash must antedate the compilation of the Yalkut in the first half of the thirteenth century. This passage interestingly assumes that not only the present Twelfth Benediction, with the eulogy 'who humblest', but also the present Eleventh, with the eulogy 'who lovest', can be construed as anti-gentile;[46] that they are recited in this order, the reverse of that which became standard;[47] that, if the initial reference to the sabbath is taken to qualify the whole passage, these benedictions, against normal usage (whereby the petitionary benedictions are omitted on sabbath, cf. Tos. Ber. iii. 13), are retained in the sabbath Tefillah; and that the Prayer itself is followed by a curse with scroll in hand, a ceremony associated with the ban.[48] Whether a sabbath Tefillah is meant is debatable, but the association of the Twelfth Benediction with the Eleventh, and their variable order, are confirmed by other evidence discussed below. In the present connection the passage has a twofold significance: it shows that the Benediction of the *Minim*, set in its context, could be understood as a prayer against the gentile 'insolent'; and it presupposes a separate curse 'after the prayer', as Justin envisages separate teachings of the *archisynagogi* at that point.

A specimen form of the benediction was first made widely known in the Christian west through the Talmudic and liturgical translations

[44]Second recension, c. iii, in S. Buber, *Sammlung agadischer Commentare zum Buche Ester* (Vilna, 1886), 68; *Yalkut Shimeoni* (2 vols., Vilna, 1909), vol. ii, 1058, col. 1.

[45]S. Krauss, 'Imprecation against the Minim in the Synagogue', *Jewish Quarterly Review* ix (1897), 515–17, and 'Zur Literatur', 128 f.

[46]With 'they expect ... execute judgement' cf. 'as soon as the exiled are gathered in, judgement is executed upon the wicked' in the explanation of the Eleventh Benediction at b. Meg. 17b, with the comments at Elbogen, 34, 50.

[47]Attention is drawn to this point by L. Ginzberg, *A Commentary on the Palestinian Talmud*, i (New York, 1941), 325.

[48]Krauss, 'Zur Literatur', 129 and n. 20.

by Nicholas Donin, a Jewish convert, appended to the Papal letter of Gregory IX (1239) which prepared for the Paris Disputation of 1240.[49] Here 'benediccio Mynim' runs 'Let there be no hope for the converts (*conversis*), and may all *mynym* [Donin's transliteration, which he interprets by adding (*infideles*)] perish in a moment, and may all the enemies of thy people Israel be cut asunder, and mayest thou uproot and destroy the kingdom of wickedness, and crush and bow down all our enemies speedily in our days; blessed art thou, O God, who breakest enemies and bowest down the impious.' It is quoted to support the charge that 'Three times each day, in a prayer which they assert to be more worthy than others, they curse the ministers of the church, kings, and all others who bear enmity towards the Jews themselves'. This expresses what became also a standard view of the purpose of the benediction. By a combination of the objections noted so far, it is regarded as a curse on both church and king and all other enemies of the Jews.

The basis of this interpretation emerges in the mediaeval apologetic and polemic described by Krauss.[50] Apostates and *minim* were thought to refer to converted Jews (or the apostles) and the clergy, respectively, and the kingdom of insolence to the civil power. Thus the Hebrew account of the Paris Disputation rebuts the charge that 'the kingdom of insolence' is that of France; on the contrary, Jews pray for this kingdom, and for their protector the Pope, as directed in Aboth iii. 2 'Pray for the peace of the kingdom'.[51] Lipmann Mühlhausen (early fifteenth century) sardonically asserts that all Christians themselves say 'Let there be no hope for apostates' – to return to Judaism; if by *minim* the Jews meant idol-priests (*komerim*, a regular opprobrious Hebrew term for the clergy), they would have used the word, as Scripture does at II Kings xxiii 5 (where their abolition is described).[52]

Lipmann's point that words unambiguously referring to Christians are not found in the benediction was repeatedly made by Reuchlin in his defence of Jewish literature. Its strength lay in the fact that the forms under discussion did not contain the word *noṣerim*. Reuchlin could write, therefore, that 'no word is to be

---

[49]Latin text published by I. Loeb, 'La controverse sur le Talmud sous Saint Louis', *Revue des études juives*, iii (1881), 39–57 (50 f.); discussion at Merchavia, 278–80.

[50]Krauss, 'Zur Literatur', 129–37.

[51]Text reprinted by J. D. Eisenstein, *Oẓar Wikuḥim* (New York, 1928, repr. Israel, 1969), 86.

[52]T. Hackspan, *Liber Nizachon Rabbi Lipmanni* (Nuremberg, 1644), 193; this section is reprinted by Eisenstein, 116 f., who calls his answers (115) 'wonderful, even if unreliable'; a similar view at Krauss, 'Zur Literatur', 130 f.

found therein which means or signifies the baptized, or apostles, or Christians, or the Roman Empire'.[53] He qualified this by noting that God alone knows the thoughts of those who use this prayer, but felt able to placard the anti-Christian interpretation of the benediction as the first of thirty-four *Unwahrheiten* perpetrated by Pfefferkorn.[54]

This argument was essential for the protection of synagogue worship and Jewish literature. Reuchlin's saving clause on the thoughts of the heart was none the less echoed, in respect of another disputed prayer, the *Alenu*, by a notable seventeenth-century defender of the Jewish liturgy, J. C. Wagenseil.[55] His adoption of Reuchlin's concession to the possibility that Christians may be intended, even though not named, reflects the continuing debate on synagogue prayers. The view that their condemnations of the insolent and idolatrous could apply to Christianity was strengthened by the growing seventeenth-century knowledge of Hebrew polemical literature, a genre of which Reuchlin had also been aware. Of special note in the present context, however, are the concomitant appeals to rabbinic comments on the Eighteen Benedictions. Disputation on the meaning of contemporary prayers had long raised the question of their origin,[56] but the studies of the Christian Hebraists gave new impetus to this inquiry.

Hence Ber. 28b 'they ordained it at Jamnia' repeatedly figures in debate. Within the Babylonian Talmud itself these words on the Twelfth Benediction agree with the baraitha 'Simeon ha-Paqoli arranged the Eighteen Benedictions in order before Rabban Gamaliel in Jamnia' and the story of Samuel the Small, in the same passage, but appear to be inconsistent with 'the men of the great synagogue ordained Prayers for Israel' (Ber. 33a) and 'one hundred and twenty elders, prophets among them, ordained the Eighteen Benedictions in order' (Meg. 17b). These two ascriptions to Jamnia, on the one hand, and the time of Ezra, on the other, are harmonized, as Elbogen points out, by the statement in Meg. 18a that the Benedictions had been forgotten, but were then set in order again by

---

[53]*Doctor Johannsen Reuchlins ... Augenspiegel* (Tübingen, 1511), f. 5a; I have used the facsimile edition, n.d., 'mit einem Nachwort von Dr Josef Benzing'.

[54]*Augenspiegel*, ff. 24a–b, 32b–35a.

[55]J. C. Wagenseil, *Tela Ignea Satanae* (Altdorf, 1681), 'Confutatio Carminis R. Lipmanni', 215–24.

[56]Ibn Verga, *Shebhet Yehudah*, ed. S. Wiener (Hanover, 1855), 108, as reprinted by Eisenstein, *Wikuḥim*, 161, col. 2, envisages a late fifteenth-century defence of the Second Benediction on the ground that the first three of the Eighteen come from Abraham, Isaac, and Jacob.

Simeon.[57] Jewish apologetic of the sixteenth and seventeenth centuries leans naturally towards the ascription to the pre-Christian 'men of the great synagogue', whereas Christian criticism stresses the evidence for Jamnian origin.

Thus Ishmael Valmontone in Bologna, 1568, anticipates objections based on Rashi on Ber. 28b. Rashi's comment that the Benediction of the *Minim* was ordained 'when the disciples of Jesus had multiplied' had been printed, in slightly varying forms, in the Soncino, 1484, edition of Babylonian Talmud, Berakhoth, in the Babylonian Talmud of Bomberg (Venice, 1522), and in the Mishnah with Alfasi (Sabbioneta, 1559).[58] Valmontone nullifies it by the mediaeval argument that another Jesus is intended.[59] When in the following century Salman Zevi (1615) defended the benediction against S. F. Brenz by ascribing it to Ezra's time, Johannes Wülfer, in a generally sympathetic examination of his arguments, here concluded against him on the basis of Samuel the Small's story with Rashi's comment.[60] The Buxtorfs similarly cited Ber. 28b in their argument that the benediction was directed against Christianity.[61] It is not surprising that the apologetic of Isaac Lopez (1695) is entirely Talmudic, based on the harmonizing passage in Meg. 18a: the benediction was composed in Ezra's time and then forgotten; Samuel the Small was simply the sage who remembered it at the time when the ancient benedictions were being arranged in order.[62] A distinction between usage and origin was drawn, however, in the discussions of Ber. 28b by the Cistercian bibliographer Giulio Bartolocci.[63] He held that the contemporary benediction, which he quoted in two forms (including that with 'apostates' and *minim*), did indeed refer to Christianity and the Roman Empire; but he identified Samuel the Small's Gamaliel with the New Testament figure, and so argued, in anticipation of modern views, that the benediction was first composed not against Christians principally, but against others

---

[57]Elbogen, *Gottesdienst*, 28 f.

[58]The point is specially noted by G. B. De Rossi, *Annales hebraeo-typographici saeculi xv* (Parma, 1795), 33, no. 8; Strack, p. lxvii.

[59]Eisenstein, 168, cols. 1–2; background illuminated in publication of related work of Solomon Modena by D. B. Ruderman, 'A Jewish Apologetic Treatise from Sixteenth Century Bologna', *Hebrew Union College Annual* l (1979), 253–74.

[60]J. Wülfer, *Theriaca Judaica, ad examen revocata* (Nuremberg, 1681), 'Animadversiones', 327–32.

[61]J. Buxtorf, *Synagoga Judaica* (5th edn., revised by J. J. Buxtorf, Basle, 1712), 209–13.

[62]Isaac Lopez, *Kur maṣreph*, as reprinted in Eisenstein, 221, cols. 1–2.

[63]G. Bartolocci and C. G. Imbonati, *Bibliotheca Magna Rabbinica* (4 vols., Rome, 1675–93), i, 730 f.; iii, 319–23.

82   JEWS AND CHRISTIANS IN CONTACT AND CONTROVERSY

known by all to be heretics – such as Theudas, mentioned in
Gamaliel's speech (Acts v 36).

The long debate just briefly surveyed thus tends finally towards
the historical orientation of current study. Throughout, however, it
has raised questions about the prayer in mediaeval and Renaissance
Jewish usage which continue, with only slight alterations, to be
pertinent in discussion of the Jamnian benediction. Was it, as
Schäfer argues, directed against the gentile government (Pirqoi ben
Baboi, Midrash Panim Aherim) as well as heretics, or against
Christians especially (Agobard), or a combination of these (polemists from Nicholas Donin onwards)? For confirmation of these
charges appeals were made to Rashi and the rabbinic texts on the
Tefillah, evidence still of concern to the historian and considered
below. Lipmann's defensive argument that Christians were not
specifically named is now qualified, since some formulations have
noṣerim, but remains relevant in view of the fluidity of the Eighteen
Benedictions in the Jamnian period, and the lack of evidence for
formulations contemporary with Justin and the later books of the
New Testament (Hoennicke, Kimelman) – even though the patristic
evidence makes it probable, as argued above, that Nazarenes were
sometimes specified at this stage. The main objection to an argument
on Lipmann's lines remains that envisaged by Reuchlin, that Christians may have been intended in Jamnian formulations even though
unnamed. The alternative argument, whereby the benediction is
referred to the time of Ezra, survives in the view discussed below
that Samuel the Small reshaped an existing benediction. These
points are now taken up in an examination of the setting of the
Twelfth Benediction among the Eighteen, and Jewish testimony on
its origin and purpose.

II

The Twelfth Benediction is directed, according to Schäfer, as much
against the Roman government as against heretics,[64] who are in any
case heretics in general rather than Christians in particular. His
contention is based especially on the formulations of the benediction
itself, and is supported by such an interpretation as that already
noted in Midrash Panim Aherim, as well as by other material
discussed below. Yet there are grounds for thinking it an over-

[64]'Heretic' is kept as a rendering of *min*, since differences of belief as well as conduct are
likely to be in question (cf. Heinemann, *Prayer*, 31 f., for the confessional character of many
early Jewish prayers); debate on this subject is surveyed by F. Dexinger, 'Die Sektenpro-
blematik im Judentum', *Kairos* xxi (1979), 273–87.

simplification. Rather, it appears, a benediction 'of the *minim*', constituting a curse on heretical members of the congregation of Israel, was included at Jamnia within a contextual invocation of divine judgement on both Israel and gentiles, in a prayer for messianic redemption. This anti-heretical purpose was not forgotten in Jewish interpretation of the Twelfth Benediction.

The origin of the benediction was reconstructed with great textual precision by K. G. Kuhn. On the basis of Schechter's Geniza formulation he argued for a Jamnian addition 'and may the Nazarenes ... and let them not be written with the righteous' to two pre-Jamnian prayers against apostates and against the gentile government, now together forming the first part of the Twelfth Benediction.[65] The place of an anti-gentilic prayer in the benediction will be considered shortly. At this stage, when origins are about to be discussed, it should simply be noted that the textual precision of Kuhn's suggestion is hardly attainable in view of the fluidity of the Tefillah at the end of the first century. Kuhn took account of rabbinic evidence for varying formulation, but its importance has been made far more obvious since he wrote. The fixed number of Eighteen Benedictions may itself be a presupposition of the end of the second century rather than the first, and the benedictions themselves varied in order, content, and combination.[66] As has been emphasized since the beginning of the century, the formulations in liturgical MSS, from the Geniza or elsewhere,[67] cannot be taken *tout court* as reflecting a Jamnian text. Hence an attempt to ascertain the purpose of the Jamnian benediction depends on the combination of a circumspect use of liturgical texts with an examination of material, some of which has already been noted, in the Talmud and its interpreters.

Maimonides offers an explanation of the origin of the benediction. In his Code he follows the view, already assumed in the introduction to the story of Samuel the Small at Ber. 28b, that the framing of this benediction 'of the *minim*' under Gamaliel is the

[65]Kuhn, *Achtzehngebet*, 18–21.

[66]R. S. Sarason, 'On the Use of Method in the Modern Study of Jewish Liturgy', in W. S. Green (ed.), *Approaches to Ancient Judaism: Theory and Practice* (Missoula, 1978), 161 n. 179; J. Heinemann, *Prayer in the Talmud* (E.T. Berlin, 1977), 45–51.

[67]Hebrew texts of the Twelfth Benediction are collected by S. Baer, *Seder 'abodat yisra'el* (Rödelheim, 1868), 93–5; additions from the Geniza and elsewhere in L. Finkelstein, 'The Development of the Amidah', *Jewish Quarterly Review* N.S. xvi (1925–6), 1–43, 127–70, = J. J. Petuchowski (ed.), *Contributions to the Scientific Study of Jewish Liturgy* (New York, 1970), 91–177 (163 f.); Marmorstein, 'The Amidah', n. 9 above; S. Assaf, 'Mi-seder ha-tefillah b'ereṣ yisra'el', in Y. Baer, Y. Guttmann, and M. Schwabe (edd.), *Sefer Dinaburg* (Jerusalem, 1949), 116–31 (118).

reason why the 'Eighteen' Benedictions in fact, in the Babylonian tradition, number nineteen. 'In the days of Rabban Gamaliel', he writes, 'the *minim* multiplied in Israel, and were afflicting Israel, and leading them astray (*mesithim*) ... He arose, he and his court, and ordained (*hithqin*) another benediction, which would contain a petition to the Lord to destroy the *minim*, and he set it in the Prayer ...'[68] The heretics are thus thought to have constituted so great an affliction in Gamaliel II's time that an entirely new benediction was added. Maimonides may be thinking of the Sadducees, whence this benediction was sometimes called 'of the Sadducees' (Baer, *Seder*, p. 93); but there is fair probability that, like his earlier contemporary Judah ha-Levi (p. 94 below), he also has Christianity in mind; for his description of the heretics as arising from within Israel and afflicting the Jews is strikingly reminiscent of the Toledoth Jeshu,[69] the leading of Israel astray recalls Sanh. 43a (p. 105 below), and Maimonides assumes, with a large part of the Toledoth tradition and named authors from Saadia onwards, that Christians are foretold at Dan. xi 14, 'the children of the violent *of thy people* shall lift themselves up to establish the vision'.[70] At any rate, he clearly considers the multiplication of unbelievers in Israel, rather than oppression by an external 'kingdom of insolence', to be the occasion of the benediction.

The Talmudic evidence on the benediction, to which allusion is made in this account, includes the story of its 'ordering', regulations for its recital, references to its title and eulogy, but no specimen formulation of it other than that in *habinenu*, an early brief paraphrase of the Tefillah taught by Mar Samuel (early third century).[71] Formulations of the benediction itself are handed down outside the Talmudic textual tradition, in liturgical MSS. Their

[68]Maimonides, *Mishneh Torah*, 11. ii. 2, 1; *Mishneh Torah* ... photographed from the Rome edition of the year 5240 (1480) (Jerusalem, 5715 (1955)), 53 f. On this edition, issued without date or place, see H. M. Z. Mezer, 'Incunabula', *Encyclopaedia Judaica* viii (1971), cols. 1319–44 (1323, par. 2).

[69]See the texts in S. Krauss, *Das Leben Jesu nach jüdischen Quellen* (Berlin, 1902), 47, 82, 121, with editor's summary, 176, and discussion, 193 f., 283 f. (on the Twelfth Benediction). Indications of Toledoth influence elsewhere in Maimonides are noted at W. Horbury, 'A Critical Examination of the Toledoth Jeshu' (diss., Cambridge, 1970), 509.

[70]*Mishneh Torah*, xiv. xi. 4 (Amsterdam, 1702, iv, f. 307a); interpretations of the verse in this sense are gathered by Judah Rosenthal, *Studies and Texts in Jewish History, Literature and Religion* (Hebrew: 2 vols., Jerusalem, 1967), i, 204.

[71]Ber. 29a, jBer. iv. 3, 8a, translated and discussed by B. M. Bokser, *Post Mishnaic Judaism in Transition: Samuel on Berakhot and the Beginnings of Gemara* (Chico, 1980), 26–30; vocalized texts in W. Staerk, *Altjüdische liturgische Gebete* (Kleine Texte, 58: Bonn, 1910), 20.

variations confirm the view that rabbinic regulations affected sub-ject-matter more than wording.[72] The frequency of 'insolent' (*zedim*) or 'kingdom of insolence' in the texts of the benediction itself is the main ground of Schäfer's argument for the importance of an anti-Roman intention behind it. He also notes, however, that part of the Talmudic tradition on benedictions with which 'of the *minim*' might be combined may support his interpretation, for one of them is named 'of the wicked' or 'of the sinners'.[73] This tradition is important for the question of origin, and it will be convenient to note the ways in which it has been understood in modern inter-pretation of Gamaliel II's measures, before considering the texts of the benediction itself.

Maimonides, as noted already, follows the Talmudic view that this benediction was newly added under Gamaliel II, and increased the total number of benedictions in the Tefillah. Elbogen accepted this view in a form suggested by the Palestinian Talmud, that until this time there were only seventeen of the Eighteen Benedictions.[74] He held that a new formula 'of the *minim*' was combined at Jamnia with an existing prayer for the punishment of the wicked at the last judgement, hitherto part of the Eleventh Benediction 'Restore our judges'.[75] These elements, with the eulogy 'who humblest the insolent', formed a new Twelfth Benediction. At the same time the curse on apostates was balanced by a new prayer for a blessing on proselytes, inserted in the Thirteenth Benediction 'Upon the right-eous'.[76] Elbogen cites in support jBer. iv. 3, 8a '"of the *minim*" and "of the sinners" are included in "who humblest the insolent"', with a reference also to ii. 4, 5a (the same, with 'wicked', *resha'im*, for 'sinners', *poshe'im*), and the similar but divergent Tos. Ber. iii. 25 '"of the *minim*" is included in "of the *paroshim*", and "of the proselytes" in "of the elders"'.[77]

Others had understood these passages to mean, rather, that Samuel the Small revised a benediction which already existed separately.[78] Saul Lieberman, taking up this view, argues that 'of the

[72]Heinemann, *Prayer*, 51–3.
[73]Schäfer, 51 and n. 35.
[74]Elbogen, 36–9; at 40 he quotes jBer. iv. 3, 8a 'If a man says to you, There are seventeen benedictions, say to him, The Wise set "of the *minim*" in the Prayer at Jamnia', on which see Heinemann, *Prayer*, 225 n. 20.
[75]Elbogen, 34; a poetic version of this benediction, asking for an end to the haters of Zion, is quoted by Bokser, *Samuel*, 137 n. 50.
[76]Elbogen, 38 f.
[77]Ibid., 38, and 517 n. 10.
[78]Earlier supporters of this view are listed by Aptowitzer, 109 n. 3 and Jocz, 54.

separatists (*paroshim*)', as in the Tosefta, was its pre-Jamnian title;[79] Joseph Heinemann regards both 'of the separatists' and 'of the wicked' (jBer. ii. 4, 5a) as possible.[80] Although 'wicked' has been explained by Ginzberg as a scribal correction for *minim* which has crept into the Palestinian Talmud's text,[81] its possible currency as a title is supported both by *habinenu*, as quoted below, and by the eulogy 'who breakest the wicked' which sometimes precedes 'who humblest the insolent' at the end of the prayer.[82] Ginzberg, although he doubts the originality of 'the wicked', otherwise takes the evidence in what seems to be its most natural sense when he says that separate benedictions 'of the *minim*', 'of the sinners', and 'of the proselytes' may have been repeated in some places, each on its own.[83] The combinations of particular petitions are likely to have varied well into the Amoraic period.[84]

The pre-Jamnian fluidity of the Tefillah was therefore probably still greater than Elbogen allowed. Those who differ widely from him on the development of the prayer as a whole nevertheless agree to a considerable extent with him on the means whereby this particular benediction was introduced. A new formula 'of the *minim*' was combined with existing material, in Elbogen's view extracted from the Eleventh Benediction, in the view of Heinemann and others already current as a benediction on its own. Yet the Tosefta and Palestinian Talmud suggest, as Ginzberg noted, that the new formula was also recited separately, without the associated material. In this respect their evidence, like that of Midrash Panim Aherim on Esther, reflects an even greater degree of variableness than does the textual tradition of the Tefillah itself. The extant formulations of the Twelfth Benediction correspond to a later time, when it had become regular practice to combine 'of the *minim*' with another benediction. The evidence to be compared with the New

---

[79]S. Lieberman, *Tosefta ki-fshuṭah*, *Order Zera'im*, Part 1 (New York, 1955), 53 f., followed by E. Bickerman, 'The Civic Prayer for Jerusalem', reprinted from *Harvard Theological Review* lv (1962) in Bickerman, *Studies in Jewish and Christian History*, ii (Leiden, 1980), 290–312 (298 n. 34), and Frend, 179.

[80]Heinemann, *Prayer*, 225 f. and nn. 20, 23, and in J. Heinemann and J. J. Petuchowski, *Literature of the Synagogue* (New York, 1975), 32 f.

[81]L. Ginzberg, *A Commentary on the Palestinian Talmud*, vol. i (New York, 1941), 336 (on Ber. ii 4, 5a).

[82]Ginzberg, *Commentary*, i, 335; examples at Baer, 95, and Marmorstein, 'Amidah', 414 (last line) and 416, no. 10; 'who breakest the wicked alone, ibid., no. 9; most rites according to Marmostein, ibid., 415 (examples, including a Yemenite text) have the double eulogy 'who breakest *enemies* and humblest the insolent' found also in Nicholas Donin's version (p. 79 above) and printed by Baer, 95.

[83]Ginzberg, *Commentary*, i, 335.

[84]Heinemann, *Prayer*, 223 f. (cf. 43–8); Midrash Panim Aherim (pp. 77–8 above).

Testament and patristic passages under consideration is therefore not simply that of the Twelfth Benediction in its extant forms, but rather a benediction specially directed against heretics, which was recited in the Prayer on its own as well as in combination with other benedictions. Before its introduction Christians could have been condemned under the heading of 'separatists' or 'wicked', and the use of such a curse in some synagogues would be consistent with New Testament evidence (p. 103 below).

This benediction of the heretics was associated with those on separatists, wicked men, and sinners. What was their larger context? The section on the Tefillah where the relevant benedictions are gathered expresses, like other prayers considered to be of comparable age, a longing for messianic redemption, with its accompanying judgement.[85] At Ezek. xx 34–8 the gathering of the dispersed is followed by judgement on the house of Israel, whence transgressors are purged. Gathering and judgement are similarly linked in the present Tenth, Eleventh, and Twelfth Benedictions. The Eleventh echoes the language in which judgement on Zion is described in Isa. i 26 f., and the condemnation of apostates in the Twelfth corresponds to that of those who forsake the Lord (Targum, '*the law of the Lord*') at Isa. i 28. The 'proud' and 'wicked' of the Twelfth are the object of judgement at Mal. iii 19–21 (iv. 1–3), quoted at Tos. Sanh. xiii. 5 in a description of Gehenna with a list of sinners including those named in the Twelfth Benediction.[86] The interconnection of the Eleventh and Twelfth Benedictions has already appeared from their mention in reverse order in Midrash Panim Aherim on Esther. There, however, they are both applied to the gentiles. In the explanation at Meg. 17b (parallel text at jBer. ii. 4, 5a) these benedictions are firmly anchored, by contrast, in the prophecy of the purging of Jerusalem herself. 'When the exiles are gathered in, judgement is executed on the wicked, as it is written (Isa. i 25 f.) ... when judgement has been executed on the wicked, sinners come to an end, and the insolent are included with them, as it is written (Isa. i 28).' The scriptural echoes in the extant texts of these benedictions suggest that this application is to be preferred, and that consequently the context of the malediction on sinners,

[85]Elbogen, 33–5; Kuhn, p. 25; Sarason, 107 and n. 63, 115; Heinemann, *Prayer*, 34 f. The day of judgement is pictured, with quotations of Isa. lxiii. 4 and Ps. lviii. 1, in the paraphrase of the Twelfth Benediction in the mediaeval Targum to the Tefillah edited from a Yemenite text by M. Gaster, 'Ein Targum der Amidah', *Monatsschrift für Geschichte und Wissenschaft des Judentums* xxxix (1895), 79–90(89).

[86]Text and translation, with parallel from R.H. 17a, at Strack, *Jesus*, lvii f., cf. Schäfer, 50 f.

with whom the *minim* came to be associated, is that of prayer for judgement upon God's people themselves at the redemption. A comparable combination of malediction with prayer for messianic redemption appears at I Cor. xvi 22.[87]

The texts of the Twelfth Benediction itself, however, name not only various kinds of sinners in Israel, but also the gentile 'kingdom of insolence'. The phrase is indeed very frequent, as Schäfer points out; it should also be noticed that formulations which he does not cite mention the expulsion of oppressors, the perishing of the heathen from God's land, and the breaking of the gentile yoke – thoughts which are sometimes emphatically expressed even without the phrase 'kingdom of insolence' itself.[88] Further, *habinenu* has just 'and against the wicked raise thy hand',[89] which could readily refer to Jews, gentiles, or both; in a paraphrase attributed to Saadia this benediction is simply concerned with the wicked and the enemies of Israel;[90] and among explanations of the benediction the Buxtorfs noted that of Bahya ben Asher (Spain, end of thirteenth century): 'they ordained it to uproot the kingdom of wickedness' – the phrase which stands for 'kingdom of insolence' in a Sephardi recension of the Tefillah.[91]

Such evidence appears to support Kaufmann Kohler's adaptation of Elbogen's exposé of the importance of the last judgement in this section of the Prayer. Kohler held that the judgement meant in the Twelfth Benediction is that awaiting Syria or Rome, envisaged as the Danielic fourth kingdom to be overthrown at the end of days.[92] Kuhn similarly notes the frequency of 'proud' and 'insolent' in Maccabaean literature, and sets 'kingdom of insolence' in an originally anti-Seleucid prayer which continued in use against Rome.[93] 'Insolent', 'wicked', and 'sinners' could obviously be applied to gentiles as sinners *par excellence* (Gal. ii 15). How readily judgement on the nations could figure in such a context appears from Ecclus. xxxvi 3 'Lift up thy hand against the strange nations'

[87]On the setting of this verse see C. F. D. Moule, 'A Reconsideration of the Context of *Maranatha*', *New Testament Studies* vi (1959–60), 307–10.

[88]Marmorstein, 'Amidah', pp. 414 (reprinted at Elbogen, 586); 416, nos. 2, 8, and 9; and 417, first quotation.

[89]Elbogen, 34, links these words with the Eleventh Benediction; they correspond to the Twelfth in the division of the prayer by Bokser, n. 71 above.

[90]Heinemann–Petuchowski, *Literature*, 43.

[91]Buxtorf, *Synagoga*, 210; Bahya b. Asher, *Kad ha-qemaḥ* (Venice, 1546), f. 80a, col. 1; Finkelstein, 'Development', in Petuchowski, *Contributions*, 151.

[92]K. Kohler, 'The Origin and Composition of the Eighteen Benedictions', *Hebrew Union College Annual* i (1924), 387–425 (401 f.).

[93]Kuhn, 20 f.

(close to the wording of *habinenu*[94]) and II Macc i. 28 'Punish those who oppress us, and wrong us in pride', in two passages with many resemblances to the Tefillah. Midrash Panim Aherim on Esther assumes that the gentiles will indeed think that the present Twelfth and Eleventh Benedictions do refer to themselves. Yet the texts of the benediction also offer support to the inner-Jewish interpretation found at Meg. 17b, for they continue to list sinners of Israel, especially apostates and heretics. Bickerman indeed suggested that '*kingdom* of insolence' was a later addition to the formula, on the basis of the mention of 'the insolent' in the eulogy.[95] The early fluidity of the Prayer means that, as in the case of Kuhn's reconstruction, this conjecture can hardly be more than speculation; but the fact that it can be made draws attention to the importance of references to sinners of Israel in formulations of the benediction.

An identification of the judgement as that impending upon Rome is thus too restricted to cover by itself the evidence for the wording of the benediction. Judgement is envisaged, according to that evidence, as the purging of Israel as well as the downfall of the heathen. A third, individual and ethical, aspect of judgement should probably also be taken into account. It is notable that the end of the domination of the four kingdoms could be connected, in the thought of the rabbinic period, with the ethical theme of the destruction of the evil impulse. Thus a prayer attributed in Ber. 17a to R. Alexandri (fourth-century Palestine) runs: 'Lord of the worlds, it is manifest and known to thee that our will is to do thy will. What prevents us, but the yeast in the dough [the evil impulse] and subjection to the kingdoms? Let it be thy will to deliver us from their hand and we shall return to do the ordinances of thy will with a perfect heart.'[96] The high-holy-day prayer 'Now therefore put thine awe upon all thy works', held to be comparable in age and themes with the Eighteen Benedictions, suggests that the phrase 'kingdom of insolence' in the Twelfth Benediction could evoke these ethical overtones of the annihilation of evil. Within a setting of God's claim upon all his works, asserted at the beginning and end, the prayer asks favour for 'thy people' and 'thine anointed', so that 'the

---

[94]Compared by M. H. Segal, *Sefer Ben Sira ha-shalem* (2nd edn, Jerusalem, 1958), 226, ad loc.

[95]Bickerman, 'Civic Prayer', 293 n. 15.

[96]Introductory comments in Heinemann-Petuchowski, *Literature*, 47–51; the same train of thought occurs at Luke i 74 f. (Qumran parallels noted by D. R. Jones, 'The Background and Character of the Lukan Psalms', *JTS*, N.S. xix (1968), 35); cf. Yose ben Yose, *'anusah le-'ezrah*, ll. 50 f. (A. Mirsky, *Yosse ben Yosse: Poems* (Jerusalem, 1977), 111 f.); at the redemption the heart will no longer be led astray from keeping the law.

righteous shall see this and rejoice' but 'iniquity shall shut her mouth, and all wickedness shall be consumed like smoke, when thou makest the dominion of insolence (*memsheleth zadon*) to pass from the earth'.[97] Here an unmistakable emphasis on the overthrow of the heathen, for which the prayer has been attacked conjointly with the Twelfth Benediction which it resembles in this phrase,[98] receives an equally marked ethical colouring from the use of abstract nouns for wickedness. Moral interpretation of the benediction itself on these lines was naturally found conducive to edification and apologetic; so 'in this petition is included prayer for the subduing of the evil impulse' (Bahya, loc. cit.), and 'we pray for the destruction of sin, not the death of sinners' (Seligman Baer, loc. cit.). Further, such interpretation contrasts strongly with the numerous specifications of classes of wrongdoer to be prayed against, found accumulated in texts of the benediction itself. On these grounds an ascription of ethical overtones to the imprecation against 'the kingdom of insolence', might well be treated with reserve. Nevertheless, its claims are substantial enough to indicate that it should indeed be envisaged by the interpreter. It has roots, as already noted, in rabbinic thought about the last things. Traces of the view that evil itself, not simply evildoers, will be overcome in the last days are also found in non-rabbinic descriptions of judgement likely to be close to the Jamnian period.[99] Lastly, it coheres with the universal outlook attributed to the Tefillah and high-holy-day prayers, in contrast with the much more obviously particularist tone of later prayers and poetry (echoed also in some texts of the benediction).[100]

An anti-gentilic imprecation thus has a place within the Tefillah, but its meaning is affected by its larger context of prayer for messianic redemption and judgement. The purging of the house of Israel is envisaged first, and the judgement on the nations can be connected with the ethical theme of the destruction of evil itself. The emphasis laid from time to time on these different aspects of judgement will have varied according to circumstances. Rabbinic attitudes to Rome appear to have hardened during the third

[97]Heinemann-Petuchowski, *Literature*, 62; the prayer is quoted, to show that 'kingdom of insolence' in the Twelfth Benediction is ethical rather than national, by Baer, *Seder* 95.

[98]Wülfer, 'Animadversiones', 340 f., decides against it; it is defended by Wagenseil and Valmontone, as cited at pp. 80–81 above.

[99]I Enoch lxix. 29 'everything evil will pass away' from before the Son of Man (M. A. Knibb, *The Ethiopic Book of Enoch* (2 vols., Oxford, 1978), ii p. 165); II Esdras vii. 113 f., xvi. 52; II Baruch lxxii–lxxiii; cf. Luke i 74 f. (n. 96 above), Rom. xvi 20, I Cor xv 25 f., Rev. xx 14.

[100]Heinemann, *Prayer*, 32 f.; Heinemann-Petuchowski, *Literature*, 60; Mirsky, *Yosse*, 16 f.

THE BENEDICTION OF THE *MINIM*

century.[101] Even then, however, peaceful submission to Rome is repeatedly urged by the rabbis,[102] and favourable attitudes emerge clearly together with hostility in the earlier centuries. The Jamnian period is notable for patriarchal co-operation with Rome.[103] These varied rabbinic attitudes suggest that the Tefillah in the second and third centuries will not infrequently have been recited in congregations which were being encouraged to manifest civic loyalty. These rabbinic sources, illustrating Palestinian conditions in the first instance (although not without relevance to Jewish attitudes elsewhere in the empire), are complemented by Diaspora evidence for the importance attached to the benefits of Roman rule. Roman justice, still praised in third-century Palestine,[104] embraced the protection of synagogues both in Palestine and the Diaspora, as the story of Callistus' punishment for interrupting a sabbath service in Rome, c. 185–90, vividly illustrates.[105] The custom of praying for rulers is stressed in ancient as in mediaeval Jewish apologetic, and ancient Jews also evinced their civic loyalty in the dedications of synagogues and the inscription of honorific decrees.[106] The wording and interpretation of the Eighteen Benedictions, which could be recited in any language (Mishnah, Sotah vii. 1), will in the Diaspora have been subject to the considerations, already evident at Rom. xiii 1–7,[107] which led to the emphasis on civic loyalty in mediaeval and modern Jewish liturgy. Hence, both in Palestine and the Diaspora, the external circumstances of synagogue worship would favour the interpretation of judgement on the nations in the Tefillah in a larger sense than that of a simple expression of hostility to Rome. This larger sense is implied, as seen already, in the biblically moulded context provided by the Prayer itself.

It appears, therefore, that the context of the Twelfth Benediction

[101]Stemberger, 'Rom', 390; de Lange, 'Attitudes', 269, suggests that the turning-point was Hadrian's suppression of the Second Revolt.

[102]de Lange, 'Attitudes', 275–81.

[103]Stemberger, 'Rom', 382 f.

[104]Simeon b. Laqish on Gen. i. 31 'very good' at Ber. R. ix. 12, commented upon by Stemberger, 'Rom', 390 and de Lange, *Attitudes*, 275.

[105]Hippolytus, *Refutatio*, ix. xii. 7–9 (ed. P. Wendland, *GCS* xii, Leipzig, 1916, 247); the importance of the passage in this respect is noted by E. M. Smallwood, *The Jews under Roman Rule* (Leiden, 1976), 524 f.

[106]Exod. xxii. 28(27) LXX; Josephus, *Ap.* ii 6 (77); Aboth. iii. 2; 'in many places they pray a special prayer for the king and the prince of the city when the scrolls of the law are brought forth', Valmontone in Eisenstein, 168; cf. J. Bergmann, *Jüdische Apologetik im neutestamentlichen Zeialter* (Berlin, 1908), 158 (prayers); Juster, i 346–8, and S. Krauss, *Synagogale Altertümer* (Berlin and Vienna, 1922), 160–3, 346 (dedications and inscriptions).

[107]For this passage as apologetic see E. Bammel, 'Ein Beitrag zur paulinischen Staatsanchauung', *Theologische Literaturzeitung* lxxxv (1960), cols. 837–40.

in the Tefillah, and the circumstances of synagogue congregations in the Roman Empire, would have tended to restrain or modify the identification of judgement especially or exclusively with the end of gentile rule. The formula 'of the *minim*' approved under Gamaliel II thus came to be linked with imprecations against sinners of Israel, in the context of a larger prayer for redemption and universal judgement. Rabbinic lists of sinners suggest how readily 'of the *minim*' could be combined with 'of the wicked' or 'of the separatists'. In descriptions of Gehenna '*minim* and apostates and the wicked of Israel' are grouped together (Exod. R. xix. 4, on xii 43 f., in the name of R. Berekiah (fourth-century Palestine);[108] and whereas more commonplace sinners are reduced to ashes finally after a year below, there is a continuing punishment for '*minim*, apostates, delators, *epikurosim*, deniers of Torah, and those who separate themselves from the congregation' (Tos. Sanh. xiii. 5, see p. 87 and n. 86 above). Already in this life, therefore, 'hate *minim*, apostates, and traitors', as David said in Ps. cxxxix 21 f. (*Aboth deRabbi Nathan*, First Recension, xvi (ed. S. Schechter, repr. New York, 1967), p. 64); the text is applied just to *minim*, in the name of R. Ishmael (second-century Palestine), at Tos. Shabb. xiii. 5). As this advice suggests, sinners offending so gravely may be treated as gentiles (apostates may not eat the Passover, Exod. xii 43 in Targums Onkelos and Pseudo-Jonathan; '*minim*, apostates, and traitors' do not benefit from the injunction to help 'him that hateth thee', Exod. xxiii 5 as interpreted in Tos. B.M. ii. 33); they may be ranked beneath non-Jews ('*minim*, traitors, and apostates' in the estimation of Abbahu (third-century Caesaraea), A.Z. 26b); and they can readily be associated with gentiles in thought (thus the destroyers of the Temple are added at the end of the list in Tos. Sanh. xiii. 5). These passages, like the New Testament treatment of both false teachers and apostates as liable to summary expulsion,[109] do something to reveal the thread linking the categories of sinner listed in texts of the benediction. It is of interest, however, that whereas such texts in the earlier period begin 'for the apostates', and later on 'for the slanderers' (*la-malshinim*, Baer, 93), and both these types of sinner are in the catalogues just quoted, neither figures among the early titles of benedictions discussed above. On the other hand *minim*, which comes to prevail over the other titles, is also first in all five lists of sinners, being followed immediately in four of them by 'apostates', the first category to be named in texts of the benediction

---

[108]E. E. Hallevy (ed.), *Shemoth Rabbah*, i (Jerusalem, 1959), 247.
[109]Lampe, 'Discipline' (n. 127 below), 358.

itself. So far as they go, the five passages quoted, taken in conjunction with the texts of the benediction, suggest that *minim* whose special importance is indicated by their place at the head of each list, rated a benediction which could be independent, but which could appropriately be combined with condemnations of other sinners incurring comparable odium – as has happened in our texts of the Twelfth Benediction.

Thus the origins of this section of the Tefillah, so far as they can be reconstructed, suggest that the imprecation against *minim* approved at Jamnia was included in a prayer invoking judgement on the wicked, both inside and outside the congregation of Israel. It could be combined with another benediction within this context, and the textual tradition of the present Twelfth Benediction witnesses to the period after such combination had become regular. Although the combined Benediction now included the condemnation of other sinners in Israel and gentile oppressors, it continued to be understood especially as an anti-heretical measure. Some illustrations of this point conclude the present discussion of the benediction in Jewish tradition.

First, the ancient title 'of the *minim*' (not 'of the government') became standard. The titles with which it is associated in Palestinian Talmud and Tosefta are 'of the separatists', 'of the wicked', and 'of the sinners'. In the context of the Tefillah these presuppose, as already noted, a universal judgement in which Israel itself is sifted.

Secondly, Talmudic regulations connect this benediction with heresy. The reader who fails to say 'who givest life to the dead', 'who humblest the insolent', and 'who buildest Jerusalem' (the eulogies of the Second, Twelfth, and Fourteenth Benedictions) should be dismissed, on the presumption that he is a *min* (jBer. v. 4, 9c). In the Babylonian Talmud a similar ruling attributed to Rab (early third century) states that if the reader errs in any other benediction, he is not dismissed, but if he errs in that of the *minim*, he is dismissed, for he himself may be a *min* (Ber. 29a). This saying is introduced to explain the story, also at jBer. v. 3, 9c, that Samuel the Small himself erred in the benediction he had formulated, and looked at the congregation to see if he would be dismissed; but an exception was made for him.[110] Tanhuma Buber, Wayyiqra, 3 supplies a reason for Rab's ruling: if the reader is inclined to heresy, he will be cursing himself, and the congregation will give the Amen

---

[110]Texts of both passages in Strack, *Jesus*, 31; comments by Elbogen, 517 and (followed here) Ginzberg, *Commentary*, iv (ed. D. Halivni, New York, 1961), 276.

[111]Elbogen, 37 f.

to what he says.[111] Maimonides sums up and decides: 'If he who recites the Amidah should make a mistake ... and delay for an hour, then let another stand up in his stead. But if he made a mistake in the benediction of the *Minim*, let another stand up in his stead, for perhaps he is infected with heresy.'[112]

Thirdly, Maimonides' account of the origin of the benediction (pp. 83–4 above) is by no means isolated in its allusion to unbelief arising within Israel. Earlier in the twelfth century Judah ha-Levi, discussing prayer in his *Kuzari*, brings out the background thought of judgement when he says that in the Twelfth Benediction the Jew prays 'for the purging of dross and the removal of thorns from the midst of the children of Israel' (Isa. i 25, xxxiii 12). Later on, in a chronicle of Jewish history tied to the tradition-chain of Aboth, he notes that the Sadducees and Boethusians are 'the *minim* for whose destruction we pray in the Prayer; and as for Jesus and his companions' – already mentioned, like the two sects, a little earlier – 'they are the "baptized" (*meshuʿmadim*) who joined themselves to the sect of those who perform immersions in the Jordan'.[113] It seems probable, although no comment on this point is known to the writer,[114] that ha-Levi is here continuing the explanation of the Twelfth Benediction which he has begun with his reference to the *minim*. He now identifies another prominent word in the formula, 'apostates' (*meshummadim*), on the basis of the Geonic derivation of the word from *meshuʿmad*, 'baptized'.[115] The Benediction thus involves, in his eyes, an imprecation against Sadducees, Boethusians, and Jesus and his companions. The Geonic understanding of *meshummadim* is paralleled in the west, as appears from Amulo's complaint, in ninth-century Lyons, that *apostoli* are impiously called by the Jews *apostatae*.[116] The explicit mention of Nazarenes in some texts of the benediction could no doubt, especially under Byzantine

[111]Elbogen, 37 f.

[112]*Mishneh Torah*, II. ii. 10, 3 (*Mishneh Torah* ... photographed from the Rome edition, 59, col. 2).

[113]*Kuzari*, iii. 19 and 65, in the translation (based on a fresh evaluation of the text of censored passages) by Y. Even Shmuel (Tel Aviv, 1972), 117, 144.

[114]In the first edition with Judah Moscato's commentary (Venice, 1594), also the first censored edition, the passage from *minim* onwards (f. 188b) is omitted from the text (Ibn Tibbon's version) and receives no comment; Ibn Tibbon in J. Buxtorf, Fil., *Liber Cosri* (Basle, 1660), 241, identical with the edition of Venice, 1547, as quoted by Even Shmuel, 280, is fuller but still lacks the words 'Jesus ... *meshuʿmadim*', for which see both Arabic and Hebrew in H. Hirschfeld, *Das Buch Al-Chazari ... im arabischen Urtext sowie in der hebräischen Übersetzung des Jehuda Ibn Tibbon* (Leipzig, 1887), 170–3.

[115]Hai Gaon, at A. Kohut, *Aruch Completum*, v (Vienna, 1889), 85, s.v. *md*; cf. S. Bernfeld, 'Apostasie', *Encyclopaedia Judaica*, ii (Berlin, 1928), cols. 1197–1219 (1198).

[116]Strack, *Jesus*, p. xvi.

rule, be associated with prayer against oppressors;[117] but, as the widespread application of Dan. xi 14 to Christianity confirms (p. 84 above), it will have encouraged the interpretation of the formula as a curse on unbelievers. In the Geonic period *Halakhoth Gedoloth*, followed later in the west by the Mahzor Vitry, says that the benediction was ordained 'after Jeshu bar Pandera'.[118] Hence Rashi builds on tradition when, as already noted, he explains the ordering of the benediction in Jamnia from the increase of the disciples of Jesus. Thus an anti-heretical intention was continuously identified in the Benediction from the Amoraic period, and from the time of the mention of Nazarenes in the formula it is linked in interpretative tradition with Christianity in particular.

The conclusions of the foregoing discussion may now be briefly recapitulated. In the second century the 'Eighteen Benedictions' still varied very considerably in order, content, and combination. The origin of the Twelfth Benediction was ascribed by Maimonides, summing up Talmudic evidence, to the time of Gamaliel II, when heretics from within the house of Israel were troubling the Jews. The Palestinian Talmud and Tosefta suggest that, for a considerable time after Gamaliel II, a benediction 'of the *minim*' could be recited on its own as well as in combination with other benedictions. The present Twelfth Benediction results from such a combination.

The section of the Tefillah with which the Jamnian formula 'of the *minim*' was associated appears from the present Tenth, Eleventh, and Twelfth Benedictions to be a prayer for redemption and judgement. An Amoraic tradition, following scriptural allusions in these benedictions, interprets it as a prayer for judgement on Israel. In the textual evidence for the Twelfth Benediction, however, imprecations on gentile oppressors are also prominent, as Schäfer has emphasized. The extant formulations of the prayer are best accounted for when the judgement in question is envisaged as universal; it begins from the house of Israel, and the thought of its application to the gentiles is not devoid of ethical overtones concerning the end of evil itself. The emphasis laid on different aspects of judgement will have varied according to circumstances, but the dependence of synagogue congregations upon Roman protection will sometimes have encouraged attention to the larger view implicit in the Tefillah itself.

---

[117]The (?seventh-century) poetical paraphrase edited by Marmorstein, 'Attitude' (n. 9 above), and quoted in his 'Amidah', 415, no. 1, runs 'I will humble the Nazarenes and the *minim* from *my* borders.

[118]Strack, *Jesus*, 40.

Within the Twelfth Benediction, the association of *minim* with sinners of Israel and with gentiles is comparable with the link between *minim*, apostates, and gentiles in rabbinic lists of specially hateful sinners. Although the combination of the Jamnian formula with another benediction meant the condemnation of this range of Jewish and gentile offenders, the combined benediction was understood from the Amoraic period onwards as an anti-heretical measure, and a substantial part of later interpretation associated it with Christianity in particular.

Hence, to describe the Twelfth Benediction as an anti-Roman as much as an anti-heretical prayer is to narrow its large biblical scope misleadingly, and to put second the purpose which from the Amoraic period onwards appeared primary.[119] In any case, however, the datum for comparison with second-century Christian evidence is not the Twelfth Benediction as we have it, but the formula 'of the *minim*' approved at Jamnia, which could be recited on its own as well as in combination with other benedictions. This formula was certainly anti-heretical, as its name implies; the question remains whether, as Rashi and others thought, it was in the second century also anti-Christian.

III

The examination of patristic evidence in Part I supported the view that, from Justin's time onwards, an imprecation against Christians was pronounced in synagogue. A somewhat earlier origin of this practice would be consonant with his allegations, but in his own time it was both regular and resented. By the second half of the fourth century the prayer mentioned Nazarenes and *minim*, and was recited thrice daily. Consideration of the Twelfth Benediction and rabbinic evidence about it has now suggested that a petition 'of the *minim*', with a primarily anti-heretical intention, was included in the thrice-daily Tefillah, on its own or in combination with other petitions, at least from the end of the first century. As in the case of other benedictions, its wording long continued to be variable. The petition came to be part of the present Twelfth Benediction, some formulations of which mention Nazarenes as well as *minim*; but

---

[119]This primacy survives in the explanation of the seventeenth-century Yiddish ethical writer Isaac b. Eliakim of Posen, *Leb Tof*, c. ii, that the benediction 'ist gemacht geworden gegen den *Minim*, und gegen die bösen Leut / und gegen die da Israel wehe thun' (transliterated quotation by Wülfer, 'Animadversiones', 331; small variations, not affecting this point, in *Leb Tof* (Fürth, 1765), f. 14a).

these texts cannot be taken to reproduce wording from the Jamnian period.

So far as the fourth century is concerned, the two sets of evidence clearly refer to the same synagogue prayer. The argument of Part I would suggest that this is true for the early second century also, and that the scope of the prayer involved all Christians, not just those of Jewish birth. Both these points might now be thought to be consistent with observations made in Part II. The variableness of the prayer would cover specific references to Christians such as Justin attests, and are later found in texts of the Twelfth Benediction; and the direction of the imprecation against Christians in general would be consonant with its inclusion in a section of the Tefillah invoking universal judgement upon the Jew first, but also the gentile. Nevertheless, the credit given above to Justin's evidence, although it is based primarily upon the specificity of his reports and the sense of immediacy which they convey, must depend in some measure upon an over-all view of early Jewish–Christian relations. In conclusion, therefore, attention is recalled to the broader significance for this subject of the sources already discussed, especially the Tefillah and Justin's *Dialogue*.

It should first be noticed that the combination of Jewish and Christian evidence throughout this section might be questioned on the ground that the texts differ widely as to origin and transmission. J. Maier, stressing the difference between the Jewries of Palestine and the western diaspora in the second century, has argued for the impropriety of comparing Justin's evidence on Judaism with rabbinic texts which may have been edited in Babylonia at the end of the Talmudic period.[120] It is true that the comparison requires care, but the attempt to make it seems to be amply justified by the degree of solidarity between Jewry in dispersion and in the Land assumed in ancient sources. Roman legislation presupposes a scattered but unified Jewish *ethnos*, and this unity was held to be maintained by messengers (Justin, *Dial.* cviii) and letters (Acts xxviii 21).[121]

Jewish attitudes to emergent Christianity are indirectly illuminated by both Ber. 28b and the Tefillah. The Talmudic report that Gamaliel II approved a benediction of the *minim* is seen in S. Kanter's study (n. 2 above) as consistent with this patriarch's special respect for the Tefillah as a focus of unity; his liturgical regulations suit the larger purpose of unifying Judaism which his legal traditions

[120]Maier, *Jesus*, 249 f., 257 f.
[121]Juster, i, 234 f.; Derrett, 545 f.; on the striking extent to which Acts is unaffected by anti-Judaic commonplaces, Harnack, *Die Apostelgeschichte* (Leipzig, 1908), 8 f., 214–16.

seem to express. The Tefillah itself underlines congregational solidarity. In the Twelfth Benediction apostates from the congregation stand out among the wicked, in the Thirteenth proselytes are prominent among the righteous. The divine judgement invoked in the Prayer is thus anticipated in the make-up of the congregation. These emphases clearly reflect characteristics of Judaism in the early Christian centuries. Philo's condemnation of apostasy, with which the Twelfth Benediction was linked by Juster,[122] is borne out by evidence for lapse from Judaism in the western diaspora of the first and second centuries,[123] and is paralleled in rabbinic and Targumic passages just noted (p. 92 above). A favourable attitude to proselytes is reflected also in the *Alenu* prayer (nn. 97–8 above)[124] and in early Christian sources mentioned below. In all, this section of the Tefillah breathes the spirit of intense solidarity which, as Horace, Tacitus, and Juvenal back-handedly attest, inspired formidable pressure-groups and a zeal for increase, seconded by the fascination of Jewish practices.[125] The view of Christianity which it could imply emerges when the gravamen against St. Paul, in the eyes of Jerusalem Christians zealous for the law, is represented as his teaching ἀποστασία from Moses (Acts xxi 21).

The same spirit of intense solidarity in the expectation of judgement passed into early Christianity. O. Böcher has shown how the rabbinic injunction to hate heretics and apostates finds analogies both at Qumran and in I John ii 15 (cf. II John 10), Rev. ii 6;[126] the curse on *minim* has already been compared with I Cor. xvi 22, and apostasy seems to be the unforgivable sin at Heb. vi 4–8, x 26–31.[127] The encouragement of proselytes is comparable with the assurance of deliverance from wrath given to pagans who join the congregation, I Thess. i 9 f. The Apostle's complaint that the Jews prevented him from preaching to the heathen, I Thess. ii 16, begins

[122]Juster, i, 272 f.; it is tempting to connect the saving clause 'if they do not return', in some texts of the benediction (Marmorstein, 'Amidah', 416, no. 5; Assaf, 118) and at Ps.-Jon. Exod. xii 43 (p. 92 above), with the provision for Jews baptized under constraint to return to the Synagogue, C. Th. xvi. 8. 23 of 24 Sept. 416, quoted by Juster, i, 273 n. 2.

[123]Smallwood, 376, 507.

[124]W. G. Braude, *Jewish Proselytism in the First Five Centuries of the Common Era* (Providence, 1940), 17.

[125]Horace, *sat.* i. iv. 143 f. 'veluti te Iudaei cogemus in hanc concedere turbam'; Tacitus, *Hist.* v. 5 'augendae … multitudini consulitur'; Juvenal, *Sat.* xiv. 99 'mox et praeputia ponunt'.

[126]O. Böcher, *Der johanneische Dualismus im Zusammenhang des nachbiblischen Judentums* (Gütersloh, 1965), 142–5, 152 f.; Böcher, 'Johanneisches in der Apokalypse des Johannes', *New Testament Studies* xxvii (1981), 310–21 (304, 317 and n. 17).

[127]G. W. H. Lampe, 'Church Discipline and the Interpretation of the Epistles to the Corinthians', in W. R. Farmer, C. F. D. Moule, and R. R. Niebuhr (edd.), *Christian History and Interpretation: Studies presented to John Knox* (Cambridge, 1967), 337–61 (355–61).

a series of attestations that church and synagogue long continued to compete in their appeal to non-Jews. Trypho is represented as saying that Justin might have hoped for salvation, if he had remained a good pagan; but now that he has allowed himself to be deceived, his only hope lies in circumcision and keeping the law (*Dial.* viii). Justin claims that proselytes blaspheme the name of Christ twice as much as born Jews (*Dial.* cxxii), Tertullian envisages a proselyte arguing against Christianity (*Adv. Iud.* i), and Origen, who reports the Jewish claim that the dispersion was providentially intended as a means for the gaining of proselytes, complains of pagans who go over to Judaism without considering Christianity (*c. Celsum* i. 55; *in Matt. ser.* 16). Justin has to consider the case of gentile *Christians* who become proselytes (*Dial.* xlvii).[128]

This missionary rivalry between two bodies, each with an equally formidable *esprit*, is placed in its larger historical setting by Simon and Frend.[129] Here, however, it is significant as itself affecting many of the congregations in which the Prayer was recited, and as the background against which Justin wrote. The section of the Tefillah to which the benediction of the *minim* belongs exhibits the same combination of missionary zeal with condemnation of heresy and lapse as is attested from without by Justin, who reports the curse against Christians. Two questions about the benediction are best viewed against this background. Was it directed, as argued above, against gentile as well as Jewish Christians? Secondly, how is it related on the one hand to New Testament and patristic reports that Christians are excluded from synagogue and from converse with Jews, and on the other hand to patristic complaints that Christians do attend synagogue?

For both these questions it is important that the synagogues, where the Prayer was recited, were also places where non-Jews drawn to Judaism congregated. The evidence of Acts on this point is confirmed by inscriptions and rabbinic sources.[130] The Prayer, itself a badge of Jewish loyalty, condemned heretics in the presence of the non-Jews for whose allegiance church and synagogue were vying.

---

[128]To the passages compared by Harnack, *Trypho*, 86 f. add Barn. iii. 4; on New Testament evidence for lapse into Judaism, Lampe, 356, 358.

[129]Simon, 432–46; Frend, 178–201. The measures deplored by Justin and anti-Jewish statements in Revelation express the separation of church and synagogue with 'fanaticism on both sides', according to the unsympathetic but illuminating summary by Ed. Meyer, *Ursprung und Anfänge des Christentums*, iii (Berlin, 1923), 589 f.

[130]Acts xiv. I, xviii. 4 ('Greeks'); xiii. 16, 43, xvii. 4 ('godfearers'); cf. Juster, i, 413 and M. Hengel, 'Proseuche und Synagoge', in G. Jeremias, H. W. Kuhn, and H. Stegemann (edd.), *Tradition und Glaube: Festschrift für K. G. Kuhn* (Göttingen, 1971), 157–84 (173 f.).

Gentiles who choose to become Christians are worse than pagans, in Jewish opinion as represented by Justin (*Dial.* viii, cited above). That the benediction should condemn *all* Christians, as its context in the Tefillah allows and as Justin believed the synagogue curse to do, is entirely appropriate to this *Sitz im Leben*.

On the second question, the apparent conflict of evidence on the admission of Christians to synagogue is stressed by Kimelman, 234–40. He argues that the Johannine complaints of exclusion are dubious in their isolation within the New Testament and their lack of rabbinic support, whereas patristic sources make it clear that Christians were welcomed in synagogues – a fact which itself casts doubt on the cursing of Christians therein. Due weight can, however, be given to all these pieces of evidence, once it is recognized that they reflect situations both before and after separate Christian and Jewish worship had become normal. From the first period, the New Testament envisages the punishment of Christians in synagogue, implying continued membership of the congregation (e.g. Mark xiii 9 and parallels; Acts xxii 19; II Cor. xi 24); but their exclusion is also attested. In a convincingly differentiated series of reports Acts describes local opposition resulting in the withdrawal of Paul from the synagogue (Acts xviii 7, xix 9) or his forced departure from the town (xiii 50 (expulsion), xvii 10, 14); and at Luke vi 22 exclusion is expected generally (Derrett questions whether the social ostracism involved could be effected without an institutional sanction).[131] Such exclusion is the step reluctantly taken when punishment fails to correct. The Johannine evidence stands out not for any lack of other New Testament indications of Jewish institutional opposition, but because, as Lindars emphasizes, it alleges a definite policy of excommunication based on a confessional test, a Jewish agreement to put out of the synagogue any who confessed Christ (John ix 22; cf. xii 42, xvi 2).[132] Such a measure, unattested in rabbinic sources (like much Jewish history of the second half of the first century), is nevertheless consistent with the probably second-century Jewish evidence for prohibition of converse with heretics noted below. The Johannine passages give the clearest sign of the enforced separation of the Christian body from Jewish worship; as Lindars notes, they probably reflect concerted action throughout the regions known to the evangelist. Their complaint is of exclusion, rather than cursing. The Jamnian benediction, consistent as it is with such a result, hardly suffices of itself to bring it

---

[131]Derrett, 548 n. 3.
[132]Lindars, 49 f.

about; incidental exclusion of heretical prayer-leaders, even if they are accompanied by other members of the congregation, falls short of the Johannine grievance. These points favour Lindars's suggestion that the Jamnian regulation simply reinforced an earlier, more drastic exclusion of Christians, although the imprecise dating of both the gospel and Gamaliel II's ordinance leaves open the view that the two measures were contemporaneous.

After separate worship had become customary, Justin does complain of cursing in synagogue, and the benediction now provides clearly apposite material for comparison. As noted at the beginning, Justin also mentions Jewish anti-Christian propaganda and a prohibition of converse with Christians, to be related to the benediction shortly. For the moment it is enough that these measures reinforce the separation already carried out. The prohibition of converse was clearly compatible with a good deal of Jewish–Christian contact; Justin's two references to it (*Dial.* xxviii (Trypho), cxii) might suggest that it was principally invoked to prevent Jews hearing Christian preachers or entering inadvisedly into discussion. Corresponding motives on the Christian side led to the patristic condemnation of synagogue attendance by church members. In the situation of rivalry just described, the measures of which Justin complains may be said to form the precondition under which Christian visits to synagogue, deplored by Origen, Chrysostom, and others,[133] could be tolerated or even encouraged by the Jewish authorities. As has appeared from *Dial.* xlvii, gentiles, including some who had joined the church, were inclined to regard Judaism and Christianity as alternative versions of the same biblical faith, over against paganism.[134] So long as the claims of Judaism were secured by measures disallowing Christian pretensions, Christian visitors could be regarded by Jews as witnesses to popular reverence for the synagogue, and as possible future proselytes. The condemnation of Christianity in the Prayer would attest to Jews and gentile sympathizers the exclusive rights of Judaism in the biblical inheritance, and knowledge of the attitude which this practice expressed might shake the visitors' confidence in the Christian surrogate. Such visitors are of course to be distinguished from those who disturbed the service as Callistus was charged with doing.

The apparently conflicting evidence is thus all comprehensible within the development of Jewish–Christian relations. That for exclusion refers to the Christian loss of any right to synagogue

---

[133]de Lange, *Origen*, 86 f.; Kimelman, 239 f.
[134]Harnack, *Trypho*, 86; Abrahams, *Studies*, Second Series 64.

membership, in the late first century; that for a prohibition of converse, limited in its effect, to the defence and confirmation of Judaism by these and other means, including the Benediction, in the early patristic period; and that for Christians in synagogue to the missionary rivalry of the same period, when such visitors, like other interested gentiles, could be regarded as potential proselytes. The malediction on Christians in the Prayer is therefore not inconsistent with the presence of Christian visitors in the synagogues. Rather, it is one expression of those exclusive and universal claims of Judaism which form the presupposition under which such visits can be encouraged.

Lastly, the view that Christians were particularly envisaged in the benediction of the *minim* is strengthened by Justin's evidence for other anti-Christian measures. The cursing of *Christ*, as noted in connection with I Cor. xii 3 and Justin, *I apol.* xxi (p. 75 above), is probably a test of synagogue loyalty going back to the apostolic age; to these passages may be added Acts xxvi 11, where Saul's opposition to 'the name of Jesus the Nazarene' is thought to have meant that 'in all the synagogues often punishing them I compelled them to blaspheme'.[135] Justin thinks that the Jewish dissemination of a negative account of Christian origins dates from the same period (*Dial.* xvii, cvii, cxvii). His occasion for this repeated claim is doubtless his indignation at what he believes to be happening in his own day.[136] Nevertheless, there is evidence, besides that for the cursing of Christ, to support the view that the propaganda of which Justin complains did indeed begin well before his time. G. W. H. Lampe has interpreted a range of energetic and sometimes enigmatic warnings in the New Testament and Apostolic Fathers as indicating a prophetically-backed Jewish countermission to Christians, especially in the late first and early second centuries.[137] Thus the prophet bar-Jesus who opposes Paul in Paphos on behalf of Judaism is described in Acts xiii 6–12 in terms reminiscent of the warnings against deceivers, whose activities seem to be accompanied by persecution, at II Tim. iii 8–13; false teachers 'of the circumcision'

---

[135]This link is made in M. Pole (Poole), *Synopsis Criticorum aliorumque Sacrae Scripturae Interpretum* (5 vols., Utrecht, 1684–6), v, col. 485 (on I Cor. xii 3).

[136]C. K. Barrett, 'Shaliaḥ and Apostle', in E. Bammel, C. K. Barrett, and W. D. Davies (edd.), *Donum Gentilicium: New Testament Studies in Honour of David Daube* (Oxford, 1978), 88–102 (96).

[137]Lampe, 'Discipline', 358–60, developed in G. W. H. Lampe, '"Grievous wolves" (Acts 20:29)', in B. Lindars and S. S. Smalley (edd.), *Christ and Spirit in the New Testament: Studies in Honour of C. F. D. Moule* (Cambridge, 1973), 253–68; J. Lightfoot comments similarly, on I Cor. xii 3, *Opera Omnia* ed. J. Leusden (2 vols., Utrecht, 1699), ii, p. 915.

are especially to be countered, Titus i 10 f.; in I John false prophets fail to acknowledge that the Messiah has truly come in the person of the historical Jesus (iv 1–6), false teachers have left the congregation (ii 19, perhaps an instance of the transition from gentile Christianity to Judaism condemned by Justin), and the burden of their message is denial that Jesus is Messiah (ii 22); I Clement, warning against the 'envy' regarded as the motive of Jewish opposition at Acts v 17, xiii 45, argues above all for the Christian claim to be truly the people of God; and Ignatius specifically opposes 'Judaism' (e.g. *Philad.* vi 1, 'it is better to hear Christianity from a circumcised man than Judaism from an uncircumcised man').[138] In the light of this interpretation, into which he also draws Hebrews (compare the passages cited at p. 98 above), Jude, and II Peter, Lampe convincingly suggests that Justin's assertions may authentically echo an earlier Jewish counter-action more aggressive than such defensive measures as persecution (Acts ix 1–2, I Thess. ii 14–16), the exclusion from the synagogue discussed above, or malediction in the Tefillah (with which he compares *Dial.* xvi).

Justin's claim is supported in a different way by the content of the propaganda which he reports. His account coheres with the New Testament on one side, and later Jewish and Christian sources on the other. The Jewish statement spoke, according to *Dial.* cviii, of a godless and lawless *hairesis* arising from one Jesus, a Galilaean crucified by the Jews; his disciples stole his body by night from the tomb, and now deceive men by saying that he is risen and ascended. Most of this could have been derived by Justin directly from Matt. xxvii 63 f., xxviii 13–15; but the opening words, the combination of the rare 'Galilaean' with the Matthaean 'deceiver', and the charge that the disciples themselves are deceivers, suggest that allegations circulated viva voce are reflected. Continued repetition of the story which the First Evangelist believed to be told among the Jews (Matt. xxviii 15) cannot therefore be ruled out as a source.

The view that Justin preserves authentic traces of Jewish propaganda receives confirmation from later evidence. A Jewish variant of the story alleged in Matthew, related to Johannine tradition but unmentioned in the New Testament, is found in the *Toledoth Jeshu*

---

[138]Barrett, *John and Judaism*, 53 f., and in R. Hamerton-Kelly and R. Scroggs (edd.), *Jews, Greeks and Christians* (Leiden, 1976), 234 f., finds here a syncretistic Judaism in which circumcision was not required. It may be suggested, however, that the passage is intelligible, without this inference, as a gibe against Gentile sympathizers with Judaism, who might be uncircumcised, but were 'plus royalistes que le roi' in opposing Christianity (so Abrahams, *Studies*, Second Series, 64).

and quoted by Tertullian (n. 21 above). Jewish responsibility for the crucifixion is assumed, as in Justin's report, at Origen, *c. Celsum* ii. 5, 9 (Celsus, in a context of hostile narratives of Christian origins attributed to a Jew) and at Sanh. 43a, discussed below. The charge of deceit related by Justin, attested already by Matthew and at John vii 12, 47, reappears in later Christian reports of Jewish opposition (e.g. Apoc. Joh. i) and may well have stood in the original text of the Testimonium Flavianum.[139] It is connected with Christ's execution, as in Justin, in the tannaitic tradition that 'on Passover Eve they hanged Jesus', proclamation having been made that he was to be stoned, 'because he practised sorcery and deceived and led astray Israel' (Babylonian Talmud, Sanhedrin 43a). Here 'deceived' and 'led astray' refer to the offences condemned at Deut. xiii 6–11, 12–18 (7–12, 13–19) respectively, and discussed at Mishnah, Sanh. vii. 10. In the list at Sanh. 43a they follow that of sorcery (Deut. xviii 10; Mishnah, Sanh. vii. 11), frequently linked with Christ's ministry from New Testament times.[140] This order of reference reverses that of Deuteronomy and the Mishnah, but agrees with that in Justin's summary of the reaction of those who saw Christ's miracles, and 'dared to call him a magician and a deceiver of the people' (μάγον ... καὶ λαοπλάνον, *Dial.* lxix).

Thus Justin's alleged Jewish statement appears to be confirmed as a genuine reflection of Jewish propaganda not only by Christian and pagan reports of Jewish criticisms from the first and second centuries, but by tannaitic tradition. The latter point, however, has recently been questioned by Maier on two main grounds. First, in *Dial.* cviii deceit, in Maier's view, means primarily a magician's imposture (with reference to the prediction of the resurrection, as in Matt. xxvii 63 f.) rather than the Deuteronomic enticement to idolatry envisaged at Sanh. 43a; and the penalty named is crucifixion rather than the Mishnaic stoning, with subsequent hanging, of the Talmudic passage.[141] To these objections it may be answered that the distinction between imposture and enticement is hardly to be maintained in contexts where, as in Deut. xiii, followed by Matthew and Justin, miracle and prediction are regarded as authentications of prophecy; and that Sanh. 43a may be counted among the passages where hanging is mentioned as though it were an

---

[139]M. W. Meyer (ed.), *The Nag Hammadi Library in English* (Leiden, 1977), 99; Bammel, 'Testimonium', n. 37 above.

[140]Examples from Mark iii. 22 onwards at W. Bauer, *Das Leben Jesu im Zeitalter der neutestamentlichen Apokryphen* (1909, repr. Darmstadt, 1967), 465.

[141]Maier, 250.

independent mode of execution, crucifixion,[142] for the passage introduced as tannaitic begins with the separate sentence 'they hanged Jesus', taken up again at the end, and only the words linking the list of charges with the Mishnaic institution of the herald, as noted below, indicate that the Mishnaic penalty of stoning is to be inflicted.

Secondly, and more fundamentally, Maier contends that Sanh. 43a did not originally refer to Jesus of Nazareth.[143] He notes that the tannaitic material is only quoted in this Talmudic context for the sake of halakhic debate on the proclamation prescribed at Mishnah, Sanh. vi. 1; the identification of the condemned man as Jesus has nothing to do with that context, and should probably be ascribed, in Maier's view, to post-Talmudic redaction; the list of charges, also found applied to Jesus at Sanh. 107b (where Maier believes it originally referred to Gehazi) cannot have been uncommon in the rabbinic period, and the anecdote at Sanh. 43a will originally have been told of a second-century magician, ben Pandera.

Maier's closely-argued revival of an influential mediaeval view on new tradition-historical grounds deserves fuller consideration. Here it must suffice to note reasons why the traditional application of the passage in Sanh. 43a seems the more probable. First, Maier's general view (pp. 14 f., 255–8) that Palestinian Jewry was unconcerned with Christianity before Constantine is inconsistent with the solidarity attested between Jewry in the Land and elsewhere in the Roman Empire (p. 97 above) and with evidence that Christians attracted adverse Jewish attention in Palestine (e.g. Gal. i 13 f., I Thess. ii 14, Acts xxi–xxvi; Josephus, *Ant.* xx. 200; Justin, *I Apol.* xxxi). Secondly, the earlier history of the baraitha in Sanh. 43a can be more satisfactorily reconstructed than Maier allows on the assumption that, as the uncensored text affirms, Jesus of Nazareth is indeed intended. Thus there are indications that the sentences 'on Passover Eve they hanged Jesus of Nazarene' and 'Jesus the Nazarene ... practised sorcery and deceived and led astray Israel' may be older than their immediate context. The first sentence, as already noted, is not wholly consistent with its sequel 'and the herald went before him forty days ...', which is phrased in accordance with the

---

[142]D. J. Halperin, 'Crucifixion, the Nahum Pesher, and the Penalty of Strangulation', *Journal of Jewish Studies* xxxi (1981), 32–46; at 45 he treats Sahn. 43a as a rabbinizing reinterpretation of a tradition of crucifixion. This is true of the central passage, but not necessarily (see below) of the sentences which frame it, where the original tradition probably survives. Graetz (Maier, 217) made this point with regard to the parallel formulation on Ben Stada, Sanh. 67a.

[143]Maier, 219–37.

halakhah; the argument that what is anti-Mishnaic is likely to be pre-Mishnaic applies here.[144] The second sentence begins in Sanh. 43a, where an omission is indicated in the rendering above, 'Jesus the Nazarene *goes forth to be stoned, because* he ...'. The italicized words are not found when the sentence is quoted on its own in Sanh. 107b, and only serve to bind it to its context in Sanh. 43a. The tradition given as an independent sentence in Sanh. 107b could have been quoted selectively from the narrative now found in Sanh. 43a, but it is perhaps more likely that it circulated as a separate saying. An early stratum of the Sanh. 43a narrative would then have consisted of these two sentences, stating that Jesus was hanged for sorcery and deception. The view ultimately approved in the Mishnah, however, is that these offences are punished by stoning (Sanh. vii. 4), which in all cases, or only those of blasphemy and idolatry (both opinions at Mishnah, Sanh. vi. 4), is followed by the hanging of the corpse. Hence, at a secondary stage in the composition of the narrative, it was supposed that the known 'hanging' of Jesus was that which follows stoning, according to the halakhah. Now Mishnah, Sanh. vi. 1, ordains that the man sentenced to stoning should be preceded to his place of execution by a herald, announcing his offence and summoning any who, even at the last moment, can testify in favour of his acquittal. This procedure being assumed, the story now arose that the herald announced for forty days that 'Jesus the Nazarene goes forth to be stoned, because he practised sorcery and deceived and led astray Israel' – but still they found no cause for his acquittal. The point of this story, now in Sanh. 43a, is to show that he was guilty beyond a peradventure; comparably exaggerated narratives with the same point assert that he led nine hundred brigands (pagan source quoted by Lactantius, *Inst. Div.* v. 3, 4)[145] or that he suffers a specially loathsome torment in Gehenna (Gittin 57a–b). Finally this story, now combined with the two earlier sentences, was quoted in the Talmudic tractate at the point where the herald of Mishnah, Sahn. vi. 1 is being discussed, because, as Maier rightly notes, it raises the halakhic question whether the herald should go forth before the day of execution itself. Hence Justin's report can still be seen as substantiated by tannaitic as well as pagan and Christian tradition; and it can now also be seen that

---

[144]Discussion of this argument, in which the law of hanging is an important instance, by J. Heinemann, 'Early Halakhah in the Palestinian Targumim', *Journal of Jewish Studies* xxv. I (1974) (= *Studies ... in Honour of David Daube*), 114–22 (116–21).

[145]Assigned to a Jewish source, comparable with that in Celsus, by the present writer (pp. 162–75, below).

his link between execution and deception, and his specification in *Dial.* lxix of charges of sorcery and deception at the time of Christ's ministry, are paralleled in precisely those sentences of Sanh. 43a which have appeared on critical grounds to be earlier.

The third in Justin's group of allegations of anti-Christian measures concerns a prohibition of converse with Christians, already discussed above in relation to the evidence for Christian synagogue attendance. Trypho is made to exclaim (*Dial.* xxxviii) that 'it would have been well if we had been persuaded by the teachers, who ordained (τοῖς διδασκάλοις, νομοθετήσασι) that we should enter into discussion with none of you, not even to hold this conversation with you'. Justin later asks (*Dial.* cxii) whether 'your teachers' (διδάσκαλοι) do not deserve to be called blind guides, when they never even dare to mention or expound the great matters of the law of Moses, and 'when we expound them, they forbid you entirely to listen, or to enter into conversation'. This ordinance of the *didaskaloi* against hearing sermons from Christians or entering into discussion with them was compared above in respect of motivation with the patristic warnings against attending synagogue. Like Justin's report of propaganda, however, it recalls traditions preserved in rabbinic texts. Graetz long ago identified the ordinance mentioned in Trypho's speech with the prohibition of dealings with *minim* at Tos. Hullin ii. 20f. and elsewhere.[146] The sequel in Tosefta points the moral by two anecdotes on the rejection of healing and teaching offered in the name of ben Pantera (Tos. Hullin ii. 22f., 24; Strack, pp. xxi–xxiv, 2–4). The probable interpretation of these passages is that Palestinian Christians are among the *minim* to be shunned.[147] The attitude behind such a prohibition, further illustrated by the association of *minim*, apostates, and gentiles discussed in connection with the Tefillah (p. 92 above), is exhibited in the saying ascribed to the conservative, priestly Tarfon (early second century) that *minim* are worse than idolaters,[148] closely paralleled by Trypho's cutting

---

[146]H. Graetz, *Gnosticismus und Judenthum* (1846, repr. Farnborough, 1971), 21; texts cited below translated by J. Neusner, *The Tosefta: Fifth Division* (New York, 1979), 73–5.

[147]So Kimelman, 231 f. For Maier, 264 f. (cf. 175–7, 197 f., 251 f.), ii. 24 refers to an otherwise unknown Yeshua ben Pantiri, of *c.* A.D. 100, and ii. 22 f. to a second-century magician, ben Pandera; they were identified with Christ in the post-Talmudic period on the basis of the tradition going back to Origen, *c. Celsum*, i. 32, itself a mistaken application of a Palestinian story about ben Pandera to Jesus. The present writer (pp. 177–8 below) regards the Tosefta stories and that ascribed to a Jewish source by Celsus as alike indebted to a widely current Jewish allegation on Christ's birth.

[148]Tos. Shabb. xiii. 5, ed. S. Lieberman (New York, 1962), 58; translation and analysis by J. Gereboff, *Rabbi Tarfon* (Missoula, 1979), 43 f.

reference to Justin's conversion from paganism (*Dial.* viii).[149] The impression given by Justin of the Jewish teachers' ordinance and the attitude behind it is thus borne out by rabbinic rulings and strictures on *minim*, among whom Christians are specified.

The allegations of propaganda and disciplinary measures made by Justin in connection with his complaints of the cursing of Christians in synagogue are thus supported in each case by other evidence. This observation strengthens in turn the credibility of his belief in the synagogue malediction; and the correspondences noted between two of his other claims and rabbinic tradition encourage the identification of this curse as a form of the 'benediction of the heretics' known from Jewish sources. At the same time Justin's evidence sheds light on the development of Jewish–Christian relations from the second half of the first century. Emergent Christianity, inheriting the same intense congregational self-consciousness and universal claim reflected in the Eighteen Benedictions, was met by defensive measures and active counter-propaganda. A curse upon Christians in the Tefillah, such as the convergence of evidence suggests, can now be seen to have its place among measures which reinforced the exclusion of Christians from synagogue membership, and expressed, for the benefit of both Jews and gentiles, the sole rights of Judaism in the biblical inheritance and its promise to the nations.

The history of the benediction in relation to Christianity may now be briefly resumed. Justin, the first non-Jewish witness who directly alleges a synagogue curse, was right in supposing that Christians, both Jewish and gentile, were cursed in synagogue. The curse, one of a number of measures against emergent Christianity, was a form of the Benediction of the *minim*. This malediction on heretics was approved at Jamnia under Gamaliel II and incorporated in the Tefillah, which at this time was gaining an importance as a bond of Jewish unity. The wording of the benediction was variable, and no surviving text can be assumed to reproduce a specimen form of the Jamnian prayer. As has often been noted, it could apply to heretics other than Christians; but the impression of Jewish opposition given by Christian sources from Paul to Justin, confirmed by the scattered but hostile references to Christianity in early rabbinic literature, suggests that Christians were prominently in view at the time of the benediction's approval.

Related maledictions on 'separatists' or 'wicked' were probably already current, and applied in some synagogues to 'the sect of the

---

[149] Abrahams, 64, cites Eusebius, *Pr. E.* i. 2 for the argument that a heathen should remain a good polytheist or turn to Judaism.

Nazarenes' (Acts xxiv 5, xxviii 22), whose members had suffered persecution in Palestine (I Thess. ii 14, p. 105 above). The Johannine evidence, together with that from the sub-apostolic period collected by Prof. Lampe, reflects the impact of measures more drastic than such a benediction alone. The Jamnian ordinance belongs to this more systematized opposition of the late first century, and probably reinforces an earlier exclusion attested in John, although uncertainties of dating leave open the possibility that these two measures may be contemporaneous.

During the second century the wording and combination of benedictions in the Tefillah varied widely; the formula 'of the *minim*' was recited on its own as well as in combination with other benedictions, and could be worded so as to condemn Christians in particular. Within the Tefillah it belonged to a general context of prayer for redemption, with accompanying judgement on Jew and gentile, and in this section of the Prayer it came to be regularly incorporated in the present Twelfth Benediction. The application of the benediction to gentile as well as Jewish Christians is consistent with this context.

In the fourth century Nazarenes and *minim* were specified in this benediction in Palestine. Part of the evidence to this effect from Epiphanius and Jerome suggests that a Jewish-Christian sect was intended; but their conflicting remarks on this point are second-hand, and conditioned by their immediate aims. Justin, believing that the curse applies to all Christians, and Tertullian, assuming that all Christians are meant by *Nazareni*, are better guides to the scope of the benediction.

This interpretation is supported by ancient non-Christian recognition of the church of Jews and gentiles as a single tribe or race. It also suits the Judaism of the early Christian centuries, when, as the relevant section of the Tefillah attests, proselytism remained important. The benediction thus understood is not inconsistent with reports of Christian visitors in synagogue during the patristic period. It was one of a number of expressions of the sole and universal claims of Judaism, whereby such visitors could be encouraged as potential proselytes.

The Twelfth Benediction includes prayer against gentile pride, but it was not solely or mainly an anti-Roman curse; the large biblical scope of its contextual prayer for judgement, vindication, and the end of evil was not forgotten, and from the Talmudic period onwards it was viewed primarily as an anti-heretical benediction.

Its continued application to Christianity after the fourth century is attested by formulations of the benediction itself. In some settings the Christian empire will have been especially in view, but Geonic and mediaeval interpretations show that Christ and the apostles were also envisaged.

From the Paris Disputation of 1240 the benediction was at the heart of debate on the legitimacy of Jewish literature and synagogue prayer. Hence formulations of this benediction were drastically modified, Talmudic tradition on the venerably pre-Christian age of the Prayer as a whole was emphasized, and the ethical overtones genuinely present in the context of the benediction and treasured in devotional commentary upon it were made to rule out its application to Christianity. In discussion of these interpretations the main lines of modern argument were laid down, and the historical question of the purpose of the Jamnian ordinance came to the fore.

In these pages it has been urged that more can be said than recent students would allow for its association with nascent Christianity. It was not decisive on its own in the separation of church and synagogue, but it gave solemn liturgical expression to a separation effected in the second half of the first century through the larger group of measures to which it belongs. The anti-heretical benediction is interpreted by its context in the Tefillah, which is marked by the zeal for the mission and unity of the brotherhood also found in the early Christian congregations; and the effects of this zeal on both sides are illustrated by Justin's allusions to the propaganda, counter-propaganda and disciplinary measures which characterize the beginning of Jewish–Christian controversy.[150]

---

[150]The writer gratefully acknowledges comments from those who heard earlier versions of the above at seminars under the chairmanship of Professors H. Chadwick and G. N. Stanton, especially Professor S. G. Hall, Mr. H. Maccoby, Dr J. C. O'Neill, and Dr S. C. Reif.

3

I THESSALONIANS ii 3 AS REBUTTING THE CHARGE OF FALSE PROPHECY

ἡ γὰϱ παϱάϰλησις ἡμῶν οὐϰ ἐϰ πλάνης οὐδὲ ἐξ ἀϰαθαϱσίας οὐδὲ ἐν δόλῳ.

It has become commonplace to note that the charges rejected in this defence of Paul's preaching in general (vv. 3–4) recall those levelled at Graeco-Roman philosophers; just as the sequel, reverting to his Thessalonian preaching in particular (vv. 5–12), seems to echo philosophical ideals. These observations, already important in von Dobschütz's commentary on ii 1–12, govern the later expositions of verse 3 by Dibelius, Rigaux, Malherbe 'Gentile' (with fresh material from Dio Chrysostom), Best, and Friedrich; Marxsen, who deals mainly with other aspects of the passage, also applies this verse to wandering philosophers.[1] Schmithals, *Paul*, however, building on patristic exegesis, links it with other Pauline self-defences, notably II Cor. iv 1 f.; he goes on to identify the opponents as the 'Gnostics' also encountered in Corinth. Lastly, by contrast, the apostle's debt to Old Testament prophetic self-awareness is determinative for Denis, 'Prophète', who is followed by Henneken, *Verkündigung*.

The well-known post-biblical developments of Hebrew prophecy are not usually considered in this connection, but may also be relevant to a decision on the background of the passage. In Jewish and Christian apologetic the Old Testament prophets appeared, by a stylization applied also to Christ and the apostles, as intellectual guides outshining the philosophers. The terms of praise and blame bestowed on philosophers in any case overlap with those applied to prophets, and in this context the vocabularies begin to merge. At the same time the claim to prophecy had not ceased. Lev. xix 31, xx 27, on divination; Deut. xiii, on false prophecy and enticement to idolatry; and Deut. xviii 10–22, on divination, the prophet like Moses, and the false prophet, lost none of their importance. Deut. xiii is linked with Lev. xx 27 in CD xii. 3, with Deut. xviii in Philo, *Sp.L.* i. 54–65, and with both passages in Mishnah, Sanhedrin vii 4. 10 f. Popular presentation of the prophets, as exemplified in the Martyrdom of Isaiah, makes the debate on false prophecy crucial (iii. 6–10). As appears in different ways from Philo, the Qumran

---

[1] Writings cited by author's name only are listed at the end of the chapter, those cited with short title in the bibliography; on comment since 1982 see pp. 14–16, above.

writings, and the rabbis, a prophetic claim could arise in the business of biblical exposition (Meyer, cols. 813–28); it was significant in Josephus' career, and was also evident, as Acts xiii 6 memorably shows, in Jews of a less literary cast; and it was well known in the early Christian congregations (I Thess. v 20). In all these settings the question how to tell true prophecy from false remained vividly actual.

The line of interpretation adopted by Dibelius and his followers draws on abundant references to the failings of wandering philosophers. Ancient criticisms include all the charges noticed in I Thess. ii 1–12, as is emphasized by Malherbe and Best. The weakness of such an interpretation in vv. 3 f. is that Septuagintal and post-biblical usage associates *paraklesis* with prophetic address, and *plane* with false prophecy – the cognate verbs both occur in the fundamental legislation on false prophecy, Deut. xiii (vv. 6 f., LXX); and this usage might be expected to be significant for Paul. On the other hand the prophetic interpretation, as expounded by Denis, leans too heavily on the view that the apostle elaborated a consciousness of himself as eschatological 'messianic prophet' from passages, not all of equally certain relevance, in Isaiah, Jeremiah, and Wisdom. May it be that the passage does reflect the apologetic of prophecy, as Denis well suggests (so, earlier, Zimmer, 250 f.); but that the apostle is primarily concerned not with biblical hints of opposition to the prophets, but with contemporary charges of false prophecy?

Despite the familiarity of the wandering philosopher in late antiquity, he was not clearly identified by the early Pauline commentators as the figure from whom the apostle wished to dissociate his preaching. Chrysostom indeed says, in his second homily on the Epistle, that the practices rejected in verse 3 are those of charlatans and wizards, γοήτων καὶ μάγων.[2] This comment is quoted by Dibelius, 9, together with anti-philosophical polemic from Lucian of Samosata and others. The standard pejorative terms used by Chrysostom would clearly suit this context; the Epistle to Diognetus, vii 4, condemns philosophers' opinions on divine substance as πλάνη τῶν γοήτων. It is doubtful, however, whether Chrysostom or his hearers would have viewed these terms as distinguishing a philosophical charlatan in particular; for, in the merging of vocabularies noted above, both words had long also been applied to false prophets. The seducer to apostasy should not be listened to, says Philo, paraphrasing Deut. xiii 1–3, 'for such a one is a *goes*, not a

---

[2]F. Field (ed.), *Sancti Patris Nostri Joannis Chrysostomi ... Interpretatio Omnium Epistolarum Paulinarum per Homilias facta* (7 vols., Oxford, 1849–62), vol. v (1855), 329.

prophet' (*Sp.L.* i. 315); Balaam is a *magos* (Philo, *Vit.Mo.* i. 276), the proscription of divination at Deut. xviii 10–14 includes in Aquila 'one who inquires of a *magos*' (verse 11, for *sho'el 'ob*),[3] and the diviner, counterfeiting prophecy, is rightly called a false prophet (Philo, *Sp.L.* iv. 48f., 51); hence 'wizard' and 'prophet' are antonyms in the view, rejected at *Rec.Cl.* i. 58, that Christ worked his miracles 'ut magus, non ut propheta'.

This view of Chrysostom's language is confirmed by his continuation: '"nor in guile" – nor for a revolt, like Theudas'. The name offers a clue to the opponents whom he believes the apostle to envisage. In the previous homily, on i, verses 3 and 6 (ed. Field, ibid., pp. 316, 318), he has recalled from Acts xvii 5–9 how 'those fighting against the *kerygma*' sought for Paul in Thessalonica, and how they stirred up the politarchs to bring persecution upon the brethren. The Jewish accusation by which this is inspired (Acts xvii 6f.) is, of course, that Paul and Silas are raising sedition against Caesar, 'saying that there is another king'. Hence Theudas is probably named in the second homily as a rebel leader with whom the apostles were indeed compared by a Jewish councillor, Acts v 36.

In his homily on this section of Gamaliel's speech (*in Acta hom.* xiv. 2) Chrysostom refers his hearers to Josephus for fuller information. The relevant passage would have been especially well-known to him through Eusebius' chapter (*H.E.* ii. 11) 'on Theudas the charlatan (*goes*)'. Here Acts v is quoted first, followed by Josephus' description of Theudas as a 'charlatan' who promised a miracle and 'said he was a prophet' (*Ant.* xx. 97). The final impression left by Chrysostom on I Thess. ii 3 is thus that the apostle has in mind the charges of sedition brought by Thessalonian Jewry; he therefore dissociates himself from men like Theudas, who 'claimed to be somebody' – a prophet, according to Josephus – but was in truth a 'charlatan'.

A group of early commentators find the clue to the background in the Epistles rather than the Acts. For Theodore of Mopsuestia the apostle is claiming to have taught the Thessalonians 'not as those are accustomed to teach, who wish to lead astray (*seducere*) those whom they teach, or to tell them something untrue; who also often conceal "with guile" the things that they say'.[4] *Plane* here is 'leading astray' (cf. Deut. xiii 6) to uncleanness spiritualized as untruth, an

[3] F. Field (ed.), *Origenis Hexaplorum quae supersunt* (2 vols., Oxford, 1875), vol. i, 299.
[4] H. B. Swete (ed.), *Theodori Episcopi Mopsuesteni in Epistolas B. Pauli Commentarii* (2 vols., Cambridge, 1882), vol. ii, 9.

interpretation possibly based on II Thess. ii 11 combined with II Cor. vi 8, Eph. iv 14f.; and the understanding of guile as conceal-ment (cf. Deut xiii 7, 'secretly') clearly derives from II Cor. iv 2f. (especially close in thought to I Thess. ii 3) and xi 13. Hence the practices rejected by Paul are those of the 'false apostles' of II Cor. xi 13. This exegesis of I Thess. ii 3 is given explicitly by the Ambrosiaster: 'hoc propter pseudoapostolos dicit'.[5]

II Cor. iv 2, with i 12, probably also inspires Pelagius' 'not against our conscience' for 'nor in guile'; but he defines the error rejected earlier in I Thess. ii 3 as the view that the evil can reign with Christ, supporting this with a quotation of Gal. vi 7.[6] For Theodoret, Paul rejects the lying and improper *mythologia* of the poets (*P.G.* lxxxii, col. 633); Philo condemns the mythographers as idolatrous image-makers (*Sp.L.* i. 28), and Theodoret is probably taking *plane* at I Thess. ii 3, as he does at Rom. i 27f., Eph. iv 14, to mean the denial of God (*P.G.* lxxxii, col. 536). He goes on, however, to interpret 'nor by guile' as 'we do not lure you to destruction', and here he clearly thinks of the common denigration of sectarian leaders as subversive, which the Ambrosiaster imagines being applied to St. Paul (comment on Phil. i 17, ed. Vogels, vol. iii, p. 134). Theodoret may have in mind Acts xvii 6f. and Theudas, like Chrysostom; but his comment is too brief for specification of the type of false teacher envisaged.

The teaching from which the apostle differentiates his *paraklesis*, according to these early comments, is therefore either that of seditious persons (Chrysostom, Theodoret), the charges of Thessa-lonian Jewry being in view (Chrysostom); or that of the false apostles (Theodore, the Ambrosiaster) or antinomians (Pelagius) mentioned elsewhere by Paul; or that of the poets (Theodoret). There is no clear reference to wandering philosophico-religious teachers, although, like other types of false teacher, they could be envisaged in Theodoret's second comment. Chrysostom's earlier comment might suit this interpretation; but his continuation gives the example of a Jewish false prophet, and shows his awareness that his pejorative terms belong equally to the biblically rooted vocabu-lary of true and false prophecy, to which the interpretations of *plane* by Theodore and Theodoret are also indebted.

Can this vocabulary further illuminate Paul's defence of his

---

[5]H. J. Vogels (ed.), *Ambrosiastri qui dicitur Commentarius in Epistulas Paulinas*, iii (CSEL. lxxxi (Vienna, 1969)), 215.

[6]A. Souter, *Pelagius's Expositions of Thirteen Epistles of St. Paul*, Texts and Studies, ix. 1–2 (2 vols., Cambridge, 1922–6), vol. ii, 421.

preaching? Existing studies have abundantly illustrated the nouns of verse 3, and their links with the prophetic *books* have been noted by Denis. The examination which follows may occasionally offer fresh material, but its principal *raison d'être* is to consider the words with regard to the discussion of the *validity* of prophecy. The Pentateuch and its interpretations therefore bulk more largely than is usual in study of this verse. The apologetic of prophecy, with which the apostle's purpose has obvious affinities, emerges as a thread binding together much ancient usage of the words he chooses.

Paraklesis and its cognate verb, studied by Schmitz and Stählin and by Bjerkelund, *Parakalo*, are linked with prophecy in the senses both of comfort and of exhortation. The prophets console with their promise of redemption, whence consolation comes to be used for redemption itself (Luke ii 25, and rabbinic usage). So, according to Ecclus. xlviii 24 f., Isaiah 'by a great spirit saw the last things, and comforted (*parekalesen*) the mourners in Zion' – his vision of the end constituting consolation. The twelve prophets also 'comforted Israel', Ecclus xlix. 10. Similarly the early Christian prophets provide 'edification, *paraklesis*, and encouragement', for their hearers 'learn, and ... are consoled', I Cor. xiv 3, 31; and the apostolic teachings about the end, like Isaiah's, are the means of consolation (I Thess. iv 18, v 11). Hence, for both Jew and Christian, the biblical books, all of them prophetic (Josephus, *Ap.* i. 37; Heb. i 1), constitute *paraklesis*, I Macc. xii 9, Rom. xv 4; and the word is used of the exposition of these books, Acts xiii 15 (probably, like Heb. xiii 22, reflecting a Jewish word use; so Rigaux, 406).

Here the sense of 'exhortation' becomes important, although it does not drown the biblical overtones of 'comfort' (compare Bjerkelund, *Parakalo*, pp. 26 f.). This *paraklesis* is a gift of the spirit, distinguished from prophecy but associated with it, Rom. xii 8. The Pauline usage may build on a Jewish use of the verb for the prophet's characteristic form of address. The Baptist is *parakalon*, Luke iii 18. In the Septuagint of Isaiah the consolation of Israel, which is given even more prominence than it has in the Hebrew, may be 'vain' (xxviii 29, xxx 7; Ottley, *Isaiah* vol. ii, pp. 245 f.) rather than God-given and 'true' (lvii 18) *paraklesis*. Similarly, the prophetic *paraklesis* may not be genuine. The verb is used for the enticement to apostasy practised by the false prophet, Deut. xiii 7, LXX ἐὰν δὲ παρακαλέσῃ σε. Likewise, Cain entices, *parakalon*, all whom he meets into luxury and brigandage, Josephus, *Ant.* i. 61. Thus *paraklesis*, when applied to the apostolic preaching in I Thess. ii 3, suggests a claim to be giving true prophetic exhortation and comfort; but the Septuagintal and Josephan employment of both noun and verb in bad as well as good senses shows that the question whether the Pauline *paraklesis* is a false prophet's enticement need not be remote.

The apostle's vindication of his *paraklesis* therefore follows appropriately. *Plane*, as noted already, is the standard term for the seduction to idolatry constituted by false prophecy. The false prophet of Deut. xiii 6 (E.VV., verse 5) 'spoke to seduce you', ἐλάλησεν ... πλανῆσαί σε, 'from the Lord your God'. The corresponding Hebrew *dibber sarah*, 'spoke rebellion', is used as shorthand for 'prophesied falsehood' in CD v. 21 f., xii. 3. The Septuagintal use of the πλανάω word-group suggests that it had acquired a similarly regular association with false prophecy (Braun, p. 236, noting that the Septuagint also applies it comparably to bad rulers). Thus at Deut. iv 19 images are prohibited lest, seeing the host of heaven, 'being seduced (*planetheis*) you should worship them'. Here the Hebrew is *niddahta*, part of the verb used in a later clause of Deut. xiii 6 (5) for 'to thrust you out' (LXX *exosai se*) and in xiii 14 (13) for those who led astray a whole city to idolatry (LXX *apestesan*, cf. Acts v 37 on Judas the Galilaean); from this latter verse the Mishnah defines such an offender as *maddiah*, Sanh. vii. 10. Isa. xxx is unified by the LXX as a vision of false prophecy rejected by the 'holy people' (verse 19); whereas they used to say to the prophets, 'Tell us another *planesis*' (verse 10), now 'no longer shall those who lead thee astray draw near' (verse 20), and idols shall be removed (verse 22). In Josephus, reflecting the same usage, Moses vindicates his mission by asserting that his miracles are not 'according to wizardry and seduction of true judgement', κατὰ γοητείαν καὶ πλάνην τῆς ἀληθοῦς δόξης (*Ant.* ii. 286).

The spirit causing the Egyptians who resort to divination to err is πνεῦμα πλανήσεως, Isa. xix 14. This phrase is applied to punitive delusion visited on sinful Israel, Ps. Sol. viii. 15 (compare the work of the 'energy of deception', II Thess. ii 11); but its development also leads to what one may call, adapting a phrase of G. W. H. Lampe, 'Martyrdom', 119, the 'demonology' of prophecy. The πνεύματα τῆς πλάνης mentioned throughout the Testaments of the Twelve Patriarchs (Braun, 239, n. 38) inspire false teaching, among other evils; and Justin Martyr ascribes to these spirits the falsehoods which Christ foretold would be taught in his name, *Dial.* xxxv. Judah grieves because his children follow diviners and '*demons of seduction*', Test. Judah xxiii. 1. These may be compared with the 'spirits of Belial' who have dominion over the false prophet according to CD xii. 2, and contrasted with the truly prophetic spirits who are *subject* to the prophets, I Cor. xiv 32. 'The spirits of *plane* and of Beliar' are classed together for judgement at the last, Test. Levi iii 3.

In the New Testament the influence of Deut. xiii and its related passages on the πλανάω-group is evident in the Jewish estimates of Christ and his teaching recounted at Matt. xxvii 63 f. ('deceiver', 'seduction') and John vii 12, 47 ('lead astray'); compare the epithets *planos* and *laoplanos* ascribed to Jewish critics at Apocr. John i and Justin, *Dial.* lxix, and Sanh. 43a, 'he deceived and led astray Israel' (*hesith we hiddiah*, the verbs being those from Deut. xiii 7, 14 used to define the offences of beguiling to idolatry at Mishnah, Sanh. vii. 10). Of false prophets in general the word-group is used at Mark xiii 5 f., II Tim. iii 13, II Peter ii 15 (after a probable reference to Deut. xiii at ii 1), I John ii 26, iv 6 ('the spirit of deception', cf. Isa. xix 14, whose work makes it necessary to 'try the spirits' and expose false prophets, iv. 1), Jude 11 'the deception by Balaam', Rev. ii 20, xix 20 (cf. xiii 14).

The use of the words from this group to express straying, or being led astray, rather than the act of deception, appears in Wisdom and Philo. It is close to the usages discussed so far, because idolatry is the characteristic and fundamental straying. In Wisdom the active sense, 'deception', may well survive at xii 24, where the heathen 'were led very far astray in the ways of *plane*'; but it is their 'going astray (*planasthai*) concerning the knowledge of God' which leads to all evils, including madness and false prophecy, at xiv 22, 27 f. Philo, who prefers the form *planos* for the abstract noun (Braun, 239), quotes Deut. iv 19 'being seduced' to show that idolators have been led infinitely far astray, πλάνον ἐπλανήθησαν ἀνήνυτον (cf. Wis. xii 24); they should have taken care to walk by the way whence there is no straying, διὰ τῆς ἀπλανοῦς ὁδοῦ (compare ἀπλανεστάτη ... ὁδός, *Dec.* 81). This phrase has probably moved, by 'the way' of Deut. xiii 6, to Isa. xxxv 8 LXX, the 'pure way' in which 'they shall not be led astray'. Similarly, in Philo, *Dec.* 52, idolatry is *planos*, 'error'; and *plane* at Rom. i 27 (cf. verse 25), in a context thematically close to these Sapiential and Philonic passages, bears the same sense of 'straying' into idolatry.

This sense of 'error' is preferred by a number of commentators on I Thess. ii 3. The context here, however, is closer to that of Moses' defence of his divine legation by a demonstration that his miracles involve no 'seduction of true judgement' (Josephus, *Ant.* ii. 286, quoted above). This active sense of *plane*, bound up with the influential Deuteronomic terminology just considered, commends itself at I Thess. ii 3. The passive sense is nevertheless advocated by von Dobschütz, 87 f., because this first section of the sentence is objective, and subjectivity only comes in with the second and third sections; by Zimmer, 251 and Best 93, because 'deception' would make 'nor in guile' superfluous; and by Braun 251 n. 152, because, as others also note, the passive sense is more frequent in the New Testament. To the first two objections it may be answered that, in a defence of 'our' *paraklesis*, subjective reference can hardly be ruled out at any point; and that 'deception' in the sense of seduction to apostasy would be expected to involve 'guile' (see below), but by no means covers all the semantic range of the latter word. Best is rejecting 'deception' in the sense preferred by Schmithals, who rightly replies (*Paul*, 144) to the objection represented by Braun that New Testament usage varies sufficiently to allow the active sense, preferred also by Schlier, 31, but more questionably restricts the 'deception' to a particular charge brought against Paul with regard to the collection.

Plane may therefore be taken in the active sense at I Thess. ii 3. It was thus understood by Tertullian, who quotes the verse (*Pud.* xvii) with the rendering 'ex seductione', and by Theodore (discussed above), who paraphrases 'docuimus, non sicut illi ... qui seducere volunt illos quos docent'. Theodoret's 'denying God' evokes the close connection with apostasy which *plane* has from Deuteronomy onwards, and which comes out so formidably in Philo's paraphrases of Deut. xiii (*Sp.L.* i. 54–7, 315 f.). Paul's opening words may then be rendered: 'Our prophetic exhortation arises not from seduction to apostasy ...'

'Ἀκαθαρσία, however, might seem at first to point to the 'philosophical' interpretation, for it implies charges of impure life and false teaching ('evil opinions are the uncleanness of the soul', Epictetus[7] in Arrian iv. 11. 1). Yet, in biblical usage it is associated with false prophecy. This is true both of its sense of ritual uncleanness, whether literally or spiritually understood, and of its sense of moral licence.

The latter sense is represented at Rom. i 24, where the word sums up the moral consequences of idolatry, the archetypal *plane* (verse 27). For post-biblical writers *akatharsia* appears in Israel, especially through the licence and ritual malpractices of rulers and priests (Ps. Sol. viii. 12, 22; Test. Levi xv 1); but it is characteristic of Gentile idolaters. 'May God ... deliver us from the uncleanness of polluted enemies!', Ps. Sol. xvii 45. With a more ethical stress, it epitomizes Gentile sin at Rom. vi 19 (cf. I Thess. iv 5–7) and Eph. iv 19. As

---

[7]The passage is quoted ad loc. by G. Raphelius, *Annotationes Philologicae in Novum Testamentum* (2 vols., Leiden, 1750), vol. ii, 539.

appears in Rom. i and I Thess. iv, it can refer to sexual licence in particular; when Potiphar's wife tempts Joseph by offering to convert, he replies that the Lord does not want those who revere him to be in uncleanness, Test. Jos. iv. 6. Such licence is linked with false prophecy above all in 'Balaam's deception' (Jude 11), a great *exemplum*. The story is told at Num. xxv, xxxi 16; Hos. ix 10 (Israel are 'alienated to shame', LXX); Ps. cvi 28–31: Rev. ii 14, and elaborately recounted by Josephus, *Ant.* iv. 126–58 and Philo, *Mos.* i. 295–311; *Virt.* 34–44. By the false prophet's counsel the Midianite women lured Israel to idol-sacrifice. Greek-speaking Jews understood this as a lapse to the mysteries. 'Israel became initiate (ἐτελέσθη) to Baal-peor' (Num. xxv 3 LXX), language repeated at Ps. cv 28 LXX and Philo, *Sp.L.* i. 56. Philo strongly condemns the mysteries for their licence in the same book, 319–23, immediately after his paraphrase of Deut. xiii, and he exemplifies the duty of punishing apostates (ibid. 55 and 316) from the hero of this episode, Phinehas (ibid, 56 f.). Similarly, idolatry leads not only to false prophecy, but also to fornication and carelessness of marital purity, at Wis. xiv 12, 24. St. Paul links fornication with idolatry at I Cor. x 7 f., where, in contrast with Rom. i 24 (echoing, as Hooker, 'Romans i' shows, Ps. cv 14 LXX, on Num. xi), he alludes to Num. xxv.

The licence understood as *akatharsia* is therefore regularly connected with pseudoprophetic seduction to apostasy. In the standard biblical *exemplum*, a false prophet makes licence the means of *plane*; in Wisdom, false prophecy and licence are parallel results of having gone astray; for Philo, following the Septuagint, the licence of the mysteries is a temptation to apostasy, and is banned by Moses in the same way as the idolatry preached by the false prophet. A train of thought originating in the Bible and familiar to St. Paul therefore links the two nouns juxtaposed in I Thess. ii 3. Their appearance together is not surprising. Nevertheless, 'uncleanness' here is unlikely to mean licentious behaviour in particular. More light is shed on its meaning in this verse by the sense of ritual uncleanness, instanced in a spiritualized form later in the Epistle.

In I Thess. iv 7 f. the immediate reference of *akatharsia* is to moral licence, the argument being close to Joseph's in Test. Jos. iv 6. The Pauline context, however, is governed by levitical language, and abstinence from fornication has been urged as a particular implication of a more broadly understood sanctification (verse 3). In verse 8 the argument has returned from the particular to the general exhortation (Best, p. 168). Hence, in verse 7, *akatharsia* is not completely rendered by 'fornication', but retains its levitical overtones of 'uncleanness' in contrast to 'holiness', spiritually understood. God's gift of his holy spirit to the congregation is immediately mentioned (verse 8). This sequence implies an opposition between uncleanness and the spirit, such as is reflected in the terminology of false prophecy.

False prophecy is regarded as defiling. To be joined together with diviners is 'to be defiled' (ἐκμιανθῆναι) by them, Lev. xix 31. The warning that the soul that follows diviners shall be destroyed from his people is underlined by 'And ye shall be holy ...' at the beginning of the next verse (Lev. xx 7 f.). It is the 'holy people' who reject false prophecy, Isa. xxx 19 LXX; and the way of holiness whence Israel shall not be led astray is *pure*, Isa. xxxv 8 LXX; both adjectives are Septuagintal additions. In Ecclus. xxxiv 1–8 it is taught that 'divinations and soothsayings and dreams are vain' (verse 5; cf. Deut. xviii 10, on divinations, and Deut. xiii 2, 4, 6 LXX, on dreams). This line is immediately preceded by the couplet 'From the unclean thing, what can be cleansed? From the lie, what can become true?' (verse 4).

In the Septuagint the language of the dietary laws, forbidding defilement of the human psyche, is close to that of I Thess. iv (cf. II Cor. vii 1). 'You shall not make your souls abominable by beast, or by fowl, or by any creeping thing which I have separated from you in *akatharsia*; and you shall be holy to me, for I am holy' (Lev. xx 25, cf. xi 43 f.). It comes to be held that ethical misconduct, too, 'defiles the soul' (Test. Asher ii. 7). This defilement of the human spirit is the counterpart of false teaching in CD v. 11–13. 'They also have made their holy spirits unclean, and with a blasphemous tongue they have opened their mouth against the ordinances of the covenant of God ... and they are speaking error against them'. The first clause echoes Lev. xi 43, xx 25; the last, Isa. xxxii 6 (LXX *planesis*).

False prophecy thus defiles the human spirit; but in this respect among others, as the last quotation vividly illustrates, the consideration of the human spirit approximates to that of the divine (the analogy between the two is discussed by Moule, *Holy Spirit*, 7–17). Impurity is inimical also, and eminently, to God's holy spirit, in familiar passages at Ezek. xxxvi 26–9, echoed at I Thess. iv 7 f. (the gift of the divine spirit saves Israel from her uncleanness); Ps. li (1) 12 f.; Wis. vii 22–5. Whereas true prophets speak by God's holy spirit (II Kingdoms xxiii 2, Acts xxviii 25, II Peter i 21), their opponents speak by 'the spirit of uncleanness' (Zech. xiii 2), which the Qumran psalmist names together with Satan and the evil impulse (11QPsᵃ, col. xix, l. 15). So it is promised that, with the end of idolatry, 'I will take away the false prophets and the unclean spirit' (Zech. xiii. 2 LXX). The charge of false prophecy levelled against Christ can take the form 'he has an unclean spirit' (Mark iii 30; cf. 'demon', John vii 20, viii 48–52, x 20). Similarly, the false prophet, the dragon, and the beast of Rev. xvi 13 f. have 'unclean spirits' which are 'spirits of demons'; thereby the false prophet works miracles (Deut. xiii 2 f. (1 f.)) to lead men astray to idolatry, Rev. xix 20 (cf. xiii 13 f.). Divination is associated with 'the spirit of uncleanness', in express contrast with 'the holy spirit', in an anecdote told in Sifre of R. Eliezer (end of first century, if to be identified with Eliezer ben Hyrcanus); a variant in Sanh. 65b refers it to R. Akiba. When he reached the verse Deut. xviii 12, 'he used to say, woe upon us, for he who cleaves to uncleanness, the spirit of uncleanness rests upon him; he who cleaves to the Shekhinah, it is just that upon him the holy spirit should rest. And who brings it about [that this is not the case]? "Your iniquities have separated between you and your God" (Isa. lix 2)' (Sifre Deut. 173, on xviii 12: ed. L. Finkelstein (Berlin, 1939; repr. New York, 1969), 220).[8]

Thus, just as the immorality understood as uncleanness is linked with false prophecy, so false prophecy itself is ascribed to the spirit of uncleanness. The adjective *akathartos* in St. Paul retains marked traces of Semitic, biblical usage (I Cor. vii 14, II Cor. vi 17). Similarly, it may be suggested, *akatharsia* here is best understood as 'spiritual uncleanness', approximating to the 'spirit of uncleanness' of Zech. xiii 2, the source of false prophecy.

The meaning is proximate rather than identical. There is no *pneuma* to make explicit the thought of uncleanness as a power, still less the demonological expression 'unclean spirit'. Nevertheless, the use of *ek* with *akatharsia*, as with *plane*, indicates that these vices are considered here as originative, in the vivid, personificatory biblical tradition of speech.

Bultmann, *Theologie*, §§ 14 (pp. 157–9; E.T., vol. i, 155–7), distinguishing 'animist' conceptions, wherein spirit is an independent and personal power, from 'dynamist' ones, wherein it is an impersonal force, notes that both coexist in St. Paul, but that expressions like 'the spirit of gentleness' may be animist in form rather than content. In I Thess. ii 3, it may be suggested, the opposite is the case. *Plane* and *akatharsia* should be located within

---

[8]That the version in Sifre, which has 'holy spirit', is likely to be more original than that in the Talmud, which has 'spirit of purity', is shown by A. M. Goldberg, *Untersuchungen über die Vorstellung von der Schekhinah in der frühen rabbinischen Literatur* (Berlin, 1969), 413 f.

the animist range of meaning, although its formal, verbal indication is lacking. As just noted with regard to *akatharsia*, their meaning should not be pressed into a strict animism, even though it is in speaking of prophecy that the apostle comes particularly close to this (I Cor. xiv 12, 14, 32, cited by Bultmann, ibid.). Rather, they are instances of the personificatory tendency which affects the use of *akatharsia* at Rom. vi 19, 'enslaved to uncleanness', and of *plane* at II Thess. ii 11, 'the effective working of deception'. So at I Thess. ii 3, where the thought of an energetic spirit of uncleanness is almost, but not quite, expressed, *akatharsia* may be rendered 'the spiritual uncleanness which possesses the false prophet'.

Denis, 'Prophète', 281 f., understands *akatharsia* as 'the unclean profanity of paganism' which co-operates with 'eschatological error' (*plane*) to combat 'messianic action' – the large sense which Denis gives to *paraklesis*, because of its Isaianic echoes and its equivalence to *euangelion*. He therefore finds the significance of Zech. xiii 2 in its demonstration that God's messianic action is against idolatry, against false prophets, who represent error, and against the unclean spirit, who is Satan, present amid error. The over-inclusive definition of *paraklesis* (267 f.) paradoxically obscures its particular association with prophecy, which is an aspect of the valuable point rightly made by Denis, the apostle's debt in this passage to biblical thought. Hence in Zech. xiii 2, as in other important passages which he brings forward, he looks for messianism and eschatology rather than the specifically prophetic links wherein, it has been suggested here, the significant thread is to be found. A scrap of later evidence, to be quoted after consideration of *dolos*, may bear out the 'prophetic' interpretation of *akatharsia* advanced above.

The progression from uncleanness to guile is natural, apart from any other consideration, because the antonymous 'pure' and 'guileless' figure as a pair of adjectives or adverbs. For Philo, monotheism provides for 'guileless and pure' piety (compare 'reasonable, guileless milk', I Peter ii 2), and idolatry should be far from the man seeking truth 'purely and guilelessly' (*Dec.* 58, 65). The adverbial pair is quoted by Denis, 'Prophète', n. 182, from Dio Chrysostom, *Or.* xxxii. 11: it is rare to find a philosopher speaking 'purely and guilelessly'.

This passage in Dio Chrysostom is used by Malherbe to explain the Pauline apologia in philosophical terms. The biblical usage of *dolos* nevertheless repays attention. 'You shall not walk in guile' (Hebrew *rakhil*, 'as a talebearer') 'among your people', Lev. xix 16 LXX. The preceding verse commands righteousness in judgement, without respect of persons. The two verses are echoed in the

Testament of Benjamin, subtitled in part of the MS tradition 'concerning the pure mind' (compare the association of purity with guilelessness noted above). In Test. Benj. vi. 2 'the good disposition receives no glory or dishonour from men, and knows no guile or lying . . .' Philo uses the two verses, quoting the second, to show that a ruler should preside over his subjects like a father, not doing wrong craftily (*doleros*); good rulers sometimes show a more than fatherly affection; these injunctions apply to those who exercise authority in every branch of life (*Sp.L.* iv. 183–6). These developments of Lev. xix 15 f. LXX are of interest at I Thess. ii, where the apostle, having mentioned *dolos* in verse 3, protests in verses 4–7 that he speaks not as pleasing men, and in Thessalonica has not sought glory from men – compare John v 41, on the sincerity of christ, and xii 43, on the insincerity of secret believers – but has shown the (more than paternal?) affection of a nurse.

It is perhaps in its capacity as the characteristic failing of the ruler or teacher (compare the association of the ruler and prophet in the Septuagintal usage of *planao*) that guile attains in Wisdom the position of a primary, representative sin. 'The holy spirit of discipline shall flee from guile', the youth of unspotted life is snatched away by death 'lest guile should deceive his soul', and Solomon learns wisdom 'guilelessly', without ulterior motive (Wis. i 5, iv 11, vii 13). Guile, like uncleanness, is especially inimical to the spirit, human and divine.

Correspondingly, the false prophet is marked by guile. He does his enticing 'secretly', *lathra(i)*, Deut. xiii 7 (6). In Philo's interpretation of this passage, he is 'putting on the name and guise of a prophet, making pretence to be possessed by inspiration', 'lying with his invention of oracles and pronouncements'; the brother who acts in this way may well be 'appearing to have a good intention' (*Sp.L.* i. 315 f.). Potiphar's wife's guile (Test. Jos. iii 9, iv. 1, 3) gives the parallel in 'profane' seduction. False teachers, comparable with the false prophets of old, will bring in heresies of destruction 'on the side', II Peter ii 1. There is no *dolos* in the mouth of the true servant of the Lord, Isa. liii 9 LXX. At one remove from the false prophet himself, Balaam's counsel leads to the *doliotes* of the Midianites, 'the things they did to you in guile because of Peor', Num. xxv 18 LXX. The closeness of the link between guile and lying emerges from the treatment of the guile of the kings of the last days, Dan. viii 25, xi 23; in both verses a word rendered by Theodotion as *dolos* (which LXX have at another point in viii 25) appears in LXX as *pseudos*. Similarly, Isa. liii 9 is quoted at I Peter ii 22 with *dolos*, and Rev. xiv 5 with *pseudos*, the distinguishing mark of the pseudo-prophecy so important in the Revelation. Hence 'guile' is the first charge said to be brought by St. Paul, 'filled with the holy spirit', against the *pseudoprophetes* Elymas, Acts xiii 10. It is the insincerity which covers seduction from the truth with the semblance of genuine prophecy.

Guile came to be a charge of which the apostle was especially conscious (II Cor. iv 2, xii 16), so that he insisted on his own sincerity (II Cor. i 12, ii 17). He levelled it himself at the false apostles, II Cor. xi 13. Schmithals, *Paul*, pp. 143 f., refers *dolos* at I Thess. ii 3 to the charge, inferred from II Cor, xii 16, that he had renounced financial support in order to benefit from the collection. The biblical associations of guile with abused authority and false prophecy favour a less precise reference. A rejection of *plane* is naturally followed by a repudiation of the concomitant guile. St. Paul disowns the guileful insincerity which would give seduction the appearance of prophecy. Such insincerity is the principal charge rebutted in the Pauline passage closest in thought to this one, II Cor. iv 1 f. The last two words of I Thess. ii 3 may then be rendered '[Our exhortation] is not preached with the guileful insincerity which would cover falsehood.'

This interpretation of the verse receives a measure of encouragement from a passage of Justin's *Dialogue*. It is not cited in commentaries used by the present writer, but an unknown former owner of his copy of Justin has pencilled the reference to I Thess. ii 3 in the margin. The problem of true and false prophecy is important to Justin (*Dial.* xxxv, lxxxvii f.), and near the beginning of the book he raises it in connection with the prophetic writings, which he describes as instrumental in his own conversion. He was directed to them, he says, by an old man with whom he had profitable discourse in a quiet place not far from the sea. In the climax of their dialogue the old man says of the prophets that they did not offer demonstrations of their sayings, for they were trustworthy, above all demonstration, and events agreed with their predictions; 'although they were also worthy to be believed because of the miracles [*dynameis*] which they performed, since they both glorified the maker of all as God and Father, and announced the Christ his son, sent from him. The false prophets, filled with the seducing and unclean spirit [ἀπὸ τοῦ πλάνου καὶ ἀκαθάρτου πνεύματος] neither did nor do this; but they dare to work certain miracles for the confusion of mankind, and glorify the spirits of seduction [*tes planes*] and demons' (*Dial.* vii). Here, if the suggestions made so far have any force, Justin takes one step more than St. Paul, but a step on the same way; for the Pauline sequence of seduction and uncleanness is now set explicitly in the demonology of prophecy.

The verse may then be rendered periphrastically: 'Our prophetic exhortation arises not from seduction to apostasy, nor from the spiritual uncleanness which possesses the false prophet; it is not preached with the guileful insincerity which would cover false-hood.'

This interpretation of the verse within the biblically rooted discussion of false prophecy may be held to agree with three other features of I Thessalonians. First, the prophets, past and present, are important (ii 15, v 20), and the apostle both transmits and recalls teaching about the last things which, by the analogy of Rev. i 3, could be regarded as prophecy (iv 15–17, v 2 f.). Secondly, immediately before ii 3, the apostle has again recalled as 'not empty' (ii 1–2) his coming to Thessalonica, which according to i 5 was 'in power and in holy spirit and in much assurance'; if, as is probable, this refers to miracles[9] (so Schmithals, *Paul*, pp. 140 f., and Schlier, p. 21, following most Fathers; Lampe, p. 91 thinks that this view may well be right; cf. Rom. xv 18 f., II Cor. xii 12, Mark xvi 20, Heb. ii 4), the reference falls into place as a proof of true prophecy. Thirdly, ii 14 f., in conjunction with Acts xvii 1–10, show that bitterly-resented Jewish opposition hindered the apostle; defence against a charge of false prophecy would fit not only his own biblically-conditioned self-awareness, but also the kind of charge likely to be made by Jews: seduction to apostasy (so Jerusalem Christians, according to Acts xxi 21) under the guise of proselytizing (i 9 f., ii 16), this charge also covering, as Chrysostom shows, the sedition (Acts xvii 6 f.) readily associated with false prophecy (Acts v 36 f., xxi 38).

The danger of confusing different kinds of ancient religious propaganda in Pauline study has been indicated by Bowers, 'Propaganda'. He accepts, with emphasis on Pauline distinctiveness, that itinerant philosophers are envisaged at I Thess. ii 3. It has been suggested here that the danger to which he rightly points may imperil this interpretation as a whole. The philosophical exegesis,

---

[9]So, on i. 5, Theodore (Swete, vol. ii, 4), Theodoret (*P. G.* lxxxii, col. 632), Severian of Gabala (K. Staab, *Pauluskommentare aus der griechischen Kirche* (Münster, 1933), 329), the Ambrosiaster (Vogels, vol. iii, 212 f.); on ii. 1 f., Chrysostom (Field, vol. v, 328). Pelagius on i. 5 (Souter, vol. ii, 418) gives as alternatives the 'power' of miracles or of patient suffering; the latter is adopted by Chrysostom on this verse. Rigaux, p. 376, and Best, p. 75, exclude 'miracle' from the Pauline range of meaning of *dynamis* in the singular, unless (Rigaux adds) it is specified, as at Rom. xv 19, II Thess. ii 9. This distinction seems over-sharp in view of the well-attested Jewish and early Christian connection of power with miracle.

attractive as it seems, may in truth lead astray from the prophetic apostle.[10]

WORKS CITED BY AUTHOR'S NAME

E. Best, *A Commentary on the First and Second Epistles to the Thessalonians* (London, 1972)

H. Braun, s.v. πλανάω, etc., TWNT vi (Stuttgart, 1959), 230–54

M. Dibelius, *An Die Thessalonicher I-II; An Die Philipper*, 2nd edn. (Tübingen, 1925)

E. von Dobschütz, *Die Thessalonicher-Briefe* (Göttingen, 1909)

G. Friedrich, 'Der erste Brief an die Thessalonicher', in J. Becker, H. Conzelmann and G. Friedrich, *Die Briefe an die Galater, Epheser, Philipper, Kolosser, Thessalonicher und Philemon* (Göttingen, 1976)

W. Marxsen, *Der erste Brief an die Thessalonicher* (Zürich, 1979)

R. Meyer, s.v. προφήτης, TWNT vi (Stuttgart, 1959), 813–28

B. Rigaux, *Saint Paul: Les Épîtres aux Thessaloniciens* (Paris, 1956)

H. Schlier, *Der Apostel und seine Gemeinde* (Freiburg i.B., 1972)

O. Schmitz and G. Stählin, s.v. παρακαλέω, TWNT v (Stuttgart, 1954), 771–98

F. Zimmer, 'I Thess. 2. 3–8 erklärt', in C. R. Gregory *et al.*, *Theologische Studien Herrn Wirkl. Oberkonsistorialrath Professor D. Bernhard Weiss zu seinem 70. Geburtstage dargebracht* (Göttingen, 1897), 248–73

[10]The writer is most grateful to Professor C. F. D. Moule for commenting on a draft of this note.

4

JEWISH–CHRISTIAN RELATIONS IN BARNABAS AND JUSTIN MARTYR

The ways have parted already, for the writers considered here. The author of the Epistle of Barnabas saw Christian and Jews as 'us' and 'them' (αὐτοί, ii 7, xiv 1, 4; the more adverse ἐκεῖνοι, iii 6, viii 7, x 12, xiii 1, xiv 5). Justin Martyr wrote that Christians who adopted Judaism had 'gone over' (μεταβάντας) to the polity of the law (*Dial.* xlvii 4). For both authors, however, the ways still run close together.

To proceed from these writings to the relations of Jews and Christians in the second century is not, of course, straightforward. A. von Harnack, for example, allowed that Justin's *Dialogue* reflected genuine Jewish–Christian contact, and that it therefore formed one of the exceptions to his view that most writing *adversus Iudaeos* was really for internal consumption or *adversus gentes*; but he thought that the Judaism described in the Epistle of Barnabas was indeed abstract, standing for the influence of the scriptures inherited by Christians rather than the way of life of flesh-and-blood Jews.[1] His judgement remains influential in the study of patristic anti-Jewish writing in general and of Barnabas in particular, for instance in the commentaries by H. Windisch (1920) and K. Wengst (1984); but reasons for a different opinion in this instance have often been noted, perhaps especially fully and creatively in S. Lowy's reconstruction of a Jewish situation to which the Epistle responds.[2] Some of the arguments are reconsidered below, and it is urged here that Barnabas as well as Justin probably reflects the importance of the contemporary Jewish community for the early Christians; but Harnack's view serves to underline the truth that the writings in question are literature, not slices of life.

---

[1] A. Harnack, *Die Altercatio Simonis et Theophili nebst Untersuchungen über die antijüdische Polemik in der alten Kirche* (TU iii 1, Leipzig, 1883), 73–4, 78 n. 59; Harnack, *Chronologie der altchristlichen Litteratur bis Eusebius* (2 vols., Leipzig, 1897, 1904), i, 415–16. On these questions see also pp. 21–5, above.

[2] H. Windisch, *Der Barnabasbrief* (1920), in W. Bauer, M. Dibelius, R. Knopf, H. Windisch, *Die apostolischen Väter* (Handbuch zum Neuen Testament, Ergänzungsband, Tübingen, 1920–23), 299–413 (322–3); K. Wengst, *Didache (Apostellehre), Barnabasbrief, Zweiter Klemensbrief, Schrift an Diognet* (Darmstadt, 1984), 112 (Wengst's view of the aims of the Epistle, as advanced in his earlier *Tradition und Theologie des Barnabasbriefs* (Berlin & New York, 1971), is criticized by Scorza Barcellona (as cited in n. 4, below), 166–170; S. Lowy, The Confutation of Judaism in the Epistle of Barnabas', *JJS* xi (1960), 1–33.

Barnabas and Justin as Christian Authorities

First, then, it may be noted that Barnabas and Justin have an importance for Jewish–Christian relations in antiquity, and in the second century in particular, simply by virtue of their places in the Christian *literary* inheritance. The Epistle of Barnabas went up to a very high place, being venerated as the work of an apostle or an apostolic man, and accordingly transmitted, as in Codex Sinaiticus and the biblical text followed in Jerome's *Hebrew Names*, at the end of the New Testament books; its wide circulation and high repute are confirmed by the early Latin version, and by remarks in Origen and Jerome.[3] Its striking judgement that the ritual and dietary laws were never meant to be kept literally was taken in a refined form through Origen into the Alexandrian stream of Christian assessment of the Old Testament, and it must be reckoned a considerable influence on early Christian views of Judaism and the Jewish scriptures.[4] Its specifically second-century éclat is marked by Clement of Alexandria's acceptance of the attribution to Barnabas (n. 3, above), and by the making of the Latin version in the early third century, or even before Tertullian;[5] moreover, its transmission with the New Testament books in the fourth century, despite the currency of criticism like that expressed by Eusebius, is most easily understood if its repute for apostolicity had been widespread since early times.

[3]Eusebius, *H.E.* iii 24, 4 reckons it himself among the νόθοι, but when later writing on Clement of Alexandria (vi 13, 6; 14, 1) puts it higher, among the ἀντιλεγόμεναι γραφαί – this is probably a tribute to the respectable company shared by Barnabas in Clement – in the course of recording how Clement of Alexandria cited some of these, including Barnabas, in his *Stromateis* (Wisdom, Ecclesiasticus, Hebrews, Barnabas, I Clement, Jude) and in his *Hypotyposes* (Jude, the other catholic epistles, Barnabas and the Revelation of Peter); apostolic authorship is affirmed by Clement of Alexandria, *Strom.* ii 20 (116–17) and elsewhere; Origen, *Contra Celsum* 63, quotes 'the general epistle of Barnabas' without comment, as if it were undisputed, going directly on to cite Luke and I Timothy, and envisaging that Celsus might himself have known the Epistle of Barnabas; according to Jerome, *vir. ill.* vi, the Epistle is read among the apocrypha, but the apostle Barnabas was the author – and when commenting on Ezek. xliii 19 Jerome finds it natural to say that the bullock offered for us is mentioned in 'many places of the scriptures, and especially the Epistle of Barnabas, which is included among the apocryphal scriptures'.

[4]The success of the Epistle in the early church was emphasized by J. Armitage Robinson (with Preface by R. H. Connolly), 'The Epistle of Barnabas and the Didache', *JTS* xxxv (1934), 113–46 (122–3).

[5]J. M. Heer, *Die Versio Latina des Barnabasbriefes* (Freiburg i. B., 1908), 59 (before Cyprian, probably after Tertullian) (references to the Latin text below are to this edition); Wengst, *Didache* ..., 105, n. 4 notes that Heer later (*RQ* xxiii (1909), 224) allowed with caution that the version might possibly be earlier than Tertullian; F. Scorza Barcellona, *Epistola di Barnaba* (Turin, 1975), ascribes the version to the second or third century.

Justin's lower place among the Christian authors was still the honourable position of a philosopher-martyr, and his works, including writings now lost, were current among 'many of the brethren' in the time of Eusebius (HE. iv 18, 8–9). Tatian and Irenaeus had quoted Justin, and for the present purpose it is also notable that his biblical interpretation often overlaps with that of Irenaeus and Tertullian; there is a fair case for literary debt on the side of Tertullian, but in any case Justin is clearly representative of widespread second-century exegesis.[6] The writings here considered, therefore, all had a high repute among Christians in the second century; Barnabas was then widely accorded the lofty rank of an apostolic epistle, and Justin's work was both well known and representative. These writings will have been correspondingly influential in forming second-century Christian attitudes to the Jews and Judaism.

Questions to be Considered

Secondly, however, it can be asked what pre-existing attitudes these writings reflect, and how far they illuminate Jewish–Christian relations in the earlier second century. These are the main questions considered below. Barnabas and Justin can reasonably be reviewed together, for although the Epistle of Barnabas is probably about fifty years earlier than Justin's writings (see below) they share so much in subject-matter and biblical testimonies that it is asked whether Justin used the Epistle.[7] (With different aims, but with a comparable linkage, Barnabas and Justin's Dialogue were translated and issued together in Switzerland towards the end of the Second World War as the two earliest post-biblical Christian statements on Christian as opposed to Jewish understanding of the scriptures.[8])

Justin is generally considered, as by Harnack, to reflect genuine

---

[6]A. Lukyn Williams, Justin Martyr: The Dialogue with Trypho. Translation, Introduction and Notes (London, 1930), p. xiv (overlaps with Tertullian and Irenaeus not amounting to clear evidence for literary dependence); T. D. Barnes, Tertullian (Oxford, 1971), 106–8 (Tertullian did not use Justin's Dialogue for his Adversus Iudaeos, but did use the First Apology in his own Apology).

[7]O. Skarsaune, The Proof from Prophecy (Supplements to NT lvi, Leiden, 1987), 110–113 (on shared Old Testament quotations), 307–11 (on similar treatments of the Day of Atonement) and 393–9, with n. 61 (on similar treatments of Amalek and the brazen serpent), concluding that Justin has never copied an Old Testament quotation from Barnabas, inclines to the view that for testimonies and other material too they had shared sources rather than direct contact.

[8]K. Thieme, Kirche und Synagoge. Die ersten nachbiblischen Zeugnisse ihres Gegensatzes im Offenbarungsverständnis: Der Barnabasbrief und der Dialog Justins des Märtyrers, neu bearbeitet und erläutert (Olten, 1945).

contact with Jews, and so to promise some light not only on the Christian but also, with due allowance for his limited candle-power as an outsider, on the Jewish side of the relationship. On the Epistle of Barnabas opinions diverge, as already noted. It is not a defence of Christianity 'against the Jews', although such defence forms a large part of its content, but a scriptural instruction which is also an earnest exhortation to a moral life, appropriately concluded by a version of the Two Ways. Despite the clear internal direction of its teaching and exhortation, the series of lively and embittered references to 'us' and 'them' cited from it above form one of the main grounds for thinking it a source for Christian attitudes not just to the scriptures and morality, but also and especially to the flesh-and-blood Jewish community.

With regard to Christian attitudes, it will be urged here that all these writings evince an outlook which, despite anti-Judaism, is formed by Jewish culture and influenced by Jewish public opinion. The Jews are in the majority as compared with the Christians: unlike the Christians, they are recognized as an ancient nation loyal to their ancestral laws and customs: and despite their revolts (themselves no small proof of Jewish strength and numbers) they enjoy a public prestige symbolized by the general knowledge of their assemblies for the reading of the law ('palam lectitant ... vulgo aditur sabbatis omnibus', Tertullian, *Apology* xviii 8).

In the Epistle of Barnabas, after the suppression of the first Jewish revolt against Rome, and probably before those which broke out under Trajan, the writer thinks that Christians are in danger of going over to the Jewish community, and for Justin too this is a live possibility. Christians accordingly share in prevailing moods of Jewish communal feeling, notably in excitement at the prospect of a rebuilt temple and in the related patriotic hopes for the redemption of Israel current during this epoch of Jewish upheavals (66–70, 115–18, 132–5). It seems likely that differences in attitude among Christians on these subjects correspond to contemporary differences in the Jewish community.

The less-documented Jewish side of the relationship with the Christians has left some traces in Barnabas, but is much more fully documented in Justin. His writings, like the Epistle of Barnabas, evince a marked share in Jewish public opinion. A brief reassessment of his knowledge of the Jewish community leads to consideration of his report of Jewish reaction to Christianity. The Jewish measures against Christian dissent which he describes (measures thought by Justin to be of long standing) resemble those suggested by some New Testament passages. They will have derived their effectiveness, it is suggested, from a communal solidarity which was no doubt enhanced by the strong patriotic feeling already noted, but in any case involves intercommunal communication and cohesion.

Dating

The works of Justin considered here, the Apologies and the *Dialogue with Trypho*, were written between 151 and Justin's death, which occurred when Junius Rusticus was prefect of Rome (162–8).[9] The *Dialogue* was probably composed after the *First Apology*, and has many links with it, especially in proof-texts. Both these works refer to the 'war in Judaea', Bar Cocheba's revolt of 132–5; in the *First Apology* (xxxi) it is spoken of as recent, and the *Dialogue* is envisaged as taking place not long after it had broken out (i 3, cf. ix 3; xvi 2 seems to presuppose the suppression of the revolt). These evocations of the wartime and post-war situation underline the significance of the works, despite their later date, for the period (ending in 135) primarily considered in this volume. Jewish questions are important in the *First Apology*, but become the main subject of the *Dialogue*, which according to Eusebius (*HE.* iv 18, 6) was set in Ephesus. The interchanges of the speakers are marked by a striking and lifelike contrast between the personal courtesy for the most part maintained by Justin (and especially by Trypho), and the bitterly harsh remarks of Justin (and occasionally of Trypho too) when they are speaking as representative of their communities. The *Dialogue* is an artistically contrived literary work, and one which has not survived in its entirety; but behind it there are genuine Jewish–Christian communal contacts, and the author had his own experience of them.[10]

The date of the Epistle of Barnabas cannot be treated so rapidly. J. B. Lightfoot signalled the principal internal evidence when he stated that 'it was certainly written after the first destruction of Jerusalem under Titus to which it alludes, and it was almost as certainly written before the war under Hadrian ending in the second devastation, about which it is silent, but to which it could hardly

---

[9]Harnack, *Chronologie*, i, 274–84; H. Chadwick, 'Justin Martyr's Defence of Christianity', *BJRL* XLVII (1965), 275–97 (277–8); G. Visonà, *S. Giustino, Dialogo con Trifone* (Milan, 1988), 18–19 (with discussion of literature).

[10]For discussion see Williams, *Dialogue*, xi–xix (on the text and its sources); Chadwick. 'Defence', 281–2 (testimony-collections probably used in both Barnabas and Justin); G. N. Stanton, 'Aspects of Early Christian–Jewish Polemic and Apologetic', *NTS* xxxi (1985). 377–92 (378), P. R. Trebilco, *Jewish Communities in Asia Minor* (Cambridge, 1991), 29–30, and especially Visonà, 46–57 (the Dialogue includes genuine reflection of Jewish–Christian contacts in general and in Justin's own experience).

have failed to refer, if written after or during the conflict.[11] Attempts at greater precision in dating turn mainly on two pairs of passages. First, there are possible but not certain allusions at xi 9, to the Syriac Apocalypse of Baruch lxi 7 (this passage from Barnabas is taken over without reference to a source by Clement of Alexandria, *Strom.* iii 12(86)); and at xii 1, to II Esdras iv 33 and v 5, but with a clause not in our II Esdras v 5. Literary contact between Barnabas and these two apocalypses is indeed far from certain; at xi 9 there is a fair argument for allusion, rather, to Ezek. xx 6, 15, for a later chapter in Ezekiel is clearly in view in verse 10, and at xii 1 an apocryphal Jeremiah may be the source.[12] Even if the two allusions were certain, however, the dates of the Syriac Apocalypse of Baruch and II Esdras iii–xiv could only be said to be soon enough after A.D. 70 for the destruction of Jerusalem to be acutely resented, with a strong argument for placing the eagle vision of II Esdras xi–xii in the reign of Domitian (81–96).[13] More important than the limited significance of these passages for dating is their manifestation of some kinship in the choice of material between Barnabas and Jewish apocalypses from the years after 70.

Secondly, another pair of passages in Barnabas probably refer to contemporary events. At iv 3–5 the Epistle gives a prophecy, veiled in the language of Dan. vii 7 f., 24, and recalling the oracle based on this passage in Sib. iii 396–400, that three horns out of ten horns will be humbled under one 'little horn'. The 'little horn' in Daniel is illomened, and strong candidates for identification with it are therefore Vespasian, destroyer of Jerusalem and humbler of the three emperors who preceded him in quick succession, or Nero redivivus, awaited as humbler of the triad of Flavian emperors; but the passage cannot be confidently assigned to a particular reign. The second of the two passages offers more hope in this respect. In xvi 3–4 the writer holds that the prophecy 'they who destroyed this temple shall themselves rebuild it' (an adaptation of Isa. xlix 17 LXX) is now being fulfilled; 'because they [the Jews] went to war, it

---

[11]J. B. Lightfoot, *The Apostolic Fathers, Part I. S. Clement of Rome* (2nd edn, 2 vols., London, 1890), ii, 505.

[12]The evidence is set out and discussed by Heer 67–8, Scorza Barcellona, 151–2, and Wengst, *Didache …,* 171 n. 185, 200 n. 189; the suggestion of Ezek. xx 6 at xi 9 goes back at least to the early eighteenth–century W. Lowth, cited by J. Potter, ed., *Clementis Alexandrini Opera* (2 vols., Oxford, 1715), ii, 550, n. 2. That no literary dependence on the two apocalypses can be established was the conclusion of J. A. T. Robinson, *Redating the New Testament* (London, 1976), 318, n. 34.

[13]On the date of II Esdras, E. Schürer, G. Vermes, F. Millar, M. Black, M. D. Goodman & P. Vermes, *A History of the Jewish People in the Age of Jesus Christ*, iii. 1 (Edinburgh, 1986), 297–300.

was destroyed by the enemy; now they themselves, the servant of the enemy, will build it up again'. The reference (further discussed in section II, below) is probably to the temple of the Jews at Jerusalem. If so, the passage can be associated with the reign of Nerva (18.ix.96–27.i.98), who favoured the Jews by removing the 'calumny of the Jewish exchequer', and was well remembered by Christians too (Eusebius, *HE*. iii 20, 8–9); a belief that the temple would be rebuilt can readily be envisaged in his reign.[14] The early years of Hadrian are often suggested (especially on the basis of the praises of Hadrian at the beginning of the fifth Sibylline), and they are certainly likely to have revived Jewish hopes; but Nerva's reign seems preferable, not only because his CALVMNIA SVBLATA coinage was a particularly clear public sign of favour to the Jews, but also because the growth of the great reputation of the Epistle as apostolic is easier to understand if its date is earlier than the time of Hadrian.[15] If this is right, the interpretation of Daniel in iv 3–5 will have been re-applied from Vespasian to Nerva, who does not suit the bad character of the little horn, but is as well qualified as Vespasian (for neither could claim to rule by right of descent) to be called an offshoot 'on the side'.[16] The Epistle could then be assigned, with fair probability, to the very end of the first century.

Barnabas

(i) The Epistle and the sources

The Christian outlook on Judaism represented in Barnabas and Justin can now be considered further. An attempt to reconstruct something of this outlook from Barnabas will be made through

[14]For the importance of Nerva's action to the Jews, see M. D. Goodman, 'Nerva, the *fiscus Judaicus* and Jewish Identity', *JRS* lxxix (1989), 40–44.

[15]Theories of dating are reviewed, with preference (following Lightfoot) for Vespasian's reign, by J. A. T. Robinson, *Redating*, 313–19, and with preference (following A. Hilgenfeld) for Nerva's reign, by P. Richardson & M. B. Shukster, 'Barnabas, Nerva, and the Yavnean Rabbis', *JTS* NS xxxiv (1983), 31–55; the argument for the early years of Hadrian (following W. Volkmar and J. G. Müller, with L. W. Barnard and others noted by Wengst, *Tradition*, 107–8, nn. 25–6) is put by G. Al(l)on, *The Jews in their Land in the Talmudic Age* (edited and translated by G. Levi, repr. Cambridge, Mass., 1989), 448–52. M. Hengel, 'Hadrians Politik gegenüber Juden und Christen', in *Ancient Studies in Memory of Elias Bickerman* [= *JANES* xvi–xvii (1984–5)] (1987), 153–82 (160 & n. 36), gives no special discussion of the date of Barnabas and regards xvi 4 as obscure ('dunkel'), but accepts it as one of the indications that Jews between 117 and 130 possibly hoped for the rebuilding of Jerusalem and the temple.

[16]The argument is more fully presented by the present writer (arguing that Ber. R. lxiv 10, an anecdote also implying belief that the temple would be rebuilt by Roman permission, more probably reflects conditions under Nerva than under Hadrian) in *The Jewish Revolts under Trajan and Hadrian*, forthcoming.

attention, first, to the fear of assimilation manifest, it will be argued, especially in a controverted passage, iii 6; then to the radical theory of the Jewish scriptures developed throughout chapters ii–xvi; and finally to the dependence of the writer on Jewish culture and opinion.

The wide differences in estimate of Barnabas have been noted already. Rabbinic students have repeatedly suggested a Jewish background for its exegesis, and have also noted rabbinic responses to the polemical positions it represents; notable predecessors of S. Lowy (n. 2, above) include M. Güdemann, K. Kohler, A. Marmorstein and G. Al(l)on, and at least one New Testament student with strong rabbinic interests, Adolf Schlatter.[17] This position is reflected in H. Veil's introduction (in E. Hennecke's handbook to the New Testament apocrypha), G. Hoennicke's book on Jewish Christianity, B. Reicke's study of early Christian 'zeal',[18] and, in fuller treatments of the Epistle, in the work of J. Muilenburg (n. 15, above) and F. Scorza Barcellona (n. 4, above). On the other hand, Harnack's position was developed in Germany not only in the commentaries by Windisch and Wengst (n. 2, above), but also in the church history of Hans Lietzmann (who saw the writer of the Epistle as a 'learned manikin', unable to resist composing a pamphlet); it has also influenced the French commentary by R. A. Kraft and P. Prigent.[19] In England, however, the importance of the Jewish community for the author found greater recognition; W. J. Ferrar summed up the setting of the Epistle in the words 'Its bitterness and contempt for the Jewish polity must have been stirred by real danger of a relapse to Judaism among Christians', and Armitage Robinson, although he found no bitterness or animosity in the severe things said about the Jews as a people, agreed that the writer's situation was one in which

[17] M. Güdemann, *Religionsgeschichtliche Studien* (Leipzig, 1876), 99–131, known to me only as reported by K. Kohler, 'Barnabas', *JE* i (1902), 537–8 and J. Muilenburg, *The Literary Relations of the Epistle of Barnabas and the Teaching of the Twelve Apostles* (Marburg, 1929), 98–100; A. Marmorstein, 'L'Épître de Barnabé et la polémique juive, *REJ* lx (1910), 213–20 [rabbinic polemic attacks positions which are represented in Barnabas]; G. Allon, 'The Halakhah in the Epistle of Barnabas' [in Hebrew], *Tarbiz* xi (1939), 23–8; A. Schlatter, *Die Tage Trajans und Hadrians* (1897), reprinted in id., *Synagoge und Kirche bis zum Barkochba Aufstand* (Stuttgart, 1966), 9–97 (63 f.).
[18] H. Veil, 'Barnabasbrief', in E. Hennecke (ed.), *Neutestamentliche Apokryphen* (2nd edn., Tübingen, 1924), 503–18 (503–4, with a brief criticism of Windisch); G. Hoennicke, *Das Judenchristentum im ersten und zweiten Jahrhundert* (Berlin, 1908), 95–7, 284–6 (inclining to the view that the author of Barnabas was Jewish); B. Reicke, *Diakonie, Festfreude und Zelos in Verbindung mit der christlichen Agapenfeier* (Uppsala Universitets Årsskrift 1951:5, Uppsala, 1951), 378–82.
[19] H. Lietzmann, *The Beginnings of the Christian Church* (E.T., 2nd edn, London, 1949, repr. 1961), 217: P. Prigent & R. A. Kraft, *L'Épître de Barnabé* (Paris, 1971), 29 & n. 1.

Judaism might be perceived as 'after all a nobler and more sustaining creed than the Christianity which, since it had broken away from its original stock, was already showing signs of decay' in moral decadence.[20]

The literary basis for this disagreement over the setting of Barnabas lies especially in the possibility of distinguishing between the framework of the Epistle, with its emphasis on the right understanding of the scriptures by the writer's spiritual 'sons and daughters' and on godly living (for example at i 1,5–8; iv 9–14; xviii–xxi), and the more polemical contents of chapters ii–xvi, the anti-Judaism of which may then be assigned to the past setting of the sources employed (especially the testimonies) rather than to the present situation of the author (the argument is concisely stated by Windisch, 322–3 and Wengst, 112–13).

The author as well as his source seems to be involved in anti-Judaism, however, for example at iii 6 (considered in the following paragraph), iv 6, xv 8–9, xvi 1, and, although he certainly presents his teaching as 'knowledge' in general, it often involves rebuttal of the Jews in particular, and his own attitude cannot readily be distinguished from that which emerges from the whole series of passages on 'us' and 'them' noted already. It is perhaps unlikely, in any case, that so much lively polemic should have been gathered together in circumstances to which it did not speak. Accordingly, the repeated assertion in Barnabas of the Christian claim to the Jewish scriptures should not be too confidently assessed as an academic exercise, for this assertion was fundamental *adversus Iudaeos*, as Justin shows (Dialogue xxix 2). In general, it is worth noting that the view represented by Harnack, Windisch and Wengst originated when an early and decisive separation of the Christians from the social influence of the large Jewish population in the eastern Roman provinces was more widely accepted than would now be the case.[21] Lastly, as Armitage Robinson stressed, the author's concern with moral exhortation coheres with his anxiety about Judaism, for it presupposes a precarious state of Christian morals which might well

[20]W. J. Ferrar, *The Early Christian Books* (London, 1919), 38–9; Armitage Robinson 'Barnabas', 121, 125–6, 145–6 (his stress on the writer's moral concern coheres with his view that the author of Barnabas originally composed the treatise on the Two Ways; the present writer would view the treatise as a pre-Christian Jewish work taken over in the Epistle).

[21]Thus, in a repristination of Harnack's general view of the *adversus Iudaeos* texts, live Jewish–Christian polemic is allowed for up to the middle of the second century by D. Rokeah, *Jews, Pagans and Christians* (Jerusalem & Leiden, 1982), 9–10, 61–5; there is of course a strong case for important contacts throughout the patristic period, as J. Juster, Marcel Simon, B. Blumenkranz and others have shown.

have made the Jewish community appear more honourable in life-style as well as prestige.

(ii) Fear of Christian assimilation to the Jews

A striking characteristic of the outlook on Judaism in the Epistle, then, can provisionally be identified as a combination of evident fear of Christian assimilation to the Jews with the radical view of the ritual laws noted already. Fear of assimilation, the first point to be considered, emerges when the initial argument of the Epistle that sacrifices were never needed and are done away (chapter ii) culminates in a section on fasting (chapter iii). Here the declaration of the fast which the Lord has chosen (consisting of charitable works) in Isa. lvii 6–10 is taken as a manifestation of God's will beforehand 'to us' (the Christians), ἵνα μὴ προσρησσώμεθα ὡς ἐπήλυτοι τῷ ἐκείνων νόμῳ, 'lest we be shipwrecked as (if) proselytes to their law' or 'lest we be dashed against their law as (if) proselytes' (iii 6). (Compare the Latin 'ut non incurramus tamquam proselyti ad illorum legem', 'that we may not rush in as (if) proselytes to their law' or 'that we may not run up against their law (if) proselytes'.) The clause is sometimes understood, as by Windisch and Wengst in their comments ad loc., as a warning against Judaistic Christianity rather than lapse into Judaism. It is certainly likely that Judaizers within the Christian fold are among envisaged here, for in the next chapter (iv 6) there is a condemmation of those who say that 'the covenant is theirs and ours' (not 'ours' only, as the author would maintain). In this instance, however, as is shown by the context of 'us' and 'them' (iii 1, 3, 6; iv 6–8), any Judaistic Christianity known to the writer would clearly be not simply a response to the literal sense of the ritual and dietary laws, but a response made in awareness of 'them', the Jewish community, and in the knowledge that this is the way in which the Jews observe 'their law'.

This observation is underlined by the consideration that fasting, the matter in view, was much more prominent in ancient Jewish custom than it is in the Pentateuchal laws. Fasting is not a main subject of the Pentateuch, apart from the fast of the Day of Atonement, Lev. xvi 29, xxiii 26–32 and elsewhere, and the recognition that women's private vows may involve fasting, Num. xxx 13. Although the Day of Atonement is not mentioned in Barn. iii (a point emphasized by Lowy [n. 25, below]), it is indeed likely that fasting owes its original connection with the sacrifices here in Barnabas to that Day, with which an underlying testimony-chain will have linked the sacrifices, newmoons and sabbath condemned in

Isa. i 11–13 (Barn. ii 4–6); this is suggested not only by the inclusion of the Day of Atonement in Isa. i 13 LXX (the quotation in Barn. ii 5 stops just before the relevant words),[22] but also by the use made of Isa. lviii in comparable sections of Justin's *Dialogue* (xl 4, and in the scheme underlying xii 3–xv) and of Irenaeus (*Haer.* iv 17, 3).[23] Nevertheless the choice of this text from Isa. lviii on fasting as the final link in the underlying chain implies a view of the Day of Atonement as 'the Fast' par excellence (the name of the Day as found for example in Philo, *SpecLeg* ii 193, 200; Acts xxvii 9) which itself reflects the great importance of fasting in general in current Jewish practice.[24] Moreover, this chapter of Barnabas as it now stands is on fasting in general rather than on the unmentioned Day of Atonement in particular, although the Day will become the main subject, with emphasis again on the fast, in chapter vii; and the space given to fasting in chapter iii is accordingly best understood, as Lowy showed, against the background of other regular (probably weekly) communal fasting by Jews, such that the fasts, of which the unmentioned Day of Atonement would simply form the supreme example, could seem to belong to the staple of 'their law'.[25]

Lastly, the importance of Jewish custom in the setting of Barn. iii is further suggested by Jewish use of the prophetic passage which forms the Christian proof-text. The prophecy in Isa. lviii, quoted at length in Barnabas iii and Justin, *Dialogue* xv, and forming the standard

[22]I. L. Seeligmann, *The Septuagint Version of Isaiah* (Leiden, 1948), 102–3, on ἡμέραν μεγάλην and νηστείαν.

[23]Skarsaune, 168–9, 179.

[24]Compare, for instance, Philo's statement that sacrifices are offered 'some daily, some on the seventh day, some on new moons and holy days, some at fast-days (νηστείαις), some at the three seasonal festivals' (*SpecLeg* i 168); Philo apparently is thinking principally of 'the Fast', the Day of Atonement (ibid 186), but his language recalls the association of sacrifices, festivals and fasting in Barnabas ii–iii, and suggests the general importance of fasts, on which see also the following footnote. Similarly, the spiritual interpretation of fasting and its association with the Day-of-Atonement laws as a Pentateuchal focus is illustrated by Philo, *Post. Caini* 48, taking the commandment 'to humble the souls on the tenth of the month' (Lev. xxiii 27) in an inward and moral sense.

[25]Among the material considered by Lowy, 2–10 note Josephus, *Ap.* ii 282 (Jewish pious observances widely adopted in Greek and barbarian cities are specified as the sabbath rest, fasts, lighting of lamps and many of the dietary customs); the inclusion of material under the healing 'fasting' (Taanith, Taaniyoth) in the Mishnah and Tosefta, and the assumption therein that Monday and Thursday are appropriate days for a fast (M. Taanith i 6, TosTaanith ii 4); and Didache viii 1 (fast on Wednesdays and Fridays, for 'the hypocrites' fast on Mondays and Thursdays). Lowy well suggests, following and adapting G. Al(l)on, that the Jewish custom of Monday and Thursday fasting reflected in the Didache is attested in a baraitha in Shabb. 24a, and is also in view in Barnabas; he adds that it is likely to have had special significance as the accompaniment of urgent prayer for messianic redemption. Compare Luke xviii 12 (the devout Pharisee thought to fast twice weekly), Matt. vi 16–18 (Christian fasting).

proof-text here and elsewhere in Barnabas and Justin for the Christian interpretation of fasting, was used, according to the Tosefta, in a form of the admonition to be addressed by the elders to a community beginning a fast (TosTaanith i 8); it was also read, as is still the case, on the Day of Atonement (baraitha in Meg 31a, designating the passage beginning Isa. lvii 15). These passages probably represent usage well established in the early third century, and likely to go back at least to the second. The liberal second-century Christian recourse to Isa. lviii on fasting therefore corresponded to contemporary and later Jewish association of this passage with communal fasts, an association which, when the second-century and earlier Christian material is viewed in conjunction with the rabbinic texts, seems not unlikely to be pre-Christian.[26]

Rebuttal of Christian Judaizing in respect of fasts, which was probably one object of the warning in Barnabas here, would therefore necessarily have been at the same time an attempt to neutralize the overshadowing presence of the Jewish community. To summarize, Christian awareness of the Jews is already plain in the contextual references to 'us' and 'them' (iii 1, 3, 6); further, the remarkable prominence of fasting in Barnabas iii corresponds not to its relatively modest place in the Pentateuchal laws, but to its high importance in contemporary Jewish custom; lastly, the prophetic text used in Barnabas to justify Christian deviation from this custom was one associated in Jewish usage with communal fasts. These points together confirm that the Jews themselves, not simply Christian Judaizers, concern the author. It is therefore reasonable to take iii 6 in the sense which its vigorous language most naturally suggests: namely that, although the writer would certainly condemn Judaizing practices, one of his main purposes was to ward off the danger of Christian lapse to the Jewish community; the Greek, followed in this by the Latin, neatly combines the thoughts of violent and disastrous motion to, and of becoming a proselyte to, 'their law'.

Finally, there is a good case for supposing that the assimilation feared in iii 6 was encouraged not just by the attraction of the old paths and the more honoured society, but also by active propaganda. Reicke, noting that the ethical interpretation of the unclean beasts, fishes and birds in chapter x of the Epistle recalls vices often

---

[26]The association of Isa. lviii with the Day of Atonement explains the incorporation of Isa. lviii 6 into the quotation of Isa. lxi 1–2 (linked with Atonement as the beginning of Jubilee) at Luke iv 18, according to C. Perrot, 'Luc 4, 16–30 et la lecture biblique de l'ancienne synagogue', in J.-E. Ménard (ed.), *Exégèse biblique et judaisme* (Strasbourg, 1973), 170–86 (178–9).

attributed to political intriguers, finds that internal agitation and propaganda by Christian Zealots is being countered in chapters vi, xv and xvi.[27] His view is supported by the clear indication of internal strife at iv 6. It is by no means inconsistent with Lowy's suggestion of propaganda by Jews themselves; for Lowy, the lawlessness leading to the final stumbling-block (iv 1–3) is constituted by Jewish movements towards national messianic redemption, accompanied by propaganda which is the πλάνη to be resisted at all costs (ii 10, iv 1, cf. iv 10–13), and was very possibly voiced by Jewish prophets in oracles like those preserved in the apocalypses and the Jewish Sibyllines.[28] This view is supported by the association of πλάνη and its cognates elsewhere, from the LXX Pentateuch onwards, with false prophecy and mutual Jewish and Christian charges of false teaching, notably in the strong sense of seduction to apostasy.[29] Lowy's interpretation would cohere closely, also, with G. W. H. Lampe's later suggestion that Jewish anti-Christian propaganda, including prophecy, is to be discerned behind I Clement, Ignatius, the Johannine Epistles, and many of the later New Testament writings (Lampe does not discuss Barnabas).[30] The content of the propaganda denounced in Barnabas could be envisaged partly as argument for the law, the land and the temple-service (central points in the author's own apologetic), and partly, perhaps, as criticism of the teaching of Christ and the disciples, such as is attested in Justin and Celsus (the references in Barnabas to Christ's expected advent (vii 9, xii 9, xv 5–7) and his love for Israel (v 8) on the one hand, and to the lawless character of his disciples (v 9) on the other, might then represent, respectively, response and concession to such polemic). However the content is to be envisaged, propaganda from Jews and from Christians close to their position is likely to have strengthened the tendency towards assimilation to the Jews evident at iii 6.

The Epistle therefore reflects a Jewish encouragement of prose-lytes which is often ruefully attested from the early Christian standpoint. Justin in the Dialogue represents Trypho as exhorting him to join the Jews (viii 3–4); Justin himself exhorts Trypho 'and

---

[27]Reicke, 378–82.

[28]Lowy, 9–10, 13–17, 26, 31.

[29]W. Horbury, 'I Thessalonians ii. 3 as Rebutting the Charge of False Prophecy', *JTS* N.S. xxxiii (1982), 492–508 (497–9, on seduction to apostasy) (chapter 3, pp. 116–18, above); Stanton, 'Aspects' [n. 10, above], 379–82 (on Jewish anti-Christian polemic).

[30]G. W. H. Lampe, '"Grievous Wolves" (Acts 20:29)', in B. Lindars & S. S. Smalley (edd.), *Christ and Spirit in the New Testament: Studies in Honour of C. F. D. Moule* (Cambridge, 1973), 253–68.

those who wish to be proselytes' (to the Jews, probably, rather than the Christians)[31] to come over (xxiii 3, xxviii 2), and complains that proselytes blaspheme the name of Christ twice as much as born Jews (cxxii 2); proselytes, says Tertullian gloomily, usually hope not in Christ's name, but in Moses' ordinance, and the 'large people' ('populus amplus') to be confuted by the new law in Christ going forth from Zion (Isa. ii 3–4) is 'first of all that of the Jews and their proselytes' (*Adv Marc* iii 21, 3); comparably, Tertullian envisages in his *Adversus Iudaeos* that the Jewish case is being argued with a Christian by a proselyte.

Such early Christian evidence supplies part of a fuller picture of Jewish–Christian missionary rivalry, in competition for the same potential non-Jewish adherents, and not without hope for converts from the other side.[32] These attitudes emerge clearly from the passages just cited from Justin's *Dialogue*. In Barnabas, however, the stance is notably defensive. Hopes for fresh adhesion by Jews are not expressed. The overriding necessity is to justify the position of 'us' *vis-à-vis* 'their' law, and to ward off the peril of assimilation to and absorption in the Jewish community. The attack on the Jewish position represented by the Epistle's exclusive claim to the Jewish scriptures can be classified, in the context provided by the Epistle, as the best form of defence.

(iii) Theory of the Jewish Scriptures

The anxiety at the prestige and influence of the Jews among the Christians evident at iii 6 thus in turn helps to explain the second characteristic of the Epistle to be considered here, its radicalism on the Jewish scriptures. For this author, the seemingly literal sense of the ritual laws was never divinely intended, and within the law and the prophets this truth, now recognized by 'us', was continually indicated in vain to 'them'.

[31]Arguments for this view of *Dialogue* xxiii 3 are set out by Skarsaune, 258–9; Jewish προσήλυσις to Christianity is envisaged at xxviii 2, and the phrase 'Christ and his proselytes' occurs at cxxiii 5 in a deliberate contrast with the Jewish proselytes who are being discussed, but comparison of xxiii 3 with the opening of the *Dialogue*, and Justin's usage of 'proselyte' simply for Jewish proselytes (as in cxxii 1–cxxiii 2), support the view that Jewish proselytes are intended at xxiii 3.

[32]See Simon, *Verus Israel*, 271–305, 390–5, with special reference to rivalry at 135, 284; B. Blumenkranz, 'Die christlich-jüdische Missionskonkurrenz (3. bis 6. Jahrhundert)', reprinted from *Klio* xxxix (1961), 227–233 in id., *Juifs et Chrétiens: Patristique et Moyen Age* (London, 1977); W. H. C. Frend, *Martyrdom and Persecution in the Early Church* (Oxford, 1965), 186–93.

The covenant, indeed, according to this Epistle, belonged to the Jews only for the brief time until they worshipped the golden calf and Moses broke the tables (Exod. xxxii 7, Deut. ix 12 as interpreted in Barn. iv 4–6, 14 and xiv 3–6); the Christian inheritance of the covenant was prophesied in what the scripture says concerning Isaac and Rebekah, Ephraim and Manasseh, and Abraham himself (xiii). The ceremonies, biblical and post-biblical, of the Day of Atonement were simply intended to foretell the Lord's passion and kingdom (vii); the same applies to the related rite of the Red Heifer (viii);[33] an evil angel misled the Jews to understand circumcision carnally, despite biblical injunctions on the circumcision of the heart (ix 4–5; does this view depend on an unmentioned interpretation of the giving of 'statutes that were not good' in Ezek. xx 25, on the lines of that given by Origen, *Contra Celsum* vii 20?[34]); the dietary laws were never meant to be literally observed, as again the biblical text itself indicates (Deut. iv 1, 5 and perhaps 14 interpreted in Barn. x 2 as 'I will make a covenant of my ordinances with *this* people', cf. Barn. i 2); on the other hand, the scriptures (here mainly in the prophets and the Pentateuch) clearly foretell the Christian rite of baptism in its association with the cross (Barn. xi–xii); the sabbath commandment in the Decalogue cannot be observed now, during 'the era of the lawless one', because (as Gen. ii 2 shows) it refers forward to the time of the Lord's Advent, and Christians can accordingly meanwhile observe their own 'eighth day' (xv, cf. vi 19).

This series of radically spiritual and ecclesiastical interpretations suggests that already in chapter ii the testimony-chain is probably understood in a particularly negative way when, after a typical Christian application of Isa. i 11–14, it is added that the Jews always erred in offering sacrifices rather than the oblation of a godly life (Jer. vii 22–3 taken, no doubt in the light of Amos v 25, as a *question* whether the forefathers who came out of Egypt were commanded to offer sacrifices, and interpreted in Barn. ii 7–9 as a divine declaration 'to them'). The linked testimonies from Isa. i and

---

[33]For illustrations (including Mishnah, Parah iii 1) of the association between the Red Heifer and the Day of Atonement assumed at Heb. ix 13 see W. Horbury, 'The Aaronic Priesthood in the Epistle to the Hebrews', *JSNT* xix (1983), 43–71 (51–2).

[34]Christian exegesis of this verse in Ezekiel as signifying a divine punishment of the Jews is reviewed by F. Dreyfus, 'La condescendance divine (*synkatabasis*) comme principe herméneutique de l'Ancien Testament dans la tradition juive et dans la tradition chrétienne', in J. A. Emerton (ed.), *Congress Volume, Salamanca 1983* (SVT xxxvi, Leiden 1985), 96–107 (98–9); this chapter of Ezekiel was probably used at Barn. xi 9 (n. 12, above). On Barn. ix 5 see n. 44, below.

Jer. vii would be later used elsewhere to show that the sacrificial laws, literally intended, were a concession to the Jews' weakness (Justin, *Dial.* xxii 1–6; Irenaeus, *Haer.* iv 17, 1–3);[35] but in Barnabas it seems likely that the true meaning of the sacrificial laws is thought to have been, from the beginning, their moral significance (compare x 27). A contrast with Justin comparable with that which has been suggested regarding Barn. ii 7–9 comes out more plainly at Barn. ix 6. An objection to the interpretation of circumcision noted above is there envisaged as: 'the people received circumcision as a seal' (the mystical description of circumcision also attested at Rom. iv 11, and applied to baptism in Christian tradition). The objector's view of circumcision is in fact a view accepted by Justin in the *Dialogue* (xvi 2, xix 2), with the harsh polemical twist that it was meant to permit the Jews to be singled out for their present sufferings (in the aftermath of the Bar Cocheba revolt). In Barnabas, however, the possibility that circumcision was a divine mark of distinction is wholly and contemptuously dismissed (ix 6) with the argument that, if so, even Syrians, Arabs and Egyptians, circumcised as they are, should all be regarded as heirs of the covenant. In this remark, perhaps a sign of the Egyptian setting of the Epistle,[36] there is a hostility which recalls the scorn for Jewish 'bragging about circumcision' in the Epistle to Diognetus (iv 1, 4). Comparably, the author can adopt the adverse phrase '*their* law' in iii 6, considered above, here it will mean the law as understood and observed by Jews, but in the anger of the moment this qualification is left unspoken.

How then is the theory of the Jewish law in Barnabas to be classified? Its exceptional character has probably sometimes been over-emphasized. P. Prigent assessed it as much more moderate than the attitude taken in the Epistle to Diognetus,[37] and it certainly allows to the ritual laws an abiding value – but only as encoded moral commandments and prophecies, the meaning of which was declared in vain to the Jews in the law and the prophets, but is now understood by the Christians. Herein Barnabas takes up a primitive

[35]Dreyfus, 97–9, 102–3.

[36]Syrians, named first in ix 6, were disliked by the Greeks in Egypt (E. J. Bickermann, *The Jews in the Greek Age* (Cambridge, Mass. & London, 1988), 184; compare the mockery of Agrippa I by the Alexandrians as a Syrian king, Philo, *Flacc* 39); 'all the priests of the idols', mentioned without reference to nationality after Syrians and Arabs, can well be understood as Egyptian priests; and the crowning absurdity of pride in circumcision here is the fact that 'even Egyptians' – particularly despised by Greeks and Jews in Egypt – are circumcised.

[37]Prigent & Kraft, *Barnabé*, 158–9, nn. 4 & 5 (also contrasting the comparably scornful Tertullian, *AdvMarc* v 5).

Christian theme classically expressed in II Cor. iii 12–16,[38] and becomes the forerunner of the harmony of the Old and New Testaments as it was achieved by Origen and his successors in Alexandria and the west; for them the hidden spiritual sense of the law was that primarily envisaged by Moses, its true *raison d'être*, and in this truest sense the law was fulfilled by Christ.[39] The Epistle of Barnabas can perhaps be detected in the background of the passages in Origen (cited in the previous footnote) in which it is recalled that the giving of the Mosaic law was followed by the sin of the calf, but Jesus gave the second law and covenant, or in which it is stressed that Moses himself intended the spiritual sense when he spoke of circumcision, Passover, new moons and sabbaths, and when he broke the tables of the *written* law. However that may be, the continuity between the Epistle and later Alexandrian and western exegesis in attitude to the law might seem to lend support to the view that its theory is relatively moderate, because of its great respect for the scriptures; although the strongly anti-Jewish aspect of this later exegesis would itself suggest that in the Epistle too this theory could subserve anti-Jewish polemic. At any rate, Barnabas can be seen to offer an early example of the allegorical and timeless harmonization of the testaments, as opposed to the more historical harmonization (adumbrated in Justin and developed by Irenaeus and others, following Gal. iii–iv) which divides the legislation into moral and ceremonial laws, and allows that the latter were valid in their literal sense for a limited time.[40]

[38]In its context in II Corinthians this passage subserves Paul's self-defence, as shown by E. Bammel, 'Paulus, der Moses des Neuen Bundes', *Theologia* liv (Athens, 1983), 399–408 (401–2), but its reference of testimony-linked commonplaces on Jewish hardening (and blinding, iv 4, which may still refer to Jews, cf. Rom. xv 31) to Jewish (mis-)understanding of the law is paralleled at Acts vii 51–3, and is likely to be pre-Pauline; II Cor. iii and Acts vii 1–53 are both Moses-centred passages (Bammel, 399; M. Simon, *St Stephen and the Hellenists in the Primitive Church* (London, 1958), 44–5).

[39]Among passages from Origen, Didymus the Blind, Cyril of Alexandria, the Ambrosiaster and Marius Victorinus gathered by M. F. Wiles, *The Divine Apostle* (Cambridge, 1967), 64–6, note Origen, *Hom. in Num* v 1 (PG xiii 603 'Moyses intelligebat sine dubio quae esset vera circumcisio' etc.) and *Comm. in Rom* ii 14 (PG xiv 917 'Moyses et sprevit, et abiecit, et contrivit litteras legis, hoc sine dubio iam tunc designans, quod honor et virtus legis non esset in litteris, sed in spiritu'). On the sin of the Calf as response to the law-giving, and the second law and covenant given by Christ, see also Origen, *Contra Celsum* ii 74–5. Origen's treatment of the law is discussed with reference to predecessors, including Barnabas, by C. P. Bammel, 'Law and Temple in Origen', in *Templum Amicitiae: Essays on the Second Temple presented to Ernst Bammel* (Sheffield, 1991), 464–76 (469, n. 22 gives a more negative interpretation of 'their law' in Barn. iii 6 than that ventured in the text above).

[40]An attempt to sketch these two approaches to the harmony of the testaments is made by the present writer, 'Old Testament Interpretation in the Writings of the Church Fathers', in M. J. Mulder & H. Sysling (edd.), *Mikra* (Assen & Philadelphia, 1988), 727–87 (746, 759–61).

Important though it is to notice how Barnabas's view suited the later Christian mainstream, these observations so far do less than justice to the anti-Jewish aspects of the theory, as the contrasts with Justin sketched above may already have suggested. First, the theories such as this, which have contributed towards resolution of the inner-Christian problem of the harmony of the testaments, all betray in their early history a considerable tension over the law as understood by the Jews; thus, in the 'historical' solutions just noticed, the ceremonial laws can be harshly designated, as in Irenaeus, as bonds of servitude imposed on the Jews as a punishment.[41] A similar tension is likely to have affected Barnabas, and it seems to appear especially in the historical element of the Epistle's theory, the contention that the breaking of the tables of the law cancelled the covenant with Israel (iv 7–8, xiv 1–4), but the Beloved gave the covenant to 'us' (iv 8, xiv 4). This second making of the tables of the commandments and the associated covenant, including festival and sabbath laws (Exod. xxxiv 1–28, cf. Deut. x 1–5) is not expressly mentioned in Barnabas, as Simon emphasizes;[42] but it seems likely that, as Simon also argued,[43] it is assumed to be the covenant given by the Beloved, which was at the same time the ritual law misunderstood by the Jews. This assumption could arise naturally from Exod. xxxiv 27–8 (linking the renewed covenant with the Decalogue rewritten by God and with mainly ritual laws written by Moses).

On such an interpretation, Barnabas would be familiar with the concept of a 'second law', but would differ from the treatment of it in the Didascalia, and the closely allied views of the ritual law in Justin and Irenaeus; it was widely held, following biblical hints like that in Deut. iv 14 noted above in connection with Barn. x 2, that the second law-giving by Moses himself after the incident of the Golden Calf, a legislation marked especially by the ritual and dietary laws, was punitive, disciplinary or educative (so Irenaeus, *Haer.* iv 15, 1 & 5, appealing to the interpretation of the Calf incident in Stephen's speech, Acts vii 38–43).

[41]Irenaeus, for example at *haer* iv 16, 5; see Horbury, 'Interpretation', 760–1, Dreyfus, 'Condescendance', 99, and, for surveys of the development of theories of the ritual law in the context of anti-Jewish polemic, M. Simon, *Verus Israel* (E.T. Oxford, 1986), 85–91, 163–9.

[42]Simon, *Verus Israel*, 88 treats failure to mention the second law-giving as the main weakness of the Epistle's argument, but his stricture seems to be implicitly modified by his suggestion that the remaking of the tables is perhaps envisaged in references to the testament of the Beloved (see the following footnote).

[43]This view was briefly put forward by Simon, *Verus Israel*, n. 125 to p. 88, and p. 149 (Barnabas seems to find in Exod. xxxiv 1–10 a symbolic prefiguration of Christianity; it is the testament of the Beloved), and stated more fully by Simon, *Stephen*, 106.

In Barnabas, then, it may be suggested, the familiar concept of this second law, which according to Exod. xxxiv 10–28 was given together with the renewed covenant, is unmentioned but assumed; and it is identified with the legislation constantly misunderstood by the Jews, but really ab initio meant for the Christians and accompanying the covenant given to *them*. Consequently, although the Epistle seeks the inward meaning of the ritual law and refrains from scoffing at its superstition, this respect for scripture takes the form of a Christian claim to this law and its associated covenant, which is also an exclusion of any Jewish claims whatever to the covenant and the law.

Secondly, the Epistle is concerned not only with the scriptures inherited by the church, but also with the customs currently observed by the Jews, and in line with Jewish practice it treats the scriptures and the customs as a unity, as already noted in connection with the fasts, the Day of Atonement and the Red Heifer. (There is a striking contrast here with such New Testament passages as Mark vii 3–15, Matt. xv 1–9.) This way of thinking is back-handedly exemplified, the present writer would suggest, in the angry reference at iii 6 to 'their law' – 'the law as they keep it'. It is accepted that, for those who think differently from the author, the standard interpretation of the law is summed up by the contemporary Jewish polity. The theory of the law sketched in the Epistle, therefore, is not just a theory of the Christian Old Testament, but a theory of the whole Jewish constitution and way of life, of what Justin would later call 'the polity of the law' (ἡ ἔννομος πολιτεία, *Dial.* xlvii 4). Thus defined, however, the Epistle's theory seems more strongly anti-Jewish as well as Jewish; if accepted, it exposes the Jewish way of life as a demonic illusion (see Barn. ix 5), and validates the Christian polity.[44]

Thirdly, in accord with this conclusion, the theory is accompanied by hostile comments on 'them'; in accord with their regular failure to understand, *they* smote the shepherd of Zech. xiii 7 (v. 12, adapting the second person plural imperative of LXX; contrast with Barnabas the first person singular divine subject given to the verb (now in the indicative) when the text is quoted in the New Testament, and Justin's second person *singular* imperative[45]). Similarly, they bound the righteous man of Wisd. ii 12 (vi 8), their

---

[44]See also p. 17, above, and J. N. B. Carleton Paget, *Barnabas*, 105–7, 144–7.

[45]Skarsaune, 121; for the likely origin of the New Testament wording in emphasis on a divine plan when the text was quoted in isolation, see B. Lindars, *New Testament Apologetic* (London, 1961), 131.

circumcision is no seal of election (ix 6), and their temple was heathenish (xvi 2). Correspondingly, the radical and influential theory of the scriptures in Barnabas can be seen to have anticipated the golden age of patristic exegesis in securing a significance, albeit a Christian one, for the whole Mosaic code as currently interpreted by Jews; but at the same time it excludes the Jews from the covenant and law they think to be theirs, and can be seen to have arisen from the Christian need for justification *vis-à-vis* the Jews, and to present a sharply anti-Jewish cutting edge.

(iv) Dependence on Jewish culture and opinion

The anxiety about assimilation to the Jews which is one aspect of this theory of the scriptures is consistent with the last characteristic of the Epistle to be reviewed, its marked dependence on Jewish culture and public opinion. Some signs of literary dependence on ultimately Jewish material have already appeared, notably in the use of the Two Ways (Barn. xviii–xxi)[46] and of descriptions of the rites of the scapegoat[47] and the Red Heifer (vii–viii). A sharing in contemporary Jewish opinion is also evident, as the passages considered above for guidance on dating show. It was clear that Barnabas xi 9 and xii 1 have material in common with Jewish apocalypses of the end of the first century A.D., and a similar bond emerges from the passage on the Roman emperors in iv 3–5, interpreting Dan. vii; here the Epistle, like the book of Revelation, expects the imminent fall of Rome, to be followed by the messianic reign of the saints, when the Beloved comes to his inheritance (iv 3); and it therefore shares the outlook of Jewish apocalypses such as II Esdras xi–xii, xiii and Sib v 403–33.

Future expectations which the writer shares with the Jews and assumes that his readers also share reappear elsewhere in the Epistle. Thus, the Son of God will tear up Amalek by the roots at the end (Exod. xvii 14 as interpreted in Barn xii 9). This passage in Exodus received comment in the name of rabbis of the turn of the first and second centuries; Elizer ben Hyrcanus and Joshua ben Hananiah

---

[46]See S. P. Brock, 'The Two Ways and the Palestinian Targum', in P. R. Davies & R. T. White (edd.), *A Tribute to Geza Vermes* (JSOT Supplement Series, 100, Sheffield, 1990), 139–52 (distinguishing the form of the treatise used in Barnabas as presupposing not only a link between Jer. xxi 8 and Deut. xxx 15, 19 to give the concept of two ways, as found in the Didache, but also a description of the ways in dualistic terms of light and dark, as found in a developed form (lacking the idea of just *two* ways) in 1QS).

[47]Barn. vii 6, Justing, *Dial.* xl 4, and Tertullian, *Adv Iudaeos* xiv 9–10 = *Adv Marc* iii 7, 7–8 state without express biblical warrant that the two goats must resemble one another; this practice is recommended in M. Yoma vi 1.

both ascribe the cutting-off of Amalek to the time when the kingdom of God is established (Mekhilta, Beshallah, Amalek, ii, on Exod. xvii 14 & 16, respectively).[48] Amalek can stand in rabbinic thought for Rome or for the power of evil, and a similar range of meaning seems possible in Barnabas, in the light of Justin's association of Amalek both with the demons and with the earthly authorities whom they influence.[49] Similarly, when Barnabas looks forward to the true sabbath-rest of the messianic millennium (xv 5–8), sabbath observance is indeed being rebutted, but the expectation of a thousand-year sabbath to come is shared with the Jews.[50]

The extent of the dependence in Barnabas on Jewish culture and opinion goes far to explain the explain the vigour of the Epistle's argument for divergence from the Jews on points thought vital for the continuance of the Christian community. One strand of this argument suggests strong Christian attraction to the patriotic Jewish outlook glimpsed in the shared expectations just discussed, in a development described by Reicke as an 'anti-Roman Zionism'.[51] In vi 8–19 the command to enter the 'good land, flowing with milk and honey' (Exod. xxxiii 1, 3) leads to the thought of the Christians as a new creation, so that 'the habitation of our heart is a holy temple to the Lord' (vi 15); this passage probably counters Jewish emphasis on the duties of possessing the land and building the temple, such as is seen, close to the probable date of Barnabas, at the beginning of the summary of the law in Josephus's *Antiquities*.[52] In xvi 4–10, also

---

[48]J. Z. Lauterbach, *Mekilta de-Rabbi Ishmael*, ii (Philadelphia, 1933), 158–60; that the exegesis ascribed in the text (Lauterbach, ii, p. 158, line 155) to Eleazar (of Modin) should be in the name of Eliezer (ben Hyrcanus), for Eleazar's exegesis is given immediately before, is shown by W. Bacher, *Die Agada der Tannaiten*, i (2nd edn, Strassburg, 1903, repr. Berlin, 1965), 142, n. 1.

[49]L. Ginzberg, *The Legends of the Jews*, vi (1928, repr. Philadelphia, 1968), 24–5, nn. 141, 147; Justin, *Dial* xlix 8, cxxxi 4–5 with Williams, 99, n.3.

[50]For example, in the interpretations of the title of Ps. xcii 'for the sabbath day', in S. Buber (ed.), *Midrash Tehillim* (Wilna, 1891, repr. Jerusalam, 1977), 402 foot (ii 22, the seventh age is all sabbath and rest), 405 (v, the day when Isa. xxxii 15 if fulfilled, and wars cease), cited among other passages including Barn. xv 4 by Ginzberg, *Legends*, v (1925, repr. Philadelphia, 1968), n. 140. A. Hermans, 'Le Pseudo-Barnabé est-il Millénariste?' (*Analecta Lovaniensia Biblica et Orientalia* iii 15), *ETL* xxxv (1959), 849–76 gives the answer No, but 7–8 can be read without difficulty as envisaging a millennial sabbath leading to a new world beginning, like the old, on the first (eighth) day.

[51]Reicke, *Diakonie*, 381–2; this aspect of early Christian thought is further studied by R. L. Wilken, 'Early Christian Chiliasm, Jewish Messianism, and the Idea of the Holy Land', *HTR* lxxxix (1986), 298–307.

[52]Josephus, *Ant.* iv 199–201 (when you have conquered the land, found one city chosen by God, with one temple and one altar); similar emphasis is later exemplified in the developments of Exod. xv 16–19 into different versions of a saying 'Let Israel come into the land and build the temple', in Mekhilta, Beshallah, Shirata, ix & x (Lauterbach, ii, 75–6, 78).

discussed in section I, above, the writer takes pains to show that opinions of this kind on the Jerusalem temple should not be shared. The presupposition here is that Jews are rebuilding the temple, with Roman sanction, and therefore as 'servants of the enemy' (xvi 4). The Romans are 'the enemy', as in chapter iv. The author of Barnabas insists that the true temple is inward and spiritual, as at vi 15, probably attempting, in line with the interpretation of iii 6 advanced above, to check Christians who are attracted to the Jewish community when its hopes appear to be fulfilled by the prospective revival of the temple-service.[53] Jewish hopes centred on the land and the temple are rejected, therefore, but assumptions about Rome as 'the enemy' are still unquestioningly shared, as in iv 3.

(v) The Christian and Jewish settings of Barnabas's outlook

These impressions of fear of assimilation to the Jews, of an anti-Jewish theory of the Jewish polity, and of a dependence on Jewish culture and public opinion in Barnabas together suggest a reasonably coherent outline of the defensive outlook on the Jewish community manifest in the Epistle. Admittedly, it represents only one section of Christian opinion. The Christians form a divided minority over against the Jews; some Christians admit that the Jews are the people chosen to receive the covenant, and simply claim for the Christians a share in it (iv 6); some, perhaps an overlapping group, are strongly attracted to go over to the Jewish community (iii 6; Christians in this position are probably also envisaged in xvi). This division of the Christian community into Judaizers, non-Judaizers and potential Jewish proselytes is reflected again in Justin's Dialogue (xlvii 1–4); the author of the Epistle was not far from the opinion of those mentioned by Justin who thought that Judaizing Christians could not be saved, and those attracted to Judaism in Barnabas may be compared with those in Justin who have gone over to the polity of the law. Christian Judaizers reappear in Celsus and Origen (Origen, Contra Celsum v 61, cf. ii 1), and the various positions emerging in Barnabas doubtless long continued to be represented among the Christians, although the proportion of Christians who took the Judaistic view was probably declining, like

---

[53]The present writer has argued this more fully in 'Messianism among Jews and Christians into the Second Century', *Augustinianum* xxviii (1988), 71–88 (82–3); the widely held view that the reference is to Hadrian's construction of a temple of Zeus, mentioned by Cassius Dio lxix 12, 1 (so Wengst, *Didache* ..., 114–15), makes the text in Barnabas so harshly paradoxical that one would have expected a phrase of elucidation.

the (not identical) proportion of Christians who were of Jewish birth, during the second century.[54]

At the time of the Epistle, however, these divisions are likely to have involved considerable proportions of the small Christian population. The Epistle can give some guidance to the outlook on the Jews even among Christians whose view the author rejects, for these Christian divisions are all determined by the attitude taken to the Jewish polity. They will have contributed accordingly to a sense that the Christians were weak and upstart by comparison with the large, ancient and determinative Jewish body. This sense, in conjunction with the cultural dependence of the Christians on the Jews and the experience of propaganda by Jews and Judaizers, explains the fear of assimilation to the larger body evident in Barnabas.

Correspondingly, the Epistle's theory of the Jewish law is a justification of the non-Judaizing practice which rapidly became the Christian norm, denying the Jews' claim to their ancestral covenant and law in a vigorous attack by the smaller body on the greater. Its thoroughgoing adoption of the law made it a particularly useful key to scripture in later Alexandrian exegesis, and a particularly powerful instance of the widespread ante-Nicene assertion that the Christians have replaced the Jews as the elect people of God.[55] As in some other polemic of this period, the name 'Israel' is conceded without hesitation to the Jews, as at v 8 (one more example of the Epistle's indebtedness to Jewish usage);[56] but the Christian claim to the Jewish heritage is nonetheless total and exclusive, and (by contrast with a good deal of anti-Jewish writing, including Justin's work) there is no explicit reference to a return of Israel, whether in the near future by baptism or in the last days; it is particularly notable that

[54]The variety of Christian attitudes is emphasized by B. L. Visotzky, 'Prolegomenon to the Study of Jewish–Christianities in Rabbinic Literature', *AJS Review* xiv (1989), 47–70 (49–63), and (with special reference to the Nazoraeans) by W. Kinzig, '"Non-Separation": Closeness and Co-operation between Jews and Christians in the Fourth Century', *VC* xlv (1991), 27–53 (35).

[55]The argument is important in Justin's *Dialogue* (xii 4–5 and elsewhere); in Tertullian, Cyprian, the pseudo-Cyprianic *Adversus Iudaeos* and *de Montibus Sina et Sion* (see W. Horbury, 'The Purpose of Pseudo-Cyprian, *Adversus Iudaeos*', *Studia Patristica* xviii.3 (1989), 291–317 (302–3, 305) (chapter 7, below); and in Aphrahat and Ephrem Syrus (R. Murray, *Symbols of Church and Kingdom* (Cambridge, 1975, corrected repr. 1977), 56–60, 67).

[56]This usage recurs in Melito's Paschal Homily, in the later second century, and the pseudo-Cyprianic *Adversus Iudaeos*, probably of the early third century. Lowy, 29 urges that 'Israel' in Barnabas is always linked with scripture rather than contemporary life, and is on the way to being appropriated as a Christian title, but this may be too much to conclude from a text in which it is never easy to find anything unconnected with scripture; as occurrences bearing on the present, note specially v 2 ('Israel' contrasted with 'us'), xvi 5.

this theme is not mentioned in chapter xi, on baptism, where the refusal of Israel to accept baptism is the point of departure. The setting of this lively contention is a dependence on Jewish culture such that, when there is no reason to differ, Jewish opinion remains the norm, as has emerged from passages on the fall of Rome and the hope for redemption. Hence, although with regard to Justin it seems appropriate to speak of Jewish–Christian missionary rivalry, Barnabas seems primarily a work of defence.

The success of the Epistle in the later church should not obscure the connections between its outlook on the Jews and its contemporary setting. These appeared especially in the writer's need to counter excitement at the prospect of a rebuilt temple. If the Epistle was written for a readership in Egypt, as suggested by its early attestation and perhaps also by internal evidence (ix 6 and n. 36, above), it would have formed a suitable response to currents of Jewish opinion in Egypt towards the end of the first century. The temple of Onias at Leontopolis formed such a focus of Jewish unrest that it was closed by imperial order in 73 (Josephus, *B. J.* vii 420–35), and comparable zeal for national redemption would have been stirred again among Egyptian Jews by hope for the rebuilding of the Jerusalem temple twenty-five years later; in Sib. v 403–33, cited above, and probably reflecting Egyptian Jewish thought before the revolt under Trajan, the messiah is to rebuild Jerusalem and the temple. It is likely that the inner-Christian divisions apparent in Barnabas are themselves related to differences of opinion in the Jewish body; and on this view of the setting, the writer's check on excitement over the temple could be compared up to a point with attempts by the Alexandrian Jewish communal leadership to quell enthusiastic Jewish reception of refugee Sicarii and their message in 72–3 (Josephus, *B. J.* vii 409–19). Similarly, the treatment of the laws in Barnabas is to some extent comparable with an attitude deplored by Philo, allegorical interpretation treated as justifying neglect in observance (*Migr. Abr.* 89–93). The Judaizing Christians, again, will reflect within the Christian community the zeal of the Jewish multitude who, according to Philo (ibid., 93), would censure such neglect.

These possible links between the Epistle's outlook and various currents of opinion among Jews in Egypt would not lose all their force if the setting were in fact to be sought elsewhere, for they relate to trends which can be envisaged as widespread in the Jewish community. A similar consideration applies to Lowy's suggestion, followed here in many respects, that the Jewish messianic movement which looked for national restoration forms the background of the

Epistle; the view would suit an Egyptian setting, given the Egyptian manifestations of this way of thinking noted above, but the Jewish hopes concerned were very widespread, as is confirmed by the far-flung Jewish revolts under Trajan, and the centrality of redemption in the Eighteen Benedictions.[57]

Justin Martyr

(i) Overlap with Jewish opinion

Justin evinces a similar cultural debt and a similar overlap with Jewish public opinion. His cultural dependence is most obvious when he has to come to terms with Jewish revision of the LXX in the *First Apology* (xli) and the *Dialogue* (lxvi–lxviii, lxxi–lxxiii, lxxxiv, cxx), and when in the *Dialogue* (vii–viii) he presents his conversion as a learning to know the prophets. In both cases, however, he makes an independent Christian contention from within his indebtedness. He argues for Jewish doctrinal alteration and mutilation of the LXX, and himself quotes the text together with Christian interpolation, notably in Ps. xcvi;[58] and he says that he was possessed by love of the prophets 'and of those men who are the friends of Christ' (*Dialogue* viii 1).

His overlap with Jewish opinion can be traced, as in the case of Barnabas, with regard to future hopes and with special reference to the fate of Rome. Here again there are distinctive Christian touches. So Amalek is fought 'with hidden hand' (Exod. xvii 16 LXX), and Justin assumes that Trypho will agree that this will take place at the war of the glorious Advent, for Christians the second Advent; but in the cause of Christianity Justin goes on to ask how this interpretation can satisfy the expression 'with *hidden* hand', especially as the text describes a victory over Amalek in the past. He therefore applies it, rather, to the hidden power of God which was at work in the crucified Christ, before whom demons and all powers and authorities tremble (*Dialogue* xlix 8, resumed in cxxxi 5).

This Christian exegesis as presented by Justin includes phrases recalling the New Testament, but seems ultimately to depend on the all-important interpolated text of Ps. xcvi (xcv), in which Christ

---

[57]On prayer for redemption in the Amidah, W. Horbury, 'The Benediction of the *Minim* and Jewish–Christian controversy', *JTS* N.S. xxxiii (1982), 19–61 (38–9, 47, 49–50) (Chapter 2 above pp. 87–90, 93, 95).

[58]R. Petraglio, 'Le interpolazioni cristiane del salterio greco', *Augustinianum* xxviii (1988), 89–109 (101–5 on Ps. xcvi).

reigns from the tree (verse 10), terrible over all demons (verses 4–5) and worshipped by the nations of the whole earth (verses 7–9).[59] Two aspects of the interpretation are notable here. First, with the Epistle of Barnabas (notes 48–9, above), but independently of it (n. 7, above), Justin here treats a Pentateuchal narrative on which comparable vestiges of early rabbinic commentary survive;[60] both Barnabas and Justin draw on very early Christian comment of the Amalek episode, and their interpretations suggest, as noted already, that Christian and Jewish comments were closely similar, Christians and Jews alike in this case setting the overthrow of Amalek in the messianic age. Secondly, Justin's alternative and preferred exegesis keeps the thought of divine victory over the powers, implicitly including the present Roman order, which belongs to his first exegesis and to Jewish interpretation of Amalek.

Dan vii, once more, is quoted at length in the *Dialogue* (xxxi–xxxii) to include the downfall of the Fourth Beast;[61] and the event symbolized by this downfall is in mind in the First Apology (xii 7), when the Word – in scripture and in Christ's saying – is said to foretell that Rome cannot stop the Christian movement. Correspondingly, the Romans are told a little later in the First Apology (xlv) that Ps. cx foretells the apostolic preaching of the powerful word; but if they want to read these words (that is, the prophecy of David, as the context suggests, rather than Justin's own words) from a hostile viewpoint, they may – presumably then taking the psalm as a militant prophecy of the kingdom of Christ. When Justin uses this boldness of speech, he has just mentioned Roman suppression of prophecies, specifying the books of Hystaspes, the Sibyl and the biblical prophets as prohibited on pain of death by the agency of the demons (*First Apology* xliv, cf. xx). We read them none the less, he says, and submit them for inspection by the Romans; and he evidently takes the prophets of Israel to have the downfall of Rome as a main subject, in the manner of Hystaspes and

---

[59]This suggestion, supported by the association elsewhere in the Dialogue (lxxxiii 4) of Ps. xcvi 5 with Ps. cx as a prophecy of the power of Christ, may perhaps be added to the discussion of the Jewish background of this exegesis by Skarsaune, 394–5.

[60]Bacher, *Tannaiten*, i, 141 (Exod. xvii 16 interpreted of the messianic age, in the name of Joshua b. Hananiah; cf. n. 48, above); 196–7 (remains of early rabbinic commentary preserved).

[61]This explanation of the long quotation is accepted, and linked with the alternations between discretion and *parrhesia* on Rome in the First Apology, by E. dal Covolo, '"Regno di Dio" nel Dialogo di Giustino con Trifone Giudeo', *Augustinianum* xxviiii (1988), 111–23 (117–19, with n. 34), following and discussing E. Bodenmann, *Naissance d'une Exégèse* (Tübingen, 1986), 227–31, on Dan. vii in Justin.

the Sibyl.[62] The downfall is no doubt implied in the many references in the *Dialogue* to the millennial reign of Christ in Jerusalem (notably at xl 4, lxxx–lxxxi, lxxxiii 3, lxxxv 7, cxxxviii 3, cxxxix 4–5).[63] Their political aspect is indicated by Justin's Christian reapplication of a nationalist Jewish exegesis of Micah iv 1–7, on future restoration and reign in Jerusalem the text is said in the *Dialogue* (cix–cx) to apply to the Christians' persecution and glorious millennium rather than to Jewish suffering, with a view to divinely aided messianic restoration, after the war of Bar Cocheba.

Justin shares with Barnabas, therefore, a general dependence on Jewish culture and a particular accord with Jewish hopes for redemption, evident especially in expectations of the fall of Rome and of a millennial reign in Jerusalem (the latter theme is present but not so strongly emphasized in Barnabas (n. 50, above)). Justin is nearer to the Jews than Barnabas in one important respect: he allows the legitimacy of Christian observance of the ritual law (*Dialogue* xlvii 1–2). What is striking is the extent to which both authors, amid their engagement with Christian modification of Jewish tenets and customs, unquestioningly accept a Christian form of Jewish 'zeal', a messianism in contact with the anti-Roman feeling behind contemporary Jewish upheaval. It is striking less perhaps in its contrast with the emphasis also placed by Justin on the complementary biblically derived commonplaces on obedience to rulers, for the contrasting emphases are equally held together in the scriptures, than in its reflection of characteristics which seem to have marked the Jews more clearly than other subjects of the Roman empire: a consistently sustained mood of opposition to Rome and readiness for revolt, and a self-awareness resembling nationalism in the modern sense.[64]

The attitude shared by Barnabas and Justin may shed light on the fate of Christians under Bar Cocheba, as the writer has tried on the basis of this evidence to argue elsewhere.[65] Justin says in the First Apology (xxxi) that the Jewish leader punished Christians, if they would not deny Christ and 'blaspheme'. In view of the Christian share in Jewish hopes and Jewish hostility to Rome considered here,

---

[62]A brief conspectus of these works as 'resistance literature' is given by G. E. M. de Ste. Croix, *The Class Struggle in the Ancient Greek World* (London, 1981), 442–3, with nn. 7–8.

[63]Justin's millenarianism is considered (not with special reference to this aspect) by Skarsaune, 401–9 (cf. 338–44).

[64]The Jews were unique in combining a common culture with traditions of political unity, and in mounting a general revolt in 66 after prolonged acquiescence in Roman rule, according to P. A. Brunt, *Roman Imperial Themes* (Oxford, 1990), 517–19 (cf. 126–8).

[65]Horbury, 'Messianism', 83–4.

it would not have been unreasonable for participants in the revolt to expect that some Christians in Judaea would come over to the Jewish community at the time of its apparent success. The view expressed in Eusebius's *Chronicle*, Hadrian xvii, that Bar Cocheba killed 'Christians who were unwilling to help him against the Roman army' perhaps therefore conveys less of the inwardness of the transaction than Justin's report in the *First Apology*. In the *Dialogue*, as already noted, Justin condemns Christians who go over to the Jews (xlvii 4); and in Judaea under Bar Cocheba, a situation in many ways comparable with that addressed in Barn. xvi, some are likely to have done so, whereas others refused to 'blaspheme' by uttering the curse-formula which will have been the effective sign of the transition from the first century onwards (as suggested by Acts xxvi 11, on compulsion 'to blaspheme' in the purging of Christians from the synagogues, viewed in conjunction with the formula ἀνάθεμα Ἰησοῦς, I Cor. xii 3).[66]

(ii) Jewish reaction to Christianity

The report in the First Apology on Christians under Bar Cocheba introduces the second main topic in Justin to be considered, his notices of Jewish reaction to Christianity; but it also raises the frequently-considered question of his sources for Jewish and Palestinian matters, and his personal knowledge of the Jews and Palestine.[67] O. Skarsaune thinks it likely that existing Jewish–Christian material was used for his passages on the cursing of Christ by Jews and on the revolt under Hadrian, and suggests that it could have come to Justin through his Christian education; this might well have included teaching from Palestinian gentile Christians who had themselves made Jewish–Christian exegetical traditions their own.[68] Similarly, Justin would have used possibly Palestinian gentile traditions for his emphasis on the exclusion of Jews from Jerusalem when the revolt was suppressed, although these traditions are also in touch with Jewish exegesis, and it is hard to distinguish between gentile material and Justin's own contribution.[69] A strength of Skarsaune's proposals lies in their allowance for Justin's personal involvement in

---

[66]Horbury, 'Benediction', 53–4 (102, above).

[67]Studies of Justin's contacts with Judaism, including A. Harnack, *Judentum und Judenchristentum in Justins Dialog mit Trypho* (TU 39, Leipzig, 1913), are listed by Visonà, 72–3; on the haggadah, see also Ginzberg, *Legends*, vii (*Index* by B. Cohen, 1938), 594–5 (index of passages in Justin).

[68]Skarsaune, 290–5, 371–4.

[69]Skarsaune, 372–3, 428–9.

these subjects as well as his indebtedness to earlier teaching. Justin certainly used sources, especially the testimony traditions illuminatingly reconstructed by Skarsaune, but on some of these topics his personal contribution is also likely to have been important. The Bar Cocheba war, for instance, figures in his own narrative framework in the *Dialogue* (i 3, ix 3), and as a Palestinian he could have had his own information about it. Again, the subject of cursing crops up so many times, in varied ways but always with vehemence of expression, that it is natural to think that Justin himself, as well as his source, knew something of it.

To recall his background, he says at the beginning of the *First Apology* that his father and grandfather were 'from Flavia Neapolis, a city of Palestinian Syria', present-day Nablus. He could associate himself in the *Dialogue* with the Samaritans (cxx 6), and he names in the First Apology (xxvi 3–4) the villages from which the Samaritans Simon and Menander came; he himself, however, was an uncircumcised gentile (*Dialogue* xxviii 2, xli 3). He mentions various Palestinian localities, including the cave of Bethlehem (*Dialogue* lxxviii 5). He gives the name of Bar Cocheba (in the report discussed above); this becomes a notable point when one considers that Cassius Dio, to judge by the account of fair length and detail surviving in epitome (lxix 12–14), described the whole Jewish revolt under Hadrian without mentioning the name of the Jewish leader. Justin's specifically Jewish knowledge ranges in the *Dialogue* from the description of a phylactery (the lettering of which 'we [the Christians] assuredly consider holy', xlvi 5) to what sounds like an early form of the mystical reckoning of the divine stature later known as Shi'ur Qomah (cxiv 3, denouncing Jewish anthropomorphism in connection with Ps. viii 3).[70] It seems likely that he learned even his Platonism in a school which was sympathetic to Jewish teaching.[71] His Palestinian and Jewish knowledge should not be exaggerated, but it is not negligible, and it is aided by Justin's

---

[70]Second-century figures discussed in connection with the origins of the Shi'ur Qomah include Elchasai and the Gnostic teacher Marcus. Origen's comments on anthropomorphism, Jewish and Christian, at one point seem to echo this passage in Justin (N. R. M. de Lange, *Origen and the Jews* (Cambridge, 1976), 44); but they are circumstantial enough to make it possible that they preserve authentic information on a Jewish mystical practice (M. S. Cohen, *The Shi'ur Qomah* (Lanham & London, 1983), 40, n. 65, on Origen, *in Gen. hom.* i 13). The same can be said of Justin here.

[71]M. J. Edwards, 'On the Platonic Schooling of Justin Martyr', *JTS* N.S. xlii (1991), 17–34, argues that Justin's Platonism belongs to the school represented by his contemporary Numenius of Apamea in Phrygia, cited by Clement of Alexandria, Origen and Eusebius as a philosopher who honoured Jewish beliefs and writings (e.g. Clem Alex, *Stromateis*, i 22, 150 (Numenius calls Plato 'Moses Atticizing'); Origen, *Contra Celsum* i 15, iv 51).

own considerable overlap with Jewish ways of thinking.[72] If compared with the knowledge exhibited by a slightly later Palestinian gentile Christian, Julius Africanus of Aelia, in his letters on biblical subjects preserved by Origen and Eusebius, it can perhaps be said to show less classical and historical erudition bearing on the Jews, but a fuller acquaintance with Jewish exegesis and ethos.[73]

Justin's notices of Jewish reaction to Christianity can therefore be approached in the expectation that, although defective reporting is inevitable in the circumstances, he will have had some good sources and some personal knowledge. Special interest attaches to his indignant remarks on specific communal measures. In the present context two aspects of them only can be considered: first, their witness to the great importance of corporate Jewish reaction for the Christians; secondly, the contact between Justin and other sources in the allegations of particular measures.[74]

First, there are traces of a probably testimony-linked tradition on an organized Jewish rebuttal of the apostolic preaching; the passages are comparable and sometimes co-ordinated with the prominent tradition of the apostolic mission, already noticed in connection with Ps cx in the *First Apology* (xlv), and have a similar air of legendary development. Twice in the *Dialogue* (xvii 1–2, cviii 2, recalled at cxvii 3) Justin asserts that, after the crucifixion, the Jews sent chosen men throughout the world to denounce the appearance of the godless sect of the Christians, whose teaching is deception. Justin links the apostolic mission which they rebutted not only with Ps cx, but also with Isa. ii 3 'out of Zion shall go forth the law', a text appearing as a quotation in the *First Apology* (xxxix) but only as an allusion in the *Dialogue* (xxiv 1, cf. xi 2), although the parallel Micah iv 2 is quoted in this connection at cix 2, shortly after the passage on Jewish criticism in cviii. The counter-mission is linked at xvii 2 with the texts Isa. iii 9–11 and v 18–20, used in connection with the death of Christ and Jewish criticisms of Christianity in the *First Apology* (xlvii–xlix),[75] but it seems likely that it also became attached to Isa. xviii 1–2, which in the LXX becomes a woe on

---

[72]Justin's inherited material shows that he was strongly influenced by Christianity evincing close gentile–Christian contact with Jewish exegesis (Skarsaune, e.g. 326, 429), and he continued to breathe this atmosphere.

[73]On Africanus's letter to Origen, see M. Harl & N. R. M. de Lange, *Origène, Philocalie 1–20, sur les Écritures, et la Lettre à Africanus sur l'Histoire de Suzanne* (SC 302, Paris, 1983); on his letter to Aristides (in Eusebius, *H. E.* i 7), R. Bauckham, *Jude and the Relatives of Jesus in the Early Church* (Edinburgh, 1990), 355–63.

[74]For further discussion see Horbury, 'Benediction' and Stanton, 'Aspects'.

[75]On their possibly Jewish–Christian background see Skarsaune, 290–1; Jerome comparably refers to Jewish cursing of Christians in his comment on Isa. v 18.

those responsible for the despatch of papyrus letters overseas. In Eusebius's commentary on Isa. xviii 1–2, and in an exegesis of this passage in the tract on Antichrist in the name of Hippolytus (58), the counter-mission envisaged by Justin is conducted by Jewish emissaries sent overseas with letters. One may suspect a testimony-registration of the story of the anti-Christian emissaries, using texts from Isaiah, a book widely read as a prophecy of Jewish–Christian relations.

The connection of an imagined scene of organized Jewish response with the testimony tradition suggested here may be compared with early Christian treatment of the complementary theme of the repentance of the Jews and their acceptance of Christianity by baptism. This theme complements the denunciation of their hostility in Justin's *Dialogue*, as in other Christian writings, often on the pattern of the testimony Isa. i 14–16 (e.g. xii 3–xiii 1, xiv 1 (based on Isa. i 14–16); cviii 3, immediately after the story of the counter-mission, cf. cxviii 3); and the elaboration of an imagined testimony-based scene in which Jews in fact seek Christian baptism can be traced in Cyprian.[76] It seems likely, then, that the story of organized Jewish denunciation twice told by Justin had similarly gained incorporation into the testimony traditions, and thereby into catechises as well as apologetic. If so, the weight attached by the Christians to Jewish response makes itself most plainly felt.

Secondly, however, these passages are among a number of references to organized and corporate Jewish reaction which have some contact with other sources.[77] The story of official denunciation immediately after the crucifixion is told in the context of complaints about contemporary Jewish criticisms, which the Christians think to be disseminated among the gentiles by the community as a body (*Dialogue* xvii 1–2, cviii 2, cf. *First Apology* xlix). Despite the legendary character of this story, it corresponds to the currency of Jewish anti-Christian statements from an early period, as suggested by Matt. xxviii 15; items of propaganda listed at cviii 2 recur elsewhere, and overlap with the rabbinic tradition according to which Jesus was executed because he practised sorcery and deceived and led astray Israel (Babylonian Talmud, Sanhedrin 43a).[78] Comparably, other references to communal measures in Justin find external correspondence. The curses on *Christians* in the synagogues often

---

[76]Horbury, 'Pseudo-Cyprian', 304–5 (chapter 7, below).
[77]They are surveyed by Harnack, *Trypho*, 78–81 and Horbury, 'Benediction', 19–23, 48–59 (chapter 2, above).
[78]For the details see Horbury, 'Benediction', 54–8 (chapter 2, above pp. 77–8).

mentioned in the *Dialogue* (especially xvi 4, xcvi 2) can be compared either with the Birkath ha-Minim or with cursing such as that associated with the cursing of Haman at Purim.[79] The blasphemy or anathematization of *Christ* in the synagogues (xxxv 8, xlvii 4) can be connected, as noted already, with a long-established purgation formula indirectly attested in Acts xxvi 11 and I Corinthians xii 3; what appears to be a related practice is described in the *Dialogue* as reviling of the Son of God and mockery of the king of Israel, 'such things as your rulers of synagogue (ἀρχισυνάγωγοι) teach, after the prayer' (cxxxvii 2). This too may be compared, following T. C. G. Thornton, with Purim cursing;[80] but Justin alleges a frequently- followed practice, and it is therefore also worth noting, despite its late date, a midrashic reference to curses uttered with scroll in hand at the end of the Eighteen Benedictions.[81] The prohibition of converse with Christians decreed by Jewish teachers (διδάσκαλοι, xxxviii 1, cxii 4) is comparable with the prohibition of dealings with *minim* attested at Tos Hullin ii 20–21.

From Justin, therefore, it emerges that corporate Jewish rejection of Christianity had so deeply impressed itself on Christians as to find a place in the testimony tradition, and that it was possible in his time to point to specific Jewish measures which expressed this corporate attitude. Further, his statements on these matters find some support in other sources, Jewish as well as Christian. It can be added that some kind of corporate Jewish antagonism to the Christians would accord with two features of the Jewish situation which, as noted already, were strikingly reflected and reproduced in the Christian sub-group itself: the zeal and national solidarity of the period of the

---

[79]T. C. G. Thornton, 'Christian Understanding of the *Birkath ha-Minim* in the Eastern Roman Empire', *JTS* N.S. xxxviii (1987), 419–31 (429 and n. 5) prefers the second possibility, and envisages spasmodic and informal cursing on the lines of the cursing of Christ later attested in probable connection with Purim; he stresses the lack of evidence, apart from Jerome, for later Christian understanding of the Benediction of the *Minim* as including a curse on the Christian body in general. The intensity of the Christian reaction reflected in Justin speaks, however, for a regularly-encountered Jewish response, and Justin and inner-Jewish evidence on the Benediction point to the same setting, the synagogues of the second century. I would therefore still incline to find the Benediction reflected in the *Dialogue*, and to associate later Christian silence on it with silence on the synagogue service in general, but the main point asserted in the text above – the correspondence of Justin's evidence with other sources – is not affected if Thornton's explanation is preferred.

[80]T. C. G. Thornton, 'The Crucifixion of Haman and the Scandal of the Cross', *JTS* N.S. xxxvii (1986), 419–26 (425).

[81]Midrash Panim Aherim on Est iii 8, quoted in Yalkut Shimeoni ad loc; one of the midrashic versions of Haman's anti-Jewish charges, discussed by S. Krauss in connection with the Benediction of the *Minim*, but of interest here as presupposing curses 'after the prayer' (Horbury, 'Benediction', 29–30; chapter 2, above, pp. 77–8).

Jewish revolts, and the welcome being extended to proselytes. These features reappear in the Eighteen Benedictions, in which prayer for national redemption (especially in the Tenth Benediction and onwards) includes a blessing on proselytes and a curse on apostates, oppressors, and heretics (*minim*) (the Eleventh and Twelfth Benedictions). Is it possible, however, to go beyond this appeal to the general atmosphere, and to attempt, on the basis of the specific allegations in Justin, more precise suggestions on organized Jewish reaction?

A start could perhaps be made with the suggestion that Justin's references to 'ruler of synagogue' and 'teachers' point to two related but distinct intercommunal networks of communication. *Archisynagogi* held an office which could involve supervision of the synagogue service (including a kind of teaching in the synagogue, according to Justin here), but was distinguished enough to be suitable for leading members of the community. So, to take one famous example, the Theodotus inscription shows a priest and *archisynagogus* wealthy enough to build a synagogue with appurtenances, and proud enough of his title to record that it was held by his father and grandfather before him.[82] Holders of this office would often be among the group of principal persons in the community, those πρῶτοι who are envisaged in the case of the Roman Jews in Acts as being in a position to receive 'letters from Judaea' or messengers concerning Jewish visitors (Acts xxviii 21). Such diaspora contacts with the Holy Land did not necessarily come to an end in 70, and it would be speculative but not unreasonable to envisage communication by way of Caesarea between western diaspora notables and the patriarchate emerging in Galilee.[83]

'Teachers', on the other hand, are said to have decreed the prohibition of converse. The authority ascribed to them recalls that claimed in Justin's time by members of the nascent rabbinic movement. In the Fourth Gospel, διδάσκαλος is given as the rendering of the title Rabbi (John i 38, cf. xx 16); and the Greek title also occurs in Jewish inscriptions, while the respect it engendered is strongly suggested by the Aphrodisias inscription recording members of a Jewish group of φιλομαθεῖς.[84] It is likely that diaspora

---

[82] E. L. Sukenik, *Ancient Synagogues in Palestine and Greece* (London, 1934), 69–70 and Plate XVIa.

[83] For the probably third- or fourth-century Beth She'arim epitaph of a 'Caesarean *archisynagogos*, [a native] of Pamphylia' see M. Schwabe & B. Lifschitz, *Beth She'rim* (Jerusalem, 1967), 91, no. 203.

[84] J. Reynolds & R. Tannenbaum, *Jews and Godfearers at Aphrodisias* (Cambridge, 1987), 30–34.

teachers would have had some direct or indirect contact with the rabbinic schools of Galilee and Judaea; Trypho is represented in Justin's *Dialogue*, presumably not implausibly, as a refugee from Judaea in Greece and Corinth (i 3), Aquila is depicted in the haggadah as a proselyte of Pontus who travels to the Holy Land to get instruction, and a practice of making journeys to the diaspora will underly the legends of rabbinic travel.[85]

The Jewish communal recognition of such measures will have depended not only on these networks of inter-communal contact, but also on the constituency of the more zealous in each place. Their importance as watchdogs on law-breaking is chillingly evoked by Philo; with *Migr. Abr.* 93, cited above, compare *Spec. Leg.* ii 253, on the thousands of watchful 'zealots of the law, most exact guardians of the ancestral traditions'. In Acts xxi 20–21 a comparable group among the Christian Jews of Jerusalem is mentioned in order to induce Paul to demonstrate his own observance, although it is Jews from Asia who then accuse him (verse 27). The continuation of this mood of zeal after the First Revolt is both reflected and reproduced in Barnabas and Justin, as noted above.

Groups of synagogues and communities are likely, therefore, to have put these measures into action, partly by the authority of office-holders and teachers, partly through the solidarity of the more zealous. Cursing and prohibition of converse will have built on and reinforced earlier measures against the Christians, notably the exclusion from synagogue complained of the New Testament (Luke vi 22; John xi 22, xii 42, xvi 2). Although the ancient constitutional rule of high priest and king was lost, except for a brief revival under Bar Cocheba, it is likely that Diaspora contact with the Holy Land continued, and that office-holders and teachers in the communities began to form links with the nascent patriarchate and rabbinic movement.

Justin therefore witnesses not only to the profound significance of the Jewish reaction in Christian eyes, but also to continuity and cohesion in the second-century Jewish community. At the same time he presents a Christianity which is as much determined by Jewish culture and thought as that of Barnabas, but which breathes a less strictly defensive atmosphere, despite the context of missionary rivalry with the Jews. Justin can allow the validity of varied

---

[85]A. E. Silverstone, *Aquila and Onkelos* (Manchester, 1931), 24–6, 30–31, quoting Tanhuma Buber on Exod. xxi 1 and Sifra Lev. xxv 7; the anecdotes of Akiba's journeys are examined by P. Schäfer, 'Rabbi Aqiva and Bar Kokhba', in W. S. Green, ed., *Approaches to Ancient Judaism*, ii (Chico, 1980), 113–130 (113–17).

positions in the Christian camp, thereby drawing nearer than Barnabas to observant Jewish attitudes, and he can express hopes for Jewish conversion where Barnabas is preoccupied with resisting the strength of Jewish influence. The Christian future was with Barnabas's claim to the entire Jewish scriptures in their spiritual sense, but there would be an important place too for the more historical approach of Justin. Yet, for all their contribution to the Christian inheritance, the Epistle of Barnabas and Justin's works in their second-century setting are Jewish as much as Christian documents. Despite and partly because of their anti-Judaism, they attest the overshadowing spiritual power of the Jewish polity, and could properly be assigned to a Christian sub-section of Jewish literature.

5

CHRIST AS BRIGAND IN ANCIENT ANTI-CHRISTIAN POLEMIC

The ancient world described Christ in language also readily associated with criticism of government. Christian apologists used words such as 'prophet', 'teacher' or 'wonder-worker' to present Christ as a divinely-authenticated philosophical guide.[1] Domitian's expulsion of philosophers and astrologers from Rome is simply one instance of a general recognition that such teachers might be significant politically. Their followers' terms of praise had well-worn pejorative counterparts suggesting deception and subversion. The very words which offered the apologists common ground with paganism could therefore facilitate their opponents' depreciation of Christ's teaching.[2] Justin's *teacher* and doer of *mighty works*, Tertullian's *illuminator and guide of humanity*, is Lucian's *crucified sophist* and Celsus's *charlatan* and *leader of sedition*.[3]

This polemic (see pp. 17–20, above) links Jesus with Jewish nationalism or, in its own terms, with the sedition considered characteristic of Jewry.[4] Robert Eisler took early *antichristiana* of this kind to confirm his own derivation of Christianity from a messianic independence movement.[5] This chapter is devoted to one such pagan criticism singled out by Eisler.[6] Cited in Lactantius,

---

[1]For apologetic based on Christ's predictions see Justin, 1 *Apol.* i. 12, *Dial.* xxxv, li (ed. J. C. T. Otto (Jena, 1843) i, 162: ii, 118, 164), with the title *prophet* at Origen, *Contra Celsum* ii. 13 f (cp. *In Jo.* xiii. 54, on 4:44) GCS, Origenes 1, 143 f; 4, 285, and Eusebius, *D.E.* ix. 11, *PG* xxii, 689; for *teacher* Justin I *Apol.* i. 12f, xxxii, pp. 162, 164, 204, Otto; *Justin* ii. 5, and *Apollonius* xxxvi–xli in H. Musurillo, *The Acts of the Christian Martyrs* (Oxford, 1972), 42, 100, Arnobius, *Adversus Nationes* i, 63, ii. 11 (CSEL 4, 44, 55 f), Lactantius, *Div. Inst.* iv. 24 f (CSEL 19, 371–7); with *wonder-worker* (in a defence of the cursing of the fig-tree), Chrysostom, *Hom. in Matth.* 67: I, on 21: 18 (*PG* 58.633). For apologetic on the miracles, G. W. H. Lampe and M. F. Wiles in C. F. D. Moule (ed.), *Miracles* (London, 1965), 205–34.

[2]For polemic against philosophers, magicians and prophets see R. MacMullen, *Enemies of the Roman Order* (Cambridge, Mass., 1967), 46–162.

[3]Justin, n. 1 above and 1 *Apol.* xxx, 200 Otto; Tertullian, *Apol.* xxi. 7 (CCL 1, 123); Lucian, *Per.* xiii (Loeb Classical Library v, 14); Origen, *C. Cels.* i. 71, etc., viii. 14 (R. Bader, *Der ΑΛΗΘΗΣ ΛΟΓΟΣ des Kelsos* (Stuttgart–Berlin, 1940), 62, 197).

[4]'Non cessat gens illa habens seditiones, et homicidia, et latrocinia', Origen, *Comm. ser. in Matth.* 121, on 27: 16 f (GCS 38, p. 256); cp. J. Juster, *Les Juifs dans l'Empire Romain* (Paris, 1914), i, 147, n. 1[9] and 220, n. 8: ii, 182, n. 2.

[5]R. Eisler, ΙΗΣΟΥΣ ΒΑΣΙΛΕΥΣ ΟΥ ΒΑΣΙΛΕΥΣΑΣ (Heidelberg, 1929–30), i. xiii–xxxv (ET *The Messiah Jesus and John the Baptist* (London, 1931), 3–21).

[6]Eisler, ΙΗΣΟΥΣ i, xxv f, E.T. 10 f; further references in section III below.

DI v 3, 4, it attaches to Christ's ministry the heavily-loaded term of *brigandage*. Some remarks on the historical context of this charge (I) may serve to introduce an examination of the text (II), followed by an estimate of its significance (III).

I

Assertions about *Christ* such as this occur in polemic which is anti-*Christian*, concerned primarily not with history but with the contemporary church. The Christian *secta*, like others, might be expected to imitate its founder; 'they worship their crucified sophist and conform their lives to his precepts' (Lucian, *Per.* xiii; see n. 3 above). Two facts of Christ's life freely admitted by Christians proved especially useful to their opponents: his crucifixion and his gathering of disciples. Sources ranging from a rabbinic text of the tannaitic period to Celsus, an oracle ascribed to Apollo and the anti-Christian *Acts of Pilate* view the cross as a just punishment.[7] The consequent labelling of the crucified as a criminal – κακὸν ποιῶν, βιοθανής, κακούργος, *noxius* – was easily transferable to his followers; 'they worship what they deserve' (Minucius Felix, *Oct.* ix. 4).[8] Again, on the call of the disciples, Tertullian and Christians in general stress that 'a vast multitude' turned to Christ, while rabbinic sources see him as, *inter alia*, the leader-astray of whole communities, and for Celsus he is the initiator of *stasis*.[9] The contemporary force of these historical claims appears when we find the church likewise designated *factio*, and the judicial estimate of St Cyprian's episcopal work related as 'You have gathered to yourself many other vicious men in a conspiracy'.[10] Such early non-Christian interpretations of Christ's ministry were offered in a period when persecution was

[7]Sanh. 43a; Origen, *C. Cels.* ii. 5, 63 Bader, *Kelsos*; Porphyry in Augustine, *Civ. Dei* xix. 23 (ed. B. Dombart and A. Kalb (Leipzig, 1929), ii, 393); Rufinus's version of Eusebius, *H.E.* ix. 6 (GCS 9.1, 813, 815).

[8]For the epithets see John xviii 30, *Martyrium Cononis* IV. 6 (188 Musurillo, *Martyrs*), *Acta SS. Tarachi, Probi et Andronici* in T. Ruinart, *Acta primorum martyrum sincera et selecta* 2nd edn. Amsterdam, 1713), 442, and Minucius Felix, *Octavius* xxix. 2 (ed. J. P. Waltzing (Leipzig, 1912), 50); for the passage cited in the text see Waltzing, *Octavius*, 12.

[9]Tertullian, *Apol.* xxi. 18; (CCL 1, 126); for a 'multitude' of disciples see already Luke vi 17 (contrast Matthew iv 25, Mark iii 7). The multitude fed with loaves and fishes are disciples at Origen, *C. Cels.* ii. 46, iii. 10 (GCS 168, 210). For Jesus as leader-astray of communities see Sanh. 43a; the offence is described in M. Sanh. vii. I0, Deut. xiii 13–18, EVV. 12–17. Celsus is cited at n. 3, above.

[10]Tertullian, *Apol.* xxxix. 1 (CCL I, 150); Minucius Felix, *Octavius* viii. 3, 10 Waltzing; *Acta … Cypriani* iv. 1, 172 Musurillo, *Martyrs*.

commonplace.[11] It is a paradigm of the close relationship which could obtain between assertions about Christ and attacks on the church that the fabricated *Acts of Pilate* were circulated to support the persecution under Maximin Daia.[12]

The claim that Christ practised brigandage, a further hostile interpretation of the gathering of disciples, should therefore be considered in relation to anti-Christian charges. It specifies Christ's offence unusually. The general term 'evil-doer' was commonly particularized with words like those already noted applicable to dubious teaching and wonder-working (see n. 8 above).[13] Here Christ is identified as a violent criminal. That remains damaging to the church, however brigandage is understood; but, as Eisler did not fail to note and as recent study has amply documented,[14] the charge of brigandage may of course in ancient usage amount to that of sedition.

The innuendo of sedition readily adhered, as noted above, to anti-philosophical and anti-Christian charges of deception and magic. It already figures alongside deception and magic in the gospels as an express allegation.

Brigandage, however, although it may overlap with sedition in usage, remains distinct. *Stasis* in this sense and *seditio* commonly retain some reference to faction, *lesteia* and *latrocinium* to robber-like activity. Thus in polemic *stasis* may be used of the church's emergence from Jewry (Celsus, see n. 3 above), seen as the revolt and secession of a new party, while *latrocinium* typically denotes brigand-like political violence (so in Cicero of the Catilinarian conspiracy),[15] misgovernment (St Leo the Great had many precedents in pagan political satire when he applied it to a church synod),[16] or misappropriation (as in critiques of territorial gains in

---

[11]The chief evidence for this view is summarised in K. Aland, 'The Relation between Church and State in Early Times: a Reinterpretation', *JTS*, N.S. xix (1968), 115–27 (120–2).

[12]Eusebius, *H.E.* i. 9, i. 11, ix. 5 (GCS 9.1, pp. 72, 80, 810).

[13]W. Bauer, *Das Leben Jesu im Zeitalter der neutestamentlichen Apokryphen* (repr. Darmstadt, 1967), 484 f.

[14]R. MacMullen, 'The Roman Concept of Robber-Pretender', *RIDA* 3rd series, 10 (1963), 221–6; M. Hengel in O. Betz, K. Haacker and M. Hengel (eds.), *Josephus-Studien* (Göttingen, 1974), 176 f, n. 7.

[15]Cicero, *Pro Murena*, 39 (84) 'hoc Catilinae nefarium latrocinium', cited among other passages by I. Opelt, *Die lateinischen Schimpfwörter and verwandte sprachliche Erscheinungen* (Heidelberg, 1965), 132.

[16]Leo, *Ep*, xcv. 2 (ACO 2. 4, 51); parallels in MacMullen, *RIDA* 3rd series 10 (n. 14 above) and Opelt, *Schimpfwörter*, 132 f, 168 f. Comparably, 'MP likens leadership to thugs', part headline in *The Times* of 13 March 1976, 1.

Roman or Jewish origins).[17] It accords with this usage when jurists treat pretenders as brigands (n. 14 above). Josephus touches this range of meaning, but remains close to the literal sense of the word, when he calls rebel-bands *lestai*.[18]

With this distinction in mind it can be understood that up to the time of our citation brigandage is not prominent in anti-Christian charges of sedition.[19] The necessary points of comparison were not well marked. Unlike Josephus' rebels or the factions of the late Roman republic, Christians were not notorious for resort to arms, being indeed well known for the numbers of women and children in their churches.[20] Unlike emperors, imperially-summoned synods at a later date, or pretenders to power, the third-century church did not exercise what was recognisably established government or tyranny. Unlike Rome or Jewry, it had no territorial claims. It looked to hostile observers like a people scattered everywhere, comparable with the Jews in atheistic and anti-social exclusiveness,[21] or like a network of secret societies,[22] or like a quarrelsome religio-philosophical party.[23] Words like *genus, stasis, factio, conspiratio* suited these points of view better than *latrocinium*.

An instance in which Christians were accused as brigands shows the unusual circumstances in which the charge might become plausible. A body of Syrian Christians, according to Hippolytus, followed their bishop into the desert in expectation of Christ's coming and were in danger of being massacred by the governor as brigands and arousing general persecution.[24] It can be inferred that enthusiastic groups, especially where Christianity had penetrated the

---

[17]For Rome parallels to Augustine, *Civ. Dei.* iv. 4 (i, 150 Dombart-Kalb) are collected by MacMullen, *Enemies*, 350, n. 30; for Jewry see Ber. R. 1. 2 (ed. A. A. Halevy (Tel-Aviv, 1956), 2) discussed with parallels in W. Bacher, 'The Supposed Inscription upon "Joshua the Robber"', *JQR* 3 (1891), 354–7.

[18]For the importance of the literal sense in Josephus see M. Smith, 'Zealots and Sicarii, Their Origins and Relations', *HTR* 64 (1971), 1–19 (14); S.J.D. Cohen, *Josephus in Galilee und Rome* (Leiden, 1979), 211–14.

[19]Its absence from Celsus (see pp. 168–9 below) and Minucius Felix is especially striking. For polemic on Christians as public enemies see A. Harnack, *Der Vorwurf des Atheismus in den drei ersten Jahrhunderten* (TU 28.4, Leipzig, 1905), 8–15 and *Die Mission und Ausbreitung des Christentums in den ersten drei Jahrhunderten* (4th edn. Leipzig, 1924) i, 281–9: E.T. *The Expansion of Christianity in the First Three Centuries* (London, 1908) i, 266–78).

[20]Lucian, *Per.* xii, Loeb Classical Library v, 12; Minucius Felix, *Octavius* viii. 4, 11 Waltzing.; Origen, *C. Cels.* iii. 55 f (GCS pp. 250 f).

[21]Harnack, *Mission* i, 281 f (E.T. i, 266–8).

[22]Celsus in Origen, *C. Cels.* i. 1, viii. 17, 39, 198 Bader; Minucius Felix, *Octavius* ix. I f, 11 f Waltzing.

[23]Celsus, n. 3 above.

[24]Hippolytus, *In Dan.* iv. 18 (GCS 1, 230–2).

countryside,[25] might despite discouragement from within the church[26] sometimes lay themselves open to the charge of brigandage by looking like robber-bands. The failure of brigandage to bulk large in anti-Christian polemic nevertheless indicates that such cases will have been exceptional.

Brigandage is however mentioned when Christians complain, and their opponents stress, that Christ and members of his church have been put to death in a way appropriate to robbers (see, with other examples,[27] Origen, *C. Cels.* ii. 44, n. 51 below). The tone of the complaints (n. 26 above) confirms that the point at issue is the moral disgrace implied in such a death and emphasized in the polemic on the cross discussed above. The innuendo of sedition may be present, but is unexpressed.

To assert Christ's brigandage would certainly have contributed to the general impression that Christians were seditious. J. A. Fabricius compared our passage with Suetonius on the Roman Jewish riots *impulsore Chresto*, understood as a reference to Christians.[28] However Suetonius is to be interpreted, the comparison identifies the damaging aspersion of threat to public order cast by this polemic. Our passage might even recall, although the likelihood has not seemed great, an instance of Christians being charged with brigandage. Yet in view of its failure to correspond to any frequently attested form of the anti-Christian charge of sedition, its value to the polemist seems likely to have lain principally in its moral denigration (n. 8 above). We may then compare the eagerly pressed claim of the anti-Montanist writer Apollonius that Alexander the Montanist martyr had once been convicted not for his faith but as a brigand (*lestes*).[29]

It is relevant here that the universally encountered brigand[30] held a sure place in popular imagination. Robbers are the villains of the Midrash and the New Testament Apocrypha as well as of pagan

---

[25]The extent of rural Christianity at the end of the third century is estimated by Harnack, *Mission* ii, 948 f (E.T. ii, 327).

[26]Hippolytus, *In Dan.* iv. 18; Eusebius, *H.E.* v. 16, 18 (episcopal attempts to restrain Montanism), VII. 24 (Dionysius of Alexandria rebuts chiliasm in Arsinoe) (GCS 9.1, 459–68, 472–8, 684–90).

[27]Eusebius, *H.E.* vi. 41 (martyrdom of Nemesion) GCS 9.1, 608); Lactantius, *DI* v. 20, 6 (SC 204, 242).

[28]J. A. Fabricius, *Salutaris Lux Evangelii* (Hamburg, 1731), 158n.

[29]Eusebius, *H.E.* v. 18 (GCS 9.1, 474–6).

[30]To the rich material in MacMullen, *Enemies*, 255–68 add the adoption of *lestes* as a loanword in Hebrew, Aramaic and Syriac: S. P. Brock, 'Greek Words in the Syriac Gospels', *Le Muséon* 80 (1967), 389–426 (406).

romance.[31] Their resemblances to established government are a standing joke[32] and their rivalry with it may win sympathy from those who feel oppressed,[33] but they remain the archetypal evil-doers. When Clement of Alexandria tells of a Christian youth who defects to become a brigand-chief, his bishop is made to say that the young man is 'wicked, abandoned, and more than all, a robber'.[34] For the wicked man and shedder of blood *par excellence* of Ezek. xviii 10, where the Greek versions render *pariṣ* with words for evil-doer in general (LXX has *loimos*, applied to St Paul at Acts xxiv 5), St Jerome keeps the specific *latro*.[35] In *Cena Cypriani*, when the biblical characters attend a fancy-dress party, it is Cain who comes attired as a brigand.[36]

II

An anti-Christian work by a writer who later helped to implement the Diocletianic persecution affirmed, according to Lactantius, 'that Christ, driven out by the Jews, gathered a band of nine hundred men and committed acts of brigandage': 'Christum ... a Iudaeis fugatum collecta nongentorum hominum manu latrocinia fecisse.'[37]

The writer, not named by Lactantius here, is probably to be identified with Sossianus Hierocles, governor of Bithynia in 303 and prefect of Egypt in 307.[38] He led the persecution in both provinces.

---

[31]S. Krauss, *Griechen und Römer* (Monumenta Talmudica V. i, repr. Darmstadt, 1972), 161–3, nos. 383–90; R. Söder, *Die apokryphen Apostelgeschichten und die romanhafte Literatur der Antike* (Stuttgart, 1932), 168 f.

[32]Eisler, ΙΗΣΟΥΣ i, xxv (E.T. 10) and n. 17 above; cp. Stith Thompson, *Motif-Index of Folk-Literature* (revised edn. Copenhagen, 1955–8), v. 418 U11.2: 'He who steals much called king; he who steals little called robber.'

[33]On Palestine before the First Revolt see Josephus, *BJ* ii. 253 with A. Schlatter, *Die Theologie des Judentums nach dem Bericht des Josefus* (Gütersloh, 1932), 171.

[34]Clement of Alexandria, *Quis Dives Salvetur*, xlii. 9 cited in Eusebius, *H.E.* iii. 23 (GCS 17, 189).

[35]Jerome, *In Ezechielem* vi, on 18: 10 (CCL 75, 242).

[36]A. Harnack, *Drei wenig beachtete cyprianische Schriften und die 'Acta Pauli'* (TU 19.3b, Leipzig, 1899), 5 (dating the work *c.* 300–600), 12 (text). For Cain as brigand cp. Josephus, *AJ* i. 61, 66.

[37]Lactantius, *DI* v. 3, 4; P. Monat, *Lactance: Institutions Divines, Livre V*, 2 vols., SC 204–5 (Paris, 1973) i, 140 f: ii, 44, 50.

[38]A. H. M. Jones, J. R. Martindale and J. Morris, *The Prosopography of the Later Roman Empire* (Cambridge, 1971), 432, summarize evidence for the identification further discussed by Monat, *Lactance*, ii, 44 and T. D. Barnes, 'Porphyry *Against the Christians*: Date and the Attribution of Fragments', *JTS* N.S. xxiv (1973), 424–42 (437 f, 441). J. Geffcken, *Zwei griechische Apologeten* (Leipzig and Berlin, 1907), 291 n., not discussed by the foregoing, doubts the identification because Eusebius (see following note) says that Hierocles admits Christ's miracles and calls him a man of God; but polemic is not always consistent, and admission of the miracles is regularly allied as in Celsus with grave moral charges.

His work addressed to the Christians appears like that of Celsus to have attacked the New Testament both by criticism and – as our passage indicates – by counter-assertion. Eusebius wrote a reply in which he claimed that, apart from its comparison of Christ with Apollonius of Tyana, the book was entirely derivative.[39] Internal evidence at any rate suggests that the passage cited by Lactantius here did not originate with Hierocles.

It consists of three articulated statements: Christ was expelled by the Jews, he gathered his band, he committed acts of brigandage.[40] To be 'driven out by the Jews' implies withdrawal by Jesus some time before the end of the ministry as a result of opposition from the nation as a whole. Such collective opposition at an early stage is envisaged at John v 16, 18 (cp. the opposition from more limited circles at Mark ii 6 and parallels). Withdrawal, at a later stage in the Johannine tradition as we have it, but before the end of the ministry, is described at John xi 54.[41] Retrojection of collective opposition is as natural to the narrator as it is useful to the polemist. Hostile accounts from that of the Jew of Celsus onwards link it with the withdrawal.[42] The closest parallel to our statement is in Toledoth Jeshu where Jesus flees from Israel, represented by the Wise, near the beginning of his ministry, and gathers a band of evil disciples.[43] This first statement in Lactantius is then one instance of a development of traditions which received a different treatment in the gospels as we now have them.

The gathering of nine hundred stands in contrast with the minimizing of the disciples' numbers in Celsus (i. 62, 65; ii. 46; iii. 10; pp. 58, 76, 86 Bader). It may perhaps have arisen from the early emphasis on large numbers (n. 9 above). This emphasis reappears in Christian sources up to Hierocles's time, Origen replying to Celsus that there were not merely ten disciples, nor only a hundred, nor only a thousand[44] and Eusebius envisaging many apostles in addition to the twelve and the seventy.[45] In Jewish tradition large numbers are assumed in one of the charges against Jesus formulated in the tannaitic period (n. 9 above). Samuel Krauss compared with

---

[39]Eusebius, C. Hieroclem 1 (PG XXII. 797).

[40]Eisler, ΙΗΣΟΥΣ i, xxv: E.T. 10 obscures the order of events by a mistranslation.

[41]E. Bammel, 'Ex illa itaque die consilium fecerunt ... ', in E. Bammel (ed.), The Trial of Jesus (London, 1970), 11–40 (35, 38).

[42]Bammel, in Trial, 30–2.

[43]P. 170 below and the texts printed in S. Krauss, Das Leben Jesu nach jüdischen Quellen (Berlin, 1902), 40 f, 68 f.

[44]Origen, C. Cels. ii. 46; cp. iii. 10 (GCS 168, 210).

[45]Eusebius, H.E. i, 12 (GCS 9.1, 82).

our passage the number 310 or 320, or general references to large numbers, found in descriptions of the disciples in Toledoth Jeshu.[46] Here again the statement in Lactantius is a not unparalleled instance of development of tradition attested in the New Testament.

Acts of brigandage, the theme of the third statement, are not clearly asserted of Christ in earlier polemic as now preserved (n. 19 above).[47] It has however been claimed, in line with Eusebius's judgment of the work in general, that Hierocles simply took over the charge from Celsus.[48] The *Alethes Logos* in fact appears to preserve Celsus's own view of Christian origins,[49] together with the independent view of his Jewish source[50] – both close to our passage in different ways – as well as incidental remarks from both Celsus and the Jew likening Christ or Christians to robbers.[51] None of the passages concerned, however, can be said to offer an exact parallel.

That most closely related to our citations is likely to be i. 62, where the Jew of Celsus claims that the disciples were ten or eleven infamous men who got their living by disgraceful and importunate beggary. It belongs to the same class of narrative polemic and, like the two statements of Hierocles already considered, finds a parallel in inner-Jewish tradition.[52] Yet it seems improbable that Hierocles has himself adapted the text in Celsus. That would have meant not only changing beggary to robbery, but also contradicting the

---

[46]Krauss, *Leben Jesu*, 173.

[47]Bauer, *Leben Jesu*, 468.

[48]G. Loesche, 'Haben die späteren neuplatonischen Polemiker gegen das Christenthum das Werk des Celsus benutzt?', *ZWT* 27 (1883), 257–302 (284) finds the germ of the idea in *C. Cels*. ii. 12, viii. 14; Geffcken, *Apologeten*, 291 also pointed to ii. 12; Bauer, *Leben Jesu*, p. 468 saw it as impossible to identify the source, but referred in a footnote to *C. Cels* i. 30, ii, 12 and 44, iii. 59. Among the passages cited by these scholars, i. 30 (GCS i, 81) is Origen's own statement that Christ's persuasiveness was not that of a tyrant, a robber, or a rich man; the others, all from Celsus or his source, are summarized in the three following notes.

[49]The faction-ridden church (iii, 10, 12; viii. 49, 86, 205 Bader) began from Christ's *stasis* against Jewry (iii. 1, 5; viii. 14, 85, 197 Bader, cp. p. 163 above); the few early Christians (iii. 10, presumably including the disciples, see next note) must then by inference be regarded as seditious, but this is not made explicit.

[50]The disciples numbered ten or eleven (i. 62, 65; ii. 46, 58, 76 Bader) and lived by begging (i. 62).

[51]Christians being self-confessed sinners are the sort of people a robber would call, Celsus in ii. 59, 97 Bader, perhaps dependent on ii. 12, 44, 65 f, 76 Bader, where the Jew claims that Jesus did not keep his followers' loyalty even as well as a *lestarchos* might have, and that anyone as shameless as the Christians could assert that a punished robber and murderer was a god, because he foretold his sufferings to his *syllestai*. For the moral burden of this polemic see p. 166 above.

[52]J. J. Huldricus, *Historia Jeschuae Nazareni* (Leiden, 1705), 51–3.

argument on numbers to which Celsus clung (p. 168 above). It is more likely that Hierocles reproduces an existing variant of the Jew of Celsus's story.

This third statement, based on an existing narrative as it thus appears to be, nevertheless lacks the degree of contact with New Testament traditions noted in the two preceding clauses. It makes both Christ and the disciples men of habitual robber-like violence. The New Testament shows the disciples as (to begin with) multitudinous (n. 9 above, and Monat, *Lactance* ii, 50), ready to use arms for defence at Christ's arrest (Luke xxii 35–8, 49; John xviii 10), expecting an earthly kingdom and opposed at least in Peter's case to Christ's will to endure (Mark viii 32).[53] For Christ himself, however, we can only compare his suffering a robber's death, as is underlined by the Barabbas story (Monat, ii, 50) and the crucifixion between two robbers or malefactors 'in the same condemnation', Luke xxiii 40 (Eisler and Bauer, n. 40 and n. 47 above). The narrative of the two swords, Luke xxii 25–38, linked with our statement by Eisler, ii, 270: E.T. p. 370, needs drastic exegesis (two swords for each disciple, Eisler, ii, 268: E.T. p. 369) before it gains close resemblance. Christians continue to admit the disciples' sinfulness (Barn. viii 9) and the shame of the cross, and polemists fasten as seen already on these points (n. 8 above). In the fifth-century *Altercatio Simonis et Theophili*,[54] as E. Bammel notes,[55] the Jewish debater is depicted as drawing an implicit comparison between Christ and Absalom the parricide. Yet apart from our citation surviving polemic does not attach the charge of brigandage to Christ or the disciples in the ante-Nicene period.

For passages of more marked similarity we must turn, as Eisler and M. Lods both observed, to later Jewish material.[56] Huldrich's text of Toledoth Jeshu (n. 52 above) makes the ministry begin when Jesus kills his father. Israel refuses to associate with him, 'vain and wanton men', 'violent men' (*pariṣim*), and finally a brigand chief (*r'osh beryonim = archilestes*) join him, and he flees with 'his men' to the desert.[57] In other text-forms, as Eisler noted, Jesus's numerous followers (n. 46 above) use force against the Jews, attempts to rescue

---

[53]C. H. Dodd, *Historical Tradition in the Fourth Gospel* (Cambridge, 1963), 77–80.

[54]B. Blumenkranz, *Les auteurs chrétiens latins du moyen âge sur les juifs et le judaisme* (Paris, 1963), 27–31, no. 13.

[55]E. Bammel, 'Christus Parricida', VC 26 (1972), 259–62.

[56]Eisler, ΙΗΣΟΥΣ ii, 253, n. 3 (E.T. pp. 363 n. 2, 370 n. 1); M. Lods, 'Etude sur les sources juives de la polémique de Celse contre les chrétiens', RHPR 21 (1941), 1–33 (18 f).

[57]Huldricus, *Historia*, 35 f.

him during the ministry developing into a war after his death.[58] The standard designation of the disciples in these texts is *parişim*, which in biblical Hebrew, as in Jer. vii 11 (LXX σπήλαιον λῃστῶν, cited at Mark xi 17 and parallels), may denote robber, but also comes to mean (cp. the Greek versions of Ezek. xviii 10, p. 167 above) any violent transgressor. The same word is applied to 'Jesus and his companions' who encourage Gaius Caesar to impose emperor-worship on the Jews in a story related to Toledoth Jeshu found in two texts of Josippon.[59] Dan. xi 14, where the word is used for 'The men of violence', is regularly applied to Christians by Jewish writers from Saadia (tenth century) onwards.[60] Thus used it was no doubt often taken, as by Jefet b. Ali (tenth century),[61] of breach of religious law; but its wider application is illustrated by Josippon's use of it for Josephus's *lestai*.[62] *Latrocinia* in the sense of highway robberies are not specified of Christ in these sources; but the disciples use violence during the ministry, although, at this stage of the narrative, as opposed to that dealing with events after the crucifixion, the theme is subordinate to the ruling emphases on miracle and false teaching. These thematically-related passages may be held to strengthen the likelihood that the source of Hierocles's third statement is Jewish.

The three statements may now be considered as a unity. They look like a fragment of a longer story. A comparable fragment-like series, relating events from the conception to the first self-predication of Jesus, occurs among the passages ascribed by Celsus to the Jew (ii. 28, 53 Bader) and is fully paralleled in inner-Jewish sources.[63] Similarly the statements in Hierocles are only paralleled with the same interconnection in inner-Jewish sources. Recalling other patristic evidence for Jewish accounts of Christ[64] we may propose an ultimately Jewish source for this citation. The narrative could then have reached Hierocles directly from a Jew or through a

[58]Eisler, ΙΗΣΟΥΣ ii, 516–18, citing Krauss, *Leben Jesu*, 42, 45, 47, 76 f, 72, 120 f; further texts in W. Horbury, 'A Critical Examination of the Toledoth Jeshu' (Diss., Cambridge, 1970), 188, 192, 195, 242–4, 246 f, 291, 295.

[59]Eisler, ΙΗΣΟΥΣ i, 498; I. Lévi, 'Jésus, Caligula et Claude dans une interpolation du Yosiphon', *REJ* 91 (1931), 135–54 (139).

[60]The list in Judah Rosenthal, *Studies and Texts in Jewish History, Literature and Religion* (2 vols., Jerusalem, 1967) i, 204 includes among others Maimonides, Rashi, Ibn Ezra and Abravenel.

[61]D. S. Margoliouth, *A Commentary on the Book of Daniel by Jephet ibn Ali the Karaite* (Oxford, 1889), 61 f.

[62]G. D. Cohen, *The Book of Tradition by Abraham Ibn Daud* (London, 1969), p. xxxix.

[63]Lods, *RHPhR* 21 (1941), 31 f.

[64]E.g. H. L. Strack, *Jesus, die Häretiker und die Christen nach den ältesten jüdischen Angaben* (Leipzig, 1910), 8*-11*, 14*; B. Blumenkranz, *Die Judenpredigt Augustins* (repr. Paris, 1973), 87 f.

pagan, and it could have arisen at any time up to shortly before the date of his book.

Its potential in the hands of a polemist was obviously considerable. The Jews, to whose writings Christians constantly appealed, could be shown to have lost no time in rejecting Christ's claims. The numerous disciples vaunted by the Christians were engaged in nothing else than brigandage. As already noted, the charge of sedition was thus reinforced; and, most importantly, both Christ and his followers were branded with the mark of the most cordially detested class of violent evil-doers (section I above).

In the context of the present enquiry the historical value of the story especially concerns us. The first two items in the narrative may be considered as hostile interpretations of traditions which also entered the gospels (notably John xi 54, Luke vi 17, see p. 168 above). Brigandage, the third item, whether taken as robbery or insurrection, by contrast necessarily implies habitual acts of violence on the part of Jesus. It thereby conflicts with the range of New Testament traditions on his character. The Pauline epistles already presuppose a portrait of the earthly Christ with which this implication would be wholly inconsistent. Appeals to the self-abnegation and gentleness of Christ such as those of Rom. xv 3, I Cor. x 33 to xi 1, II Cor. x 1, even if they allude to the condescension of the nativity as well as to the ministry, would have been stultified, as C. K. Barrett points out, had it been known that the life of Jesus differed in character from what the gospels now depict.[65]

This discord with the range of New Testament evidence, then, makes it probable that we have here later invention, perhaps in a development, out of contact with Christian tradition, of the tale of beggary cited by the Jew of Celsus (i. 62). The crime of the crucified has been made to fit his punishment.[66]

III

For Eisler[67] Hierocles stood pre-eminent among ancient non-Christian witnesses to Christ, Josephus of course excepted. Eisler linked our passage with the charge of magic in Celsus and Lucian, and with

[65]C. K. Barrett, *A Commentary on the Second Epistle to the Corinthians* (London, 1973), 246, on x 1. For Paul's concern with the character of the earthly Jesus see G. N. Stanton, *Jesus of Nazareth in New Testament Preaching*, SNTS Monographs 27 (Cambridge, 1974), 99–110.
[66]P. 166 and p. 169, n. 51, and Bammel in *Trial*, p. 165.
[67]Eisler, ΙΗΣΟΥΣ, i, xxvi: his words on the importance of this passage are omitted in E.T. 11.

Celsus's phrase *leader of sedition* (see n. 3 and n. 49 above), as typifying the pagan estimate of Jesus. He valued our passage especially, however, because he took it as a clear exposition of the Roman view of Jesus as a rebel, and the best commentary on Pilate's *titulus*.

Eisler took *latrocinia* here in the legal sense of high treason. He pointed out that for the jurists (n. 14 above) a pretender is *latronum dux*, his adherents *latrones*. Elsewhere in his book he gathered modern instances of the same nomenclature, including contemporary newspaper reports of the Nicaraguan independence movement.[68] He thrice suggested in passing that the passage illuminated other aspects of the ministry. Thus he thinks, (see the passage cited in n. 6 above), that armed disciples would have been called *sicarii* by Josephus, just as Hierocles terms them robbers. Indeed, Christ's several hundred followers begging their way must have been called *latrones*, their importunity being comparable with that of mediaeval 'sturdy beggars'.[69] Lastly, he sees general agreement between our citation and the report in Slavonic Josephus that a hundred and fifty helpers and a multitude of the people joined Jesus on the Mount of Olives.[70] In this instance Eisler's mistranslation (n. 40 above), that Jesus 'was *defeated* by the Jews *when he had been* committing robberies', may by wrongly referring our passage to the arrest have caused him to see a greater resemblance between the two texts than really obtains. His rendering does not, however, seriously affect the argument for his main contention, that the passage rightly expounds Jesus's offence under Roman law. While Jews saw Christ as a leader-astray, for pagans, Eisler claimed (over-estimating the distinctiveness of their polemic), he was a magician, an instigator of rebellion, and a leader of robber bands. This pagan interpretation, especially as exemplified in our passage, closely approximated in Eisler's view to a true estimate of Jesus's ministry.

Eisler's keen eye for whatever might support his theory rightly discerned that this passage deserves attention. It is his merit to have shown that, so far from being a wholly isolated absurdity,[71] it has links with the common anti-Christian charge of sedition and with the sketch of the disciples as men of violence in Toledoth Jeshu. Our present study of the passage in the same context of pagan and Jewish polemic has suggested that it is older than Hierocles, forming in all

---

[68]Ibid. i, 194, n. 3 (this section omitted in E.T.).
[69]Eisler, ΙΗΣΟΥΣ, ii, 253 f, n. 3 (E.T. 363 (lacking the mediaeval analogy)).
[70]Ibid. ii, 440, n. 51, omitted in E.T. 457.
[71]So for example P. de Labriolle, *La Réaction paienne* (Paris, 1942), 310.

probability a fragment of an originally Jewish narrative of Christ's life taken up, like the stories of the Jew of Celsus, by a pagan polemist. Yet it has also seemed probable, in contrast with Eisler's view, that as polemic the passage aims more directly at moral denigration than the charge of sedition, and that as historical assertion it rests in its most important detail, *latrocinia fecisse*, on hostile invention. Its significance for the historian lies rather in its interconnected but fragmentary character, suggesting the existence of a fuller story and confirming that narrative polemic on Jesus, comparable with that current in later Jewish–Christian debate, must be reckoned with in any account of contacts between Jews, pagans and Christians in the ante-Nicene period.

The New Testament evidence on the questions raised by our passage is examined elsewhere in this volume. Within the limits of the present study we may note one final consideration arising from the material under review. Early anti-Christian polemic as preserved to us in respect of the life of Jesus concentrates to a marked degree on teaching and wonder-working. So already where the New Testament records corroborative evidence for the charge 'king of the Jews' it refers to what an opponent would have called charlatanry or deception rather than brigandage, γοητεία or ἀπάτη rather than λῃστεία.[72] Luke xxiii 2, 5, 14 speak of *teaching* such as might raise sedition,[73] in John xi 47 f *miracles* are specified; in John xix 7 the accusers bidden to support their charge, point to *teaching* in breach of the Torah. These are simply negative views of the activities identified in Luke xxiv 19 as prophetic *deed and word*. Despite the innuendo of subversion in polemic on these points (n. 2 above) and the recurrent charge of sedition (p. 163 and nn. 9 and 10), polemical

---

[72]For the distinction see Josephus, *BJ* ii, 254–64, where the *sicarii*, 'another kind of λῃσταί' (254), differ from another body of villains, with purer hands but more impious intentions' (258) who pretend to inspiration but are πλάνοι ... ἄνθρωποι καὶ ἀπατεῶνες (259); 261–3 deal with the Egyptian false prophet (γόης, 261); and finally γόητες and λῃστρικοί band together (264). (This passage is misleadingly said to equate the two, in E. Schürer, *History of the Jewish People in the Time of Jesus Christ*, as revised by G. Vermes and F. Millar (Edinburgh 1973–9) i, 462, n. 29; but they are justly distinguished with reference to *BJ* vi, 286, ibid. ii, 605 f. (by C. T. R. Hayward). The men of violence are likewise linked but contrasted with teachers and wonder-workers at the parallel *AJ*. xx, 167 (the distinction is overlooked by Eisler, ΙΗΣΟΥΣ i, 512 f. (E.T. (abbreviated) 110)): τὰ μὲν οὖν τῶν λῃστῶν ἔργα defiled the city, οἱ δὲ γόητες καὶ ἀπατεῶνες persuaded the people. On γόης as the pejorative equivalent of προφήτης (n. 3 above) see E. Fascher, ΠΡΟΦΗΤΗΣ (Giessen, 1927), 207 f.; for γοητεία as primarily referring to self-proclamation, ἀπάτη to its effect E. Bammel in Betz-Haacker-Hengel (eds.), *Josephus-Studien*, 13 and n. 34.

[73]That this language was probably taken by the evangelist to signify a political charge, but may in fact preserve a trace of an accusation under Jewish law, is suggested by Dodd, *Historical Tradition*, 117 n. 1, 217 n. 2.

accounts of Christ's life continue to depict him as a false prophet rather than a bandit. W. Bauer's collection of material shows that, even allowing for possible loss, our passage is exceptional.[74]

There are instances, as we have seen, where polemical narratives of Christ seem to depend ultimately on traditions incorporated into the New Testament rather than the New Testament writings themselves. It is the more striking that pagan and Jew, no less than Christian, appear to have proceeded from data on the life of Christ in which practices definable as the sorcery and deceit of a false prophet predominated over activity which could be straightforwardly identified as insurrection.

[74]Bauer, *Leben Jesu*, 468.

6

TERTULLIAN ON THE JEWS IN THE LIGHT OF
DE SPECTACULIS XXX. 5–6

Jewish–Christian relations in Tertullian's Carthage have received considerable attention. (On comment since this chapter was first published, see p. 18, nn. 46–7, above.) Renewed comparison of Tertullian with the *haggadah*[1] and *halakah*[2] has emphasized exegetical similarities, but seems to fall short of establishing direct influence of post-biblical Jewish tradition on his writings.[3] Archaeological evidence is likewise inconclusive.[4] The chief body of data is therefore formed by Tertullian's specific references to Jews. These have been taken to show close and hostile contact between church and synagogue.[5] Alternatively, it is argued that Tertullian was chiefly concerned with biblical as opposed to contemporary Judaism.[6] His allusions to Jewish antagonism[7] refer to New Testament times,[8] and, when he does clearly speak of contemporary Jews, the references

[1] L. Ginzberg, *The Legends of the Jews*, v (Philadelphia, 1925), p. ix: J. M. Ford, 'Was Montanism a Jewish-Christian Heresy?', *JEH* xvii (1966), 145–58 (155–7).

[2] Y. (F.) Baer, 'Israel, the Christian Church and the Roman Empire from the Time of Septimius Severus to the Edict of Toleration of A.D. 313', *Scripta Hierosolymitana*, vii (1961), 86–95; J. J. Petuchowski, 'Halakhah in the Church Fathers', in W. Jacob–F. C. Schwartz–V. W. Kavaler (edd.), *Essays in Honor of Solomon B. Freehof* (Pittsburgh, 1964), 264–8: Ford, 155–7.

[3] Cf. E. E. Urbach, 'The Laws of Idolatry in the Light of Historical and Archaeological Facts in the Third Century', *Eretz-Israel* v (1958), 202, n. 116: T. D. Barnes, *Tertullian* (Oxford, 1971), 100, 273.

[4] No indubitably Christian epitaph is known from the Jewish cemetery at Gammarth, according to J. Ferron, 'Épigraphie juive', *Cahiers de Byrsa*, vi (Paris, 1956), 99–103, followed (with further references) by Barnes, 273 f. On the Carthaginian lamp which may symbolize the triumph of Church over Synagogue see M. Simon, *Recherches d'histoire judéo-chrétienne* (Paris, 1962), 182, 187, 203 f.

[5] P. Monceaux, 'Les colonies juives dans l'Afrique romaine', *REJ* xliv (1902) 4, 17–19; Simon, 32; H. Z. (J. W.) Hirschberg, *A History of the Jews in North Africa* I (Jerusalem, 1965), 43–51; W. H. C. Frend, 'Tertulliano e gli ebrei', *Rivista di storia e letteratura religiosa*, iv (1968), 3–10; idem, 'A Note on Tertullian and the Jews', in F. L. Cross (ed.), *Studia Patristica* x. i (*TU* cvii, Berlin, 1970), 291–6; idem, 'A Note on Jews and Christians in Third-Century North Africa', *JTS* N.S. xxi (1970), 92–6.

[6] Barnes, 91 f.

[7] Notably *Ad Nat.* 1. xiv. 2, *seminarium ... infamiae nostrae* (similar statements, with stronger past reference, at *Adv. Iud.* xiii. 26, parallel with *Adv. Marc.* III xxiii. 3, IV. xiv. 16); *Apol.* vii. 3, *hostes ... proprii ex aemulatione Iudaei; Scorp.* x. 10, *synagogas Iudaeorum, fontes persecutionum.*

[8] H. Tränkle, *Q.S.F. Tertulliani Adversus Iudaeos* (Wiesbaden, 1964), lxxiii, followed by Barnes, 'Tertullian's *Scorpiace*', *JTS* N.S. xx (1969), 132, and op. cit., 91 f.

betray a lack of real contact. Nothing indicates, on this view, that Carthaginian Jewry exerted much influence on Tertullian or his community.[9]

The bearing of *De Spectaculis* xxx. 5–6 on this question is considered here. It has long been recognized that in this passage Tertullian cites contemporary Jewish polemic. The citation has however received the barest allusion,[10] and (so far as the writer is aware) no discussion, in recent study of Tertullian on the Jews.

At the *spectaculum* of the Lord's coming, Tertullian writes,[11] he might well wish to watch especially

eos ... qui in Dominum desaevierunt. hic est ille, dicam, fabri aut quaestuariae filius, sabbati destructor, Samarites et daemonium habens; hic est, quem a Iuda redemistis, hic est ille harundine et colaphis diverberatus, sputamentis dedecoratus, felle et aceto potatus; hic est, quem clam discentes subripuerunt ut resurrexisse dicatur, vel hortulanus detraxit, ne lactucae suae frequentia commeantium laederentur.

The τόπος of Jewish confusion at the Second Coming, linked especially with Zech. xii 10–12,[12] is here given fresh content. Tertullian makes the customary reference to the part played by the Jews in the Passion, but (in contrast with *Adv. Iud.* xiv. 6 = *Adv. Marc.* III. vii. 6) without using Zechariah. This section on the Passion (*hic est quem a Iuda ... potatus*) is sandwiched, moreover, within a collection of Jewish assertions on Jesus' origin, mission, and resurrection. Tertullian looks forward to retorting these sayings on their authors.

Clearly most of the sayings are in New Testament form,[13] although this does not exclude the possibility of their independent origin or post-biblical currency. In two cases, however, Tertullian adds an alternative which is much less closely linked with the biblical text. These additions are *aut quaestuariae [filius]*[14] and *vel hortulanus ... laederentur.*[15]

The first addition corresponds to a Jewish charge of the Tannaitic

---

[9]Tränkle, lxxiii f.; Barnes, *Tertullian*, 92 f.

[10]Baer, 88, n. 29.

[11]Minor variants are registered by E. Dekkers, in *CCL* i (Turnhout, 1954), 253, and E. Castorina, *Quinti Septimi Florentis Tertulliani De Spectaculis* (Florence, 1961), 390–2.

[12]Cf. Rev. i 7, Barn. vii. 9 f., Justin, 1 *Apol.* lii. 10–12, *Dial.* xiv. 8, xxxii. 2, lxiv. 7, cxviii. 1, cxxvi. 1, Tertullian, *Adv. Iud.* xiv. 6 = *Adv. Marc.* III. vii. 6.

[13]H. L. Strack, *Jesus, die Häretiker und die Christen nach den ältesten jüdischen Angaben* (Leipzig, 1910), 14*.

[14]Probably implied, but not stated, at Mark vi 3, John viii 41; cf. E. Stauffer, 'Jeschu ben Mirjam (Mk. 6: 3)', in E. E. Ellis–M. Wilcox (edd.), *Neotestamentica et Semitica: Studies in Honour of Matthew Black* (Edinburgh, 1969), 119–28.

[15]Cf. John xx. 15, where, however, there is no explicit indication of a Jewish charge.

period[16] which also forms an element in the *Toledoth Jeshu*.[17] This charge is attested in a number of Christian sources.[18] *De Spectaculis*, dated 196–7 by Barnes,[19] is the earliest of these, although the quotation of the Pantera-story by Celsus shows that the charge could be known to a non-Jew (who identifies it as Jewish) probably about twenty years before.[20] The currency of this account suggests that Tertullian here departs from New Testament language in order to quote a contemporary Jewish allegation.

Tertullian's second addition is comparatively unfamiliar in Christian sources. This is already suggested by its omission in St Jerome's imitation of the passage, *Ep*. xiv. 11.[21] The mention of the *hortulanus* is, as Samuel Krauss observed, the earliest attestation of a story known, once again, from the *Toledoth Jeshu*.[22] Here the gardener is a faithful Jew who disposes of the body in a watercourse. That the motif from Tertullian occurs also in the Aramaic form of the *Toledoth*[23] was emphasized by Louis Ginzberg.[24] Within Christian tradition the story is witnessed or rebutted in Commodian[25] and in various New Testament Apocrypha.[26]

---

[16]The name *ben Pantera* is applied to Jesus in Tos. Hullin ii. 22, 24 and parallels; for texts see Strack, 2–6, for discussion of the various spellings of the name S. Leibermann, 'Notes on Chapter I of Midrash *Koheleth Rabbah*', in E. E. Urbach–R. J. Z. Werblowsky–Ch. Wirszubski (edd.), *Studies in Mysticism and Religion Presented to Gershom G. Scholem* (Jerusalem, 1967), Hebrew Section, 172 f., and for a dating of the Jewish Pantera-story in the first century D. Rokeah, 'Ben Stara is Ben Pantera – towards the clarification of a philological-historical problem', *Tarbiz*, xxxix (1969–70), 9–18.

[17]S. Krauss, *Das Leben Jesu nach jüdischen Quellen* (Berlin, 1902), 187 f.

[18]Notably Origen, *Contra Celsum* i. 28, 32, 69 and *Comm. in Ioh*. xx. 16 (14); *Martyrium S. Cononis*, iv. 6 (M. Santer kindly drew my attention to this text); Eusebius, *Eclogae Propheticae*, iii. 10: Elisaeus of Vartabed, in V. Langlois, *Collection des historiens anciens et modernes de l'Arménie*, ii (Paris, 1869), 191, 195; cf. *Ev. Thom*. 105, *Acta Pilati* ii. 3, S. Cyril *ad* John viii. 39, 41, and further sources in Strack, 10*–13*, 17*.

[19]Barnes, *Tertullian*, 54 f.

[20]For the dating of Celsus' work *c*. 177–80 see H. Chadwick, *Origen: Contra Celsum* (repr. Cambridge, 1965), xxvi–xxviii.

[21]Slightly earlier, largely perhaps for stylistic reasons, St Jerome has added to Tertullian's list the charge of *magus* which was familiar to him (cf. *Ep*. xlv. 6, where different texts ascribe it either to past or to present Jews).

[22]Krauss, 3, 247 f. The *lactucae* continue to figure in Jewish tradition about the death and burial of Jesus; cf. E. Bammel, 'Excerpts from a New Gospel?', *Novum Testamentum*, x (1968), 5 f.

[23]For light from this text-form on an obscure statement of the Jew of Celsus see E. Bammel, 'Origen *Contra Celsum*, i. 41 and the Jewish Tradition', *JTS* N.S. xix (1968), 211–13.

[24]L. Ginzberg, *Genizah Studies in Memory of Doctor Solomon Schechter*, i (New York, 1928), 324, 332 n.

[25]*Carmen Apologeticum*, 440 ('infamant: in puteum misimus illum'), 477 f.; cf. B. Blumenkranz, *Die Judenpredigt Augustins* (Basel, 1946), 88 n.

[26]*Gamaliel* (the Jews show Pilate a body in a well): *Bartholomew* (the gardener is ostensibly in league with the Jews, but really intends to remove the body in order to treat it honourably);

This combination of two items known from post-biblical Jewish sources makes it highly probable that Tertullian is citing current Jewish anti-Christian polemic. An analogous allusion is his report that Jews call Christians *Nazareni*.[27]

We may conclude that Carthaginian Jews argued against Christianity. The Christological direction of their polemic is paralleled, for instance, in Smyrna[28] and in later Africa.[29] Tertullian was aware of these arguments, and hence knew that Jewish antagonism had continued into his own time. In his references to this antagonism, where the context allows, he is therefore likely to have had the present as well as the past in mind. Equally, since Jewry impinged on the Christian consciousness with these fundamental criticisms, the passages where contemporary Jews are mentioned should not be interpreted so as to suggest that Judaism was unimportant to Tertullian and his community.[30]

---

for the former see A. Mingana, *Woodbrooke Studies*, ii (Cambridge, 1928), 204, 207, and M. A. van den Oudenrijn, *Gamaliel* (Freiburg, Schweiz, 1959), 67, for the latter E. A. Wallis Budge, *Coptic Apocrypha in the Dialect of Upper Egypt* (London, 1913), 188. The passages were linked with Tertullian and the *Toledoth Jeshu* by H. J. Schonfield, *According to the Hebrews* (London, 1937), 99 f., 125–8.

[27]*Adv. Marc.* iv. viii. 1: for the equivalence to Hebrew נוצרים cf. St. Jerome's statements on the cursing of Christians under the name of *Nazareni*, referring to the mention of נוצרים in the *Birkath ha-Minim*: texts in Strack, 66* f., 30 f., and C. W. Dugmore, *The Influence of the Synagogue upon the Divine Office* (2nd edn, London, 1964), 3 f., and a further reference to Jerome in Ch. Merchavia, *The Church versus Talmudic and Midrashic Literature [500–1248]* (Jerusalem, 1970), 82, n. 61; see also pp. 10–11, 68–75, above.

[28]*Martyrium S. Pionii*, xii. 3, 8 (Knopf-Krüger, 52); for dating see Barnes, 'Pre-Decian *Acta Martyrum*', *JTS* N.S. xix (1968), 529–31.

[29]See the Augustinian references in Blumenkranz, loc. cit.

[30]*Iei.* xiii. 6, where the Jews are commended as exemplifying fidelity to ancestral tradition, is oddly cited by Barnes, *Tertullian*, 92 n., to show that for Tertullian Judaism was a faith not only 'unchanging' but also 'not to be taken seriously or deserving proper attention'.

7

THE PURPOSE OF PSEUDO-CYPRIAN, *ADVERSUS IUDAEOS*

The title *Adversus Iudaeos* was affixed in this case – before 365, as the Cheltenham list attests[1] – to a sermon which condemns 'Israel', but finally envisages Jewish conversion. Modern readers have estimated it so variously as to raise doubts about its aim. (On some relevant work published since this chapter first appeared, see pp. 20–25, above.) Considered as an anti-Judaic argument, this writing seemed to offer *'nihil congruens aut solidum'* (Ellies Dupin, who joined another anti-Judaic writing from the Cyprianic appendix, *ad Vigilium*, in the same condemnation); and Lukyn Williams, with all his sympathetic knowledge of the genre, found this 'an emotional sermon with very little in it'.[2]

The preacher has pretensions to philosophy and oratory which were dismissed by Nautin[3] as second-hand, but have helped to support a succession of attributions to authors of some repute – Hippolytus,[4] Novatian[5] and Melito of Sardis.[6] The discussion of authorship has sometimes highlighted features of the composition which seem consistent with the ancient title. Bunsen, in a comment which reflects his own outlook but is not without significance for an estimate of the work, found it 'far more interesting' than the Greek fragment *Adversus Iudaeos* attributed to Hippolytus; for the Platonizing author of the Latin text eschewed the listing of biblical proofs, and spoke to the heart of the Jews.[7] Landgraf compared this preacher's view that the Jews are guilty, but can still hope for mercy if they repent, with Novatian's references to Jewry, in which

[1] W. Sanday, 'The Cheltenham List of the Canonical Books of the Old and New Testament and of the Writings of Cyprian', *Studia Biblica et Ecclesiastica*, 3 (1891) 217–303 (278 f.).

[2] L. E. Dupin, *Nova Bibliotheca Auctorum Ecclesiasticorum*, i (Paris, 1692) 269; A. Lukyn Williams, *Adversus Judaeos* (Cambridge, 1935), 65.

[3] P. Nautin, *Le dossier d'Hippolyte et de Méliton* (Paris, 1953), 123.

[4] The history of this attribution, which arose from a gratuitous conflation of the pseudo-Cyprianic sermon with the Greek anti-Jewish fragment ascribed to Hippolytus, but was supported by other arguments, is sketched by Nautin, loc. cit.

[5] A. Harnack, *Die Chronologie der altchristlichen Litteratur bis Eusebius*, 2 (Leipzig, 1904), 402–4; the work is included as 'Auctoris Ignoti' in G. F. Diercks (ed.), *Novatiani Opera, CCL* 4 (Turnhout, 1972), 253–88.

[6] E. Peterson, 'Ps.-Cyprian, Adversus Judaeos und Melito von Sardes', reprinted from *Vigiliae Christianae* 6 (1952), 33–43 in E. Peterson, *Frühkirche, Judentum und Gnosis* (Rome, etc., 1959), 137–45.

[7] C. C. J. Bunsen, *Hippolytus and His Age* 2 vols. (London,[2] 1854) 1, 450.

condemnation is moderate and not unrelieved.[8] Harnack held that this Latin composition, developing condemnation into an appeal for conversion, could only have arisen in a great city of the west with a large Jewish population.[9] Such a view of the historical setting has been endorsed, more recently, in a general survey of Jewish-Christian relations; Blumenkranz finds that, like other writings on Judaism from the third-century western church, the pseudo-Cyprianic sermon was intended less for evangelism than for defence against the influence of the more numerous and secure Jewish community.[10]

The contents of the sermon, therefore, have not always been thought inappropriate to a preacher *adversus Iudaeos*. Such low ratings of his achievement as those of Dupin, Williams and Nautin have nevertheless encouraged much wavering of opinion on his purpose. Had he any real concern with contemporary Jewry? In recent study the question has received strikingly different but predominantly negative answers. In his informative edition and commentary D. van Damme argued that the work was a homily – the earliest Latin sermon – 'gegen die Juden*christen*'; and others responded that the preacher's interest in the Jewish controversy was subordinate to his expression of God's appeal to *all* men (S. G. Hall), or, less complimentarily, that his argument was mere *Schein-polemik*, intended mainly to show off his mastery of fashionable rhetoric (H. Tränkle; Sanday, loc. cit., had taken a similar view).[11]

In van Damme's edition, completed in 1968, no account could be taken of Blumenkranz's brief contemporaneous notice. The author of the sermon probably had more than one aim in view, but it is argued here that, as Harnack and Blumenkranz assumed, his principal concern – '*the* purpose of Pseudo-Cyprian' – was rightly identified in the old title, *Adversus Iudaeos*. It is true that the work is not a disputation, but a sermon; yet the peculiarities of this sermon may be explained on the view that the preacher, and probably his congregation, were in contact with Jewry and felt

---

[8]G. Landgraf, 'Über den pseudocyprianischen Traktat "adversus Iudaeos"', *Archiv für lateinische Lexikographie und Grammatik*, 11 (1900), 87–97 (93 f.).

[9]Harnack, *Chronologie*, 2: 402, n. 7.

[10]B. Blumenkranz, 'Kirche und Synagoge: Die Entwicklung im Westen zwischen 200 und 1200', in K. H. Rengstorf and S. von Kortzfleisch (edd.), *Kirche und Synagoge*, 1 (Stuttgart, 1968), 84–135 (89), reprinted with the same pagination in B. Blumenkranz, *Juifs et Chrétiens: Patristique et Moyen Age* (London, 1977).

[11]D. van Damme, *Pseudo-Cyprian Adversus Iudaeos, gegen die Judenchristen: die älteste lateinische Predigt*, Paradosis, 22 (Freiburg, Schweiz, 1969), reviewed by S. G. Hall in *JTS* N.S. xxi (1970), 183–9 (185), and H. Tränkle in *Theologische Revue* 67 (1971) cols. 45–8 (48).

overshadowed by it. Hence comes his opening appeal for a *spiritual* understanding, hence erupts his strong emotion on the Jewish question, and hence derives what Harnack noted as the striking concreteness of imagery in his concluding picture of the learned hierarchs of Israel humbling themselves before the simple and lowly Christians.[12] This imagery may in fact lead, so it is suggested, not only to the main purpose of *Adversus Iudaeos*, but also to the self-presentation of the Diaspora synagogue.

In an influential study Harnack argued that the early Christian literature ostensibly directed *Adversus Iudaeos* was almost entirely the church's justification of itself *to* itself – and to pagans; but that works which meet a situation in which Jews are really strong can readily be distinguished from the ruck of artificial compositions.[13] This qualification has not always been given the weight which Harnack himself attached to it, as is clear from his later work (for example, on Justin's *Dialogue*); but its importance for the patristic period in general was underlined by Juster, Blumenkranz and Simon.[14] Can a situation of Jewish strength be presupposed for the pseudo-Cyprianic sermon in particular? Harnack himself thought so, as already noted; but its date and setting have been the subject of further lively discussion since he wrote.

Van Damme proposed a date between the *Diatessaron* (*c.* 175) and Tertullian's *Scorpiace*, on grounds of literary relationship; he drew supporting arguments from vocabulary, which might suggest pre-Tertullianic usage, and from his identification of the preacher's 'Israel' as a group of Christian Jews, a phenomenon more readily to be envisaged in the second century than later. Developing Landgraf's argument from the difference between biblical quotations in Cyprian and Pseudo-Cyprian, and from the probably Roman insertion of the sermon into the Cyprianic corpus, he placed the writing in Rome; the Christian Jewish group could then be seen as continuous with that envisaged by A. Jaubert in the background of I Clement.[15]

---

[12]A. Harnack, 'Zur Schrift Pseudocyprians Adv. Judaeos', in Harnack, *Die Pfaff'schen Irenäus-Fragmente als Fälschungen Pfaffs nachgewiesen, Miscellen … , TU* xx.3 (Leipzig, 1900), 126–35 (134).

[13]A. v. Harnack, *Die Altercatio Simonis Iudaei et Theophili Christiani nebst Untersuchungen über die antijüdische Polemik in der alten Kirche, TU* i.3 (Leipzig, 1883), 57, 63 f., 73 f. and 78, n. 69, followed recently by D. Rokeah, *Jews, Pagans and Christians in Conflict*, Studia Post-Biblica, 33 (Jerusalem and Leiden, 1982), 46 f.

[14]J. Juster, *Les juifs dans l'empire romain* (Paris, 1914) 1, 53 f. (n.); B. Blumenkranz, *Die Judenpredigt Augustins* (Basle, 1946, repr. Paris, 1973), 2 f.; M. Simon, *Verus Israel* (Paris, 1948), 168 f.

[15]Landgraf, 93; A. Jaubert, 'Thèmes lévitiques dans la Prima Clementis', *Vigiliae Christianae* 18 (1964), 193–203; van Damme, 1–6, 74–91.

This dating was accepted by Daniélou, but the claim that Tertullian drew on Pseudo-Cyprian, and the principal arguments from vocabulary, were independently questioned by Hall, Tränkle and van der Geest.[16] In a comprehensive examination of the literary and linguistic points Orban concluded that, on the contrary, Pseudo-Cyprian knew or directly drew upon Tertullian, and that, since one of his non-Cyprianic biblical quotations also occurs in Tertullian, North Africa should not be ruled out as a possible place of origin.[17] The hypothesis that a Christian Jewish group aroused the preacher's concern was doubted by Hall and Tränkle, and Daniélou expressed reservations about it.[18]

The direct literary connection with Tertullian, if it could be established, would be the most decisive of these arguments for dating. Here the present writer would venture to differ from Orban, and to posit common material rather than direct influence; for the passages in question (references are to Diercks's text-division, van Damme's paragraph-numbers following in brackets) are a list of prophets (Pseudo-Cyprian, *Adversus Iudaeos*, ii.8 f. (24 f.), partly parallel with Tertullian, *Scorpiace* viii.3) and a biblical text (Isa. i. 2, quoted in Pseudo-Cyprian, *Adversus Iudaeos* iii.3 (29) in a form which could be a classicizing improvement of the quotation in Tertullian, *Adversus Iudaeos* iii.5). Hall, whose arguments are not mentioned by Orban, points out – with reference to Matthew, Hebrews, I Clement and Melito – that many early Christians had lists of prophets, and that a common source, or general traditions, could account for the similarities of the lists in Pseudo-Cyprian and Tertullian.[19] Similar considerations apply to the currency of biblical testimonies.

A second argument for a later origin than that proposed by van Damme is drawn by Orban, pp. 219–21, from the usage of 'testamentum' in Pseudo-Cyprian. Van Damme had claimed that it is consistently used for 'will, testamentary disposition', and that this is a sign of early date; he suggested that the word has twice been avoided, where we might have expected it in the theologically developed sense of 'covenant', by the employment of 'testificatio' instead (ii.3 [14], 5 [17]. Orban stands this argument on its head,

[16]J. Daniélou, *The Origins of Latin Christianity* (E.T., London, 1977), xiv, 31; Hall, 188; Tränkle, cols 47 f.; J. E. L. van der Geest, *Le Christ et l'Ancien Testament chez Tertullien*, Latinitas Christianorum Primaeva, 22 (Nijmegen, 1972), 30–35.

[17]A. P. Orban, 'Die Frage der ersten Zeugnisse des Christenlateins', *Vigiliae Christianae* 30 (1976), 214–38 (215–23).

[18]Hall, 185; Tränkle, col. 47; Daniélou, 31.

[19]Hall, 187 f.

and suggests that 'testamentum' was avoided in these passages precisely because, when it does occur in Pseudo-Cyprian, the meaning presupposed is the developed, technical 'testament', signifying either a part of the Bible or, with an ambivalence embracing this meaning, 'covenant, agreement, (Old/New) Testament'; the pseudo-Cyprianic sermon can therefore be no earlier than the later work of Tertullian, in which 'testamentum' is first found as a designation of a part of the Bible. Here too, however, doubts arise. First, it is not entirely clear that 'testificatio' is awkward or unnatural in the two passages from the second chapter noted above; for the word occurs (counting one instance of the verb 'testificor') four times in this chapter, always with reference to the witness of attestation constituted by a word of God (cf. Heb. vii 17). Secondly, however that may be, *testamentum* itself, in the twelve instances from the pseudo-Cyprianic sermon noted by Diercks, p. 346, seems to the present writer predominantly to mean, as van Damme says, 'testamentary disposition'; in at least two cases (i.5 [8], ii.1 [9]) this meaning merges with the broader 'covenant', once (vii.6 [64]) the word is the second member of the special phrase 'ark of the covenant', but nowhere does it clearly refer to a part of the Bible.

These considerations suggest that, despite the two arguments just reviewed, the possibility of a date contemporary with Tertullian's earlier work should still be left open. Tränkle notes, from a general comparison with the dating of the *spuria* of the Augustan poets, that it would be surprising if the date were very much earlier than that of the alleged author, in this case Cyprian himself; but he allows that the surprising would not be impossible.[20] Hall shows that the case for dependence of the sermon on the *Diatessaron* is unconvincing, but he suggests that, although van Damme is right in rejecting attribution to Melito, the pseudo-Cyprianic author knew and used Melito's *Peri Pascha* (which Hall elsewhere tentatively dates *c.* 160–170).[21] Hence, with a view to the question whether Jewish influence can be presupposed in the preacher's situation, his sermon may be located within certain broad limits of time – the closing years of the second century to the middle of the third – and of place – Italy or Africa.

Throughout this period of time, and in either place the synagogue congregations impinged on the Christian consciousness. For Italy this can be exemplified from the story of Callistus's interruption of a

[20]Tränkle, col. 48.
[21]Hall, *JTS* N.S. xxi (1970), 186–8; S. G. Hall, *Melito of Sardis* On Pascha *and fragments* (Oxford, 1979), xxii.

sabbath-day synagogue service in Rome (Hippolytus, *Refutatio* ix.12.7–9); from Novatian's three epistles on Jewish subjects, of which only *de cibis iudaicis* survives (Novatian, *De cibis iudaicis* i.6); and from Hippolytus on the watchfulness of the Jews who take counsel to bear false witness against the church (Hippolytus, *In Dan.*, i.14 f.).[22] For Caecilius, the pagan in Minucius Felix's dialogue, the Jews are 'cum deo suo capti', an opinion which the Christian friend Octavius readily recasts, with a reference to Josephus, as 'a deo ut disciplinae transfugae dediti' (Minucius Felix, *Octavius*, xxxiii.5, taking up x.4); but both, in a dialogue set in Italy, refer to the present state of the Jews, and their common understanding of it as a Roman captivity is not, as Hippolytus and Novatian show, the only form of Gentile–Christian awareness of contemporary Italian Jewry. This point is emphasized for modern readers by the imagined location of Octavius's debate with Caecilius on the beach at Ostia, not far from what we now know to have been an elegant synagogue, to which a new 'ark for the law' was presented about the end of the second century.[23]

In Africa, Tertullian permitted himself to refer to the Old Testament as '*iudaica litteratura*' (De cultu i.3, Adv. Marc. iii.6),[24] in which could be seen '*thesaurus ... iudaici sacramenti*' (Apol. xix.2), striking descriptions of the Christian biblical heritage which are most easily explained if Jewish communities were familiar.[25] Harnack, who did not think that the argument with a Jewish proselyte which introduces Tertullian's *Adversus Iudaeos* could be wholly dismissed as a fiction, ascribed his acquaintance with Jewish biblical interpretation partly to his dealings with Jews.[26] His awareness of contemporary Carthaginian Jewry has been confirmed, despite arguments to the contrary,[27] by more recent study.[28] The knowledge

[22]On the interpretation of Hippolytus see D. M. Scholer, 'Hippolytus on Jewish Persecution of Christians', in E. A. Livingstone, ed., *Studia Patristica* 17 (Oxford, 1982), 821–8.

[23]A. T. Kraabel, 'The Diaspora Synagogue: Archaeological and Epigraphic Evidence since Sukenik', in H. Temporini and W. Haase (edd.), *Aufstieg und Niedergang der römischen Welt*, ii.19 (Berlin, 1979), 477–510 (499).

[24]A. Harnack, 'Tertullians Bibliothek christlicher Schriften', *Sitzungsberichte der königlich preussischen Akademie der Wissenschaften* (Berlin, 1914), 303–34 (305), notes that this description would not have been endured in the Epistle of Barnabas or Justin's works.

[25]Tertullian takes over current terminology, but does himself recognize a double proprietorship of scripture, according to C. Aziza, *Tertullien et le judaisme* (Nice, 1977), 282, 284.

[26]Harnack, 'Tertullians Bibliothek', 312, n. 2.

[27]H. Tränkle, *Q.S.F. Tertulliani Adversus Iudaeos* (Wiesbaden, 1964), lxx-lxxiv; T. D. Barnes, *Tertullian* (Oxford, 1971), 92.

[28]W. H. C. Frend, 'A Note on Jews and Christians in Third-Century North Africa', *JTS* N.S. xxi (1970), 92–6; W. Horbury, 'Tertullian on the Jews in the Light of *De Spectaculis*

of African Jewry evident once again in Augustine[29] shows that, after Tertullian, Cyprian's *Ad Quirinum* belongs to a setting in which Jewish communities were well known. In both Italy and Africa, therefore, in the period to which the pseudo-Cyprianic sermon may be assigned with probability, a Christian author could have been concerned with contemporary Jewry. This possibility can now be explored, for the pseudo-Cyprianic preacher, through consideration of his sermon itself.

Its train of thought has been judged inconsequential, and inappropriate to a preacher *adversus Iudaeos*. These points are raised in the debate on literary connection and purpose noted already. Thus, to cite only recent writers who find some merit in the composition, Peterson considers that the introduction is unrelated to the main theme, and has no anti-Jewish polemic; Hall sums up the sermon as a Christian *Heilsgeschichte* embodying an universal appeal to which Jewish controversy is not more than incidental; and van Damme holds that the baptism envisaged at the end is described by the preacher as a punishment, so that he must be rebuking baptized Jews rather than expressing the hope still laid up for the unconverted.[30] First, therefore, the scheme of the sermon will be outlined, with a view to the questions of its coherence, and of its relevance to a situation in which Jewish influence can be envisaged.

In his opening exhortation to spiritual understanding (i.1–5 [1–8]) the preacher urges his hearers to recognize, with the aid of the Spirit, the rights conveyed under the New Testament, Christ's testament, and its force, which is to make over the inheritance to the gentiles. In the long central section (ii.1–vii.7 [9–66]) he then sketches the biblical history wherein the Old Testament, broken because of Israel's persecution of the prophets and of Christ, was replaced by the New Testament which rejects Israel and calls in the gentiles. Finally (viii.1–x.5 [67–82]), he envisages the pardon of penitent Israel, her purification in baptism, and the submission of her priests and learned men to the lowliest gentiles. 'Thus the Lord wished the gentiles to flourish' (the preacher ends); 'you see how Christ has loved you' (x.5 [82]).

Thus summarized, the sermon has a consistent emphasis on the New Testament, which is to be spiritually discerned, and by virtue

---

xxx. 5–6', *JTS* N.S. xxiii (1972) pp. 455–9 (chapter 6 above); Aziza, 19–43, with the review by W. H. C. Frend, *JTS* N.S. xxx (1979) pp. 318–20; W. H. C. Frend, 'Jews and Christians in Third Century Carthage', in A. Benoit, M. Philonenko and C. Vogel (edd.), *Paganisme, Judaisme, Christianisme* (Paris, 1978), 185–94.

[29]Blumenkranz, *Judenpredigt*, 59–68.

[30]Peterson, *Frühkirche*, 137; Hall, *JTS* N.S. xxi (1970), 185; van Damme, 10–13.

of which Israel are rejected and the gentiles brought in. The initial advocacy of spiritual understanding is, despite Peterson's verdict, related both to the main theme and to polemic against the Jews. It is taken up in the concluding address to Israel 'vel sero vel tarde intellegite testamentum novum' (vii.3 [70]), which introduces a picture of those who were once untaught by the Spirit teaching the scriptures; for those who were learned from the beginning 'nesciunt legem nec intellegunt spiritalia', and if they wish to understand must ask the very humblest for instruction (x.1 f. [76 f.]). Thus the *spiritales*, whom the preacher exhorted first of all to understand (i.3 [4]), must recognize the greatness of their inheritance; in the end it will be the lot of the humblest among them to explain it to the Jews who now claim it as their own. This connection between introduction and conclusion is of course also an instance of the polemical commonplace that the Jews, '*ab intellectu suae legis alieni*' (Novatian, *De cibis iudaicis* i.6), 'can understand nothing of the scriptures, unless they first believe in Christ' (Cyprian, *Ad Quirinum* i.5).[31] Its employment here subserves the preacher's consistent interest in establishing the superiority of gentile Christians over Jews. This interest can be best understood if the Jews seemed to him to overshadow the Christian body. Such a sense concerning the synagogue seems to emerge when, in Tertullian's exposition of a great proof-text of the new dispensation, Isa ii 3 f. (quoted with different wording in Pseudo-Cyprian, *Adversus Iudaeos* ix.1 f. [73]), the '*large* people' – *populus amplus* – to be confuted by God is 'in the first instance that of the Jews and their proselytes' (Tertullian, *Adversus Marcionem* iii.21, 3).

'Israel', accordingly, is mentioned throughout the sermon (fourteen occurrences, distributed among seven of the ten chapters, according to Diercks, p. 345). The opening appeal for understanding prepares, as just noted, for an anti-Judaic commonplace later on; and the specific point to be understood, at the end of the introduction (i.5 [8]), is the manner in which the gentiles inherit. The disinherited Jews are prominent as this point is explained from Jewish persecution of Christ and his prophets, which evoked the replacement of God's Old Testament by a new, embodying Christ's invitation to all, however lowly or sinful; these now enjoy the high privileges whence the Jews were dispossessed as a punishment, when Christ sent them the Caesar whom they had preferred to their own king (vi.7–11 [54–8]). The explanation has now reached the present state of the Jews – considered '*a deo ... dediti*' as in Minucius Felix

---

[31]For Tertullian on this theme, see Aziza, 75–7.

– and the preacher expresses Christ's invitation to them, now humiliated as well as sinful, to join themselves to the strangers who have been made 'genus Domini' (ix.2 [74]). The Jews thus maintain their prominence in the sermon throughout its orderly progression to this final appeal, which is crowned by the imagined scene, already noted, of Israel's submission.

The gentile inheritance, as Hall[32] well notes, is underlined by the preacher's last words 'you see how Christ has loved you' (more probably addressed to the gentile hearers of the introduction than, as van Damme suggests ad loc., to Israel). It is less clear, however, that the sermon should be viewed, with Hall, as a Christian Heilsgeschichte, culminating in the recital of Christ's invitation to all without exception (v.5, end – vi.4 [45–51]); the rest of the sermon, on Israel's rejection and the possibility that, through repentance, she may gain humble access to her old inheritance, is then seen as intended to point up, by contrast, what has gone before. Yet, the passage regarded as the culmination is itself part of the explanation of the circumstances of the gentile inheritance; it dramatically reports the universal appeal initiated by the risen Christ, but it is followed, as noted in the foregoing paragraph, by the passages on Israel's punishment (vi.5–vii.7 [52–66]) which conclude the explanation. The invitation to 'impia Jerusalem' which begins the final section of the sermon, after this description of 'haec poena in Israel' (see viii.1 [67 f.]), forms a specific application of Christ's invitation to the lowly and sinful, is complemented by the concluding scene of repentance, and emerges more plainly as the peak towards which the discourse has been climbing. This estimate of its importance is consistent with the sustained attention to Israel already noted in the sermon; the thread of 'Christian Heilsgeschichte' is indeed at the heart of the preacher's message, but it is intended to assure the congregation that they are – perhaps despite appearance – the heirs, and that disinherited Israel must – paradoxically – seek admission to their ancient heritage from the Christians.

The view that the sermon is consistently concerned with Israel may be supported if this consideration of its scheme is concluded by a reference to a comparable outline of anti-Judaic argument elsewhere. Daniélou noted that the first book of Cyprian's testimonies Ad Quirinum differs from Tertullian's Adversus Iudaeos, but resembles the pseudo-Cyprianic sermon, in its final allusion to Jewish baptism.[33] This first book Ad Quirinum is in fact drawn up

[32]Hall, *JTS* N.S. xxi (1970), 185.
[33]Daniélou, 290, n. 22.

according to a systematic apologetic and polemical scheme[34] which bears a marked resemblance, overall, to that of the sermon. Another important thematic correspondence, on the Jews' attainment of biblical understanding only through belief in Christ, has been noted above; but the similarities are more extensive. The train of thought proceeds from the Jews' insult to God and killing of the prophets (*Ad Quirinum*, i.1-2, cf. Pseudo-Cyprian ii.6-iii.2 [19-28]) to the prediction that they should neither know nor receive Christ (*Ad Quirinum* i.3, cf. Pseudo-Cyprian iii.3-iv.1 [29 f.]; both texts quote Isa. i 2), and their inability to understand the scriptures unless they first believe (*Ad Quirinum* i.4 f.; cf., as noted already, the concluding section of the sermon, from viii.3 [70]). They will lose Jerusalem, the holy land, and the light of the Lord (*Ad Quirinum* i.6 f., cf. Pseudo-Cyprian iii.2 [27], vi.6 [53]-vii.1 [59], vii.6 [64]-viii.1 [67], but note that the proof-text Isa. ii 6 is applied to loss of light in *Ad Quirinum* i.7, but to regaining of light by penitent Israel in Pseudo-Cyprian, ix.2 [73]). A spiritual will replace a carnal circumcision (*Ad Quirinum* i.8, cf. Pseudo-Cyprian x.4 [81]); the former law will cease, and there will be 'another disposition and a new testament' (*Ad Quirinum* i.9-11, cf. Pseudo-Cyprian's central claim, iii.2 [28], v. 4 [43]-vii.3 [61], ix.1 f. [72]4] – with quotation of Isa. ii 3-6, cf. Isa. ii 3 f. in *Ad Quirinum* i.10). The following section of *Ad Quirinum* (i.12-18) spells out the expectation, under the new testament, of new baptism (Pseudo-Cyprian x.4 [81]) yoke (Matt xi 30 quoted at *Ad Quirinum* i.13 and Pseudo-Cyprian, vii.4 [62]), pastors, temple, sacrifice and priest (Pseudo-Cyprian, x.4 [80]), and prophet. The central argument of Pseudo-Cyprian is then taken up again in the remainder of the first book *Ad Quirinum*, on the triumph of the gentile church and the Jews' hope of pardon through baptism. These concluding paragraphs (*Ad Quirinum* i.19-24) deal with the two nations; the fruitfulness of the church, in contrast with the synagogue; belief in Christ to be exhibited by gentiles rather than Jews (*Ad Quirinum* i.21, the largest single collection of proof-texts in this Book); the Jews' loss of Christ's bread and cup, and all his grace (Isa. iii 1 quoted in *Ad Quirinum* i.22 and Pseudo-Cyprian, vi.10); the attainment of the kingdom by gentiles rather than Jews; and the Jews' hope for forgiveness if they wash their hands in baptism (Isa. i 15-18 quoted in *Ad Quirinum* i.24 and Pseudo-Cyprian, viii.4, where the argument is developed to form the conclusion of the sermon, viii.4-x.4).

It will be noticed that, although the sermon quotes only six of the

---

[34]Harnack, *Chronologie*, 2: 335, n. 1; Daniélou, 289.

numerous testimonies in the first book *Ad Quirinum*, the two works show a high degree of correspondence in the outline of argument. Persecution of Christ and the prophets leads to loss of the blessings of election, for 'another disposition and a new testament' brings in the gentiles, and the Jews must now, if they hope for pardon, be washed in baptism and join the new people (*Ad Quirinum* i.1–3, 6–11, 19–end, cf. Pseudo-Cyprian ii–vii, viii–end). The claim that the Jews only gain scriptural understanding through belief in Christ (*Ad Quirinum* i.4 f.) appears in the sermon, as already seen, in the connection between the initial exhortation to spiritual understanding and the concluding picture of the Jews learning their own Bible from the Christians (Pseudo-Cyprian i, viii–x). Both texts strikingly conclude, as Daniélou well noted, with the Jews' recourse to baptismal washing.

The outline of the pseudo-Cyprianic sermon, therefore, shares its main features with the plan of Cyprian's own first book to Quirinus, which forms a self-contained anti-Judaic treatise. The early incorporation of the sermon into Cyprian's works (only one other spurious writing is attested in the Cheltenham list) is perhaps to be explained not simply from the prestige of Cyprian, as Nautin suggests,[35] but also from this schematic resemblance. However that may be, it should be noted that the two principal elements in the argument of both sermon and treatise, the replacement of Israel by the church and the consequent necessity of Israel's baptism, occur independently of one another elsewhere, both in Tertullian and Cyprian. The passages deserve mention, for they may be held to bear out the view that the sermon is genuinely anti-Judaic, and at the same time they offer indications of the circumstances in which argument *adversus Iudaeos* might take this particular form. Finally, the conclusion of the sermon itself will be considered, with reference to van Damme's view of its purpose, which rests especially upon this passage, and to the question of the self-awareness of the Jewish community envisaged by the preacher.

Tertullian, significantly enough, makes the replacement of the elect Jewish nation by the gentile church the very first point of his *Adversus Iudaeos* (i.3–8, resumed with emphasis at iii.9–13). The pressing importance attached to this claim is also suggested by its inculcation, probably to catechumens, in connection with the address of the Lord's Prayer to a 'Father' whom the Jews do not honour (Tertullian, *Orat.* ii, quoting Isa. i 2, this text is also quoted by Pseudo-Cyprian, iii.3). Tertullian's anti-Judaic explanation of the

---

[35]Nautin, 123.

phrase is intensified by Cyprian, who refers 'our' Father to those who believe, whereas the Jews slew Christ and the prophets, and cannot call God Father, for they are children of the devil (John viii 44, which here introduces the quotation of Isa. i 2); 'when we Christians pray to their reproof, we say 'Our Father', because he begins to be ours, and ceases to be the father of the Jews who forsook him' (Cyprian, *Orat. dom.* x). The point that the gentiles rather than the Jews should believe in Christ attracts, as just seen, the largest single collection of proof-texts in the first book to Quirinus. It was clearly of prime importance to negate Israel's claim to be God's people, and to assert the election of the church instead. The tradition of this theme of course ascends to Paul (Rom. ix 6–13, Gal. iv 22–31) and the Epistle of Barnabas (xiii–xiv) (see pp. 12–13, above); but it is obviously, as Aziza notes, close to Tertullian's heart,[36] and the passages just mentioned leave the same impression concerning Cyprian.

The straightforward negative force of this argument is its most frequently considered aspect, but it has a complement in the second main element of the pseudo-Cyprianic sermon, on the Jews' need to turn to the faith of the church. This complementary consideration does indeed continue the stress on the absoluteness of Israel's replacement, for it involves the assumption that the ancient people can only now be saved by recourse to the new; but its emphasis differs from that of the first argument insofar as it allows for the possibility of Israel's repentance. This second argument is sometimes found, as in Pseudo-Cyprian, as a continuation of the first. Thus Tertullian, expounding the standard view that Jacob, the younger son who inherits, represents the church, can contrast his blessing by Isaac, where heaven is mentioned before earth (Gen. xxvii 28), with the blessing received by Esau, in which earth is named before heaven (Gen. xxviii 39); 'for the testamentary disposition to the Jews in Esau' (*Iudaeorum enim dispositio in Esau*) ... imbued with earthly good things through the law, is afterwards led to the heavenly things through the gospel by an 'act of faith' (*credendo*) (*Adv. Marc.* iii.24, 9). Similarly, interpreting II Cor. iii 17, Tertullian proceeds from the commonplace of Jewish blindness touched upon in that verse to the hope also implied by the apostle, who 'says this to the Jew in particular, upon whom there is still the veil of Moses; but who, when he shall have passed over into the faith of Christ, understands Moses to have preached of Christ' (*Adv. Marc.* v.11, 7). Again, that the Christian should rejoice rather than grieve at the

[36] Aziza, 101 f.

restoration of Israel seems to him the prime objection against his own view that the prodigal son in the parable should be taken, contrary to custom, to stand for the Jews, the elder son, with his obedient service in the continual presence of his father, being more fitted to stand for the church (*Pud.* viii). Here the restoration in mind seems to be that envisaged, in a long perspective, in Rom xi, but in the first two passages the possibility of Jewish belief is not relegated to the last days.

That the conversion of Jews envisaged in all these passages of Tertullian was commonly described with a biblically based elaboration, on which the pseudo-Cyprianic sermon probably drew, is suggested by a passing allusion in Cyprian, *ep.* lxiii.8. Arguing for the mingling of wine in the sacramental cup, he claims that biblical allusions to water only always refer to baptism. Among them is the prophecy that 'the Jews, if they thirst and seek Christ, will drink from us (*apud nos*), that is, they will receive the grace of baptism' (Isa. xlviii 21, ending *et bibet plebs mea*). The same text is quoted to justify 'a new baptism' (Cyprian, *Ad Quirinum* i.12); and the picture presupposed in the epistle is further filled out by the prophecy of thirst (Isa. lxv 13) given under the heading 'that the Jews should lose Christ's bread and cup', and the final heading of the same first book to Quirinus 'that the Jews can only find pardon for their crimes if they wash off the blood of the murdered Christ by his baptism' (Cyprian, *Ad Quirinum*, i.22, 24). The allusiveness of all these passages, exemplified most strikingly in the incidental character of the reference to the Jews in the epistle, suggests a familiar and elaborated imagined picture of the Jews' recourse to the church's baptism. The less securely established Christian body would have cherished this cheering picture, somewhat as the mediaeval Jewish minority dwelt on the future return of Christians to the Torah,[37] but without relegating the event wholly to the last times.

The two arguments of the pseudo-Cyprianic sermon just exemplified from Tertullian and Cyprian are also found in works from the Cyprianic appendix; *de montibus Sina et Sion* is devoted to proving the replacement of Israel by the church, but says nothing of the hope of repentance, and *Ad Vigilium*, on the other hand, introduces *Jason and Papiscus* as a welcome sign that Jewish conversion is still possible. These writings confirm that the arguments were widespread in early Latin theology, but the relatively secure date of the two named authors more readily permits inference to the purpose and

---

[37]See, for example, pp. 256, 259, below; also Nizzahon Vetus, in D. Berger, *The Jewish–Christian Debate in the High Middle Ages* (Philadelphia, 1979), 80 f., 87, 156, 213, 242.

circumstances of the pseudo-Cyprianic *Adversus Iudaeos*. With regard to purpose, the combination of the sermon's two arguments in a brief form in Tertullian gives confirmation, further to that already received from the plan of the first book *ad Quirinum*, that the pseudo-Cyprianic sermon is a coherent whole. Again, the urgency of the argument for the church's replacement of Israel, evident in both Tertullian and Cyprian, makes the same argument less likely to be a mere rhetorical exercise in Pseudo-Cyprian. Further, the allusions in Cyprian's treatment of baptism show that the conversion of Israel has been pictured in some detail, and Tertullian does not treat it simply as an event of the last days (by contrast with Origen's predominantly eschatological treatment, as reported by Sgherri);[38] these characteristics suggest concern with contemporary Jewry, and the pseudo-Cyprianic preacher, who draws on the same imagined scene of Israelite baptism, and does not set it at the end of the age, may be credited with the same concern. The correspondence of his scheme with that of an anti-Judaic treatise, its coherence when viewed as such, and the urgency for contemporaries of its argument for the rejection of Israel, likewise suggest that the preacher had a genuine anxiety to counter the influence of the synagogue.

The circumstances in which he might wish to do so are illuminated by the care taken to impress upon catechumens the church's right to the biblical heritage. The interpretations of the Lord's Prayer in Tertullian and Cyprian may be associated with Tertullian's references to proselytes, already noted (*Adv. Iud.* i, *Adv. Marc.* iii.21, 3); African church and synagogue were vying for sympathizers. The scanty Italian indications are at least not inconsistent with a similar situation; the known Jewish communities outside Rome were in ports and commercial centres such as Ostia, Portus, Puteoli and Pompeii, where they were well placed to attract inquirers if they wished to do so, and catacomb inscriptions attest proselytes in Rome itself.[39] The story of Callistus in a Roman synagogue, however ludicrous it is meant to be, would fit a view of Jewry as 'populus amplus', a community which only an indiscreet Christian would thus affront.

The whole plan of the sermon, therefore, has appeared to be a coherent anti-Judaic argument, and church–synagogue relations to which it would have been relevant have been suggested. Van

---

[38]G. Sgherri, *Chiesa e Sinagoga nelle opere di Origene* (Milan, 1982), 126 f., 131 f., 428–44.

[39]A. Milano, *Storia degli ebrei in Italia* (Turin, 1963), 24–9, 35.

Damme, however, came to the conclusion that the preacher had baptized Jews rather than the synagogue in mind. His view is based on the final baptismal scene, which can conveniently be considered now that the general scheme of the sermon has been reviewed.

The invitation to 'impia Hierusalem' to wash the blood from her hands in baptism (viii.1–4 [67–71], quoting Isa. i 15 f., 18) follows the argument for her rejection, in close agreement, as already seen, with the plan of *Ad Quirinum* i, and in general correspondence with the sequence of reference to rejection and conversion exemplified from Tertullian. There is no need, therefore, to ascribe (with van Damme, p. 61) the relatively favourable attitude to the Jews, suggested by this invitation, to the supposed concern of the preacher with baptized rather than unconverted Jews.

Van Damme's main argument is drawn from the scene of Israelite baptism which is the imagined response to the invitation. It is described after the invitation has been repeated (ix.3 [75]) at the end of a further declaration of Israel's replacement by the church (ix.1–2 72–4], quoting Isa. ii 3–6). The passage runs:

Correptus ergo Israel sequitur iniecta manu ad lavacrum et ibi testificatur quod credidit ... et fit mirum spectaculum. Et qui Levitae offerebant et sacerdotes immolantes et summi antistites libantes adsistunt puero offerenti, discunt qui olim docebant et iubentur qui praecipiebant ... (x.3 f. [79–81]).

'*Correptus*', as noted by van Damme (p. 11), takes up Isa. ii 3 '*corripiet plebem multam*', just quoted (ix.1 [73]); and the Jewish baptism is presented, as he says, as the victory of the gentile church. It does not follow, however, as he suggests it does (van Damme, pp. 10 f.), that the conversion of the Jews cannot really have been in mind. This presentation is standard, as seen already; Isa. ii 3 is applied by Tertullian to divine confutation of the Jews and their proselytes, and the baptismal scene in Cyprian has a polemical emphasis on the Jews' need to drink 'apud nos' which makes it, in *Ad Quirinum* as in Pseudo-Cyprian, a fitting crown of the argument for Israel's replacement. However much the polemical attitude implied in such a presentation might have hindered understanding with Jews in practice, the passages which draw on this commonplace cannot be taken as indications that their authors were not in fact envisaging the conversion of the synagogue.

Van Damme goes on to argue that, consistently with the presentation just considered, the baptism itself is understood by the preacher as a penalty inflicted on the Jews. This contention is based (van Damme, pp. 11–13) on the observation that '*iniecta manu*' (x.3 [79]) alludes to a Roman legal custom whereby the defendant puts out his hand to admit liability. Israel accordingly 'follows, hand outstretched, to the washingplace' – to receive the penalty which ensues on admission of guilt. This punishment of baptism fulfils, van Damme suggests, the prophecy *'iudicabit in medio gentium'* which immediately precedes *'et corripiet plebem multam'* in Isa. ii 3, and is included in the preacher's quotation; the Lord's judgment 'in the midst of the gentiles' would then have been understood by the preacher as the baptism inflicted on Israel as a punishment in the midst of a gentile church. In that case, however (van Damme concludes), the sermon cannot be understood as an invitation to Jews to be baptized; it must be taken, rather, as a rebuke to baptized Jews, who probably unsettle the congregation with Judaizing exegesis, but must recognize their true place as learners, for all their ancestral privileges have been done away. They might have been the more ready to stress these privileges if, as van Damme later suggests from the passage *'Et qui Levitae . . .'* (x.4 [80]), they were of priestly descent (van Damme, p. 90).

This ingenious explanation is connected by van Damme, as will be apparent, with many aspects of Pseudo-Cyprian; but it seems to the present writer to mix up two points kept apart in the sermon, Israel's punishment – Israel is *already 'correptus'* – and the baptism to which, 'confuted', 'he follows' (x.3 [79]). In the description of the baptism there is no verbal echo which might suggest that *'iudicabit in medio gentium'* is only now being fulfilled. This first clause of Isa. ii 4 precedes *'et corripiet'*, as already noted, and van Damme's connection of it with the baptism mentioned *after* the echo *'correptus'* means debiting the preacher with a certain awkwardness. Furthermore, the clause is included by Cyprian with the previous verse under the heading *'quod lex nova dari haberet'* (*Ad Quirinum*, i.10), and it is most naturally understood in Pseudo-Cyprian (who quotes ii.3–6) as part of a summary allusion to the Lord's transference from disinherited Israel to the nations, a theme already expounded as Israel's punishment; *'haec poena in Israel est'* (viii.1 [67]).

'Iniecta manu' seems, in fact, to have a double reference. It is an admission of being in the wrong, as van Damme suggests; but the hand is also outstretched for washing. The legal allusion is combined with an echo, which van Damme does not note, of 'hands' in Isa. i 15 f., quoted (viii.4 [71]) in the invitation to which Israel now responds. Israel, having asked *'reconcilia me Domino'* (x.2 [77]), is clearly *'correptus'*, and appropriately comes to baptism admitting guilt. Israel's punishment, however, consists not of the baptism itself, but in the loss of the privileges of election which has already

been incurred, and because of which it is necessary for the nation once elect to seek baptism. The baptism is not a punishment, but a washing, after which Israel is described as '*purificatus*' (x.3 [79]).

It seems best, therefore, to take 'Israel' in the more readily expected sense of unconverted Jewry, which has already been shown to fit the context and to be supported by parallels. How does the passage '*Et qui Levitae* ... ', which van Damme incorporated into his theory, appear if 'Israel' refers, instead, to the synagogue?

This passage is the last in a striking series of sacerdotal references. The list of rejected prophets (ii.8 [24]) includes Aaron, who is not in the similar lists in Melito, Tertullian and Cyprian surveyed by Perler;[40] the passion was a sacrifice and libation (v.1 [40]); and Israel have lost the vessels, the candlestick, the ark of the covenant, the priestly vessels, and the trumpets (vii.6 [64]). The references to Aaron and the threefold Jewish ministry could be developments of I Clement (xliii, xl f.), probably available in Latin before the end of the second century,[41] and the two mentions of libation as well as sacrifice could rest on the Bible (e.g. Exod. xxix 40 f., Ecclus l 15), but the list of vessels, a combination with no obvious biblical precedent, has noteworthy correspondences with frequently-attested Jewish catacomb symbols – menorah, Torah-shrine, amphorae and shofar.[42] Can the remarkably hieratic description of Israel (x.4 [80], quoted above) offer any reflection of contemporary synagogal self-awareness?

The synagogues contained a menorah and an ark of the law (as it was called at Ostia), and the ark-procession underlined, as did these furnishings, the continuity between the contemporary and the biblical worship of Israel.[43] The same point was made by the conclusion of the Eighteen Benedictions with the Aaronic blessing. Continuing priestly prestige is attested, once more, from the catacombs.[44] These remarks are deliberately confined to evidence applicable to Italy or Africa, but they may suffice to indicate that, as has been suggested more generally,[45] the synagogue could leave an

---

[40]O. Perler, 'Typologie der Leiden des Herrn in Melitons *Peri Pascha*', in P. Granfield and J. A. Jungmann (edd.), *Kyriakon: Festschrift Johannes Quasten*, 2 vols. (Münster, 1970) 1: 256–65.

[41]C. Mohrmann, *Etudes sur le latin des chrétiens*, 3 (Rome, 1965), 74–106.

[42]Survey in E. R. Goodenough, *Jewish Symbols in the Greco-Roman Period*, 2 (New York, 1953), 3–50, 108–19; discussion of common symbols in Milano, 428–30.

[43]Milano, 428; on the ark-procession, J. Gutmann (ed.), *The Dura-Europos Synagogue: A Re-evaluation (1932–1972)*, (Missoula, 1973), 144 f.

[44]J. Frey, *Corpus Inscriptionum Iudaicarum*, 1 (Rome, 1936), c.

[45]Kraabel, 502.

impression of representing the ancient service maintained by the Aaronic ministry.

Tertullian, naming Israelite dignitaries in a list comparable with this passage of Pseudo-Cyprian, goes from patriarch and prophet to 'Levites aut sacerdos aut archon' (*De corona militis*, ix.1); he probably means to end at New Testament times,[46] but it can now be seen as possible that he also reflects synagogal self-awareness. Likewise, the earlier sacerdotal passages in Pseudo-Cyprian could now be compared, due weight being allowed to the influence of the Bible and I Clement, with post-biblical Jewish sources on Aaron[47] and on the libations (Philo, *Spec. leg.* i.70; Hullin 92a, in the name of Eleazar of Modin [early second century]). In this final scene of baptism the hierarchs of Israel would then have been imagined in terms not wholly unrelated to the self-awareness of the synagogue, and shown as subordinate '*puero offerenti*' – probably Christ, viewed as high priest.[48]

Then '*discunt qui olim docebant*' (x.4 [81]), taking up '*docti et periti et legis disciplinam scientes*' (x.1 [76]); the Jews are described as learned men as well as hierarchs. Here too the preacher may genuinely reflect contemporary Jewry, for the catacombs attest those who are remembered as νομομαθής or νομοδιδάσκαλος (Frey, i, p.cxlii). Relatively high social standing, such as must be presumed for some in the community which built the Ostia synagogue,[49] may have been found together with learning. The combination is known, in the early fifth century, among the Jews of the Balearic Islands, as E. D. Hunt has emphasized; Christians feared the formidable learning of the Jew Theodore, who was also *defensor civitatis*.[50] The peculiarities of the pseudo-Cyprianic sermon are comprehensible, to combine these points with the earlier suggestions on its circumstances, if the Jews appeared to the preacher as '*populus amplus*', a community of hierarchs and learned men, authoritative interpreters of biblical law and worship, perhaps of higher social standing than the Christians, and attracting proselytes who might otherwise have

---

[46]Contemporary Jewish organization could be reflected, according to Aziza, 35 f.

[47]Some passages are collected by the present writer, 'The Aaronic Priesthood in the Epistle to the Hebrews', *JSNT* 19 (1983), 43–71.

[48]*De montibus Sina et Sion*, xiv is compared in the argument for this interpretation by A. Jülicher, review of Harnack, *Die Pfaff'schen Irenäus-Fragmente* ... , in *Göttingische gelehrte Anzeigen*, 162 (1900), 265–73 (272 f.); this suggestion is not considered by van Damme, ad loc., who interprets *puer* as the bishop.

[49]Milano, 437.

[50]E. D. Hunt, 'St. Stephen in Minorca', *JTS* N.S. xxxiii (1982), 106–23 (111, 121, citing *Epistula Severi*, 11 and 13 (*PL* 41:826 f.)).

been baptized; and if this view had at least some correspondence with the synagogue's own self-awareness.

It has been argued that the contents of the sermons suit its ancient title. The anti-Judaic character of the arguments is recognized as genuine by Harnack, and, more recently, by Blumenkranz, but modern students have predominantly denied it.

A date as early as Tertullian should be left open for the sermon, despite Orban's attempt to show its dependence on Tertullian. It can be assigned with fair probability to the period between the end of the second century and the middle of the third, in either Africa or Italy. The Jews received attention from Christian writers of the time in both countries.

The sermon itself, however, has been held to suggest that the preacher had little or no real concern with Jews. Yet, Peterson's view that the introduction is unrelated either to the main theme or to anti-Jewish polemic seems to overlook strong links with both. The Christian *Heilsgeschichte* which Hall regards as the heart of the work is devoted, rather, to proving superiority over Israel, and the climax of the sermon is its appeal to Jews to be baptized.

The view that it is a coherent anti-Judaic composition is strengthened by the close similarity of its plan to that of Cyprian's first book *ad Quirinum*. Both consist of two main arguments, for the replacement of Israel by the church, and for Israel's consequent need of baptism. This similarity may have contributed towards the early inclusion of the sermon among Cyprian's writings.

These two principal arguments also occur, together and separately, in Tertullian, Cyprian and elsewhere. The parallels confirm the coherence and urgency of the sermon, which is therefore unlikely to be, as Tränkle held, a mere rhetorical exercise. They also suggest its relevance to a situation, which can reasonably be envisaged in Africa or Italy, wherein the synagogue with its proselytes is thought by Christians to overshadow the church.

Van Damme, however, in the most comprehensive recent study, argued that the preacher viewed the Jews' baptism as their punishment, and that, consequently, he must be rebuking Jews already baptized rather than addressing himself to the synagogue. This argument seems to confound the Jews' punishment, viewed in the sermon as exile and loss of election, with their baptism, treated separately by the preacher and described as a washing.

The striking description of the Jews, in the baptismal scene, as hierarchs and men of learning corresponds, to a considerable degree, with contemporary synagogal self-awareness, so far as this can be established for Africa and Italy. This observation combines with the indications of setting already noted to suggest that the preacher wished to counter the influence of the synagogue, which could appear *vis-à-vis* the church as the more authoritative interpreter of biblical law and worship. The purpose of the pseudo-Cyprianic sermon is therefore best summed up by the ancient title, *Adversus Iudaeos*.

8

JEWS AND CHRISTIANS ON THE BIBLE: DEMARCATION AND CONVERGENCE [325–451]

1. Jews and Christians

The phrase 'Jews and Christians on the Bible' naturally also raises the question of the relationship between Judaism and Christianity. Some hold, with historians including Heinrich Graetz, Adolf von Harnack, Yehezkel Kaufmann and Jacob Neusner, that Jews and Christians respectively represent two mainly independent movements; from this viewpoint, the signs of demarcation in exegesis too are likely to appear of primary importance. Others, however, would underline the common inheritance or the common perspective of Jews and Christians, following historians like James Parkes, Hans-Joachim Schoeps, Marcel Simon and Nicholas de Lange; and for them the convergences in biblical interpretation might be expected to stand out particularly boldly. A general view of exegesis should therefore embrace not only forms and methods, which often bring similarities to notice, but also the texts interpreted and the subjects treated, points at which the Jewish and the Christian ways often divide. In the end, however, any comparison between Jewish and Christian exegesis in the golden age between Nicaea and Chalcedon must also be an implicit appraisal of the relation between Judaism and Christianity in the ancient world.

The fourth and early fifth century were *aurea saecula* not only for Christians, but also for Jews; at the same time they were at least a silver age for pagans. This claim can be made with some assurance in respect of literary history, but up to a point it has a broader application as well. In the Roman Empire, although the Jewish patriarchate in Tiberias came to an end about 425, the Jews remained an exceedingly important minority, as the relative tolerance of the laws in the Theodosian Code attests.[1] Beyond the imperial borders, the large and prosperous diaspora in Babylonia was an outstanding centre of rabbinic study. In Galilee during these years the rabbinic movement shaped a literature which moulded all

---

[1] K. D. Reichardt, 'Die Judengesetzgebung im Codex Theodosianus', *Kairos* xx (1978), 16–39; B. S. Bachrach, 'The Jewish Community of the Later Roman Empire As Seen in the *Codex Theodosianus*', in J. Neusner, E. S. Frerichs & C. McCracken-Flesher (edd.), *"To See Ourselves as Others See Us": Christians, Jews, "Others" in Late Antiquity*, (Chico, California 1985) 399–421.

subsequent Jewish history, above all the Talmud Yerushalmi and the Midrash Rabbah on Genesis and Leviticus; in Babylonia at the same time the long drawn-out compilation of the gigantic Babylonian Talmud was probably beginning. The impression of Jewish prosperity is confirmed by excavations, such as those which have brought to light the synagogues of Sardis (fourth century) or Hammath Tiberias (buildings of the fourth and the fifth centuries).[2]

As regards the pagan population, there is much to support Sir Samuel Dill's phrase 'the tenacity of paganism'.[3] After Julian, indeed, the cult of the gods was prohibited, and their temples fell into ruins or were turned into churches, whereas synagogues, although they were also attacked, were still protected by law; but pagans, like Jews, retained political significance. Sometimes pagan reactions to the new situation seem to resemble those of the Jews. The poet Claudian, for example, still writes as though he were reciting to Virgil's audience 'cum patribus populoque, penatibus et magnis dis';[4] and rabbinic exegetes, likewise, find in their ancestral tradition a self-sufficient world: neither the pagan poet nor the Jewish teachers make more than sparing and enigmatic allusion to the Christians.

Nevertheless, Jewish–Christian controversy went on in these circumstances, as it had before Constantine. For the reader of Christian exegesis, this may sound obvious. Almost every exegetical writing has something *adversus Iudaeos*, and such controversy seems almost unavoidable on topics like the law or the messiah. Here, however, an important preliminary question for comparison of Jews and Christians on the Bible is raised. *Prima facie*, Christian exegesis seems to reflect genuine debate, and hence genuine common ground between Jews and Christians. At the same time, however, the rabbinic texts seem to offer little on Christianity, as has already been

[2] A. T. Kraabel, 'The Diaspora Synagogue: Archeological and Epigraphic Evidence since Sukenik', *ANRW* ii, 19, 1 (1979), 477–510 (483–8); M. Dothan, *Hammath Tiberias* (Jerusalem, 1983), 27–70.

[3] S. Dill, *Roman Society in the Last Century of the Western Empire* (2nd edn, revised, London 1910), title of Book I; respect for paganism in various places throughout the fourth century and sometimes still in the fifth is noted by R. MacMullen, *Paganism in the Roman Empire* (New Haven & London, 1981), 132–4; on Rome at the end of the fourth century see B. L. Visotzky, 'Hillel, Hieronymus and Praetextatus', JANES xvi–xvii (1984–85) [=*Ancient Studies in Memory of Elias Bickermann*], 217–24.

[4] Virgil, Aen. viii 679, cf. iii 12. Claudian was a pagan as Augustine and Orosius state (A. di Berardino, in A. di Berardino (ed.), *Patrology*, iv (E. T. Maryland, 1986), 308) or perhaps an unbaptized Christian of pagan education and inclination (W. Schmid, 'Claudianus I', *RAC* iii (1957), cols. 152–67 (158–65); Alan Cameron, 'Claudian', in J. W. Binns (ed.), *Latin Literature of the Fourth Century* (London, 1974), 134–59 (154–5 & n. 37), also finds an artificial air in the pagan-sounding verses).

noted. It is true that Greek and Latin writings by Jews of this period are probably lost (see below); nevertheless, it has continually been claimed that Jews, comparable in this respect with pagans like Claudian, gave no serious attention to Christian biblical interpretation. The Christian biblical exegeses and writings *adversus Iudaeos* would then have been intended for the Christians themselves, not only for instruction in the understanding of the scriptures, but also (according to Harnack's classical presentation) as an answer to pagan objections: 'der Jude aber, wie der Christ ihn sich dachte, war der Heide'.[5]

Harnack's phrases still re-echo, for example in the work of H. Tränkle and (indirectly) of H. Schreckenberg.[6] Through Harnack's pupil A. C. McGiffert these opinions spread in the English-speaking world as well, notably in the influential work of G. F. Moore.[7] More recently, Harnack's thesis has been presented afresh, with a newly-considered argument, by D. Rokeah; he holds that, after the Bar-Kokhba revolt, genuine polemic was exchanged only between Christians and pagans.[8] (Being myself an English pupil of a German scholar, I may perhaps be permitted to recall that I once laid a few pages of criticism of Harnack's thesis before my teacher. After due consideration he simply said, 'I incline more and more to the theory of Harnack'.) In summary one can perhaps say that Harnack was right in recognizing the internal importance of exegesis *adversus Iudaeos* for Christian education, but wrong in supposing that significant contact between Jews and Christians ceased. The continuation of such contact throughout the whole period of the ancient church has been shown especially by Jean Juster, James Parkes, Marcel Simon, Bernhard Blumenkranz and (with regard to exegesis in particular) R. L. Wilken and N. R. M. de Lange.[9] It is perhaps not always fully recognized that Harnack himself was ready to

[5]A. Harnack, *Die Altercatio Simonis et Theophili nebst Untersuchungen über die anti-jüdische Polemik in der alten Kirche* (TU iii 1, Leipzig, 1883), 57, 64–5.

[6]H. Tränkle, *Q.S.F. Tertulliani Adversus Iudaeos* (Wiesbaden, 1964), lxx-lxxi, n. 6; H. Schreckenberg, *Die christlichen Adversus-Judaeos- Texte und ihr literarisches und historisches Umfeld (1.–11.Jh.)* (2nd edn, Frankfurt a.M., 1990), 26–7.

[7]A. C. MacGiffert, *Dialogue between a Christian and a Jew* (Marburg, 1889), 2–4, 8; G. F. Moore, 'Christian Writers on Judaism', *HTR* xiv (1921), 198.

[8]D. Rokeah, *Jews, Pagans and Christians in Conflict* (Jerusalem & Leiden, 1982), 9–10, 209–12.

[9]J. Juster, *Les Juifs dans l'empire romain* (2 vols., Paris, 1914), i, 53–4 (note); J. Parkes, *The Conflict of the Church and the Synagogue* (London, 1934), e.g. 189–94, 374; M. Simon, *Verus Israel* (E.T. London, 1986), 137–46; B. Blumenkranz, *Die Judenpredigt Augustins* (Basel, 1946, repr. Paris, 1973), 2–3; R. L. Wilken, *Judaism and the Early Christian Mind. A Study of Cyril of Alexandria's Exegesis and Theology* (New Haven & London, 1971), 9–53; N. R. M. de Lange, *Origen and the Jews* (Cambridge, 1976), 89–135.

acknowledge such contacts in connection with particular situations
or writings, such as Justin Martyr's *Dialogue* or the pseudo-
Cyprianic *Adversus Iudaeos*.[10] Patristic and legal sources on Christian converse with Jews and Jewish proselytes and sympathizers
suggest that anti-Jewish exegesis may not be unconnected with
Jewish biblical interpretation; and this hypothesis finds confirmation
in the variety, and sometimes also the strength, with which Jewish
arguments are presented in the Christian texts.

Further, the traces of polemic on the Jewish side are rather more
diverse in date and origin than the study of rabbinic material has
sometimes been thought to suggest. On this subject, David Rokeah
can perhaps be called too systematic, Johann Maier too sceptical.
Rokeah finds that the rabbinic texts reflect a development: genuine
polemic with Christians would have lasted only until about 150, and
thereafter would have given way to cool disputation without mutual
influence. Maier, on the other hand, assumes that nascent Christianity was so unimportant to the Jewish communities of Galilee and
Mesopotamia that only after Constantine, and especially in the
period of the rise of Islam, when the political situation compelled
attention to the subject, were a few anecdotes in the rabbinic
tradition referred – incorrectly – to Jesus and his followers.[11]
Somewhat similarly, but attaching greater importance to the Christian influence, Jacob Neusner (see the following section) thinks of a
convergence of Jewish and Christian concerns in the fourth century,
under the new conditions of the Christian empire; but this convergence, in his view, does not constitute any real harmonization of
the two movements. There is no doubt that the periods of Christian
origins, of the establishment of a Christian empire, and then of the
rise of Islam, are likely to have been of special importance in Jewish–
Christian relations; but some Jewish material probably reflects other
times as well. Notably, the outspoken Jewish polemic in the
Toledoth Jeshu appears to presuppose the importance gained by
Tiberias under the Jewish patriarchs, but its agreements with the
speeches of the Jew of Celsus in Origen, with Tertullian on Jewish

---

[10]Harnack, *Die Altercatio Simonis*, 73–4, 78 n. 59; *Die Chronologie der altchristlichen
Litteratur bis Eusebius* (2 vols, Leipzig 1897, 1904), ii, 402, n. 7; W. Horbury, 'The Purpose
of Pseudo-Cyprian, *Adversus Iudaeos*', *Studia Patristica* xviii.3 (1989), 291–317 (chapter 7
above).

[11]Rokeah, 61–5, 76–83; J. Maier, *Jesus von Nazareth in der talmudischen Überlieferung*
(Darmstadt, 1978), 273–5 and *Jüdische Auseinandersetzung mit dem Christentum in der
Antike* (Darmstadt, 1982), 196–9; for criticism with regard to an important text, Sanh. 43a,
see W. Horbury, 'The Benediction of the *Minim* and Early Jewish–Christian Controversy',
JTS N.S. xxxiii (1982), 19–61 (56–8) (103–7 above), and for affirmation of Jewish awareness
of Christianity, Irsai and Visotzky as cited in nn. 13 & 37 below.

claims, and with passages in the probably third-century Commodian, indicate the currency of Jewish anti-Christian traditions in
the second century and later.[12] A similar outspokenness emerges in
classical rabbinic exegesis in Midrash Qoheleth Rabbah (compiled
in Palestine, perhaps during the sixth century); in the explanations of
Ecclesiastes i 8, anecdotes on Jesus's teaching and on Christian
witchcraft and licence are gathered together, and the appearance of
some of these in the Tosefta suggests their continuous circulation
from the pre-Constantinian period.[13]

Light is thrown on our subject by a saying handed down in
rabbinic tradition in the name of Abbahu of Caesarea, who flourished about the beginning of the fourth century. In the context it
appears that Abbahu has recommended his Babylonian colleague
Safra to the *minim* or 'heretics' (among whom, as probably here,
Christians are sometimes to be recognized), but Safra cannot give
them a good answer on the apparently anti-Jewish text Amos iii 2
'You only have I known of all the families of the earth: therefore will
I visit upon you all your iniquities'. Abbahu accordingly says to the
minim: 'We (in Palestine), because we live cheek by jowl with you,
make it our business to study (the Bible); they (in Babylonia) do not
study it' (Babylonian Talmud, A. Z. 4a).[14] In fact, although Palestine

---

[12]The view that Celsus reproduces genuine Jewish polemic is affirmed by de Lange, *Origen*,
66–9; G. Sgherri, *Chiesa e Sinagoga nelle opere di Origene* (Milan, 1982), 28–41; and E.
Bammel, *Judaica. Kleine Schriften I* (Tübingen, 1986), 265–83; it is denied, however, by
Maier, *Jesus*, 251–8; on Tertullian see W. Horbury, 'Tertullian on the Jews in the Light of De
Spectaculis xxx.5–6', *JTS* N.S. xxiii (1972), 455–9 (chapter 6 above) and Maier, *Jesus*, 69 &
258–9 (noting correspondences with the Toledoth Jeshu, suggesting polemical tradition from
Rome as a possible background, but warning (69) against the assumption that this would have
been universally current among Jews); on the relevant passages in Commodian, see Blumenkranz, *Judenpredigt*, 87–8 with *Juifs et chrétiens dans le monde occidental* (Paris, 1960),
169 (and a further note on the question of dating in his *Les auteurs chrétiens latin du moyen
âge sur les juifs et le judaïsme* (Paris, 1963), 38–9), Horbury, 'Tertullian', 458, n. 5 and E.
Bammel, 'Die Zeugen des Christentums', in H. Frohnhofen (ed.), *Christlicher Antijudaismus
und jüdischer Antipaganismus* (Hamburg, 1990), 170–80 (172, n. 6).

[13]Interpreted as anti-Christian by B. L. Visotzky, 'Overturning the Lamp', *JJS* xxxviii
(1987), 76–7; a different explanation is given by Maier, *Jesus*, 143–4 and *Auseinandersetzung*, 119–20.

[14]אנן דשכיחינן גביכון רמינן אנפשין ומעיינן אינהו לא מעייני According to Simon, *Verus Israel*,
184–6, 407–8 (where S. Liebermann also is cited for this opinion), the *minim* here are gentile
Christians; according to Maier, *Jesus*, 138–9 (collecting literature on the passage) they are
more likely to be apostate Jews, because Safra through them obtains a tax rebate, and they
must therefore have been involved in fiscal administration, which might seem questionable for
Christians about the year 300. They are well explained as Christian *agoranomoi*, however,
with reference to notices of pre-Constantinian Christian officials in Caesarea and elsewhere,
by L. I. Levine, *Caesarea under Roman Rule* (Leiden, 1975), 128. On the general question of
the interpretation of the word *minim* de Lange, *Origen*, 43–4, thinks it probable that the
word was first used for gentile Christians in the second half of the third century.

was the homeland of the midrash, Babylonian teachers, too, of course, studied the Bible, as will be noticed further below. The importance of the saying in the present connection is its demonstration that a close connection between exegesis and apologetic was recognized by Jews. Here Jewish interpretation marches together with the likewise apologetically directed Christian exegesis. Christian sources of the fifth century also depict Jews as speaking freely on Christ and the church.[15] An instance is offered by the ironic remarks of the Jew Simon in *Altercatio Simonis*, for example at vi, 22 'Erubescere poteris, Theophile, si hoc dictum [sc. potuisse Christum tam maledictam et ludibriosam sustinere passionem] minime comprobaveris. Nam scriptum est in Deuteronomio, *Maledictus omnis qui pendet in ligno*;' or at vi, 25, in the innocent query 'Ergo ecclesia fornicaria est?' (Harnack, *Die Altercatio Simonis*, 29, 34).[16] It may perhaps be suggested that just as in the pagan world the proud reserve of Claudian is flanked by the keenly critical treatment of Christians and Jews in his contemporary Rutilius Namatianus, and by the learned anti-Christian biblical exegesis of Porphyry and his successors,[17] so in the Jewish community reserve and outspokenness on the subject of Christian biblical interpretation can both now and later exist side by side.

Lastly, one may suspect that, despite their new prosperity, Christians did not immediately lose the sense of being newcomers and a minority *vis-à-vis* the Jews. One object of anti-Jewish controversy is to justify separate Christian existence, and above all the Christian claim to the Jewish scriptures. These books were the focus of a culture which Christians shared with Jews, and in which they were often dependent on Jews. There were strong motives for Christians to seek Jewish exegetical knowledge.

To sum up these introductory considerations concerning Jews and Christians on the Bible: first, one can scarcely discuss demarcation or convergence between Jewish and Christian exegesis without assessing the relationship between the Jewish and the Christian communities. Secondly, as regards the historical situation, despite

---

[15]Blumenkranz, *Juifs et chrétiens*, 269–70; note also the irony of the Jewish speeches in the *Altercatio Simonis* (in mid-fifth-century Gaul) as quoted in the text below.

[16]The bite of these passages goes unnoted in the useful summary by Blumenkranz, *Auteurs*, 27–31.

[17]Dill, 47–8, 310–12 (Rutilius); successors of Porphyry, whose work (summarized by T. D. Barnes, *Constantine and Eusebius* (Cambridge, Mass., & London, 1981, 174–9) continued to trouble exegetes in our period (notably Apollinaris of Laodicea, Didymus the Blind and Jerome), include Hierocles (possibly identical with the unnamed pagan objector answered in the *Apocritus* of Macarius Magnes) and Julian.

the ever-increasing strength of the Christians the Jews fashioned for themselves a classical exegetical literature in Hebrew and Aramaic, above all in Galilee but also in Babylonia, during just this golden age of ecclesiastical literature. There is more to be said on the geography and the languages of Jewish exegesis in this period. The period is in many respects, however, still pagan; culturally, neither Jews nor Christians are independent of the Graeco-Roman atmosphere and Graeco-Roman exegesis, and Jewish reaction to the new Christian influence may resemble one or another pagan position. Thirdly, Christian exegesis speaks most obviously of demarcation – or, more precisely, of internal needs, and, perhaps, of concern with pagans rather than Jews. Jewish exegesis is not expressly anti-Christian; but Christian literature abounds in topoi *adversus Iudaeos*. Nevertheless, these topoi reflect not only the inner need of the Christian community for scriptural proof in catechesis or in argument *adversus gentes*, and not only Christian self-definition, but also genuine shared concerns. Lastly, Christians probably retained a sense of cultural dependence on Jews, above all in respect of the Jewish scriptures, and remained eager to learn from Jewish knowledge.

To claim this much is already to affirm common ground between Jews and Christians on the Bible. This answer to the question of the significance of the countless passages *adversus Iudaeos* in Christian exegesis demands in turn, however, an examination of the phrase 'The Bible' in connection with Jews and Christians. For Christians the Jewish scriptures became an 'Old' Testament read together with a 'New', and among the Jews the written Torah was co-ordinated with traditions which took on independent literary life in the Mishnah and the Talmud. To what extent, then, did Jews and Christians truly share one Bible?

2. The Bible

Challenging the Donatists in 405 to a contest for scriptural proofs, Augustine cited the daily searching of the scriptures by believers who heard Paul in Beroea (Acts xvii 11–12).[18] 'What scriptures did they

---

[18]Augustine based his challenge on a biblical florilegium designed to prove the geographical universality of the catholic church (H. Chadwick, 'Tyconius and Augustine' in C. Kannengießer & Pamela Bright (edd.), *A Conflict of Christian Hermeneutics in Roman Africa: Tyconius and Augustine* (Protocol of the Fifty-eighth Colloquy of the Center for Hermeneutical Studies, Berkeley, California, 1989), 48–55 (51)). In Acts xvii 11–12 Jews are mentioned first as believers, some gentiles afterwards, but Augustine does not speak of the believers as Jews, and perhaps took them to be primarily gentiles; the Greek and Latin texts of verse 12 in Codex Bezae imply relatively few Jewish believers, many gentiles. Chrysostom, by contrast (*hom.* xxxvii 1–2 on Acts), notes in his exposition that there were gentiles too, but implies in a comment in his initial reading of the passage that those who searched the scriptures were Jewish.

search, but the canonical scriptures of the Law and the Prophets (nisi canonicas Legis et Prophetarum)? to which have been added the gospels, the apostolic Epistles, the Acts of the Apostles, and the Revelation of John (quibus accesserunt Evangelia, apostolicae Epistulae, Actus Apostolorum, Apocalypsis Ioannis)' [Augustine, *Epistula ad Catholicos contra Donatistas*, 51 (xix), PL xliii 430]. Augustine's question may indicate awareness that the passage in Acts could be used, as it had been by Priscillian, to assert that apocryphal prophecies were accepted by the early believers;[19] but it also expresses a standard opinion, which Augustine expects the Donatists to share, that the New Testament books were an accession to an Old Testament canon which was recognized in apostolic times, and that the whole collection was still to be read with attention to canonical questions.

In such questions the Christians of the period under review constantly followed the Jews. There were of course assertions of Christian independence, such as had earlier emerged in Tertullian's defence of Enoch, despite the fact that some rejected it 'because it is not admitted into the Jewish book-case (*armarium*)' (*De Cult. Fem.* i.3); but the Jewish canon retained such authority that departure from it continued to need defence. So, from Origen onwards, the number of 'the covenant-books, as the Hebrews hand down' (Origen on Ps. 1, quoted by Eusebius, *H.E.* vi 25, 4 and in the Philokalia, iii [Robinson, pp. 40–41]) is often reckoned as twenty-two, with Josephus, *Ap.* i 38–40, and Melito.[20] Josephus himself does not mention the total, but the number twenty-two is specified by Origen, Athanasius, Cyril of Jerusalem, Canon 60 of Laodicea,

---

[19]Priscillian, *De fide et apocryphis*, p. 52 Schepps, quoted with comments by A. Harnack, *Über den privaten Gebrauch der Heiligen Schriften in der alten Kirche* (Beiträge zur Einleitung in das Neue Testament, v; Leipzig, 1912), 76–8; the passage is noted in the course of a fuller summary of Priscillian's arguments by O. Wermelinger, 'Le canon des latins au temps de Jérôme et d'Augustin', in J. D. Kaestli & O. Wermelinger (edd.), *Le canon de l'Ancien Testament. Sa formation et son histoire* (Geneva, 1984), 153–210 (160).

[20]R. Hennings kindly informs me that, in a forthcoming publication, he will support the view that Origen derived the number twenty-two from his reading of the book of Jubilees rather than from reference to contemporary Jews. Quotations of the Greek Jubilees by George Syncellus and others indeed show that the Greek text of chapter II, and probably also the original, mentioned twenty-two biblical books at verse 23 (R. H. Charles, followed by C. Rabin in H. F. D. Sparks, *The Apocryphal Old Testament* (Oxford, 1984), 16; R. T. Beckwith, *The Old Testament Canon of the New Testament Church* (London, 1985), 235–40 prefers verse 15 as the more likely place, but regards the reference as an expansion of the original text, introduced by the Greek translator). Nevertheless, in view of Origen's concern with Jewish opinion on the canon it may be thought in general unlikely that he would have represented twenty-two as the Jewish total if the figure (however derived) did not find acceptance among the Jews whom he consulted. De Lange, *Origen*, 52–3 hold that Origen's list with its explicit total of twenty-two represents a Jewish tradition current in his day. This view gives full value to Origen's claim 'as the Hebrews hand down', quoted in the text above.

Epiphanius and Gregory Nazianzen.[21] Origen, Athanasius, Epiphanius and Nazianzen all add that this number is also the total number of the letters of the Hebrew alphabet.[22] Origen and Epiphanius add the names of the books in transliterated Hebrew, as Jerome later did; transliterated Hebrew titles are also found, but without the number twenty-two, in the list of books edited together with the Didache by Bryennius. The alternative reckoning of twenty-*four* books, which appears in II Esdras (IV Ezra) xiv 44–6, and became customary in rabbinic tradition (for example, Qoh.R.xii 1), emerges in the Christian west in connection with the twenty-four elders of the Apocalypse, in Victorinus of Pettau, the Cheltenham List and Jerome.[23] Hilary of Poitiers harmonizes the divergent traditions. In the context of a discussion of the symbolism of the alphabet in Ps. cxix (cxviii), he first of all mentions the number of twenty-two biblical books, probably in dependence on Origen or Eusebius, and in connection with the Hebrew alphabet. Then, however, he adds that some people include the books of Judith and Tobit in their reckoning, in order to reach the total of twenty-four, in agreement with the letters of the *Greek* alphabet. This double reference of the biblical book-collection is well suited (he adds) to the special relationship between gospel and the Roman empire, which governs both Jews and Greeks: 'specialiter evangelica doctrina in Romano imperio, sub quo Hebraei et Graeci continentur, consistit'.[24] The lists of books correspondingly often refer themselves expressly to Jewish tradition (so the list published by Bryennius, and Origen, Cyril of Jerusalem, Epiphanius, Rufinus, and Jerome).

Habitual reference to Jewish opinion also appears in the discussion of *non-canonical* books by fourth-century Christian authors. For an important group of writers, either in or in connection with the eastern provinces – Athanasius, Epiphanius of Salamis, Rufinus, probably

---

[21]The sources in what follows, where not otherwise mentioned, are the passages gathered in translation by E. Junod, 'La formation et la composition de l'Ancien Testament dans l'église grecque des quatres premiers siècles', Kaestli & Wermelinger, *Canon*, 105–51 (124–51) and Wermelinger, 'Canon des latins', 197–210; see also J. N. D. Kelly, *Early Christian Doctrines* (5th edn London, 1977), 53–6 and H. F. D. Sparks, 'Jerome as Biblical Scholar', in P. R. Ackroyd & C. F. Evans (edd.), *The Cambridge History of the Bible*, i (Cambridge, 1970), 510–41 (532–5).

[22]W. Sanday, *Inspiration* (3rd edn, London, 1896), 112–15 (collection of the passages; number-symbolism and cosmological speculation in connection with the Old Testament and the New Testament canon); de Lange, *Origen*, 52–3, n. 24 (Jewish analogies to the symbolism of the letters); both authors connect the Jewish count of twenty-two letters with the cosmic letter-symbolism of the Sepher Yetsirah.

[23]Sanday, *Inspiration*, 113.

[24]Hilary, *Tractatus super Psalmos*, Prol. [Instructio Psalmorum], 15 (CSEL xxii, p. 13).

also Cyril of Jerusalem[25] – the canonical books formed the first of three classes of books. The non-canonical books were divided into two classes. These two classes were sharply distinguished, sometimes with special emphasis on the rejection of apocrypha. (Earlier examples of such a division are the notices of Antilegomena in Eusebius [for example, *H.E.* vi 13, 6] and in the Muratorian Canon, in these cases with reference to the Antilegomena of both the Testaments.) Rufinus calls these three classes of books *canonici, ecclesiastici,* and *apocryphi* respectively; the name *ecclesiastici* was already traditional, he says, for the second class, comprising Wisdom, Ecclesiasticus and other Septuagintal books: 'alii libri sunt qui non *canonici* sed *ecclesiastici* a maioribus appellati sunt'.[26] The Council of Trent, however, protected the canonicity of this second class of books with an anathema, and Sixtus Senensis then introduced the names *protocanonici, deuterocanonici,* and *apocryphi* for the same three classes of books.[27] This change in the names in itself underlines the extent to which, in Rufinus's traditional terminology, 'the' canon was that of the Hebrews; other books were indeed recognized, but called 'ecclesiastical' rather than 'canonical'. For Athanasius, comparably, these ecclesiastical books are 'other books outside the canonical number', ἕτερα βιβλία τούτων ἔξωθεν – one may recall the rabbinic phrase 'the outside books', הספרים החיצונים (Sanh. x 1 and elsewhere) – and 'not canonical', οὐ κανονιζόμενα; nevertheless (he says) they were affirmed by the fathers to be suitable reading for catechumens.[28] In this last point Harnack probably rightly discerned the Christian adoption of a Jewish usage.[29] By contrast with the recommendation of the 'libri ecclesiastici', severe warnings against apocrypha (books in the third class, Enoch above all) sometimes appear (so in Athanasius, Cyril of Jerusalem, Nazianzen).

Jerome obviously stands together with these authors, and accordingly is no innovator in his contention for the 'hebraica veritas'. He forms an exception not in his theory of the canon, but in his learning, his eloquence, and his literary productivity. As regards our

[25]Cyril probably recognized the 'libri ecclesiastici', despite his warning against apocrypha (*Catech.* iv 36, xv 16), because he also speaks of books which are read in the church (so Wermelinger, 'Le canon des latins', 164–5; but Kelly, *Doctrines,* 55 and Junod, 'Formation', 129–30 hold that he rejected the *ecclesiastici*). Cyril quotes Wisdom and Ecclesiasticus to the catechumens, *Catech.* vi 4, ix 2,16, xi 19, etc.

[26]Rufinus, *Explanatio Symboli,* 36, translated in Wermelinger, 'Le canon des latins', 198.

[27]Sixtus Senensis, *Bibliotheca Sancta* (1566), i 1 (Cologne, 1626, p. 2), with special reference to early Christian terminology.

[28]Festal Letter 39.11 (PG xxvi 1437), of 367, translated with reference also to Coptic fragments in Junod, 'Formation', 141–4.

[29]Harnack, *Über den privaten Gebrauch der heiligen Schriften,* 51–2, 85.

subject, a group of important authors, Jerome included, stand out as representing a dependence on Jewish biblical knowledge which already appears in Melito and Origen, and as referring themselves in canonical questions to Jewish authority. Jews and Christians are of course divided by the Christian biblical canon; nevertheless, precisely in this context of the canon, learned Christians honour the Jews as custodians of the scriptures, and wish to accept their traditions as authoritative. Here the position of the learned was probably not far removed from the instinctive reverence for Jewish biblical knowledge found also among simpler Christians.

Nevertheless, the intellectual strength of this inclination was to be found in the eastern provinces. Augustine will have spoken for many in the west when he compiled an Old Testament list of *forty*-four canonical books, following the contents of the Septuagint without any division into two classes, and without any mention of the Jews (*De Doctrina Christiana*, ii 8, 13); this canon was endorsed by the Councils of Hippo (393) and Carthage (397), and by Pope Innocent I. Augustine did indeed wish, as it seems, to deprive the Jews of their reputation for biblical knowledge; they ought not to become a court of appeal for Christians in biblical questions. This happened, as we know from Augustine (Ep. lxxi 3–5), when the Christians of Oea in Tripolitania, hearing Jerome's new translation with some suspicion, resorted to the Jews in order to discover the true identification of Jonah's shade-tree (Jonah iv 6 קִיקָיוֹן, Old Latin *cucurbita*, Vulgate *hedera*). In this particular case Augustine was perhaps not altogether displeased that Jerome was hoisted on his own petard, but in general he wanted to depict the Jews not as authorities, but simply as 'capsarii', satchel-bearers who carried the books for the Christians without being able to understand them (*Enarr. in Ps.* xl 14, lvi 9, on Ps. xli 12, lvii 3).[30] Apart from this particular intention to deflate popular esteem for Jewish knowledge, it was of course customary to make the acceptance of books in the churches an important criterion of canonicity. However the factors in the formation of Augustine's view of the canon are to be assessed, ecclesiastical usage rather than Jewish tradition was determinative for him.

It is the more striking, therefore, that Augustine himself can appeal to a Jewish canon. He holds that the books of this canon once existed as a collection in the Jerusalem temple, protected by the care of successive high priests; Enoch's writings, however, were never accepted into this collection, and they were rightly excluded: 'non

---

[30]Bammel, 'Zeugen', 174–5 examines the implications of Augustine's terms with emphasis on their importance for Christian anti-pagan apologetic.

frustra non sunt in eo canone scripturarum, qui servabatur in templo Hebraei populi succedentium diligentia sacerdotum' (*De civitate Dei* xv 23, 4). Here Augustine seems to reflect not only what we have seen to be a standard Christian warning against Enoch, but also a contemporary Jewish tradition, which perhaps has reached him indirectly.[31] Josephus (e.g. Ant. iv 302–4) and the Mishnah (e.g. Kelim xv 6), speak of biblical MSS. in the temple, as Deut. xxxi 24–6 already do with regard to the tabernacle, but not of a collection of this kind.[32] One may compare Epiphanius's remark, perhaps of similar origin, that Wisdom and Ecclesiasticus were not laid up in the ark of the covenant (*De mens. et pond.* 4). Secondly, Wisdom and Ecclesiasticus, according to Augustine, are honoured in the western church, above all because of their prophecies of the suffering of Christ and the faith of the gentiles (Wis. ii 12–21, Ecclus. xxxvi 1–5); yet these prophecies are not written in the canon of the Jews, and therefore cannot be used in disputation: 'adversus contradictores non tanta firmitate proferuntur, quae scripta non sunt in canone Iudaeorum' (*De civitate Dei* xvii 20, 1). Here ecclesiastical opinion continues to be more important then the Jewish canon, but Augustine finds it advisable to mention this canon, and he can himself when necessary appeal to its repute for high antiquity and authenticity. In all, therefore, even Augustine is a witness to the importance of the Jewish Bible and its canon for the Christians.

These aspects of the history of the canon are not unfamiliar, but their implications for Jewish–Christian exegetical convergence probably deserve greater emphasis. The patristic comments attest a clear and widespread Christian inclination to recognize the Jewish norm of biblical literature, and therewith the position of the Jews as hereditary custodians of scripture. The Christians think that they share the Jewish Bible, and they want to share it in its most authoritatively recognized Jewish form.

On the other hand, the Jewish opinion which most immediately impinged on the Christians was sometimes at least that prevalent in the western diaspora, opinion therefore which did not come straight from the centres of Jewish study in Galilee and the east, although there is reason to think that it often represented Palestinian views. Further, for the Christians, in Augustine's phrase, there were 'added' certain other books to the Jewish number. Such qualifications of the impression of Christian dependence on Jewish definitions of

---

[31]Reports on contemporary Jews in Augustine are gathered by Blumenkranz, *Judenpredigt*, 62–8.

[32]For the passages see Beckwith, *Canon*, 80–86.

scripture naturally lead back to the question already asked: How far did Christians and Jews truly share 'one Bible'? The question is particularly sharply posed in Jacob Neusner's assessment of the situation as one in which there was very little common ground, above all in respect of the Christian and the Jewish canons.

For Neusner, to give the briefest outline of his position in *Judaism and Christianity in the Age of Constantine* and *Writing with Scripture*,[33] the Jewish canon is the twofold Torah. This canon therefore comprises the Hebrew Bible, and above all the written Torah in the Pentateuch, in close connection with the documents of the oral Torah in the classical rabbinic literature, especially the Mishnah, the Talmud and the Midrashim; but in fact it is a canon which is never closed, because of the continuing development of the oral Torah. The rabbinic documents together with the Hebrew Bible make up a single unity, just as for the Christians the two Testaments form one seamless robe. Jews and Christians therefore shared the same Bible only in appearance, because in each tradition it was united with another distinctive and very highly esteemed body of material. In the fourth century, it is true, the same themes emerged in both patristic and rabbinic literature. Thus explanation of history is found in Eusebius and also in Genesis Rabbah, the Messiah is important both for Chrysostom and for the Talmud Yerushalmi, and the identification of the true Israel is a theme common to Aphrahat, Leviticus Rabbah and Genesis Rabbah; and all these great subjects were discussed by Jews and Christians in a similar way, with reference to the scriptures. Yet this occurred only under the influence of the new political situation. The subsequent relationship of Jews and Christians was indeed moulded by the fourth-century discussions, but Judaism and Christianity remained totally diverse. If a learned Jew had been present at the Council of Nicaea, he would have understood nothing of the Christological debates, just as his Christian counterpart would have been unable to see the point of halakhic argument; neither could attain insight into the issues preoccupying the other's community. Even on a subject which on

---

[33] J. Neusner, *Judaism and Christianity in the Age of Constantine* (Chicago & London, 1987); J. Neusner, with W. S. Green, *Writing with Scripture* (Minneapolis, 1989). On the absence of genuine Jewish-Christian encounter on canonical questions, see especially *Constantine*, 114–45. In the present paper it is urged not that Jews and Christians discussed canonical matters, with reference to the distinctive Jewish and Christian traditions now associated with the Jewish scriptures (the questions on which Neusner emphasizes the absence of debate); but that Christians willingly attached themselves to what they understood to be a Jewish norm, that some Jews are likely to have been aware of Christian interest in information on the point, and that in both communities the books of the Jewish scriptures continued, despite interpretative developments, to be recognized as an independent entity.

the face of it looks both shared and fundamental, the issue of the canon, the concerns of the two communities are quite different, and there is no true exchange of opinion.

In these writings, as in his earlier book on Aphrahat, Neusner seeks to do full justice to the church fathers (and indeed he opines that, in a present-day American university, Eusebius would have needed to occupy at least six professorial chairs). His thesis receives support first of all from their common acceptance of the New Testament, an acceptance which then governs interpretation of the 'Old'; but it can also appeal to the bifocal character of rabbinic literature, in which (leaving aside the Targum) only the midrash is formally dependent on the Hebrew Bible. The two Talmuds form a kind of commentary on the Mishnah, not on the books of the written Torah. It is true that the so-called halakhic midrashim unite the Mishnah with the biblical laws, but if the biblical laws are fundamental, the presentation of the Mishnah independently of them remains noteworthy. The use of biblical interpretation in the fourth century, in the Talmud Yerushalmi and in the midrashim Genesis Rabbah and Leviticus Rabbah, to explore themes of moment to Christians as well as Jews might seem to indicate common ground with Christians; but Neusner forbids this conclusion by pointing to the political situation.

One may ask, however, if the formal dependence on scripture seen in the midrashim does not represent a pre-rabbinic attitude of veneration for the biblical books, which Christians inherited from their origins and which continued to be strongly manifested among Jews throughout the rabbinic period and in many different genres of rabbinic literature. Thus, the important collections of legal material in Philo and Josephus are presented as biblical interpretation, the Aramaic Targums on the Bible were developed concurrently with the rabbinic writings, and in the rabbinic literature itself biblical interpretation is of course found not only in midrashim, but within the Mishnah and the Talmud. In the halakhah of the Mishnah and the Babylonian Talmud a distinction can be drawn between biblical and rabbinical items, traditions 'from the Torah' and traditions from 'the words of the scribes' or 'from our teachers'.[34] Whether the oral Torah derives from the written is a great and time-

---

[34]For example, in Mishnah, Sanhedrin xi 3 and Babylonian Talmud Berakoth 20b, noted with other passages by W. Bacher, *Die Exegetische Terminologie der jüdischen Traditions-literatur* (2 parts, Leipzig 1899, 1905, reprinted in one volume, Darmstadt 1965), i, p. 134 n. 4; ii, p. 2. In discussion of the paper as delivered orally M. Jacobs drew attention to this distinction as an indication of the continuing importance of the scriptures.

honoured question, but for the present purpose it matters mainly that there was enough biblical interpretation, and enough stress on the independent authority of the written Torah, to *make* it a question.[35]

It may be asked, similarly, whether the biblically elaborated themes of Talmud and midrash in the fourth century, striking as they are in their convergence with Christian concerns and exegesis, are restricted in time and place to the new conditions of the Christian empire. To speak only of the messianic theme, the extensive messianic passages in the Targums include material which is probably partly earlier and partly later than Constantine. Messianic passages in synagogue poetry are for the most part probably later, but they diverge significantly from the emphases of the midrash without losing the close midrashic ties with the Bible.[36] Messianism is comparably important, to mention much earlier literature, in the Septuagint and its Jewish revisions in the west, and in the Peshitta Pentateuch in the east. The treatment of this theme in biblically governed ways which converge with Christian approaches seems therefore to be very widely attested.

Lastly, considerable Jewish–Christian contact and common ground emerged from the foregoing discussions of polemic and the canon. Jews would probably not have given weight to outside opinion on the number of the books, but some Jews would have known that Christians were concerned to follow a Jewish norm. Against this background it would seem possible that, although a Jew might not enter into christological argument, he could be aware of the main topics of debate (as the well-publicized character of the Arian controversy would suggest); just as a Christian, although he would not sympathize with the niceties of halakhic discussion, could have some comprehension of the importance of oral tradition in Jewish eyes (as Jerome, Augustine and others know that Jewish teachers pass on tradition called *deuterosis*, doubtless the Greek for *mishnah*, although in Christian usage *deuterosis* covered a wider range of material than that incorporated in *the* Mishnah).[37] In general, the differences between Christians and Jews were not such as to rule out some mutual knowledge, however sketchy.

[35]H. L. Strack & G. Stemberger, *Einleitung in Talmud und Midrasch* (Munich, 1982), 129–32 (8th edn (1992), 131–4); E.T. [by M. N. A. Bockmuehl, Edinburgh 1991], 141–5.

[36]W. Horbury, 'Suffering and Messianism in Yose ben Yose', in W. Horbury & B.McNeil (edd.), *Suffering and Martyrdom in the New Testament* (Cambridge, 1981), 143–82.

[37]On Jewish awareness of Christian arguments and writings, see O. Irsai, 'R. Abbahu Said: "If a Man Should Say to You 'I am God' – He is a Liar"', *Zion* xlvii (1982), 173–7 [Hebrew], and Visotzky, 'Overturning the Lamp' (see n. 13, above), 'Trinitarian Testimonies', *USQR* xlii (1988), 73–85, and 'Anti-Christian Polemic in Leviticus Rabbah', *Proceedings of the American Academy for Jewish Research* lvi (1990), 83–100; on Christian awareness of rabbinic

Christians in the period from Nicaea to Chalcedon who shared the widespread respect for the Jewish canon studied above were therefore largely justified in thinking that they shared the Jewish Bible, despite the interpretative divergence arising from the New Testament and ecclesiastical tradition on the one hand, and halakhic tradition on the other. In Judaism the written Torah did not lose independent authority. In Christianity, likewise, the 'Old Testament' was not confounded with the 'New'. The 'Old' was recognized as the nucleus to which the 'New' had been added, and as a body of literature still circulating separately among the Jews; and it therefore kept a distinctive éclat as the truly ancient and authentic repository of wisdom and oracles.[38] So Augustine could stress, in the anti-Donatist treatise already quoted (*Epistula ad Catholicos* 50 (xix), PL xliii 430), that the Lord himself (Luke xxiv 44–7) expected the disciples to be convinced not by the resurrection appearances in themselves, but because they could find the sequence crucifixion-resurrection foretold in the ancient canonical writings of the Law and the Prophets and the Psalms.

3. Demarcation and Convergence

The foregoing comparison of patristic and rabbinic attitudes to the Jewish scriptures has once again drawn attention to the geography and the languages of exegesis. To what extent were these divisive in the period under review? Christian knowledge of Hebrew was minimal, but Jewish use of Hebrew was itself restricted. Thus the Mishnah (Sotah vii 1) permits important prayers and biblical passages, including the Shema, to be recited in any language, and Greek is the principal language of Jewish inscriptions in Rome and the eastern provinces (it is followed far behind by Latin, and is strongly represented in Palestine and Syria, where Aramaic and Hebrew inscriptions are of course also numerous). Many Jews read and studied their own scriptures in translation, although by the fifth century a Jewish marriage-contract from Antinoupolis gives Greek

---

institutions, de Lange, *Origen*, 34–5 (Jerome on *deuterosis*); Strack-Stemberger, *Einleitung*, 43 (E.T. 38) and Blumenkranz, *Judenpredigt*, 65–6 (Augustine, *Contra Adversarium legis et prophetarum* ii 1 (PL xlii 637), on orally transmitted traditions as *deuterosis*).

[38]On the Jewish scriptures presented as a body of wisdom and prophecy in Christian apologetic, see W. Horbury, 'Old Testament Interpretation in the Writings of the Church Fathers', in M. J. Mulder & H. Sysling (edd.), *Mikra: Text, Translation, Reading and Interpretation of the Hebrew Bible in Ancient Judaism and Early Christianity* (Assen & Philadelphia, 1988), 727–87 (740–44).

in Hebrew transliteration.[39] By this time, therefore, there would probably be pressure, such as is later mentioned in Justinian's Novella of 553, for *public* reading of the Hebrew biblical text only, rather than the Hebrew followed by a translation.[40] For the most part, however, Christians and Jews were united in use of the languages prevalent where they lived, above all Greek in the eastern provinces and Greek and Latin in the west, but with a notable Christian as well as Jewish share in the Aramaic of the eastern frontier regions (Syria, Mesopotamia, Babylonia; in our period, Jews in Egypt also were using Aramaic as well as Greek). Among Jews in the Holy Land Aramaic and Greek were rival vernaculars, and Hebrew needed some encouragement; in a saying current from the early third century it was asked 'in the land of Israel, why speak the Syrian tongue? Use either Hebrew or Greek' (Babylonian Talmud, Stoah 49b, in the name of R. Judah the Prince).

In Greek, and probably also in Latin and Aramaic, the Jewish biblical translations were shared by Christians. The same is likely to be true of Jewish exegetical helps, to judge by the clear and abundant evidence in Greek (Christian use of Philo, Josephus, other Jewish writings, and information from contemporary Jews). On the other hand, as noted already, Jews were developing what came to be a classical literature of exegesis and legal tradition largely in Hebrew and Aramaic, and in Galilee and the east, whereas Christian exegetical culture was predominantly Greek, with increasingly important Latin tributaries, and centred further towards the west; but the eastern Roman provinces, above all Syria, the Holy Land and Egypt, formed an important area of overlap.[41] On the Jewish side, much exegesis now surviving only in Hebrew or Aramaic will probably once have been current also in Greek, not only in a city such as Caesarea, noted above, but also, as the Greek Jewish inscriptions of Galilee[42] and the many Greek loan-words in the midrash suggest, in the Galilaean centres of study like Tiberias.

---

[39]P. Col. Inv. 5853, ed. C. Sirat, P. Cauderlier, M. Dukan & M. Friedmann, *Papyrologica Coloniensia* xii (Opladen, 1986), discussed by N. R. M. de Lange, 'Judaïsmo y cristianismo: mitos antiguos y diálogo moderno', *Miscelanea de estudios arabes y hebraicos* xxxix (Granada, 1990), 5–29 (27).

[40]Such pressure is envisaged in the third century by de Lange, *Origen*, 57.

[41]On the Holy Land in our period, see G. Stemberger, *Juden und Christen im Heiligen Land: Palästina unter Konstantin und Theodosius* (Munich, 1987), with the essay under the same title by A. M. Ritter in J. van Amersfoort & J. van Oort (edd.), *Juden und Christen in der Antike* (Kampen, 1990), 116–24.

[42]Note the many Greek epitaphs of Besara/Beth Shéarim (edited by M. Schwabe & B. Lifschitz, *The Greek Inscriptions* (Jerusalem, 1967)), and the Aramaic and Greek inscriptions of the Hammath Tiberias synagogue mosaic (Dothan, *Hammath Tiberias* (n. 2 above), 53–62).

There was therefore not the great sundering of cultures and interests which is initially suggested by the contrasts between Christian Greek and Latin on the one hand, and Jewish Hebrew and Aramaic on the other, or between the Christian identification with the Roman empire, exemplified above in Hilary of Poitiers, and the Persian links of the eastern Jewish population.[43] Further, as argued in the previous section, biblical interpretation remained a central Jewish concern, integrated with yet distinguishable from the development of legal tradition. Here it is significant that, as mentioned in section (i), the midrash was developed not only in Palestine, with its strong Christian presence, but also over the Roman frontier in Babylonia; the Targum, substantially of Palestinian origin like the midrash, was also intensively studied and corrected in Babylonia.[44]

The distribution of the Jewish and Christian populations and languages was therefore not in itself divisive, and despite important differences between Jewish and Christian presuppositions the two communities can each be said to have made interpretation of the same set of scriptural books a major concern. Sometimes a common language will have meant particularly extensive common ground in exegesis, notably where both Christians and Jews habitually read the Bible in Greek.[45] Thus it is in the Greek-speaking context that one can most clearly detect the progressive influence on Christians of a Jewish tendency towards greater ἀκρίβεια, as ecclesiastical exegetes reckon more and more with the Jewish revisions of the Septuagint, and in their principles of exposition are conformed, as noted above, to the canon-based interpretation already exemplified in different ways in Philo and Josephus. As F. C. Burkitt commented, 'The Church was singularly willing to accept the verdict of Jewish scholarship, even at the cost of abandoning famous proof-texts'.[46] In Christian reception of this influence the fundamental character of

---

[43]Evidence for Sassanid favour towards the Jews is summarized by J. G. Snaith, 'Aphrahat and the Jews', in J. A. Emerton & S. C. Reif (edd.), *Interpreting the Hebrew Bible: Essays in honour of E. I. J. Rosenthal* (Cambridge, 1982), 235–50 (236–7).

[44]G. Stemberger, 'Midrasch in Babylonien. Am Beispiel von Sota 9b-14a', *Henoch* x (1988), 183–203; A. Goldberg in S. Safrai (ed.), *The Literature of the Sages*, First Part (Assen & Philadelphia, 1987), 336 (allowing for Babylonian midrashic creativity despite the Palestinian origin of much midrash in the Babylonian Talmud); P. S. Alexander, 'Jewish Aramaic Translations of Hebrew Scriptures', in Mulder & Sysling, *Mikra*, 217–53 (217–18 (Targum Onkelos), 223 (Targum Jonathan), 249 (Targumic tradition in Babylonia)).

[45]De Lange, *Origen*, 11, 51–2, 57–8 (mainly on third-century Caesarea).

[46]F. C. Burkitt, 'The Debt of Christianity to Judaism', in E. R. Bevan & C. Singer (edd.) *The Legacy of Israel* (Oxford, 1927), 69–96 (88–9).

the Hebrew text was of course implicitly acknowledged, and it seems likely that the Jewish revisions themselves reflect both a strong sense of the importance of the Hebrew among Jews, even though Hebrew was not widely spoken, and effective communication between Palestinian centres of study (themselves Greek-speaking) and the Greek-speaking western diaspora.[47]

Observations such as these have to satisfy those who look for Jewish exegetical works in Greek, and perhaps also Latin, from the same time as the great Greek and Latin writings of Christian exegesis. Some material is probably lost, some may survive in Christian transmission, for example in the Old Latin version (the *Collatio Legum* is a possible instance of the survival of a separate treatise), and Philo and Josephus will have had Jewish as well as Christian readers;[48] the Roman Jewish community, for instance, at the time (384) when Jerome was studying books borrowed from a Roman synagogue library by a Jewish acquaintance, will certainly have included scholarly members.[49] As consolation for the absence of Jewish Greek and Latin commentaries there are just the many individual cases in which a Christian writer depends not merely on Philo, Josephus or Jewish biblical versions and apocryphal writings, but also or instead on contemporary Jewish interpretation.[50] (Some non-literary confirmation of diaspora biblical study and its mediation to Christians is offered by inscriptions and remains of Jewish and Christian art, notably at Dura Europus and in the Roman

[47]The significance of rabbinic material on exchange between the Holy Land and the western diaspora, especially Rome, is emphasized by M. Hengel in M. Hengel (with a contribution by H. Bloedhorn), 'Der alte und der neue "Schürer"', *JSS* xxxv (1990), 19–72(42); the non-rabbinic evidence for patriarchal influence on the diaspora synagogues is surveyed by S. J. D. Cohen, 'Pagan and Christian Evidence on the Ancient Synagogue', in L. I. Levine (ed.), *The Synagogue in Late Antiquity* (Philadelphia, 1987), 159–81 (170–75).

[48]Some (not primarily exegetical) Jewish Greek writings later than Josephus surviving in Christian transmission are noted by de Lange, 'Mitos', 25 (add the apologia in the pseudo-Clementine *Homilies* iv–vi, discussed by Simon, *Verus Israel*, 49–50); the importance of Josephus for a Jewish readership is brought out by L. Troiani, 'I Lettori delle Antichità Giudaiche di Giuseppe: prospettive e problemi', *Athenaeum* N.S. lxiv (1986), 343–53.

[49]Jerome, *Ep.* xxxvi 1, to Damasus (Jerome was dictating a reply to Damasus, 'cum subito Hebraeus intervenit, deferens non pauca volumina, quae de synagoga quasi lecturus acceperat. Et illico habes, inquit, quod postulaveras: meque ... ita festinus exterruit, ut omnibus praetermissis ad scribendum transvolarem'), with comments in J. N. D. Kelly, *Jerome* (London, 1975), 83–4; L. Cracco Ruggini, 'La Lettera di Anna a Seneca nella Roma pagana e cristiana del IV secolo', *Augustinianum* xxviii (1988), 301–25, especially 305 & n. 9, 322–5.

[50]Studies of the material are gathered in J. R. Baskin, 'Rabbinic-Patristic Exegetical Contacts in Late Antiquity: a Bibliographical Reappraisal', in W. S. Green (ed.) *Approaches to Ancient Judaism*, v (Atlanta, 1985), 53–80.

catacombs.[51]) The agreements with rabbinic literature to be detected in many of these instances on the face of it bear out the view just expressed, that results of the studies carried on in the Holy Land, under the aegis of the patriarch for most of our period, were disseminated to the western as well as the eastern diaspora. In Persia and Mesopotamia, on the other hand, where the Christians were humbler and less numerous, Aphrahat and Ephrem Syrus have been judged to reflect Jewish, but not specifically rabbinic, contracts.[52]

Language and geography, then, do not bring about demarcation to the extent which might have been expected; but contrasts remain. Thus the company of famous named authors in the church stand over against lost or anonymous Jewish writers in Greek and Latin (But the names on the rabbinic roll of honour are scrupulously preserved). Again, rabbinical exegesis employed Hebrew, in which not all Jews were fluent, whereas patristic Greek united the majority of Christians in many places (although this contrast is modified by the presence of extensive portions of Aramaic in the midrash, and by the importance of Coptic and Syriac as Christian vernaculars).

On the other hand, there are great similarities between the forms of midrashic and later patristic literature. In particular, the midrash, with its collection of exegeses by various rabbis, corresponds closely to the catena, traditionally originating with Procopius of Gaza at the end of the fifth century; the rabbinic and the patristic representatives of the catena-form arise, as N. R. M. de Lange emphasizes, at the same place and time.[53] The so-called homiletic midrashim, based on sermons for the sabbaths and festivals, likewise resemble Christian

---

[51]Jewish inscriptions include the titles φιλομαθής (Aphrodisias), διδάσκαλος νομομαθής (Rome), μαθητὴς σοφῶν (Rome), σοφοδιδάσκαλος (Sardis), discussed by Reynolds & Tannenbaum, *Aphrodisias*, 30–34; on Old Testament scenes in early Christian art (the importance of which was emphasized in discussion of this paper by G. Kretschmar), and the question of their Jewish background, Horbury, 'Interpretation', 755–8, and nn. 138–9 (literature; see especially G. Stemberger, 'Die Patriarchenbilder der Katakombe in der Via Latina im Lichte der jüdischen Tradition', *Kairos* N.F. xvi (1974), 19–78); at Mopsuestia in Cilicia, in a fifth-century basilica identified by some as a church and by others as a synagogue, the partly-preserved Greek inscription of a mosaic depicting Samson with the harlot of Gaza offers an expanded Greek test of Judg. xvi 1–2 (R. Stichel, 'Die Inschriften des Samson-Mosaiks in Mopsuestia und ihre Beziehung zum biblischen Text', *Byzantinische Zeitschrift* lxxii (1978), 50–61, notes that, if Jewish, it illustrates diaspora exegesis, and if Christian, Jewish influence).

[52]J. Neusner, *Aphrahat and Judaism* (Leiden, 1971), especially 144–9, 187–95, 244; Murray, *Symbols*, 10, 18–19; Snaith, 'Aphrahat', 247–50.

[53]N. R. M. de Lange, 'Midrach et Byzance: une traduction française du "Midrach Rabba". Notes critiques', *RHR* ccvi (1989), 171–81 (173–5); on contemporary Jewish and Christian treatment of one book, M. Hirschman, 'The Greek Fathers and the Aggada on Ecclesiastes: Formats of Exegesis in Late Antiquity', *HUCA* lix (1988), 137–65.

collections of homilies. On the verges of rabbinic literature, biblical versions, including the rabbinically-influenced Aquila in Greek, could be shared, as noted already, and the Aramaic Targum Onkelos has affinities with the Peshitta Syriac used by Christians. Lastly, the biblically-based Hebrew poems used in synagogue hymnody (*piyyutim*) developed at the same time as their Syriac and Greek Christian counterparts, notably in Ephrem Syrus and Romanus, and likewise excel in allusive exegesis.[54] Their antecedents include Aramaic hymns handed down in the Targumic tradition, and papyrological discoveries have underlined the concurrence of Jewish and Christian developments in hymnody by exposing the circulation in our period in Egypt both of the Jewish Aramaic '*ezel Mosheh* (in a fourth–fifth century papyrus), on Moses at the Red Sea, and of a Christian Latin 'Psalmus abecedarius' (in a fourth-century papyrus), on the birth and marriage of the Virgin and the birth of Christ.[55]

With regard to the *modes* of exegesis, Jewish hermeneutical methods appear to have been derived above all from the Greek background of philosophy and rhetoric, as is the case in Christian exegesis too, and among both Jews and Christians there is the same contrast and confluence of literal and symbolic interpretation (embracing typology and allegory).[56] The Christian claim (e.g. Origen, *Contra Celsum* v 60) that the Jews stick to a literal interpretation and thereby miss the true sense refers to differences not of exegetical method but of custom and tenet, especially over the Pentateuchal laws and messianic prophecy. The important shared exegetical principle of the canon has received attention above.

Lines of demarcation appear more readily with regard to *lemmata* in combination with *themes*. Here the differing festivals and lectionary practices of the two communities are important. Thus the Psalms of dereliction and the narrative of the Exodus were for

[54]Some probably fifth-century Hebrew material is translated and studied in Horbury, 'Yose'; see also Z. Malachi, 'Jewish and Christian Liturgical Poetry: Mutual Influences in the First Four Centuries', *Augustinianum* xxviii (1988), 237–48.

[55]Y. Yahalom, '"Ezel Moshe" – according to the Berlin Papyrus', *Tarbiz* xlvii (1978), 173–84 [Hebrew]; W. Speyer, 'Der bisher älteste lateinische Psalmus abecedarius. Zur editio princeps von R. Roca-Puig', reprinted (with additional notes) from: *Jahrbuch für Antike und Christentum* x (1967), 211–16 in W. Speyer, *Frühes Christentum im antiken Strahlungsfeld*, (Tübingen, 1989), 64–9, 494.

[56]P. S. Alexander, 'Quid Athenis et Hierosolymis? Rabbinic Midrash and Hermeneutics in the Graeco-Roman World', in P. R. Davies & R. T. White (edd.), *A Tribute to Geza Vermes* (Sheffield, 1990), 101–24; Horbury, 'Interpretation', 763–70; B. L. Visotzky, 'Jots and Tittles: On Scriptural Interpretation in Rabbinic and Patristic Literatures', *Prooftexts* viii (1988), 257–69; F. M. Young, 'The Rhetorical Schools and their Influence on Patristic Exegesis', in Rowan Williams (ed.), *The Making of Orthodoxy. Essays in Honour of Henry Chadwick* (Cambridge, 1989), 182–99.

Christians linked from early times with the Passion and Easter, and the traces of Christian lectionaries from the time of Augustine show the importance of New Testament lessons, by contrast with the primacy in the synagogues of the reading of the Law. There is not a complete overlap between the texts thought specially worthy of comment by Christians and Jews.[57] Nevertheless, because the Bible is highly valued common property, texts which one might expect to be left aside are in fact interpreted. Thus, there is no marked Christian neglect of Pentateuchal passages on diet or ritual.[58] They are of course symbolically interpreted. On the Red Heifer, for example, Theodoret in a scholastic manner (*Quaest. in Num.* 35–6, on Num. xix) and Cyril of Alexandria with homiletic skill (*Glaphyra on Numbers*, PG lxix 625–36) build on ancient Christological exegesis, such as is already met in Hebrews and the Epistle of Barnabas; but the Jewish defence and commendation of such laws in the midrash can also make them symbolic, as was already the case in the Letter of Aristeas and Philo (so on the Heifer, in Pesikta de-Rab Kahana, iv and Num. R. xix 1–8). Yet, as appears from the passages just cited, the natural Christian association of these laws is with reconciliation through Christ, which is readily linked with apologetic against Judaism; so Cyril stresses that 'the purification which is in Christ is outside the synagogue of the Jews' (PG lxix 633). The Jewish associations of these laws, on the other hand, include the interpretation and defence of other laws of purity and diet; so Solomon is said to have perceived the solution of many specified problems of these laws, although the rite of the Heifer still puzzled him (Pesikta de-Rab Kahana iv 3, Num. R. xix 3). Nevertheless, the strong Christian instinct towards literal and practical interpretation of the Pentateuchal laws (part of the reason why apologetic is needed when the laws are not observed) can manifest itself freely where the mainstream Christian rejection of Jewish customs is not at stake, notably in connection with the priesthood, tithing and usury.[59] The demarcation between Christian and Jewish exegesis of biblical laws seems therefore to arise less from any special hermeneutical methods than from the differing ancestral customs and messianic interpretations of the two communities.

Johann Maier has brought out the importance of discovering the 'range of association' of any given text (its *Assoziationskontext* or

---

[57]Neusner, *Aphrahat*, 157–87 finds that a very large number of Aphrahat's anti-Jewish proof-texts receive no rabbinic comment in material likely to be before or contemporary with Aphrahat (messianic texts form an interesting exception).

[58]Horbury, 'Interpretation', 762–3.

[59]Examples are discussed by Horbury, 'Interpretation', 744–8.

-horizont) when comparing Jewish and Christian exegesis.[60] Such an exercise can reveal demarcation and convergence at the same time. The ways may divide, in particular, as noted already in connection with the festivals, because for Christian exegesis the New Testament is likely to suggest associations not available to the Jewish reader.

An example is offered in the great Torah Psalm cxix. Verse 120 'my flesh bristles for fear of thee' appears in the LXX as 'Nail (καθήλωσον) my flesh [plural] because of thy fear', and correspondingly in the Gallican Psalter as 'Confige timore tuo carnes meas'. In the LXX the Hebrew verb סמר, 'to bristle' has been given the sense 'to nail' which it has in the Mishnah (and the biblical noun for 'nail' is formed from the same consonants), and has been understood as an imperative. The meaning 'to nail', but not the imperative, is endorsed by Theodotion and Aquila (Symmachus, followed by Jerome, gives 'bristle').

Following the LXX, from very early times Christian exegesis associates this verse with the nails of the cross,[61] either as a prophetic testimony of the Passion (quoted between Pss. xxii 20 and 16 at Barn. v 13, Irenaeus, *Dem.* 79, and after Ps. xxii 17–22 at Cyprian, *Test.* ii 20, and paraphrased in one form of an early Christological interpolation in Ps. xxxviii 20)[62] or, as a prayer (here the LXX imperative is important) on the Pauline theme of crucifixion with Christ (linked in comments on the psalm with Matthew x 38 by Origen [quoted in the Palestinian catena on the psalm], and with Gal. ii 20 by Theodoret and Augustine; Chrysostom [Hom. iv on I Thess., 457A, on iii 13] calls Paul 'the man nailed by the fear of God'). In the Old Latin the association with the cross was strengthened by the insertion of 'clavis', 'with nails', after 'confige' (so in the Latin text of Barnabas and in Cyprian); Hilary of Poitiers and Augustine in their comments ad loc. both mention this form of the text and commend it as a translation of the Greek, and Augustine echoes the Old Latin when he says elsewhere that the fear of God ¬hould fasten all the impulses of pride to the wood of the cross, quasi *clavatis carnibus* omnes superbiae motus ligno crucis adfigat' (*De Doctrina Christiana* ii 7).

---

[60]Maier, *Auseinandersetzung*, 208; id., ' "Siehe, ich mach(t)e dich klein unter den Völkern ... ": Zum rabbinischen Assoziationschorizont von Obadja 2', in L. Ruppert, P. Weimar & E. Zenger (edd.), *Künder des Wortes: Beiträge zur Theologie der Propheten; Josef Schreiner zum 60. Geburtstag* (Würzburg, 1982), 203–15.

[61]Christian exegesis of the verse is summarized by M. Harl, *La chaîne palestinienne sur le psaume 118* (2 vols., Paris, 1972), ii, 706–7.

[62]R. Petraglio, 'Le interpolazioni cristiane del salterio greco', *Augustinianum* xxviii (1988), 89–109 (100, n. 20).

In these interpretations the use of the verse as a testimony is distinctively Christian, although the practice of collecting biblical testimonies was inherited from Jewish custom within the broader Graeco-Roman context of excerpting and anthologizing; but the moral and mystical understandings developed in Origen, Theodoret, Hilary and Augustine are in the end, despite their Pauline inspiration, not so far removed from the mystical as well as moral attitude to the fear of God already underlined by the imperative in the LXX. In the midrash, however, the moral element is strengthened at the expense of the mystical by interpretation of 'fear' as 'fear of Gehenna', but this in turn is linked again with the fear of heaven, a great rabbinic as well as Christian virtue, by reference to Isa. xxxiii 7 and Prov. xxviii 14 'Blessed is the man who fears continually' (Midrash Tehillim ad loc.).

In this example, then, distinctively Christian associations arising from the New Testament govern the Christian exegesis of a text from the psalter. They ensure its use as a proof-text, but otherwise – with the addition of the theme of crucifixion with Christ – they take it along mystical and moral lines already marked out in the LXX. The LXX translation itself is not fanciful, but a reasonable rendering of the Hebrew, largely endorsed in two Jewish revisions of the LXX; it is worth noting that the seventeenth-century Jewish commentator David Altschuler of Prague once again drew attention to the probable connection between the Hebrew verb in this verse and the biblical noun meaning nail. The rabbinic interpretation of the Hebrew text is predominantly moral, but so is much of the Christian comment. The Christ-mysticism which seems at first so strikingly Christian a feature of this comment is itself in this case a not wholly inappropriate development of a pre-rabbinic Jewish mystical understanding of the fear of God, which already seemed to the LXX translators to be present in the Hebrew text. As in the interpretations of the Red Heifer noted above, there is considerable overlap between Jewish and Christian understandings, and the ways diverge, once again, not primarily for exegetical reasons, but because of differences between the Christian and the Jewish inheritance, in particular the distinctive centrality of a realized messianism in Christian thought and the New Testament literature.

The study of many such examples of association would complement and check the rough outlines of demarcation and convergence which have been attempted here, with special reference to the years 325–451. It was repeatedly urged above that to see demarcation only is not enough, despite all that seems to speak for the self-contained separate development of Judaism and Christianity. Some consideration was given in particular to arguments for separation drawn from the apparent presence of Christian and absence of Jewish polemic (section (i)), from the importance of the new political situation under Constantine as suggesting special reasons for some thematic convergence between rabbinic and Christian literature (section (ii)), and from the differing views of the Hebrew Bible symbolized by the emergence of the New Testament on one side and of the Mishnah and the Talmud on the other (section (ii)). Arguments for an exegetical interrelationship drew especially on evidence for Jewish–Christian contacts in controversy and in study (section (i)), and on the noteworthy Christian desire to share the Jewish Bible in the canonical form recognized by Jews (section (ii)). Lastly, in section (iii) the geography and languages of exegesis were shown to allow convergence as well as demarcation, the great similarities in the forms and modes of exegesis were underlined, and in examination of a longer and a shorter text, from the Pentateuch and the Psalter respectively, it was argued that lemmata in combination with themes and in their Jewish and Christian contexts of association, where demarcation would be apparent, could also show considerable convergence.

The demarcation observed has arisen from the differences between Jewish and Christian custom and conviction rather than from any conflict of exegetical methods. These differences were keenly felt by Christians, and mattered also to some Jews. They did not mean, however, that the Bible was understood so differently as not truly to be shared. Exegesis for catechetical purposes would part Christians from Jews at a number of points, especially concerning the law and the messiah; but other kinds of interpretation joined hands. Of special note is the mass of exegesis from both sides devoted to moral instruction and exhortation. It is not misleading to continue to speak of Jews and Christians *on the Bible*.

Far-reaching divergence of approach to this subject was noted at the beginning of the paper and considered at the principal stages *en route*. It may therefore be helpful to conclude with some brief formulations of positions, which at least the writer thinks defensible, on exegesis in the Jewish and Christian communities between 325 and 451.

(i) Jews and Christians shared a common sub-culture, the literary focus of which was the Jewish scriptures. Jerome stood for a widespread Christian instinct of respect for the Hebrew text and the Jewish canon.

(ii) The Jewish scriptures continued to be recognized in each community as an independent body of authoritative writings, despite their close bonds with the New Testament and ecclesiastical tradition among the Christians, and with rabbinic tradition among the Jews.

(iii) The abundant rabbinic literature was in process of formation at this time. It is the best guide to Jewish exegesis in the period, but it is not a complete guide.

(iv) Particularly important supplements to the rabbinic texts are the ancient biblical versions, for the most part shared with Christians, and used extensively by the more scholarly Christian exegetes of this period.

(v) Languages and geography were not significantly divisive factors, especially in view of Jewish biblical study in the vernaculars (Aramaic, Greek, and probably also Latin).

(vi) Exegetical methods were shared, and divergent interpretation reflected differences of custom and tenet, not of exegetical principle. Jewish–Christian controversy encouraged some convergence of interest.

(vii) Jewish and Christian special interests deeply marked interpretation in each community, but did not blot out the features of a common Bible.[63]

[63]Some further work on these topics is discussed at pp. 25–36, above.

9

EARLY CHRISTIANS ON SYNAGOGUE PRAYER AND IMPRECATION

The synagogue was tolerated under Christian rule in antiquity and the Middle Ages, but much New Testament and patristic authority, including some texts reviewed below, would have weighed on the side of restriction. Early Christian comment on contemporary Jewish worship had intertwined roots in inner-Jewish controversy and in Greek and Roman anti-Jewish polemic.[1]

Yet such comment, despite its polemical character, included some genuine observation.[2] This aspect is illustrated here with two aims in view. First, evidence on Jewish worship in the ancient world is patchy, whether Jewish or non-Jewish. Christian texts are therefore potentially important to the historian of the ancient synagogue, as S. J. D. Cohen has emphasized.[3] Here some passages are reconsidered which may throw light on the rise of the synagogue and the development of Jewish prayer, including the question of anti-Christian imprecations in the synagogue. Secondly, the potentially misleading character of the image of Judaism in Christian polemic has long been noted.[4] Assessment of the Christian sources should also reckon, however, with the keen if hostile observation which they sometimes reflect.

In modern liturgical study, it has often been assumed that Christians knew a good deal about Jewish worship – enough to be deeply influenced by it in their own prayers, down to the relatively late date of the Apostolic Constitutions. A strong support for this view is the dismay expressed by a series of church fathers at synagogue attendance by Christians; the witnesses include Origen, Aphrahat, Chrysostom and Jerome. In the west, at the end of the second century, Callistus is said to have gone into a synagogue in Rome, creating a disturbance by claiming to be a Christian; whatever the truth of this story, it shows what could be envisaged as plausible (Hippolytus, *Ref.* ix 7, 7–9). In third-century Smyrna, according to the Acts of Pionius (xiii 1), Jews invited Christians in a

[1]For the latter see especially Juster, *Les juifs*, i, 45, n. 1.
[2]This point is brought out by Lieu, 'History', 85–7. See also pp. 36–7, above.
[3]Cohen, 'Pagan and Christian Evidence', 159–60.
[4]See for example, Harnack, *Altercatio*, 57, 64–5 (allowing that some Christian texts reflect real contact with Jews, ibid., 73–4, 78 n. 59); Tränkle, *Tertulliani Adversus Iudaeos*, lxx–lxxi, n. 6; Lieu, 'History' (see n. 2, above); Taylor, *Jews*; pp. 21–5, above.

time of persecution 'into the synagogues', and those who accepted would give up their Christianity.[5]

Comparably, canons of the fourth century include prohibitions of sharing feasts with Jews (Elvira 50, Laodicea 37–8 (360; also forbids acceptance of gifts from Jews for Christian feasts), Apostolic Canon 69 (also forbids fasting with Jews)), with special reference to the Passover (canon 1 of Antioch, 341) and to taking oil into the synagogue for a festival (Apostolic Canon 70), and prohibitions of entering a synagogue (Apostolic Canon 63) or having fields blessed by Jews (Elvira 49).[6] Moreover, after Constantine the Christians were only too well aware of synagogues and their prestige; zealous Christians constantly sought to annex or destroy them, and by the sixth century compulsory sermons for Jews had become normal, although the earliest known examples appear to have been preached in the open or in church, not in the synagogue.[7] Bishops occasionally moderated these actions, but often tolerated or encouraged them, as Ambrose did by his stance in the Callinicum affair. All this points to long-standing Christian acquaintance with synagogues and their rites, but the need for caution can be exemplified by J. van der Lof's conclusion that, perhaps contrary to expectation, the evidence for the cult of the Maccabees does not evince close links between Christians and local synagogues in the third and fourth centuries.[8]

The limited historical inquiry undertaken here can conveniently start from the conclusions of S. J. D. Cohen, as cited above. First, looking at archaeological and literary evidence as a whole, he notes that earlier church fathers rarely mention the synagogue or pro-seuche, and in his view it is rarely mentioned by pagan authors. On the other hand, he says, it gets fuller Christian discussion in the second part of the fourth century, notably from Chrysostom and Jerome; similarly, archaeological evidence for synagogues becomes

---

[5]According to Goodman, *Mission*, 118–19 they could only have become godfearers, not proselytes, since Roman legislation forbade the circumcision of gentiles; but his inference is doubtful, for Jews were indeed forbidden to circumcise those *non eiusdem religionis* (by Antoninus Pius, according to Modestinus, quoted in *Digest* xlviii 8, 11), but Christians might well be considered as aberrant Jews, sharing the Jewish *religio*. So Tertullian acknowledges that they might seem to shelter *sub umbraculo insignissimae religionis, certe licitae* – Judaism (*Apol.* xxi 1). Goodman's stimulating argument against identification of Jewish enthusiasm for proselytizing before the third century A.D. seems to me in general to underrate the closeness of Christians to Jews, and the implications of earlier evidence for Jewish welcome to proselytes, for example in Philo and the Thirteenth Benediction of the Amidah (p. 98, above).
[6]Parkes, *Conflict*, 381–2.
[7]Blumenkranz, *Juifs et chrétiens*, 93–4.
[8]van der Lof, 'Les liens'.

more abundant from the late third century onwards. He infers from this convergence of archaeological and patristic evidence that synagogues did not in fact attain institutional prominence until this period, when there is also evidence for authority exercised in synagogues by the Jewish patriarch. Secondly, he says that patristic authors are important witnesses to the view that synagogues were regarded as temple-like holy places – a view found also, he notes, in Jewish inscriptions and rabbinic literature. Thirdly, he judges that Christian references to Jewish customs and rites are sparse, but notes that they include mention of the public reading of the law by Roman permission (Hippolytus, in connection with the story of Callistus), of the alleged theatricality of synagogue services, with particular reference to trumpet-blowing (Chrysostom), of an Antiochene synagogue built over the remains of the Maccabaean martyrs (John Malalas), and of a Jewish ethnarch and Jewish patriarchs (Origen and Epiphanius); in all these points, he says, the Christian sources can be supported from other evidence.

I The Rise of the Synagogue

First, then, on the general question of the rise of the synagogue, it may be noted that Christian sources set a question-mark against the relatively late dating for the emergence of the synagogue into institutional prominence which Cohen and others favour, insofar as they presuppose its familiarity at an earlier time in the homeland as well as the diaspora. With regard to the Second-Temple period, although there is much in favour of the view that synagogue buildings were known in Judaea as well as the diaspora by the time of Herod the Great,[9] the lack of pre-Roman archaeological and literary evidence leads some to judge that they would have been far less familiar in Herodian Judaea and Galilee than in the contemporary western diaspora, where inscriptions and literature amply attest the buildings of the proseuche;[10] at this period the name συναγωγή appears to be associated with the homeland rather than the diaspora, but in any case it would have been understood there, on this

[9]See Hengel, 'Proseuche'; Levine, 'The Second Temple Synagogue'; Sanders, *Jewish Law*, 77–9; id., *Judaism*, 198–202.

[10]For similar views see Meyers & Strange, *Archaeology*, 140–41; Kee, 'Transformation', exhaustively criticized by Sanders, *Jewish Law*, 341–3, nn. 28–9 (with special reference to archaeology, Philo and Josephus) and by Oster, 'Supposed Anachronism' (questioning Kee's assessment of Luke-Acts); also Kee, 'Changing Meaning' (inter alia, setting the Theodotus inscription found on mount Ophel in the fourth century or later, as opposed to the usual dating before A.D. 66; the later date raises many difficulties, as noted by Sanders, *Jewish Law*, 341, n. 28).

view of the development of the synagogue, primarily as 'assembly' rather than 'house of assembly'.[11] It is true that in the Mishnah, reflecting conditions in Judaea and Galilee, the 'house of assembly' is taken for granted; thus Akiba is said to appeal in an argument to usage in *bet ha-k^{e}nesset* (Ber. vii 3). A synagogue assembly could also occur, however, in the 'open place (*r^{e}hôb*) of the town' (Meg. iii 1, if the open place is sold, a house of assembly must be bought with the price; cf. Taan. ii 1, where on fast-days the ark is carried to the open place); and the survival of this information in a work compiled seventy years after the Bar Kokhba revolt would be consistent with the view that common earlier practice was to meet in the 'open place', not a synagogue building.[12]

Cohen's summary of the evidence designedly omits New Testament texts, but their contribution on this point is important, as they refer to Judaea and Galilee as well as the diaspora, and antedate the Mishnah by a century or more. In Matthew, Luke-Acts, and John the term συναγωγή, 'assembly' or 'house of assembly', appears without any special explanation; a synagogue has been 'built' in Capernaum according to Luke vii 5, and the term can most naturally be taken to refer to a building, not simply an assembly, in a number of other passages (for example Mark i 21, 29, xii 39, and parallels; Luke iv 16, 44, xiii 10; Acts xiii 14, xviii 7). In Acts vi 9, on the other hand, 'the synagogue of the *libertini*' in Jerusalem is primarily an assembly or corporation formed by a particular group (compare the synagogues of the Augustesians and the Agrippesians in Rome), and including Cyrenians, Alexandrians and others;[13] yet in a rabbinic tradition, by contrast, it happens that a '*house* of assembly (*bet ha-k^{e}nesset*) of the Alexandrians who were in Jerusalem' (Tos. Meg. iii 6, compare j Meg. iii 1, 73d) is mentioned, by the second-century teacher Judah b. Ilai, in a discussion of the uses to which a former synagogue can be put – a discussion presupposing that it was, and may still be, in some sense a holy place.[14] This rabbinic passage is a reminder that an attestation of συναγωγή in the sense of 'assembly' by no means rules out the possibility of a room or building for the

---

[11]So Reif, *Hebrew Prayer*, 73–5, with nn. 42–3 (literature); on nomenclature see especially Hengel, 'Proseuche', and the summary of names by Levine, 'The Second Temple Synagogue', 13–14.

[12]Compare the αἴθριοι προσευχαί said by Apion to have been built by Moses (Apion, quoted by Josephus, *Ap.* ii 10); did some old proseuchae in Egypt approximate to the 'open place' by providing a courtyard used for assembly?

[13]On the interpretation of the Greek see Barrett, *Acts*, i, 323–4, ad loc.

[14]The Mishnah in this context quotes Lev. xxxvi 31 'And I will bring their sanctuaries into desolation' to show that the holiness of the synagogues abides even when they are forsaken (Meg. iii 3).

assembly. Similarly, the synagogue environment can be implied where the word does not occur at all, as in Paul's reference to the ἀνάγνωσις of the Pentateuch at II Cor. iii 14–15.[15] Finally, the organization of the assembly or corporation under ἀρχισυνάγωγοι is assumed as entirely familiar, once again with regard to the homeland as well as the diaspora (Mark v 22 and parallels, Luke xiii 14, Acts xiii 15, xviii 8, 17).

The New Testament texts bear on the question of the rise of the synagogue in at least three ways. First, they combine with Justin Martyr, Tertullian and Hippolytus to suggest that synagogues, including synagogue buildings, were taken for granted by the time of Christian origins, in the homeland as well as the diaspora, and continued to be prominent and familiar to Christians in the second century. Justin Martyr mentions synagogues as repositories of the biblical books (Justin, *Dial.* lxxii 3). Tertullian calls them *templa* (*Iei.* xvi 6, discussed below), as Tacitus did (*Hist.* v 5); and they are implied, but not mentioned by name, when Tertullian says of the biblical readings of the Jews 'vulgo aditur sabbatis omnibus' (*Apol.* xviii 8); he doubtless echoes Acts xv 21 on the sabbath reading from Moses (compare II Cor. iii 14–15, cited above), but the contemporary character of his observation emerges from his bitter allusion to Roman protection of the Jewish assemblies – 'a liberty paid for by tribute' (attested at about the same time in Hippolytus on the Roman synagogue visited by Callistus, as cited above).

Secondly, New Testament and early patristic passages cohere with and amplify Jewish and pagan evidence for the synagogue as an accepted institution about the time of Christian origins. Thus the New Testament assumption that synagogues were familiar in the Holy Land is fully consistent with Josephus on events at synagogue buildings at Dora in Phoenicia, on the coast between Caesarea and mount Carmel, under Agrippa I, and at Caesarea and Tiberias in 66–7 (Josephus, *Ant.* xix 300–311; *B.J.* ii 285–92; *Vita*, 277–303). He uses συναγωγή for the first two, προσευχή for the third (which was a μέγιστον οἴκημα, *Vita* 277); in the Caesarean narrative he implies the holiness of the place (the Jews believed it to be defiled, he says, by the Greeks who sacrificed at the entrance), and he mentions the removal of 'the laws' by the Jews for safety (*B.J.* ii 289, 291).

---

[15]This view is further encouraged if Paul's stress on the veil alludes to scroll wrappings (M. Meg. iii 1) or reflects some early form of the practice of shielding the ark with a veil (attested from the third century A.D., see Z. Safrai, 'Dukhan', 72, 74, and n. 29), as is urged by Knox, *Gentiles*, 131 (noting the symbolism of the temple veil in Philo); but the hint at synagogue practice depends on the mention of reading (Acts xiii 15, xv 21; Philo, *Hyp.* vii 12–13) rather than the question of the veil.

This last point recalls Justin Martyr on the synagogue books. Perhaps not far away in time from Josephus's narrative are the founder's inscriptions from the synagogue of Theodotus in Jerusalem and the proseuche of Papous in Egypt.[16] Again, Acts mentions diaspora synagogues in Syria, Cyprus, Asia Minor and Greece, but not in Italy. Its overlap with other sources is not complete. Thus Josephus mentions the Jews of Cyprus, but not their synagogues (*Ant.* xiii 284–7). On the other hand, the Roman proseuchae are relatively well attested outside Acts. For the Augustan period, Philo on the proseuchae in Rome tolerated by Augustus (*Leg. ad Gaium* 156) is corroborated by Ovid, implying their existence without naming them (and indicating attendance by women) when he tells his pupil in the art of love

> Nec te praetereat Veneri ploratus Adonis,
>   cultaque Iudaeo septima sacra Syro (*A.A.* i 76).[17]

No doubt, then, in Acts xxviii it is assumed that the reader will know of the unmentioned Roman synagogues, and will note that Paul seems not to have received permission to speak in them. This phenomenon of coherence without full overlap with other sources, evident as regards both the homeland and the diaspora, commends the New Testament material on the synagogue.

Thirdly, the New Testament writers might perhaps be expected to impose a diaspora or gentilic viewpoint, but they employ the term συναγωγή which seems to be less characteristic of the diaspora; it is used only once in Philo, and then of the Essenes in Palestine (*Quod Omnis Probus*, 81, again noting the synagogue as a sacred place).

The Christian sources, then, when set beside the epigraphic material and the Jewish and pagan literary evidence for the period up to about A.D. 200, do much to turn the scale towards the position represented by Hengel, Levine and Sanders (n. 9, above). They suggest that the synagogue was established at home as well as abroad by the time of Christian origins. The familiarity of the synagogue building in the homeland is assumed in the New Testament and Josephus as well as the Mishnah, and its acceptance as an institution throughout the Jewish world is assumed in the New Testament, Justin Martyr, Tertullian and Hippolytus as well as Philo

---

[16]On Theodotus see Sanders, *Jewish Law*, 341, n. 28, cited above; on Papous Noy, 'Place of Prayer'.

[17]A. S. Hollis (ed.), *Ovid, Ars Amatoria, Book i* (Oxford, 1977) notes ad loc. that although an occasion rather than a place is mentioned, synagogues are envisaged.

and Josephus. Yet the Christian texts give their own particular information, and do not simply echo the other sources.

II The Synagogue Ark

Now, secondly, the area which Cohen regards as more sparsely attested in the church fathers, that of rites and customs, can be considered with reference to prayer. It has appeared already that Christians sometimes entered synagogue assemblies, and that the general public could do so; 'vulgo aditur', says Tertullian, suggesting a continuation of the access by non-Jews attested earlier in Ovid and elsewhere. Christians by Tertullian's time were inclined to perceive the synagogue as a temple-like holy place, and its worship as continuous with the ancient sacrificial service described in the Pentateuch. Familiarity with the Old Testament would encourage such impressions, and they might be discounted were it not for their agreement with inner-Jewish views, as Cohen among others has noted; thus the holiness of the synagogue emerges from Philo, Josephus and the Mishnah, as cited above. The Christian impressions also remind one that, up to the third century, the synagogue was likely to be a much grander building than any used for Christian gatherings. This emerges from Josephus on Tiberias (cited above), with Philo's reference (*Leg. ad Gaium* 134) to 'the largest and most famous' of the Alexandrian proseuchae, and rabbinic tradition on the basilica-synagogue of Alexandria (Tos. Sukkah iv 6 and parallels).[18] The synagogue might be very large, and, at least at Alexandria, a basilica on the scale of the fourth-century basilican churches. (For Jewish use of this structural form compare Herod's great basilica, the 'Royal Porch', on the south side of the temple site in Jerusalem.) Even a smaller synagogue such as has been discovered at Ostia could display considerable elegance. The appeal of a 'holy and beautiful house' will have been among the factors encouraging pagans to embrace Judaism without considering Christian claims, a practice deplored by Origen (*in Matt. ser.* 16).[19]

Within this sometimes impressive synagogue setting, a group of Christian references attest the public reading of the law (Acts, Tertullian and Hippolytus, as cited already), the keeping of the holy books in the synagogue (Justin, *Dial.* lxxii 3, cited above; Ps.-Justin, *Cohortatio*, xiii), and in particular the ark of the law, which was

---

[18]Smallwood, *Legatio*, 222–3 discusses rabbinic passages together with Philo.

[19]Goodman, *Mission*, 137–8 rightly notes that motives other than proselytization will have influenced the construction of great synagogues, but the attractive power of such buildings is unlikely to have gone unnoticed by those responsible for them.

central both in the biblical reading and the public prayers. In Palestine at this period, according to rabbinic texts, the ark was carried in and out of the hall in which the assembly gathered, not kept there permanently. The Mishnah prescribes that, on a fast-day, the ark should be carried into the 'open place of the town' for public prayers (Taan. ii 1). The prayer leader in the Amidah (Eighteen Benedictions) was said to 'pass before the ark', to take up a position in front of it (M. Ber. v 3–4, etc.).[20] Diaspora usage need not have been identical, but passages in Tertullian noted below are illuminated if similar customs can be presupposed.

A visual impression of the synagogue ark in late antiquity can be gathered from representations in stone-carving, mural painting, mosaic and gold-glass, from the homeland and the diaspora. Temple imagery is used in them, and it is not clear whether the ark intended is the synagogue ark or that of Solomon's temple.[21] The representations will in any case, however, bear on the appearance of the synagogue ark, which was popularly connected with the ark of the covenant, as noted below. E. L. Sukenik wrote: 'It is a sort of double-doored chest with a gabled or rounded roof. Each of the door-wings was divided horizontally into a number of square or oblong panels. The door-posts were sometimes shaped like columns. The pediment was also ornamented, sometimes with a shell in the centre. A view of the interior of the ark is offered by the Jewish gilt glass vessels found in the catacombs of Rome. Here the Ark is as a rule represented with open doors, showing the scrolls, each rolled about a rod ... , lying in rows on shelves.'[22]

With this in mind, it can be seen that Tertullian probably means the synagogue ark when he mentions that the book of Enoch is not admitted to 'the Jewish chest', *armarium iudaicum*, in which biblical books are kept (*Cult. Fem.* i. 3).[23] This interpretation of the phrase is supported by Tertullian's references to two specific occasions on which the ark might have been seen by Christians. First, Tertullian was familiar with the sabbath biblical reading, as already noted.

---

[20]On usages concerning the ark in the rabbinic period see Elbogen, *Liturgy*, 359–63 (including later developments); Safrai, 'Dukhan', 71–7 (with special reference to archaeology).

[21]The former view is represented by Sukenik, *Synagogues*, 52–3 and Dothan, *Hammath Tiberias*, 32–7, with plate 27 (mosaic panel of ark); the latter by Dequeker, 'L'iconographie'. The doors incised on ossuaries cannot be interpreted with confidence as representing the ark (Figueras, *Ossuaries*, 57–8).

[22]Sukenik, *Synagogues*, 53.

[23]This interpretation is given without argument by Beckwith, *Canon*, 391. On rolls of Enoch in Tertullian's time see Hengel, with Deines, 'Septuaginta', 216–18.

Secondly, he knew that on a Jewish fast[24] the Jews leave their 'templa', as he calls them, and pray in the open on the sea-shore, and he vividly describes, not without a note of satire, how they wait for the evening star to signal the end of the fast (*Iei.* xvi 6); for the mockery implied in the thought that Jewish practice is governed by star-rise, compare the Preaching of Peter, 2, on Jewish dependence on the observation of the new moon. Such 'sea-shore prayers' (*Nat.* i 13, 4 'orationes littorales') were authentically Jewish, for (among other evidences) a decree quoted by Josephus calls it a Jewish custom to offer prayers by the sea (*Ant.* xiv 258), and synagogue remains have been found by the shore both in Galilee and the diaspora. Tertullian does not mention the ark when he describes the Jewish fast-day prayers, but perhaps it was brought out, in accord with the custom mentioned at about the same time in the Mishnah, and he had the chance of seeing it.

In the fourth century, Aphrahat and Chrysostom both take some trouble to belittle the synagogue ark. Aphrahat points out how Jeremiah prophesied that the ark of the covenant shall no more be remembered or made (*Hom.* xii, quoting Jer. iii 16);[25] contrast other writers who use this prophecy without making that particular point (Eusebius, Jerome, Theodoret). Chrysostom calls the ark no better than the little boxes you can get in the market (*c. Iud.* vi 7). Chrysostom is worried lest Christians, assured of the sanctity of the ark and its sacred books, regard it as making the synagogue holy, and he argues first against their logic (Did the ark when captured by the Philistines make the temple of Dagon holy?) and secondly against the sanctity of the contemporary ark itself (Where are the mercy-seat, the Urim, the tables of the covenant, the holy of holies, and all the other glories that went with the original ark in the first temple?).

Chrysostom's two arguments show how the deep-rooted Christian respect for the sanctity of the Bible embraced the ark, and consequently the synagogue; but they also suggest that Christians and Jews thought about the synagogue ark on the same lines. For Jewish association of the synagogue ark with the ark brought up to Jerusalem by David, compare the 'song of the kine' (Babylonian Talmud, A.Z. 24b; Ber. R. liv 4), perhaps linked with a synagogue

---

[24]Perhaps the Day of Atonement (so Aziza, *Tertullien*, 29–30), but not necessarily so, since days of fasting were common in Jewish practice at this period, as noted in connection with the Didache, below.

[25]This passage is judged by Safrai, 'Dukhan', 76 to attest a single synagogue ark-chest, and not the use of the ark together with a central chest or platform which is found in Geonic Babylonia.

ark procession,[26] and a carving from the frieze of the Capernaum synagogue which probably represents the ark being brought up on its new cart into Zion.[27] Chrysostom's word κιβωτός appears in the late second century in an inscription of the Ostia synagogue recording how Mindius Faustus 'set up the ark for the holy law'[28]; the emphasis here on the fundamental holiness of the law exactly corresponds to the belief which Chrysostom imputes to his own flock. The same emphasis occurs in the Mishnah, where a list in ascending order of esteem runs: open place, house of assembly, ark, scroll wrappings, holy books, a copy of the Torah (Meg. iii 1, cited above). Against this background it seems likely, as argued elsewhere, that the probably third-century reference to Israel's loss of the candlestick, the ark of the covenant, the priestly vessels and the trumpets, in the pseudo-Cyprianic *Adversus Iudaeos*, corresponds to frequently encountered Jewish symbols, and includes an attack on the synagogue ark.[29]

Patristic writings therefore show some familiarity with the ark, from which the biblical scrolls read in public were taken and before which, according to the Mishnah, the prayer-leader stood; this familiarity corresponds with the ancient biblical as well as contemporary liturgical associations of the ark, yet customs in which the ark was prominent themselves appear to have been known. Further, in the fourth century some Christians were inclined to the view that the ark was a focus of holiness, as the receptacle of the sacred books, and that its holiness was imparted to the synagogue as a whole; and this view corresponds to Jewish views attested earlier both in Galilee and in Italy (Mishnah, Megillah, and the Ostia inscription, cited above). Christian polemic directed at the ark suggests a non-legal dimension of the Christian treatment of the Jewish scriptures as an 'old' and superseded testament, found in St Paul (II Cor. ii 14–15, cited above) and in the Epistle to the Hebrews (especially viii 6–13) and thenceforth; it was probably not simply the scriptures that were in view, but the scriptures surrounded by the numinous aura of the ark, the synagogue, and the synagogue assembly. Some of the Christian anxiety to prove the abrogation of the law would then have been based not simply on the need to justify Christian practice over diet and worship, but also on the attraction of the

---

[26]The text is interpreted by Krauss, *Altertümer*, 369–71.

[27]Sukenik, *Synagogues*, 17–18, note, was against this interpretation, but it is accepted by Dothan, *Tiberias*, 36, with comparison of a Dura Europos representation.

[28]Noy, *Western Europe*, i, no. 13 & Plate vi.

[29]Chapter 7 above, pp. 196–7.

awe-inspiring atmosphere of holiness connected with the ark and the synagogue.

III Public Prayer

What further light do Christian texts throw on Jewish prayer? From Jewish sources it seems likely that some prayer was conjoined with the public reading of the law, both in the homeland and the diaspora, by the second century A.D., although – as S. C. Reif emphasizes – this was certainly not the only setting for common prayer.[30] Notable evidence includes the benediction and Amen described before the reading of the law in Neh. viii 5–7, Agatharchides on prayer as the sabbath duty (cited above), Philo's use of the term *proseuche* for the place in which the law was read (*Leg. ad Gaium* 156) (compare the use of προσεύχεσθαι for common prayer away from the homeland in I Kings viii 44 & 48, LXX), and Josephus's association of daily prayers with the septennial public reading of the law in his exposition of the commandments (*Ant.* iv 209–12); at the end of the second century the Mishnah, in a list of rites which need a quorum of ten, brings together – in a way which would be natural if they were already associated in practice – the Shema and the Amidah, the reading of the law and the prophets, and the priestly blessing (Meg. iv 1–5). The large number of texts of Jewish prayers and hymns from the late pre-Christian and early Christian period (for example, the Prayer of Manasses, the psalm of Tobit, the Song of the Three Children, the communal confession in the book of Baruch, the benedictions for every morning and evening of a month in 4Q 503, and the responses and canticles intermingled with the psalms in 11QPs[a]) indicate the importance of prayer in Judaism at this time, even though they also suggest variety in the places and times of prayer. Comparably, M. P. Weitzman argues that the importance of the service of prayer in the Peshitta reflects its importance in Jewish life at the time of Christian origins, especially but not only in the Diaspora.[31] Even when full weight is given to reservations expressed by writers on prayer,[32] Josephus' evidence in

---

[30]Reif, *Hebrew Prayer*, 83.

[31]Weitzman, 'From Judaism to Christianity'.

[32]Sanders, *Judaism*, 202–8, accepts that there will have been prayer in Judaean synagogues before the destruction of the temple, but stresses that it was more probably individual than unified. Salzmann, *Lehren und Ermahnen*, 451–2, judges that prayer will have been regular in the diaspora before 70, but leaves open the question whether in Jerusalem and its neighbourhood there was synagogue prayer while the temple stood. Nitzan, *Qumran Prayer*, 14, 40–45, allows slight beginnings only of fixed common prayer before the destruction of the temple.

particular, in the context of the earlier and later sources noted above, suggests public prayer in conjunction with the reading of the law in Judaea at the end of the Second-Temple period.

Three early allusions to Jewish prayer by Christians may be considered against this background. First, in the Didache 'Pray not with the hypocrites' (viii 2) follows on the warning 'Let not your fasts be with the hypocrites'; the writer knows that they fast on Mondays and Thursdays. (Compare the strong awareness of contemporary Jewish fasting practice evinced in the Epistle of Barnabas, chapter iii.[33]) Prayer is integral to fast-days, as already noted, and the transition to prayer is natural. Just as Wednesdays and Fridays are ordained as distinctively Christian fast-days, so, on prayer, the Lord's Prayer is given as the distinctively Christian form of prayer to use – perhaps by contrast with a Jewish form like one of the daily benedictions found in Qumran texts (4Q 503), or with a compressed form of the Amidah – and the Didache directs the Lord's Prayer to be used thrice daily; compare the Mishnaic direction that the Amidah is to be prayed thrice daily by every Israelite (Ber. iii 3, iv 1). Here there is a sense that communal prayer is a characteristic aspect of Jewish common life, and that Christians must have something comparable but different. It has of course been independently surmised that the prayers in Didache ix–x were originally Jewish, a conclusion which would well fit the situation suggested by chapter iii.[34] Irrespective of ix–x, however, it could be inferred from chapter iii alone that common prayer was established and central in the Jewish life known to the writer, perhaps in the early second century.

Secondly, Justin Martyr objects to the Jewish view that Mal. i 11, on the pure offering to be made in every place and among the gentiles, referred to the prayers offered by Israelites in the dispersion (*Dial.* cxvii 2, 4); this application of the verse occurs in the Targum and the midrash (Num. R. xiii, on vii 12), but Justin's is the earliest datable attestation. This Jewish interpretation will have seemed weighty if its background included not only biblical passages on diaspora prayer (such as I Kings viii 44, 48, Jer. xxix 7 & 12 and Baruch iii 6–7), but also the prayers currently offered in the proseuche. Such prayer is more definitely mentioned in a famous passage of Justin which also bears on imprecation. 'After the prayer'

---

[33]Chapter 4 above, pp. 136–7; on the importance of this point in assessment of the Epistle, Carleton Paget, *Barnabas*, 109–10.

[34]Sandelin, *Wisdom*, 186–228 (literature) reconstructs Hebrew forms of the prayers, holding that they were essentially Jewish thanksgivings used at common meals; they would have been used in Hebrew in Palestine, and in Greek among Egyptian Jews, whence they would have passed to Christians.

(μετὰ τὴν προσευχήν) the rulers of synagogue teach mockery of Christ – whether in a discourse or by means of a curse is unclear (*Dial*. cxxxvii 2). In Luke xiii 14 an ἀρχισυνάγωγος disputes with Christ, but the gospel narrative differs too much from Justin's allegation to be the source of it. Justin's use of the article shows that 'the prayer' had an accepted place. The Greek might correspond to the determinate Hebrew *ha-t^ephillah*, used in the Mishnah (e.g. Ber. iv 1) to designate *the* prayer, the Amidah; given the diaspora currency of texts exhibiting antecedents of the Amidah (Ecclus. xxxvi 1–17, II Macc. i 27–9), it is a reasonable conjecture that the topics of 'the prayer' as known to Justin would have resembled those which were prevalent in contemporary forms of the Amidah. At any rate Justin here provides, soon after 150, one of the earliest clear indications that prayer was regular in a synagogue assembly.

Lastly, Tertullian (*Orat*. xiv) makes the striking claim that the Jews do not raise their hands to the Lord in prayer – indeed they dare not, lest some Isaiah should cry out that their hands are full of blood (Isa. i 15). This claim is combined with an attack on Jewish purificatory washing, and it might perhaps be dismissed as an effort to justify the attached polemic, for the practice of lifting up the hands in prayer, often mentioned in the Hebrew scriptures, was common to Jews and non-Jews in antiquity (compare the raised hands carved over the incised Jewish imprecation of Rheneia, *CIJ* 725). The raising of hands is mentioned in descriptions of Egyptian Jews at prayer (III Macc. v 25 (supplication); Philo, *Flacc*. 121 (thanksgiving)). Scripture also attests the *expansion* of the hands in prayer (Exod. ix 29, etc). This gesture can of course merge into elevation (I Kings viii 22). It is noteworthy, however, that in the later second century B.C. the Judaean Jews are described by Agatharchides of Cnidus (quoted by Josephus, *Ap*. ii 209) as *expanding* their hands in prayer on the sabbath until the evening (ἐκτετακότες τὰς χεῖρας εὔχεσθαι μέχρι τῆς ἑσπέρας); and perhaps at about the same time or somewhat earlier 'I have spread out my hands' is the biblical expression echoed in the third of the apocryphal psalms preserved in Syriac (Psalm clv), verse 2 (Hebrew text in 11Q Ps^a, col. xxiv, line 3). Christians likewise lifted up hands in prayer (I Tim. ii 8, I Clem. xxix 1), but they also associated the raising and expansion of their hands with the cross, implying the custom of spreading out rather than raising only (Tertullian, ibid.; Od. Sol. xxvii, xlii 1–2).[35]

Yet Tertullian's claim is perhaps too unexpected to be totally dismissed. Can it be accounted for by a trend among many Jews

---

[35]On Christian practice see von Severus, 'Gebet I', cols. 1231–2.

towards restricting such gestures? This would accord with the stress on decorum evinced both in Philo on the sabbath assembly and in the Mishnah on the Amidah (and reflected in the Pauline 'decently and in order' in I Cor. xiv 40).[36] Tertullian himself does not want Christians to raise their hands too high (*Orat.* xvii). There are hints of a comparable Jewish feeling. As already noted, the expansion rather than the raising of the hands is mentioned by Agatharchides and in an apocryphal psalm. In III Maccabees and Philo, as cited above, the raising of hands is mentioned not as normal prayer practice, but as a sign of exceptionally intense emotion; the same consideration perhaps applies to the Rheneia hands, represented over a call for divine vengeance. One of the biblical phrases for raising the hands, 'to lift up the palms (*kappayim*)' (Ps. lxiii 4, etc.), has in the Mishnah (e.g. Ber. v 4) already become a technical term for giving the priestly blessing; the alternative phrase 'to lift up the hands (*yadayim*)' is linked in scripture itself with priestly blessing (Lev. ix 22, Ecclus. 1 20), and in the LXX both phrases alike are rendered with χεῖρες, 'hands'. Development of the biblical phrase into a technical term suggests that by the second century in the circles concerned it was not favoured as a general description of prayer.

Some reluctance to take the raising of hands as a description of prayer is also suggested by interpretations of scripture. Biblical references to the practice are sometimes but not always straightforwardly interpreted as such. In the Targum of Psalms only cxli 2 survives as raising of hands in prayer; at xxviii 2 and lxiii 5 'lifting up' in the Hebrew significantly becomes 'spreading out' in the Targum, and cxxxiv 2 is referred to the priestly blessing. In the haggadah Ps. lxiii 5 is referred to the Amidah (Babylonian Talmud, Ber. 16b), but this is because the lifting up of the palms is taken as a reference to the priestly blessing at the close of the Prayer. In Exodus, comparably, the *expansion* of Moses's hands is prayer (ix 29 in Targums Neofiti, Ps.-Jonathan and Onkelos, and Midrash Exod. R. xii 7); but there is variation over the great Jewish and Christian pattern of prayer, the *raising* of his hands with the help of Aaron and Hur (xvii 11–12).[37] In the Fragment Targum and

---

[36]Philo, *Somn,* ii 127, *Hyp.* vii 12–13; in rabbinic opinion the prayer leader in the Amidah is to display gravity (M. Ber. v 1) and a disciplined stance (feet straight, like those of the living creatures in Ezek. i 7: Babylonian Talmud, Ber. 10b).

[37]In the Mekhilta and in Targum Pseudo-Jonathan it is taken to be fast-day prayer 'until the going down of the sun' (verse 12) (compare Tertullian on prayer until star-rise), and a pattern for the officiating of three prayer-leaders on fast-days; Philo (*Mos.* i 216) similarly views it as supplication, adding that Moses purified himself beforehand (compare Tertullian's attack on Jewish washing before prayer).

Targum Neofiti the hands are specifically said to be raised in prayer, in both verses. In Targum Pseudo-Jonathan the hands are raised in prayer in verse 11, but they are *expanded* in prayer in verse 12. Finally, in Targum Onkelos the raising of the hands in verse 11 is mentioned but not specified as prayer, and in 12 the hands are said to be expanded in prayer. It was by no more than a very slight addition to existing interpretation that Christians found in this passage prayer with raised and expanded hands, in the form of the cross (so, among others, Barn. xii 2; Justin, *Dial.* xc 4–5; Tertullian, *Marc.* iii 18, 6). The caution evinced in the Jewish renderings is all the more striking because the narrative itself suggests that the hands cannot have been raised high.

From Jewish interpretation here and elsewhere, therefore, one can infer some feeling against taking the raising of the hands as a standard prayer posture, and a preference for spreading out the hands without raising them high. Such feeling, no doubt historically continuous with the sense of decorum evinced by Philo, was perhaps enhanced among Jews in Tertullian's environment by reaction against the Christianization of lifting up the hands; but Tertullian's own restrictions on raising the hands suggest a care for decorum which is not unlikely also to have been present among Jews. If this conjecture is on the right lines, Tertullian's startling claim that Jews do not raise their hands in prayer will attest a preference among Jews in Carthage for spreading out the hands rather than raising them, comparable with rabbinic stress on reverent prayer, and rooted in pre-rabbinic practice.

IV Imprecation

These are three early instances of a more widely attested Christian acquaintance with Jewish prayer custom. Against this background the much-discussed patristic passages on Jewish imprecations against Christ and the Christians seem likely to offer some reflection of practice, despite their polemical character. This view is supported by the fact that they find correspondence in other sources. Thus in Justin Martyr the cursing of *Christ* probably reflects a purgation formula used by Jews and Romans (compare Acts xxvi 11, I Cor. xii 3; also Pliny, *Ep.* x 96, 5–6, on *Christo maledicere* as one of the tests of those denounced as Christians). Justin once puts this curse on Christ 'after the prayer', as noted above, and in this respect his report can be compared with much later midrashic evidence for a curse on *Christians* uttered after the Amidah.[38]

---

[38]For fuller discussion see Chapters 2 and 4 above, pp. 77–8, 102–3, 157–8.

The cursing of Christians mentioned by Justin himself, however, seems likely to correspond to a form of the curse on apostates included in the Amidah, specially mentioning *minim*, 'heretics' – whence the Twelfth Benediction of the Amidah became known as *Birkat ha-Minim*. In contemporary Judaea and Galilee it seems that a benediction 'of the *minim*' could be used in the Amidah either on its own or in combination with another benediction, 'of the separatists' or 'of the wicked'; extant texts of the Twelfth Benediction show the results of such a combination.[39] The general context was a prayer for national redemption and judgement. Association of Justin's curse on Christians with the Amidah, in its fluid second-century shape as reflected in his milieu, is encouraged by the later reports of Jerome noted below, where the Amidah is almost certainly the Jewish prayer in view.

Nevertheless, Justin is widely considered to have mistaken the scope of the benediction 'of the *minim*'. He assumes that the curse applied to all Christians, but many judge that, insofar as it touched the Christian church, it would have applied to Jewish members only.[40] This judgement seems, however, not to reckon fully with the position of the church at this period as a minority closely linked with the non-Christian Jewish majority (compare Tertullian, *Apol.* xxi 1, quoted in n. 5 above). The single Christian body of Jews and gentiles, within which gentiles claimed to have been made one with Jews (Eph. ii 11–iii 11), was widely regarded by outsiders as an aberrant form of the majority Jewish community, which also had a substantial number of gentile adherents. So the Christians as a body were considered by Jews and pagans a αἵρεσις (Acts xxiv 5) or faction (Celsus in Origen, *Contra Celsum* iii 1, 5; viii 14) of the Jewish community. A Jewish attitude of this kind is suggested also by Trypho's bitter disapproval of gentile conversion to Christianity and of gentile Christians, as represented in Justin's *Dialogue*; it would have been better for the gentile Justin to have continued as a pagan, when he might have had some hope, than to be deceived by Christian error, and it would have been better if Trypho himself had obeyed the ordinance of the Jewish teachers, who forbid discussion with Christians (*Dial.* viii, xxxviii). The *Dialogue* in these passages recalls the Tosefta, on *minim* as people who are worse than idolaters, and should be steadfastly shunned

---

[39]Elbogen and Heinemann, *Liturgy*, 33–5, with n. 22; Chapter 2 above, pp. 85–8, 95–6.
[40]So Van der Horst, *Hellenism–Judaism–Christianity*, 111 (literature); for the considerations in the text below see pp. 76–7, 99–100, 107–8 above.

242 JEWS AND CHRISTIANS IN CONTACT AND CONTROVERSY

(Shabb. xiii 5; Hullin ii 20–22, where anecdotes of Christians are told to support the ban on converse with *minim*).[41]

The allegations of thrice-daily maledictions in Epiphanius and Jerome (who are perhaps indebted here to Apollinaris of Laodicaea) are likely to reflect the *Birkat ha-Minim* when repeated thrice daily as the Twelfth Benediction of the Amidah. In Jerome these allegations are part of his unceasing all-round polemic against opponents of his ecclesiastical position. Yet, as Samuel Krauss showed, Jerome had some familiarity with Jewish prayer.[42] T. C. G. Thornton has argued, nevertheless, that the allegations were invented, because the imperial authorities would have forbidden any such public prayer.[43] Yet the authorities were not always anxious to act against the Jewish communities, as the initial imperial resistance to Ambrose's pressure in the Callinicum incident shows. It has long been thought likely, however, that imperial action on the Eighteen Benedictions was indeed eventually taken in the sixth or early seventh century, perhaps in connection with Justinian's Novella of 553 on Jewish public reading of the scriptures. Pirqoi ben Baboi (eighth century) reports a tradition that the 'evil kingdom' prohibited the Shema and the Tefillah in the land of Israel before the Arab conquest. This will refer to a Byzantine measure, banning both these prayers as anti-Christian,[44] in an extension of the prohibition of objectionable Jewish interpretation in the Novella.[45]

The Christian notices of synagogue prayer illustrated above have something to offer, it has been suggested, not only on topics in Jewish–Christian relations, such as the cursing of Christians, but also on the rise of the synagogue, the significance of the ark, and the development of Jewish public prayer. Christian texts are important among the early attestations of synagogues, they cohere with archaeological and other indications of the impressive architecture

---

[41]Goodman, *Mission*, 142 suggests that the measure of acceptance of paganism in *Dial.* viii dilutes Trypho's counsel that Justin should be circumcised; but Trypho is represented as thinking that *even* a pagan is better than a Christian, not as doubting that Justin ought to accept Judaism.

[42]Krauss, 'Fathers', 233–4.

[43]Thornton, 'Understanding'.

[44]The prominence of the Shema (Deut. vi 4) in mediaeval anti-Christian polemic is noted by Lasker, *Philosophical Polemics*, 189, n. 19; comparably, in a Byzantine Christian work, the fifth- or sixth-century Greek Dialogue of Timothy and Aquila, Deut. vi 4 is the first text quoted against Christian beliefs by the Jewish spokesman (F. C. Conybeare (ed.), *The Dialogues of Athanasius and Zacchaeus, and of Timothy and Aquila* (Oxford, 1898), 65).

[45]Pp. 11, 77, above (on Pirqoi ben Baboi in the series of references to the Benediction of the *Minim*); Mann, 'Changes', 252–4, 277–8, ascribes the measure to Heraclius; Veltri, 'Novelle', 129 (literature) ascribes it to Justinian, whom he regards as seeking the conversion of the Jews.

of synagogues, and they show the prevalence of common prayer at an earlier date than most Jewish sources permit. They can also give glimpses of the style of prayer; Tertullian's notices suggest an esteem for decorum and *gravitas* recalling Philo and the Mishnah. Moreover, it is of significance for the study of the western diaspora if such Christian reports can be illuminated by rabbinic and targumic texts, as was attempted above. Links of some strength between the west and the homeland can then be presupposed. Lastly, the fact that Christian texts can offer material for consideration in the study of Jewish prayer suggests that, although Christians saw the synagogue through Old and New Testament spectacles, their eyes were not wholly blinded to their contemporary Jewish neighbours.

10

THE BASLE NIZZAHON

The name 'Nizzahon', 'confutation', was borne by several different mediaeval Hebrew works of Jewish–Christian controversy. Perhaps the best known is the early fifteenth-century Nizzahon of Lipmann Mühlhausen, edited by Theodor Hackspan (Nuremberg, 1644). Franco-German Jewish apologetic, from the twelfth century onwards, is richly attested in the earlier compilation first edited as 'Nizzachon Vetus' by J. C. Wagenseil in his *Tela Ignea Satanae* (Altdorf, 1681), now re-edited by D. Berger (Philadelphia, 1979).

An untitled work, which shares some material with Nizzahon Vetus (hereafter N.V.), is fragmentarily preserved in Rome, MS. BN Centrale or. 53 (hereafter R), ff. 31^r–65^v.[1] It forms the earliest witness, albeit indirect, to the otherwise sparsely attested text of N.V.; and it is historically significant in its own right, as a distinct but comparable compilation of mediaeval polemic from northern France and Germany.

In the present note a Basle manuscript described as Lipmann's Nizzahon (see pp. 37–9 above) is identified as a second, longer copy of the untitled work hitherto known only from R. MS. AN. ix. 4 (hereafter B) of the Oeffentliche Bibliothek der Universität, Basle, studied here from a microfilm kindly supplied by the library, derives independent interest from its preservation of some passages lacking in R and its association with a number of Christian Hebraists. Some account of the contents and history of B (section I, below) is supplemented by the text of an unpublished seventeenth-century description from the flyleaf (II), and a suggestion (III) as to how the manuscript first came to be identified as Lipmann's work (an identification already made, with an attribution to a particular member of the Lipmann family, in an old marginal note).

The assessment of B requires much further study, but here (section IV, below) a preliminary impression is given of its textual witness to the work incompletely contained in R. Lastly (V), a specimen section of B – five folios not paralleled in R – is summarized, with a view to two questions concerning the untitled work. The first is its debated literary relationship with N.V.; the second is the character of the untitled work, considered as an independent

[1]Angelo di Capua, 'Catalogo dei Codici Ebraici della Biblioteca Vittorio Emanuele', *Cataloghi dei Codici Orientali di alcune Biblioteche d'Italia*, i (Florence, 1878), 46, no. 8.

composition, in comparison with contemporary polemical writings. To judge from the specimen, it possesses a measure of distinctiveness which enhances its interest as a witness to medieval Jewish–Christian controversy.

I

Until the printing of J. Prijs' catalogue in 1994 (p. 39 above), the most accessible description of B was the notice in N. Allony and E. (F.) Kupfer, *List of Photocopies in the Institute* ii (Jerusalem, 1964), 127, no. 1553. The manuscript is there identified as Lipmann's Nizzahon, in accordance with the marginal note already mentioned. This marginal identification had similarly been accepted by the Buxtorfs, father and son, before Lipmann's work was published by Hackspan; their description is quoted in section II below. After Hackspan's edition, however, J. C. Wolf – anticipated, as shown below, by a seventeenth-century student of B – noted, on the basis of the Buxtorfs' printed account of B, that the Basle Nizzahon was unlikely to be Lipmann's work; he suggested that it might be N.V.[2] J. and B. Prijs noted more recently, in connection with Sebastian Münster's quotations of N.V. rather than the identification of the Basle manuscript, that one passage quoted by Münster finds correspondence in two widely separated pages of B.[3] Their observation, of course, also suggests that the Basle manuscript is linked with N.V. rather than with Lipmann's Nizzahon; this proves to be the case, but the link is an indirect one, for B is an exemplar of the untitled work hitherto known only from R.

Ad. Posnanski, followed now by Dr. Berger, had cited R throughout his unpublished edition of N.V. (Jewish National and University Library, MS. 8° 791). E. E. Urbach later showed that the folios of R in question, constituting a third and distinct section of the manuscript, presented an incomplete text of a work different from N.V., but sharing much of its material with N.V.; he put the proportion at 90 per cent, an estimate which seems likely to be on the high side (see section V, below). Urbach ascribed this division of R to the second half of the fourteenth century.[4]

The earlier leaves of R. contain polemic related, in the first section, to the thirteenth-century work of Joseph Official and, in the second, both to the northern French literature of the Official family

[2] J. C. Wolf, *Bibliotheca Hebraea* (4 vols., Hamburg, (1715–33), i, 737.
[3] J. and B. Prijs, *Die Basler hebräischen Drucke* (Olten and Freiburg, i, Br., 1964), 500.
[4] E. E. Urbach, 'Études sur la littérature polémique au moyen-âge', *Revue des études juives*, c (1935), 49–77 (72 f.).

and to the southern works of Nahmanides and Joseph and David Kimhi. The whole manuscript has evoked a number of studies.[5] In the present context note should be taken of Judah Rosenthal's description of the manuscript and his editions of two portions of the third section, ff. 31^r–43^v and 62^v–63^v.[6] Whereas Urbach, 77, regarded R as a source of N.V., Dr. Berger concludes, 375, that the author of N.V. used some of the material of R, but not R itself.

This question will be considered in section V below, as already noted, together with that of the characteristics of the work attested in the third part of R. Now, however, a fuller account is offered of B, the second witness to that work. B includes some material not known from R, and must rank as a source of considerable importance for the study of mediaeval Hebrew polemic.

An unnumbered flyleaf bears two owners' names on successive lines ('S. Hortini, K. / Johannis Buxtorfii 1623') above a seventeenth-century Latin description, considered below. It is followed by eighty-four numbered folios, approximately 21 cm. in depth, described by W. Schickard and the Buxtorfs as parchment,[7] and usually containing twenty-four lines to the page. A separate series of page numbers, one of which is mentioned in the flyleaf description, runs from pp. 1 to 19 = ff. 1^r to 10^r.

The text runs from f. 1^r, l. 1 והיה בית יעקב אש (Obad. 18) to f. 84^v, l. 1 (probably not continuous with the last line of f. 84^r) אמר להם ישו והלא. Another hand, probably Christian, then adds on l. 2 the Hebrew text of Job xxi 16b.

The hand of the text and its marginal appendages is an ornamental Ashkenazi cursive. The text is spaciously set out, and in the earlier folios the left margin is exactly justified with graphic fillers and other devices. Despite its handsome presentation the text has many errors, especially in biblical quotations, sometimes corrected by a second transcription of the appropriate word by the scribe himself.

The margins contain additional material from the scribe of the

---

[5] J. Rosenthal lists his editions of parts of R in 'Divre wikkuah mi-tokh sefer hameqanne', *Kobez al Yad*, N.S. viii (Jerusalem, 1975), 295–323 (295); see also Berger, 35 f., 374–80, and (mainly on the second section of R) J. E. Rembaum, 'A Reevaluation of a Medieval Polemical Manuscript', *AJS Review*, v (1980), 81–99, and R. Chazan, 'A Medieval Hebrew Polemical Melange', *HUCA* li (1980), 89–110.

[6] J. Rosenthal (ed.), *Sepher Joseph Hamekane* (Jerusalem, 1970), 30 of the Hebrew pagination; Rosenthal, 'Pirqe wikkuah', in S. Leiberman and A. Hyman (eds.), *Salo Wittmayer Baron Jubilee Volume* (Jerusalem, 1974/5), iii, 353–95 (ff. 35^r–43^v), and Rosenthal, *Kobez*, N.S. viii, 313–23 (ff. 31^r–35^r, 62^v–63^v).

[7] W. Schickard, *Bechinath Happeruschim* (Tübingen, 1624), praef., f. 4^v; J. Buxtorf, *De Abbreviaturis Hebraicis ... Item Bibliotheca Rabbinica* (2nd edn., issued by J. Buxtorf, Fil., Basle, 1640), 384f.

main text, comprising further passages comparable with the text itself, brief summaries of the subjects of some paragraphs, and the numbers of the paragraphs. The summary headings and numbers are sometimes surrounded by a decorative border.

Further marginalia in Hebrew and Latin evidently derive from readers of the manuscript. Some are corrections, others are running heads or annotations in Hebrew cursive of Italian appearance, others are Latin identifications of the subjects or texts being treated.

The beginning of the text is lacking, and the title נצחון is added in the Italianate cursive at the foot of f. 1ʳ. At the head of f. 6ʳ, in a similar cursive, is the Hebrew note 'The book of Nizzahon composed by the sage, our teacher R. Eliezer of blessed memory, called Lipmann'.

J. and B. Prijs, loc. cit., ascribe the manuscript to the fourteenth or fifteenth century, Allony and Kupfer to the sixteenth century. An early sixteenth-century dating is the latest possible, for, as Schickard, loc. cit., and the flyleaf description both attest, the manuscript was brought from Italy by Immanuel Tremellius (1510–80): that is, when he migrated to Strassburg in 1542.[8]

The contents consist mainly of two series of numbered paragraphs, the first on the Hebrew scriptures and Christian objections, the second on the New Testament and ecclesiastical teaching. They are arranged as follows:

Ff. 1ʳ–2ʳ, answers to charges of Jewish guilt and unbelief, especially concerning the cross and the immutability of the law;

ff. 2ʳ l. 9–64ʳ, first series of paragraphs, numbered 1 to 138, comprising

ff. 2ʳ–16ᵛ, nos. 1–24, principally on Psalms and Latter Prophets (the beginning of the third section of R, f. 31ʳ, printed by Urbach, p. 72 and Rosenthal in *Kobez*, N.S. viii. 313, corresponds to f. 10ʳ, 1. 6, towards the end of paragraph 12);

ff. 16ᵛ–36ᵛ, nos. 25–80, on the Pentateuch;

ff. 36ᵛ–37ᵛ, nos. 81–4, on Joshua (81–2), the pagan miracle of the fallen Vestal (83, cf. N.V., Berger paragraph 217 end; Wagenseil, pp. 131f.), and the Song of Songs (84);

ff. 37ᵛ–64ʳ, nos. 85 (on baptism)–138 (defence of the Talmud), objections and answers to Christian objections, including many on biblical texts. (No. 98 in R, f. 43ᵛ, as printed by Rosenthal in *Baron Jubilee Volume*, iii. 385, corresponds to no. 98, f. 44ᵛ, at the beginning but not the end.)

Ff. 65ʳ–83ᵛ, second series of paragraphs, numbered 1–47, on the New Testament and the Church (the opening of this series in R, as quoted by Urbach, p. 73, corresponds to f. 65ʳ, ll. 1 ff. (cf. N.V., Berger paragraph 154, beginning;

[8]J. Ney, s.v. 'Tremellius', in A. Hauck (ed.), *Realenzyklopädie für protestantische Theologie und Kirche*, xx (Leipzig, 1908), 95.

Wagenseil, p. 186); no. 35, the last paragraph in the New Testament series in R according to Urbach, p. 73, occurs on f. 78^r); Latin marginalia often note the New Testament texts and subjects.

F. 84^r, unnumbered section on Matthaean genealogy, continuing with four lines on the baptism of Christ (so N.V., paragraph 154; Berger's Hebrew text, pp. 106f., Wagenseil, pp. 187f.);

f. 84^v, two lines only, described above.

Paragraphs 12 (part)–98 of the first series are printed from R by Judah Rosenthal as follows:

Nos. 12 (part)–24, from R, ff. 31^r–35^r, in *Kobez*, N.S. viii. 313–19; nos. 25–98, from R. ff. 35^r–40^v, 34^r–43^v (sixteen folios in two numerations), in *Baron Jubilee Volume*, iii. 353–84.

The recorded owners of the manuscript are Immanuel Tremellius; S. Hortinus, perhaps to be identified with Samuel Hortinus, professor of divinity in Berne, who presented several Hebrew manuscripts to the Berne library in 1632 and compiled its catalogue;[9] and Johann Buxtorf the Elder (1564–1629), who acquired the manuscript, according to the flyleaf, in 1623. He promptly lent it to W. Schickard of Tübingen, who gratefully acknowledges the loan in his 1624 publication, loc. cit. Four years later, beginning a criticism of the Talmudic Jesus-passages, Schickard recalled how 'the abominable R. Lipmann of unhappy memory' depends on them 'in the execrable MS. book Nizzahon, than which I have never read a worse'.[10] The manuscript was returned as well as read, for a short description of it was included in the 1640 edition, issued by Johann Buxtorf the younger (1599–1664), of the elder Buxtorf's *Bibliotheca Rabbinica*, loc. cit. The *Nachlass* of the Buxtorfs, which includes some manuscripts described in *Bibliotheca Rabbinica*, was acquired by the Oeffentliche Bibliothek der Universität in 1705 (J. and B. Prijs, 324, 376). It seems likely that MS. AN. IX. 4. formed part of this acquisition.

II

Beneath the owners' names on the flyleaf is the title, struck out, 'Objectiones Judaeorum ex Veteri et Novo Testamentis'. Instead, *Sepher Nizzachon*, with the corresponding Hebrew characters before it, is written as the heading of the Latin description mentioned above. This continues:

h.e. *Victoria*, seu *Triumphus* (Judaeorum sc. super Christianos). Auctor R. Elieser,

---

[9]H. Hagen, *Catalogus Codicum Bernensium* (Berne, 1875), ix and xlv.
[10]W. Schickard, *Tarich* (Tübingen, 1628), 83.

qui vocatur Lipman, ut manu Judaica adscriptum, pag. 11. Sciendum, aliquot hujus nominis libros extare. Talem habuit Willelmus Schikhardus, quem describit in *Triumphatore* suo *Vapulante*. Alium habuit Theodoricus Hackspan, quem Norimbergii edidit. Ab utroque diversus est praesens codex, in quo primum locos Veteris Testamenti vindicare conatur a Christianorum expositionibus, et in eos retorquere deinde Historiam Evangelicam, productis ex ea variis locis, refellit; utrumque breviter facit, sed amarulenter et virulente. Videndum, an hic ille sit liber,* [*altered from, Videtur mihi hic ille liber esse] quem Sebastianus Munsterus sub hoc nomine citat in notis suis in Evangelium Matthaei Hebraicum, et passim in annotationibus ad Vetus Test.* [*altered from, et ejus est manus Latinum, quod passim ad marginem conspicitur].

R. Lipman, qui composuit Sepher Nizzachon, meminit R. David Ganz in Tzemach David, ad annum 219. h.e. iuxta supputationem Christianorum, 1439.

Citat librum Nizzachon etiam Fagius in Paraphr. Chald. ad Deut. cap. 13 et cap. 18. sed quae inde citat, non conveniunt cum iis quae sunt in hoc libro.

Fuit hic liber Immanuelis Tremellii, et ab eo ex Italia allatus est.

The writer of the description, observing that several different works bear the title Nizzahon, names those edited by Schickard (1623) and Hackspan (1644), but not Wagenseil's N.V. (1681). The description must have been drawn up between the last two dates. The mention of Ganz does not narrow this span, for his annal for 219 could have been consulted in the edition of Prague, 1592 or the translation by G. H. Vorstius, *Chronologia sacra-profana* (Leiden, 1644), 148. The dates permit the conjecture that the author of this terse and informative description was Johann Buxtorf the younger, or his son J. J. Buxtorf (1645–1704). The latter, who succeeded to the Hebrew chair on his father's death in 1664, left unpublished 'a notable supplement to *Bibliotheca Rabbinica*'.[11] It is tempting, but unfortunately purely speculative, to view the description as part of his work for the supplement; for the flyleaf corrects and supersedes the entry in *Bibliotheca*, 1640.

Buxtorf the elder, edited by his son, had there written that there are two books called Nizzahon, one printed by Schickard, the other Lipmann's. Sebastian Münster had the second. 'A copy of it [or, His copy], written on parchment, we too acquired a few years ago. This one is expressly directed against the Gospel history.' A comparison with some of Münster's quotations, such as J. and B. Prijs have made more recently, probably lies behind this statement; it will also have rested on the Hebrew marginal attribution (p. 11 = f. 6^r) to an Eliezer called Lipmann, mentioned in the later flyleaf description.

---

[11]*Athenae Rauricae* (Basle, 1778), 452.

After Hackspan's edition of Lipmann's long-awaited work it became clear, as this description notes and Wolf later suspected, that the Basle Nizzahon, marginal attribution to Lipmann notwithstanding, differs from Hackspan's text as well as Schickard's. Moreover, the author of the description thought at first that the manuscript was the book quoted by Münster. This accords with the notice in *Bibliotheca Rabbinica*, which could even be read as a statement that this manuscript belonged to Münster. The author rightly changed his formulation, however, and wrote: 'it is to be seen, whether this is the book.' He similarly struck out his first opinion, that Münster himself wrote the Latin marginalia. He may have been influenced in these alterations by his comparison of Fagius's citations on Deut. xiii and xviii, for 'they do not agree with those in this book'; yet they are, as he may have seen, almost identical with two of the many passages quoted by Münster.[12]

III

No other instance of the attribution of a Nizzahon to an Eliezer surnamed Lipmann has come to the present writer's attention. The scope for such ascriptions is large, however, for the medieval books called Nizzahon include Joseph the Zealot[13] as well as the works edited by Schickard, Hackspan, and Wagenseil, and the title could have been applied to other confutations of Christianity. On the other hand, further examination may show that there is reason for this attribution to arise from the Basle manuscript in particular. Nevertheless, so long as these uncertainties are borne in mind, it is worth noting that the attribution could have arisen simply as an identification of the particular member of the Lipmann family responsible for what became the most famous Nizzahon, that of 'Rabbi Lipmann'. In early manuscripts the author's name is given simply as 'Lipmann Mühlhausen' (MSS. Hamburg 76, of 1421, and Munich hebr. 423, of 1460);[14] in others, as in Vorstius's translation of Ganz, it is 'Rabbi Lipmann' (MSS. BL Harley 5528, of 1525, and

---

[12]Cf. P. Fagius, *Thargum . . . Pentateuchus* (Strassburg, 1546), unpaginated, on Deut. xiii 6, xviii 15, with S. Münster, *Hebraica Biblia* (2 vols., Basle, 1534), i. ff. 178^v, 183^r. The texts vary more often in the first passage.

[13]A work which appears to be Joseph's is called 'the book of Nizzahon' in a marginal note in MS. Hamburg 80, f. 50^r, quoted by M. Steinschneider, *Catalog der hebräischen Handschriften in der Stadtbibliothek zu Hamburg* (Hamburg, 1878), 71, no. 187.

[14]Steinschneider, *Hamburg*, 19, no. 48; H. Striedl, L. Tetzner, and L. Roth, *Hebräische Handschriften*, ii (Wiesbaden, 1965), 234.

Erlangen 1264, used by Hackspan, a copy of a text of 1588);[15] and
the opening cento of verses from Psalms and Proverbs (Hackspan, p.
1; MS. Harley 5528, f. 4^r) similarly gives the acrostic LIPMaN only.
His contemporaries also called him simply by his surname, sometimes distinguishing him, after the title of his book, as Lipmann
naṣṣeḥan 'Victor'.[16]

Although the author of the Nizzahon has long been identified as
Yom Tov Lipmann Mühlhausen, the name Eliezer was often given in
the Lipmann family, and Judah Kaufman has conjectured that both
the paternal grandfather and the son of the author of the Nizzahon
were called Eliezer.[17] The marginal note in B, f. 6^r, would then have
originated in a belief that the manuscript contained Lipmann's
famous work, which it resembles in its use of numbered paragraphs
as well as in matter and manner. The view that this Lipmann was an
Eliezer could easily have been held in the circumstances just
described. The margin would then combine a mistaken identification
of this work as Lipmann's with an identification of the particular
Lipmann who wrote the Nizzahon.

Thus far it has appeared that the main text of B, written not later
than the early sixteenth century, parallels R in both the first and the
second series of paragraphs, but preserves more of the first series
than survives in R. From the reformer Tremellius the manuscript
eventually passed into the hands of an owner probably to be
identified as the Bernese bibliographer and Hebraist Samuel Hortinus. Buxtorf the Elder acquired it in 1623.

At this point the marginal attribution to Lipmann first became a
source of widespread error. Buxtorf lent his manuscript to Wilhelm
Schickard, who was editing another manuscript entitled Nizzahon –
that also known as Aḥiṭub we-Ṣalmon; Schickard referred to B, in
works issued in 1624 and 1628, as the Nizzahon of Lipmann.
Buxtorf the Elder did the same in his description, printed by his son
in 1640. His generosity as an owner of the manuscript and his zeal
as a bibliographer thereby laid the foundations of the public
knowledge of B, but confused for a time the literary puzzle of the
works entitled Nizzahon.

In 1644 Hackspan's edition of Lipmann's Nizzahon permitted

[15]G. Margoliouth (–J. Leveen), *Catalogue of the Hebrew and Samaritan Manuscripts in the British Museum* (4 vols., London, 1899–1935), iii, 379 f., no. 1047; Striedl–Tetzner–Roth, ii, 53 f.
[16]Judah Kaufman, *Rabbi Yom Tov Lipmann Mühlhausen* (Hebrew: New York 1927), 13 n. 1.
[17]Kaufman, 14 n. 17, and 26.

Hebraists to see that B contained a different work. The writer of the flyleaf description printed above, not impossibly J. J. Buxtorf, correctly noted that B differs from the writings edited by both Schickard and Hackspan under the name of Nizzahon, and that further comparison is necessary with the Nizzahon quoted by Sebastian Münster. In the first volume of his Hebrew bibliography (1715) J. C. Wolf likewise suspected, from a comparison of Buxtorf the Elder's printed description with Hackspan's text, that B could not be Lipmann's Nizzahon. The influence of the marginal identification was stemmed, but reserved to the latter days.

This identification itself arose, it has been suggested, from the view that the work contained in B was Lipmann's Nizzahon, to which its layout gives it a general resemblance, combined with a naming of the member of the Lipmann family thought to be responsible, for the author is only surnamed in the manuscript tradition.

Now that B can be identified as another copy of the work attested in the third part of R, what can be said, on a first and limited examination, of B's witness to the text of this untitled work?

IV

B has eighty-four folios to be compared with the thirty-four relevant folios of R, but a typical page of R carries appreciably more than a page of B. Paragraphs 12 (part)–24 in the first series occupy about eight pages in R, ff. 31^r–35^r, but about thirteen pages in B, ff. 10^r–16^v. A rough estimate on this basis, leaving blank pages out of account, suggests that R is equivalent to about fifty-five folios of B. B would then have an excess of nearly thirty folios. Ten occur at the start, before R begins at a point corresponding to B, f. 10^r. Others may be accounted for by the last third of the first series of paragraphs in B, ff. 44^v–64^r. A combination of the descriptions by di Capua and Rosenthal suggests that the corresponding section may be the very considerably shorter R, ff. 44^r–51^r. On the other hand, the second series of numbered paragraphs occupies fourteen folios in R, ff. 51^r–65^v, but only eighteen in B, ff. 65^r–83^v; here B lacks the equivalent of about five of its own folios. I have not been able to identify passages corresponding to R, ff. 62^v–63^v, published by Rosenthal in *Kobez*, N.S. viii. 319–23. They would be expected to occur towards the end of this section of B, if it contained all the material found in the corresponding pages of R. These impressions, based on the published descriptions and printed portions of R and a first examination of B, are obviously provisional. So far as they go, they suggest that B, as compared with R, gives a much fuller presentation of the first series of paragraphs, including its introductory matter, but a shorter text of the second series. However the difference is distributed in detail, the text of B, compared with that of R, is over a third as long again.

Collations of B with Rosenthal's text of R in *Kobez*, N.S. viii. 313f. (R, ff. 31ʳ⁻ᵛ, corresponding to B, ff. 10ᵛ–11ʳ; first series, paragraphs 12 (part)–14) and in *Baron Jubilee Volume*, iii. 384 f. (R, f. 43ᵛ, corresponding to B, f. 44ʳ⁻ᵛ; first series, paragraphs 97–8) suggest that the two manuscripts in the main vary only slightly from one another. B, despite its errors, sometimes has a better reading, or one which may lead to improvement of the text. Only the more noteworthy divergences are mentioned here.

In the first passage, B has a marginal note, by the scribe of the main text, against paragraph 13 (on Dan. ix 26) 'They make a verse which is not a verse in Daniel'; this comment, not in R, is incorporated into the text of N.V. (Berger's Hebrew text, 80; Wagenseil, 137). In the same paragraph, where Rosenthal, 314 n. 99, reports that a word is obscured in R, read with B תדחם 'you shall press them', found also in N.V., loc. cit. Towards the end of paragraph 13 (Rosenthal, 314, l. 11) B omits *lishpoṭ 'eth ha-'areṣ*, which follows *'az* in R but should precede it as in N.V.; B adds *'eth ha-'areṣ* (only) between *shum* and *melekh*. B is further astray than R, but the errors in both suggest that the explanatory 'to judge the earth' may have been added in the margin of a common ancestor. The quotation of Isa. ii 11 at Rosenthal, 314, l. 12 is lacking in the text of B, but is added by a second hand in the margin.

In paragraph 14, on Isa. xi 1–2, B alone has the marginal note by the scribe of the main text 'They misapply it to Jesus'. The abbreviation *k"t* in R, resolved by Rosenthal, 313, l. 16 as *koh t'omar*, probably represents *kakh tashiv*, written out in B. At the end of the paragraph the portions of Isa. xi 12 f. supplied in square brackets by Rosenthal, 314, l. 27 are written out in full, with the addition of 'the envy also of Ephraim shall depart', in B.

In the second passage, paragraph 97, on the king of Israel as hidden but waiting to come and reign (Ps. lxxxix), for Rosenthal, 384, l. 3 of the paragraph, *ba'awonenu*, read with B כמו הירח '[but he is hidden] like the moon'. In paragraph 98, B ends with the quotation of Judg. xiii 16 (Rosenthal, 385, l. 4), a little less than half-way through the paragraph as found in R, and begins a new paragraph.

Outside these passages no systematic comparison has been made, but it may be worth noting some agreements of B with R against

N.V. in paragraphs common to R and N.V. Thus in the first series, no. 34, on Gen. xviii 2, corresponding to the first part of N.V., paragraph 13 (Berger's Hebrew text, 9 f.; Wagenseil, 12–15), B, f. 22ʳ like R (Rosenthal, *Baron Jubilee Volume*, iii. 362), omits Berger, p. 9, ll. 3–7 = Wagenseil, p. 12, five lines up, to p. 13, l. 7. In the same series, no. 37, B, f. 24ᵛ agrees with R (Rosenthal, op. cit., p. 364, l. 19) in giving the anti-Jewish charge as 'you eat human beings', without the addition in N.V., paragraph 16 'and the blood of brats' (Berger's Hebrew text, 14, l. 105; Wagenseil, 21. ll. 7 f.). Berger, 375, regards this as one of the most striking indications that, in the paragraphs common to R and N.V., the wording in R is prior to that found in N.V. Lastly, in the same series, paragraph 77, R. Abraham the Proselyte receives the further appellation 'of Hungary' in B, f. 35ʳ, as in R (Rosenthal, op. cit., 381); the words are lacking in N.V., paragraph 50 (Berger's Hebrew text, 35, l. 160; Wagenseil, 53). (The R parallel resumes after some lines not in N.V., contrary to the marginal indication in Berger, l. 158).

By contrast, in paragraph 63, on Exod. xl 34 f., wherein R. Kalonymus shows 'king Heinrich the wicked' that the new cathedral of Spires bears no comparison with Solomon's temple, B. f. 31ᵛ, like N.V. paragraph 41 (Berger's Hebrew text, 29; Wagenseil, 42), lacks the final sentence supplying a further argument from I Kings vi 7 (R in Rosenthal, op. cit., 376), and closes with the emperor's declaration 'Had I not given my word, I would have ordered your head to be cut off'. Here, however, the end of a paragraph is in question, and the anticlimactic overplus in R may well be an addition of the copyist. So far as they go, then, these instances are consistent with the view that B is close to R, as the collations suggested; but the conclusion of the matter depends on further study.

V

Lastly, a synopsis of ff. 1–5 may give some further light on the relation of B to N.V., and its characteristics as a work of controversy. The manuscript opens in the course of an introductory rebuttal of Christian charges and claims, which is followed at f. 2ʳ by the beginning of the first series of numbered paragraphs. R is not extant for the text of these early pages in B.

The typical form of argument is extended biblical quotation, followed by terse controversial application. Thus f. 1ʳ, where the large characters of the first words mark the beginning of a paragraph, opens with a full quotation of Obad. 18: 'And the house of Jacob shall be a fire ... and there shall not be any remaining of the house of Esau; for the mouth of the LORD hath spoken it.' This oracle against Edom, applied to Rome and then to Christendom,[18] is directed against 'those who endeavour to spill the blood of Israel, relying on what Elihu said in the book of Job'.

Job xxxvi 9–12 is then quoted, with its assertion that the sword is the appointed end of the disobedient. 'But say to them: if we have sinned against the law of Moses, judgment is with you ... but if you attack us for some other crime, come and let us dispute together. And if they say, Why do you not believe that Jesus is God?, reply to them, Why did he accept death?'

The adversaries' proof-text for their attack is thus turned aside by implied claims that the Jews keep the law, and are justified in their disbelief. That death is incompatible with divinity is now shown by a catena of Dan. ii 11, vi 27 (26); Jer. x 10; Deut. xxxii 40. The first, third, and fourth of these texts appear, for the same purpose but in different contexts, in N.V., paragraphs 65, 109, and 50, respectively (Berger's Hebrew text, 43, 72, 35: Wagenseil, 65, 117, 51); Dan. ii 11 was quoted to a clerk by a Jewess of Loches, according to Joseph the Zealot (Rosenthal, *Joseph*, p. 119, no. 133). Two further texts drive home the attack: Ezek. xxviii 2, where pretensions to divinity are rebuked with 'thou art *a son of* man, and not God' (B significantly inserts *ben* into the biblical text); and Ezek. xxviii 9, also applied to the crucifixion in Rosenthal, *Joseph*, 72, no. 71, where the proud prince will claim godhead in vain before his slayers (B has the plural in 9a, against the biblical singular). 'So you see that he is not God, for he was slain' (f. 1ʳ, lines 23 f.). Indeed, if he were God, why did he accept a death (f. 1ᵛ) 'more accursed than any death' – for he cursed it himself (Deut. xxi 23)?

From these ancient objections the argument returns to a theme specially well marked in mediaeval polemic, the prediction of Christendom and its end in prophecy. Just as Obadiah was thought to have foretold the punishment of the persecutors, so Isaiah is reckoned to have warned us not to revere the son of man (li. 12 f.). As for their claim that their god was born, rebut it with Isa. xliii 12 (this passage had already been written by the copyist in the margin of f. 1ʳ). Similarly, because David 'saw by the holy spirit that Jesus would lead the world astray and grow mighty in sorceries, he prayed that he might by slain' (Ps. ix 21, explained similarly, but without

[18]For a survey of the development, with literature, see J. Maier, ' "Siehe, ich mach(t)e dich klein unter den Völkern ...': Zum rabbinischen Assoziationshorizont von Obadja 2', in *Künder des Wortes: Beiträge zur Theologie der Propheten, Joseph Schreiner zum 60. Geburtstag* (Würzburg, 1982), 203–15.

any emphasis on David's foresight, in N.V., paragraph 135 (Berger's Hebrew text, 87; from Munich manuscript only, not in Wagenseil)). That verse means that, when he is slain, all will know that he is not God; and it was for the same reason that David said at the end of the psalter 'Praise the Lord ... trust not in the son of man' whose thoughts perish at his death (Ps. cxlvi 1, 3 f.). David here warned future generations not to be led astray by Jesus and his company. Matt. ix. 6 is quoted to confirm that he did call himself son of man in the gospel. The Hebrew version varies from that in N.V., paragraph 168 (Berger's Hebrew text, 117; Wagenseil, 204) and Rosenthal, *Joseph*, 132, no. 25; but all three sources quote the text for the same purpose, and all call the gospel paralytic a demoniac. Ps. cxlvi 5, where David calls him blessed who has the God of Jacob for his help, was another prophetic warning. This psalm is used to make the same points in different language at N.V., paragraph 125 (Berger's Hebrew text, 52; Wagenseil, 141 f.); but it is not there explained as David's prophetic warning.

'Blunt their teeth again and say' a further argument (f. 1ᵛ l. 24–f. 2ʳ). It also forms N.V., paragraph 9 (Berger's Hebrew text, 7; Wagenseil, 9 f.); but it is closely linked to the prophetic context of B by its point that the surprising unwillingness that man should live for ever (Gen. iii 22) is explained by divine foreknowledge of the claims of Jesus, since his death would prevent men being misled by them.

The series of numbered paragraphs now begins. No. 1, on the prohibition of apostasy from God and his law, is a longer version of N.V., paragraph 243 (Berger's Hebrew text, 162; Wagenseil, 257). The end of the introduction and this first paragraph, juxtaposed in B, are almost as widely separated as possible in N.V. The texts quoted in B are Ps. lxxviii 1–4, Deut. iv 9 f., 1 f., all in N.V.; then I Kgs. ii 3, Jer. xvi 19, Zeph. iii 8 f., Zech. viii 23, forming a passage only in B: finally, Mal. iii 22, also the conclusion in N.V. B is distinguished first by a repeated question 'Why do you seduce us to apostatize?', and secondly by its collection of the prophetic promises that 'you will return to us and our law at the end of days' (f. 2ᵛ, ll. 4 f.); at the end of all the prophecies (this point is not in N.V.) Malachi says 'Remember the law of Moses'.

Paragraph 2, ff. 2ᵛ–3ʳ, not in N.V., shows that Ps. xx cannot apply to Christ, whose request in Gethsemane was denied. (Mark xiv 36 and parallels are quoted for a different purpose in N.V., paragraphs 168 and 176 (Berger's Hebrew text, 118, 123; Wagenseil, 205, 212), and Rosenthal, *Joseph*, 135 no. 36.) Rather, 'David was prophesying concerning the resurrection of the dead, that he should return to be captain over Israel, as is written in many places of the prophets' (f. 3ʳ, l. 8); compare paragraph 87 in this series, discussed in the previous section.

Paragraph 3, ff. 3ʳ–4ʳ, not in N.V., interprets Ps. lxxxi as a warning against 'any strange god' (v. 9), 'such as Jesus and Mohammed and their like'; the two are named together in different contexts at N.V., paragraphs 80 and 135 (Berger's Hebrew text, 53, 87; Wagenseil, 80; the second passage (Munich manuscript only) is not in Wagenseil). The crucifixion and the ignoring of the Gospel miracles are justified by extended quotation of Deut. xiii. 7–10 (6–9); 2–6 (1–5). The argument is ancient (cf. Sanh. 43a, for the first-quoted verses, and Matt. xxvii 63 f., John vii 12, 47, probably reflecting the whole passage) and well-attested in mediaeval polemic (e.g. N.V., paragraph 50 (Berger's Hebrew text, p. 34; Wagenseil, 50 f.). B lays stronger emphasis on a point found also in N.V., loc. cit., the prophetic prediction of Christendom in Deuteronomy. 'We did to him as the Holy One commanded us by Moses, for he knew that Jesus would arise and lead the word astray, and therefore he wrote specifically, If thy brother entice thee … ' (f. 3ᵛ, ll. 7 ff.).

Paragraph 4, f. 4ʳ⁻ᵛ, not in N.V., refutes the Christian understanding of Ps. xxii; David spoke of his own sufferings. Verse 17 can hardly refer to the crucifixion, for the stoned were never nailed up in Israel (f. 4ʳ). This argument occurs in a different exegesis of the psalm in N.V., paragraph 145 (Berger's Hebrew text, 94; Wagenseil, 162).

Paragraph 5, ff. 4ᵛ–5ʳ, on Ps. lxxii, is partly paralleled in N.V., paragraph 150 (Berger's Hebrew text, 99 f.; Wagenseil, 174–7). It gives some of the refutations found in N.V., but then, in a passage which is not paralleled, shows that the psalm can be satisfactorily understood throughout as David's prayer for Solomon.

Lastly, paragraph 6, f. 5ʳ⁻ᵛ, on Ps. lxxxvii, not in N.V. (the psalm is differently treated in Rosenthal, *Joseph*, 113, no. 123), probably reflects a northern French background in its explanation of v. 5 'And of Zion it shall be said, This and that man was born in her'. 'The matter is thus: One who was born in France, if others who did not recognize him came and asked him, Where were you born?, might answer and say, In Paris – because Paris is the capital of France.' David foresees the time when all will say 'I was born in Zion', for the Lord will establish it as the exalted capital of all kingdoms (f. 5ʳ, last line, to f. 5ᵛ).

Even so short a section as five folios offers a good deal that is relevant to the two questions broached initially. First, the relation of B. to N.V. in these pages is one of noticeable contact, but more strongly marked independence. The northern French association of paragraph 6, not in N.V., is a further indication that the two works preserve much from a common milieu, but common literary material in these pages is restricted to three paragraphs. Two of these are juxtaposed in B, ff. 1^v–2^r, but widely separated in N.V.; the second includes a substantial passage lacking in the N.V. parallel. The third paragraph, in ff. 4^v–5^r, omits some lines of N.V.'s rebuttal, but adds its own long exegetical conclusion.

Outside these paragraphs B has many biblical texts quoted in N.V. for the same purpose (see on ff. 1^r, 1^v, and the numbered paragraphs 2, 3, and 4 (including the note on the nails)); but they appear in N.V. in passages which otherwise clearly differ from B, and the most likely explanation is that the two works are independently employing standard proofs.

It would obviously not be true of these pages that, as in Urbach's estimate concerning R, the two works have 90 per cent of their material in common. Rather, in this section they share a small proportion of common material, and a larger number of common references to standard controversial interpretations; but they are clearly independent compositions, and at least in these pages B is more given than N.V. to following up demolition with constructive exegesis.

So far as they go, these folios support Berger's view that the work fragmentarily preserved in R, now more fully attested in B, is not itself a source of N.V., but a composition indebted to material also used in N.V. It is very hard to conceive of the compiler of N.V. reading the text of these folios, picking out three paragraphs, and rearranging them so that they respectively reappear, with internal excisions and additions, at the beginning, the end, and the middle of his vast work. That the B arrangement could arise directly from N.V. as we have it is equally unlikely.

Secondly, the character of the composition preserved in B, considered as a controversial work in its own right, also receives some illumination from these pages. Several passages suggest that the adverse pressure of Christendom is felt to be particularly grievous. The cheerful sarcasm of Joseph the Zealot is not wholly lacking, but more noticeable is a sober reckoning with a proof-text threatening the Jews with the sword (Job xxxvi 9–12, f. 1^r), with charges of guilt for the crucifixion and culpable unbelief (f. 1^r), and with persistent attempts to turn the Jews from their law (f. 2^v); compare f. 24^r, on the charge of cannibalism, mentioned in the previous section.

The response to this pressure is in part an uncompromising reassertion of traditional rebuttals. Schickard rightly detected the influence on this work of the Talmudic passages on Christian origins (pp. 103–7 above). In these first pages he would have met the condemnation of the miracles as sorcery (f. 1^v, cf. Sanh. 43^a), and the claim, also upheld in Sanh,. 43a, that 'we acted according to halakhah in that we slew him' (f. 3^v); it is inscribed in large letters in the margin, by the copyist of the main text, opposite the beginning of the Deut. xiii quotations in paragraph 3. The death of the cross revealed more clearly than anything else that the crucified was not divine, and it was foreseen in divine providence with this object in view (ff. 1^{r-v}, 2^r). The comment on the non-use of nails, f. 4^r, does not come in to support a claim that no Jewish penalty was inflicted; it is meant to cast doubt on the Christological understanding of Ps. xxii, on the assumption that the hanging on a tree did indeed conform to the Deuteronomic law of stoning 'according to halakhah'. With these counter-assertions may be linked paragraph 1, also in N.V., on loyalty to the one God.

Another aspect of B's response, however, distinguishes it from N.V. Care is taken to provide a convincing interpretation of the psalms, which shall be both Jewish and messianic (f. 1^v, and the numbered paragraphs 2, 4, 5, and 6). This feature may suggest that the Christological understanding was not without a certain attraction.

A well-marked characteristic of B in these pages indicates how that might have been so, but is important irrespective of this particular speculation. It is the pervasively evident absorption with prophecy. In the last days the true king of Israel will return at the resurrection of the dead (f. 3^r), and Christendom will come to an end (f. 1^r Obad. xviii), and the numbered paragraphs 1 and 6); the temporary endurance of Christendom meanwhile, the claims to be made for it, and the necessary answers, have also been foreseen and foretold by the Holy One, Moses, and David (f. 1^v; f. 2^r, parallel with N.V.; paragraph 3). These themes are important in N.V. also, and more widely, and they have roots in the liturgy and the rabbinic developments of Obadiah noted above; but they are expounded in these pages of B with special clarity and force. The author–compiler probably shares the concern with prophecy which was a feature of mediaeval Franco-German Jewish piety, and finds the hope of Israel to be at the heart of his response to Christianity. Herein he may be compared with Joseph the Zealot, who prefaces his work with 'the consolations', prophetic promises collected in answer to the wicked who ask 'On whom do you now rely?' (Rosenthal, *Joseph*, 16).

These five folios thus represent controversy framed amid a Christendom felt to exert an especially strong and hostile pressure.

The responses reassert traditional statements of loyalty to the one God and denial of the claims made for 'the son of man'; but they add sober positive exposition to show how the biblical texts on which Christians rely, and even the temporary Christian dominance, contribute to and accord with the prophetic hope of Israel. When the responses in ff. 1–5 are compared with similar passages in N.V. and Joseph, it is in the careful reconstruction of this positive prophetic interpretation that they seem to present common themes with a measure of distinctiveness.

VI

The Basle Nizzahon demands much further study, but the conclusions of this account must now be summarized. The manuscript, not later in date than the early sixteenth century, presents a considerably fuller version of the text hitherto only known from R. It is therefore an important witness to the Jewish apologetic of mediaeval northern France and Germany.

In the sixteenth and seventeenth centuries the manuscript passed through the hands of great Hebraists. The Buxtorfs' ownership and description made it well known, but the acceptance by Buxtorf the Elder and Schickard of the marginal attribution to Lipmann (whose work had not yet been printed) tended to confuse the bibliographical puzzle of the different books called Nizzahon. After Hackspan's 1644 edition of Lipmann, and before 1681, the manuscript was accurately described in an unpublished notice on the flyleaf as neither Lipmann's work nor clearly identical with that quoted by Münster (N.V.). Wolf saw from Buxtorf the Elder's printed description that the manuscript could not be Lipmann's Nizzahon. The early marginal attribution to 'Eliezer called Lipmann' perhaps arose from the view that this work was the famous book of Lipmann, to which it bears a general resemblance, combined with an identification of the member of the Lipmann family in question, who is only surnamed in the manuscript of his Nizzahon.

The text of B is over a third as long again as that preserved in R, and consists of introductory matter followed by two series of numbered paragraphs; the first is attested more completely than in R. Specimen collations suggest that B is close to R, and that, despite fairly frequent errors, it offers some better readings and some other opportunities of improving the text.

A concluding study of ff. 1–5 shows that, so far as these pages are concerned, the work preserved in B shares a small proportion of common material with N.V., but is clearly an independent composition. This section of the manuscript supports Berger's view that N.V. and the work hitherto known only from R draw independently on a common source.

The answers to Christian objections in these pages evince a measure of distinctiveness in their constructive reassertion of the hope of Israel. The compilation most fully attested in B is important not only as an early indirect witness to N.V., but as an independent controversial work comparable with N.V. and Joseph the Zealot.

11

THE REVISION OF SHEM TOB IBN SHAPRUT'S
EBEN BOHAN

Ibn Shaprut's *Touchstone*[1] is among the most comprehensive of the apologetic handbooks compiled in mediaeval Spanish Jewry. It has aroused considerable interest, especially through its Hebrew Gospel-version.[2] Like many works of its kind, however, it has never been printed in full.[3]

The MSS. belong for the most part to two recensions, containing fifteen and sixteen books respectively. These were first clearly distinguished by Steinschneider in his Leyden catalogue.[4] In the light of a third seventeen-book form unknown to Steinschneider Alexander Marx again discussed the relationship of the different types of text, arriving at radical alterations of his master's view.[5] Whereas Steinschneider considered the sixteen-book text a revised version complete in itself, Marx held that this text-form was defective and that only the seventeen-book text represented the complete work in the author's final revision.

If Marx is right, the student of Ibn Shaprut must view almost all extant MSS. of Eben Bohan with grave reservations. The fifteen-book

---

[1] N.° 65 in Judah Rosenthal, 'Anti-Christian Polemics from its (*sic*) Beginnings to the end of the 18th Century', *Aresheth* II (Jerusalem, 1960), p. 147. See pp. 39–41, above.

[2] See P. Lapide, 'Der "Prufstein" aus Spanien: die einzige rabbinische Hebraisierung des Mt-Evangeliums', *Sefarad* XXXIV (1974), 227–72 (not examining the textual problem of the *Touchstone*) also pp. 40–1, nn. 106–7, above.

[3] For extracts see L. Dukes, 'Zusätze und Berichtigungen ...', *Literaturblatt* of *Der Orient* VIi (1845), col. 149; H. Graetz, *Geschichte der Juden* V³ (Leipzig, 1895), 412: VIII³ (Leipzig, 1890), 21 f.; Ad. Neubauer – S. R. Driver – E. B. Pusey, *The Fifty-third Chapter of Isaiah according to the Jewish Interpreters* (repr., with Prolegomenon by R. Loewe, New York, 1969), I, 88–94, II, 92–8; I, Loeb, 'Polémistes chrétiens et juifs en France et en Espagne' *REJ* XVIII (1889), 43–70, 219–42 (219–26); S. Krauss, *Des Leben Jesu nach jüdischen Quellen* (Berlin, 1902), 146–9; Ad. Posnanski, *Schiloh* I (Leipzig, 1904), 223–31, LII–LV; A. Marx, 'The Polemical Manuscripts in the Library of the Jewish Theological Seminary of America', in *Studies in Jewish Bibliography and Related Subjects in Memory of Abraham Solomon Freidus (1867–1923)*, (New York, 1929), 247–78; N. R. Frimer, cited by Rosenthal, 'Polemics', p. 132, n. 10; L. Garshowitz, cited by D. J. Lasker, review of Krauss and Horbury, *Controversy*, *JJS* xlviii (1997), 165. To the descriptions of MSS. enumerated by Marx, 265n., may now be added those cited in notes 10, 11, 17 and 24 below.

[4] M. Steinschneider, *Catalogus Codicum Hebraeorum Bibliothecae Academiae Lugduno-Batavae* (Leyden, 1858), 115–20; cf. Steinschneider, *Catalogus Librorum Hebraeorum in Bibliotheca Bodleiana* (Berlin, 1852–60) (hereafter *CB*), Cols. 2553–8.

[5] Marx, 265–70.

copies will represent the work at what proved to be only a preliminary stage in its composition, and the sixteen-book copies will offer no more than a drastically truncated form of its final version; for Marx believed that Ibn Shaprut had expanded the fifteen-book form of the work into a final form which contained not sixteen but seventeen books. This full and final seventeen-book version is now represented, in Marx's view, solely by the one seventeen-book copy which he described in his comprehensive survey of the textual evidence, Jewish Theological Seminary of America MS 2234.

This adverse verdict on the witness to the text is of moment to the historian as well as the bibliographer, but, so far as the writer is aware, it has never been reconsidered. The present footnote to the fundamental work of Steinschneider and Marx is accordingly concerned with the topic on which they differ, the nature of the revision applied to the fifteen-book first recension. Comparison of MSS. of the first and second recensions shows, it will be argued, that Steinschneider was right; and that historians of the Jews in Spain, of Jewish apologetic and of the Hebrew versions of the New Testament can draw, consequently, on a more unified and less defective witness to the text of *Eben Bohan* than Marx supposed, with a much stronger attestation of the work in its final form.

I

At first, as Steinschneider and Marx both held, the *Touchstone* may have comprised only the first twelve out of the fifteen books (*še'arim*) of the first recension: I on the principles of Judaism, II–X, based on Jacob b. Reuben's *Milhamoth ha-Shem*, on proof-texts from the Hebrew Bible, XI on the Talmudic Haggadoth and XII on the Gospels. The total of the books is given as twelve in the epigraph of the Leyden MS. (which in fact, as noted below, contains sixteen books) and (erased and corrected) in the introduction of one New York MS. (Marx, p. 268).

We may supplement these observations of Steinschneider and Marx by noting two passages of the text which seem to point in the same direction. First, the preface preceding the list of contents forecasts the material of books I–XII, but not of books XIII–XIV (XV, as noted below, is a later addition). In the preface the author tells of his copying of the Gospels and names the *Milhamoth ha-Shem* as the basis of his work.[6] He notes the defects of his source for current use as over-bold

---

[6]The preface is partly printed by Loeb, 219–21.

language,[7] failure to treat some important biblical texts and entire silence on the now vehemently attacked Haggadoth.[8] Finally he says he has prefaced his work with a treatment of Jewish principles.[9] Books I–XII on their own form a book such as this introduction leads one to expect, an exordium on principles (I) followed by the revision of the *Milhamoth ha-Shem* (II–X), this being supplemented by discussion of the Haggadoth (XI) and a much fuller treatment of the Gospels than Jacob b. Reuben's (XII). The second passage in question occurs at the beginning of book XII, where the author speaks as if this book is intended to be the last: 'I have chosen to complete this work of mine ... by copying the books of the Gospel'.[10]

It is very possible, then, that the work originally contained only books I–XII of the first recension. In any event, colophons show that a form of the work consisting of these books together with XIII, on the Resurrection of the Dead, and XIV, on the Messiah, was finished in 1385 (or 1380 according to MS Breslau[11]) at Tarazona,[12] while book XV, completing the first recension as we now have it, was added in 1400 at Lucena.[13] This last book replied in eight chapters to a refutation by the convert Alphonsus of Valladolid (Abner of Burgos)[14] of Ibn Shaprut's source, the *Milhamoth ha-Shem*. Although the Christian use of the Haggadoth which Ibn Shaprut rebutted had

[7]For the passage in this sense, as opposed to Loeb's rendering (op. cit. 220), see J. Rosenthal (ed.), *Jacob ben Reuben: Milhamoth ha-Shem* (Jerusalem, 1963), XIX. Ibn Shaprut urges the tone of servant to master (Loeb, 220 f.); compare the injunctions to restrained debate in his contemporary Moses Tordesillas, who also used Jacob b. Reuben (Loeb, 228 f.; strongly reiterated in the conclusion of the biblical section of Moses' work, MS. Parm. 2565 (De Rossi, 121), f. 97b.

[8]In his later separate apologetic commentary on the Talmudic Haggadoth Ibn Shaprut remarks that those who wish to reply to the attacks on these passages have no books to turn to: Shem Tob ibn Shaprut, *Pardes Rimmonim* (Sabbioneta 1554, repr. Jerusalem, 1968), 2a.

[9]This passage is printed by G. Margoliouth (–J. Leveen), *Catalogue of the Hebrew and Samaritan Manuscripts in the British Museum* III (repr. London, 1965), 443a.

[10]*ra'iti le-haŝlim hibburi zeh ... le-ha'atiq sifrè ha-evangelio*, Margoliouth, III, p. 444a; A. Luzzatto, L. Mortara Ottolenghi, *Hebraica Ambrosiana* (Fontes Ambrosiani XLV, Milan, 1972), p. 99a, with small variants also found in ULC Add. 1175, f., 216a (cf. n. 24 below).

[11]D. S. Loewinger, B. D. Weinryb, *Catalogue of the Hebrew Manuscripts in the Library of the Juedisch-Theologisches Seminar in Breslau* (Wiesbaden, 1965), pp. 163 f. n.° 233.

[12]For Ibn Shaprut's life here as physician and business man see J. M. Sanz Artibucilla, 'Los judios en Aragón y Navarra. Nuevos datos biográficos relativos a Sem Tob ben Ishaq Saprut', *Sefarad* V (1945), 337–66. If the 1385 date is correct, this evidence shows that the author finished his work while occupied with litigation.

[13]Marx, 266 f. A reference to Lucena like that in MS. Leyden also occurs in the Ambrosian MS. (Luzzatto-Ottolenghi, p. 99b) and in that of Cambridge (n. 24 below), f. 273a.

[14]On Alphonsus see S. W. Baron, *A Social and Religious History of the Jews* IX[2] (New York 1965), 108–11, 292 n. 2 (1), 299 f. n. 11, Y (F.) Baer, *A History of the Jews in Christian Spain* I (E.T. Philadelphia, 1966), 327–54, J. Rosenthal, *Studies and Texts in Jewish History, Literature and Religion* (Jerusalem, 1967), 324; and p. 40, n. 105, above.

been given fresh impetus by Alphonsus, and although Ibn Shaprut cites another work of Alphonsus, the *Mostrador de Justicia* in book I,[15] he says in the preface to book XV that he did not meet with the reply to *Milhamoth ha-Shem* until long after he had finished his own book based on Jacob b. Reuben's treatise.[16]

This first recension of fifteen books is represented in several MSS. enumerated by Marx, 269: Breslau, British Library, Casanata, Laurenziana, Neofiti, and Oxford Opp. Add 4.° 72 and Mich. 119. Marx notes here that one incomplete MS. of the Jewish Theological Seminary of America (Marx, p. 252, n.° 14) is also probably of this recension. To these we may add Vat. ebr. 523 (scribal colophon, f. 123b, dated Conegliano, 1589),[17] and probably also the Florentine MS. Biblioteca Nazionale II.X.143, which breaks off in book XII.ix at the translation of S. Matthew iv.9; for the Gospels form book XII only in the first recension.[18]

Most of these MSS. are incomplete. Book XV is partly lacking in Mich. 119 (Neubauer n.° 2152) and almost entirely so in Neotiti 17.2. In BL Add. 26,964 (Margoliouth n.° 1070) and Oxford, Opp. Add. 4.°. 72 (Neubauer n.° 2150) book XV is mentioned in the table of contents, but the text breaks off in or at the end of the book XII.[19] Marx, n.° 14, breaks off in book XI. The Laurentian MS., Plut. II Cod. 17, has two smaller lacunae near the beginning of and at the end of XV. viii.[20] In Vat. ebr. 523, where many leaves are missing or out of order, book XV (see ff. 82b–114b) is disordered but complete.[21]

MSS. of the second recension contain sixteen books. Books III–X

---

[15]Loeb, 221: Margoliouth, III, p. 443b. The work of לאמ״ם cited in book XIII (Marx, 266 f.) is not expressly ascribed by Ibn Shaprut himself to Alphonsus.

[16]The passage is printed from Mich. 119 in Ad. Neubauer (-A. E. Cowley), *Catalogue of the Hebrew Manuscripts in the Bodleian Library* I (Oxford, 1886), col. 745 n.° 2152.1. For a corresponding statement in the table of contents of the whole work see Margoliouth, III, p. 443a.

[17]N. Allony, D. S. Loewinger, *List of Photocopies in the Institute* III (Jerusalem, 1968), p. 69 n.° 323. I am obliged to the Biblioteca Apostolica Vaticana for answering an inquiry and supplying the microfilm to which my remarks on this MS. refer.

[18]The verse can be identified from the citation in U. Cassuto, 'Nuovi manoscritti ebraici della Biblioteca Nazionale di Firenze', *Giornale della Società Asiatica Italiana* XXI (1908), p. 106, n.° 19.

[19]The foregoing embodies slight corrections to Marx, 269 (cf. 267, n. 13).

[20]For these see A. M. Biscioni, *Bibliothecae ebraicae graecae Florentinae sive Bibliothecae Mediceo-Laurentianae Catalogus* (Florence, 1757), Part 2, 228. Citations here from this MS. are derived from personal inspection and from microfilm.

[21]The leaves should be read in the sequence 82b–102b, 111a–112b, 103a–106b, 113a–114b. Ff. 107a–110b contain the end of the book VII; f. 107a continues f. 61b, f. 110b is continued by f. 22a.

are rearranged in the conventional biblical order. (It is noteworthy that their first-recension order differs from that of Jacob b. Reuben's book as now edited.) A treatise on the articles of the Christian faith, which Steinschneider showed Ibn Shaprut had written separately and which in three MSS. of the first recension appears by itself at the end of *Eben Bohan*,[22] is now inserted after books II–IX on the proof-texts and the Talmud and takes the number XII. Old XII (on the Gospel) becomes XIII. There follows a book XIV containing three chapters against Alphonsus of Valladolid. This books is regarded by Marx as a new insertion and will be discussed below. Last come the two books on the Resurrection and the Messiah, formerly XIII and XIV but now renumbered XV and XVI.

This second recension is represented in several MSS. listed by Marx. 269: Leyden (Warner 28), Parm. 2259 (De Rossi 760), Oxford, Mich. 137 (Neubauer n.° 2151) and Jewish Theological Seminary of America, Adler 1323 (Marx, p. 252 n.° 16). The fragmentary MS. Adler 1638, which according to Marx (p. 252, n.° 17) agrees in order with Adler 1323, should probably also be assigned to this recension (cf. n. 29 below). To these may be added two MSS. to be grouped with the Leyden text, since all three contain a scribal colophon by Menahem Moscato stating that copying was finished at Portogruaro in Friuli in Sivan 5344 (1584). They are the Ambrosian MS. X. 150 sup.[23] and Cambridge University Library, MS. Add. 1175.[24]

---

[22]To MS. Casanata (Marx. 267) we may add Vat. ebr. 523 (see ff. 115a–123b), and Laur. Plut. II 17, where (in the last chapter of book XV) f. 203b is followed by a lacuna (see n. 29 above and appendix below). F. 204a begins *ha-zeh 'o yišteh ha-yayyin ha-zeh*, corresponding to ULC Add. 1175 f. 210a 1. 26 (second recension, book XII.iv). F. 208b, the last page of the MS. (the conclusion is lost), ends *we-hinneh qol qore' 'elau šeḥoṭ* (cited by Biscioni, Part 2, 228), corresponding to ULC Add. 1175 f. 215a 1. 15 (XII.viii). Ff. 204a–208b thus answer to cc. iv–viii of the treatise as incorporated in the second recension. They deal accordingly with the fourth to the eighth foundations (*yesodot*) of Christianity (the Eucharist, Baptism, the end of circumcision, the Incarnation and Atonement, and the new Law), corresponding to the fourth to eighth foundations listed in the preface from MS. Casanata printed by Ad. Posnanski, 'Sepher Kelimmath ha-Goyyim', *Ha-Zofeh* IV (1915), 130 f.

[23]Luzzatto-Ottolenghi, pp. 98–100, n.° 64: pp. 141 f., n.° XXI. This otherwise full and valuable description fails to note that the colophon in Moscato's name found in this MS. and printed on p. 100 a is identical with that of MS. Leyden, and misleadingly includes, p. 99b, the Laurentian copy among those identical with the Ambrosian text and the Leyden copy among those which differ from it. The relation of the Ambrosian, Leyden and Cambridge texts (see following footnote) awaits investigation.

[24]H. Loewe, J. D. Pearson, R. Loewe, *Handlist of Hebrew and Samaritan Manuscripts in the Library of the University of Cambridge* (MS. Or. 1770–72), n.° 860. In his later, unpublished catalogue J. Leveen showed, through restoration of two partly-erased colophons (ff. 190b and 273a), that this copy, reproducing Moscato's earlier colophon, was finished in Cairo in 1673. See also Reif, *Hebrew Manuscripts at Cambridge University Library*, no. 871.

The third form of the work, represented so far as the writer is aware only by the single New York MS. of this type described by Marx, pp. 252 (n.° 15), 268 f. (Jewish Theological Seminary of America, MS. 2234), contains the sixteen books of the second recension followed by book XV of the first recension, the eight chapters in answer to Alphonsus, as book XVII.

II

Steinschneider, who had only the second-recension Leyden MS. before him and of course did not know the third form of text, had conjectured that the second recension contained only one block of new material, the treatise on Christian belief added as the new book XII. Book XIV of the second recension, the three chapters against Alphonsus, he conjecturally identified as the last three chapters of the old book XV, suggesting that the biblical chapters of this book (the first five of the eight chapters) had been appropriately distributed by author or reviser in the second recension among books II–X on the proof-texts. These suggestions stemmed from his observation that (as he saw from Biscioni's description of the Laurentian text) the three chapters of the new book bore the same titles as the last three chapters of the old book XV, while the replies of Alphonsus to Jacob b. Reuben, restricted in the first recension to book XV, are quoted in the Leyden MS. of the second recension in the earlier books. His opinion was however advanced as conjecture because no MS. of the first recension was at hand for comparison with the Leyden MS. of the second recension, and he expressly invited revision of his view in the light of further data.[25]

Alexander Marx took up this invitation in the course of his description of the Jewish Theological Seminary's polemical MSS. Among these is the seventeen-book copy noted above, which is fundamental to Marx's view. In contrast with Steinschneider, he understood the revision applied to the first recension as consisting of the insertion into the fifteen books of not one, but two further books, the treatise on Christian belief and 'another treatise against Alfonso, which perhaps is directed against another of the apostate's writings' (Marx, 267). Marx attributes Steinschneider's different view of this book as the second part of the old book XV to the fact

---

[25]Steinschneider, *Catalogus ... Lugduno-Batavae*, 118 f. In *CB.* col. 2554 he says that the citations from old book XV in the earlier books appear to have been added in revision, but that he is not yet certain on this point.

that the old book XV did not exist in Steinschneider's Leyden MS. Thus for Marx the MSS. of the second recension, containing sixteen books, are defective as witnesses of the revision, which he believed to have resulted in a work of seventeen books.

It follows that almost all MSS. of the work, according to Marx, fail to represent what Ibn Shaprut finally wrote. Those of the first recension would lack not only the treatise on the articles of Christian belief (with the exceptions listed in n. 22 above) but also, in Marx's view, the 'other treatise against Alfonso' (XIV in the second recension), while all MSS. of the second recension would lack the reply to Alphonsus found in book XV of the first recension. Marx therefore writes. p. 269: 'The only MS. containing the complete work with all the additions in seventeen books is our MS. 15' (now 2234. of the Jewish Theological Seminary). This is the copy already mentioned as containing the sixteen books of the second recension followed by a seventeenth which corresponds to book XV of the first recension.

III

For Marx, therefore, the two most strongly represented recensions differ more markedly in content than Steinschneider had thought, and are alike defective as witnesses to the complete work, which is only found in the seventeen-book version. This view can only stand, however, if the observations on which Steinschneider based his opinion are shown to be incorrect or otherwise explained. If Marx is right, the sixteen-book second-recension MSS. such as Steinschneider's Leyden text, represent a truncated form of the complete seventeen-book work, which is held to have arisen simply from the insertion of two new books into the former fifteen. The sixteen-book texts should therefore, apart from the two new books, exactly correspond to books I–XIV of the first recension. Like these, they should contain no material from the old book XV, which is now to follow as the seventeenth book. The two new insertions, likewise, should not anticipate this concluding book. Book XIV in the second recension should, against Steinschneider's view, be entirely different from book XV in the first recension, and we should not expect to find, as Steinschneider did, citations from this book XV in the earlier parts of a second-recension text.

Marx, as we saw, assumed that Steinschneider, who had no first-recension MS. before him, was indeed mistaken in identifying the new book XIV as the last three chapters of the old book

XV.[26] He correspondingly held, in brief remarks to be considered further below, that the citations from the old book XV in the earlier books in the second recension are repetitions, probably due to a copyist. Comparison of MSS. of the first and second recensions shows, however, that Steinschneider's conjectural identification of the new book XIV with old XV, vi–viii is correct. This means that a substantial portion of the old book XV is present within the sixteen books of the second recension, and calls into question Marx's correlated view, in which as will be seen he recognized some difficulty, that the other citations of this book were inserted by a copyist.

The last three chapters (vi–viii) of book XV in the first recension deal with the parts of Alphonsus' work not directly relating to Hebrew Scripture. They treat respectively the Gospels, the Resurrection of the Dead, and the Coming of the Messiah. The titles, beginnings and endings of these chapters are appended below from the Laurentian MS. of the first recension, with the insignificant variants of the Cambridge MS. of the second recension, where the same chapters form book XIV in its entirety.[27]

The five earlier chapters (i–v) of the old book XV are concerned with scriptural texts. They answer the objections of Alphonsus to Jacob b. Reuben's treatment of Proverbs, Job, Isaiah, Ezekiel and the Minor Prophets (in that order). In the first recension these objections are not cited in the books (II–X) devoted to scriptural passages, since as noted above Ibn Shaprut was not yet aware of them when composing these books. Their placing in the second recension in these earlier books would clearly have been to the reader's advantage.

The Cambridge text presents these citations from the old book XV in the books on passages from Isaiah, Ezekiel and the Minor Prophets (books III, VIII (the old numeration being kept) and VI

---

[26]Marx, 267 and n. 15. Marx may possibly have made this assumption, which he takes as self-evident, under the influence of Neubauer, *Catalogue* I, Cols. 745 f. n.° 2152.1. Here book XV in Mich. 119 (first recension) is described as 'divided into eight chapters (only three in the MS., incomplete), different from XIV of the preceding number' (Mich. 137, second recension). The connection between old XV and new XIV is not readily apparent from these MSS. since, as Neubauer says, Mich. 119 has only the *first* three chapters of the old book XV, whereas those which make up the new book XIV are the *last* three chapters (vi–viii).

[27]That book XIV has three chapters can be verified for all second recension MSS. where it is extant. Steinschneider and Luzzatto note that the book has three chapters in the Leyden and Ambrosian MS. respectively, while the writer has been able to see Parm. 2259, Mich. 137 and ULC Add. 1175, and in all three MSS. to identify in XIV.iii the lengthy passage edited by Krauss, loc. cit. n. 3 *supra*, from XV.viii of the first recension. In the seventeen-book MS. and in Adler 1323 (Marx. p. 252. nos. 15 and 16) the beginning of XIV.i and the end of XIV.iii

respectively).[28] Only the material on Proverbs and Job is omitted. Similar citations have been noticed in almost all second-recension texts.[29] An observation of Judah Rosenthal shows that, as we should expect, they are also to be found in the earlier parts of the seventeenth-book version, the first sixteen books of which represent the second recension.[30]

It is certain, therefore, against Marx's assumption, that chapters vi–viii of the old book XV remained to form book XIV of the second recension. Again, the second-recension citations from elsewhere in the old book XV are full enough to comprise the greater part of its contents outside these last three chapters.[31] Book XV of the first recension, which Marx thought to have been retained (as in the seventeen-book New York MS., ff. 179b–200a) as the seventeenth book of the revised version, is thus already almost entirely present, divided into book XIV and the redistributed material, within the sixteen books of the second recension. To add this book as the seventeenth is to repeat almost the whole of it literally, and out of context as far as the scriptural passages are concerned. Needless repetition on this scale cannot be ascribed to the author or a responsible reviser.

The seventeen-book text, the New York exemplar of which is attributed by Marx to an oriental hand of the sixteenth or seventeenth centuries, must then in all probability be derived from

(forming in both cases the end of the book) correspond either with insignificant variants (n.° 15. ff. 158a and 166a) or exactly (n.° 16. ff. 185b and 195a) to XIV.i beginning and XIV.iii end as cited from ULC Add. 1175. ff. 247b and 255b in the appendix below. My remarks on these two New York MSS. are indebted to photocopies of various pages supplied by the Library of the Jewish Theological Seminary of America.

[28]ULC Add. 1175, book III.ii. f. 116b: iii. f. 121a: v. f. 123b: xx. f. 135a (= Neubauer-Driver-Pusey, I, 92 f.); book VIII.i. f. 164b: ii. f. 167b; book VI.ii. f. 171a: iii. f. 172a: v. f. 173b: vi f. 174a: vii. f. 174b: x. f. 177b: xiii, f. 180a.

[29]For Parm. 2259 see MSS. Codices Hebraici Bibliothecae I. B. De Rossi (Parma 1804), II, p. 153b Cod. 760; for Warner 28 Steinschneider, loc. cit. n. 25 supra: for Mich. 137 and Adler 1323 Marx. 269. The photograph of Adler 1638 (= Marx, p. 252. n.° 17). p. 52 in Catalogue of Hebrew Manuscripts in the Collection of Elkan Nathan Adler (Cambridge, 1921), plate 70 shows in book III.xx Alphonsus' objections on Isa. iii and other Isaianic texts, partly printed from Mich. 137 in Neubauer-Driver-Pusey (see preceding note). Luzzatto-Ottolenghi do not touch on this point in their description of the Ambrosian text.

[30]Rosenthal, Jacob ben Reuben, XX n. 56, lists from this MS. twelve citations of the objections of Alphonsus by name in ff. 63b–103a. before the pages containing book XVII.Ff 63b and 70a, before me in photocopy, are from book III on Isaiah. Almost all the twelve citations are probably, like these, from the objections on scriptural texts (XV.i–v in the first recension), since book XIV of the second recension, as represented in the Cambridge text, has only one such citation by name, in the heading preceding c. i. (ULC Add. 1175, f. 244a).

[31]It is possible that the second recension may originally have included the comparatively brief passages on Proverbs and Job (2¾ pages in the Laurentian text), so reproducing the whole of the old book XV.

conflation of the first and second recensions. The last book of the second recension corresponds to the penultimate book of the first, so that at first appearance the second recension lacks the book against Alphonsus which concludes the first. It can well be envisaged that a copyist with access to both recensions, as would have been possible, to give an attested instance, in the Venetian *terra ferma* towards the end of the sixteenth century (two colophons cited pp. 265–6 above), should in unawareness of the reordering of the contents attempt to supply the apparent lack.

The seventeen-book text cannot therefore, as Marx thought, represent the complete work in the author's final revision. May this claim then be made for the sixteen-book second recension? Here it will be recalled that the redistribution of the old book XV is not the only rearrangement which the second recension exhibits. The books II–X on biblical passages, where the citations from the earlier part of the old book XV now appear, are themselves now made to follow conventional biblical order; the new book XII displaces the book on the Gospels; and book XIV, the rump of the old XV, now immediately follows this book on the Gospels and thus occurs before instead of after the books on the Resurrection and the Messiah. All these rearrangements appear on examination to be clear improvements. In books II–X reference to biblical passages is expedited, and the inclusion of the replies to Alphonsus from the old book XV means that these can now be studied in the context of the scriptures and the comments of Jacob b. Reuben to which they relate. The new book XII, the treatise on the articles of Christian belief appended to the whole work in three first-recension MSS., is the only new book incorporated in the second recension. It strengthens the work by supplying what was regarded at the time as an important controversial weapon.[32] In the position assigned to it its critique of Christian fundamentals balances the assertion of Jewish principles which formed book I. As that book introduced the defence of the Hebrew Scriptures and the Talmud (books II–XI), so the new book XII opens the second of the work in which Ibn Shaprut turns to attack on Christian beliefs and writings. It is appropriately followed by the criticism of the Gospels, the book now numbered XIII. What has now become the first chapter of book XIV (old XV.vi) also deals with the Gospels, so that there is continuity of theme. Similarly the subjects of the second and third

---

[32]Joseph b. Shem Tob, Ibn Shaprut's contemporary, classifies attacks on the articles of the Christian faith as the fifth of six main categories of anti-Christian polemic. See his commentary on Profiat Duran, *'Iggeret 'al tehi ka 'aboteyka*, in A. Geiger (ed.), *Qobeṣ Wikkuḥim* (unpaginated, no date or place of publication), f. 4a.

chapters of the new book XIV, the Resurrection and the Messiah, are taken up in the two books on the Resurrection and the Messiah which now follow, renumbered XV and XVI. These arrangements together make an impression of cohesion which seems best explained if they are ascribed to a single revision.

The revision applied to the first recension will then be witnessed by the sixteen-book rather than the seventeen-book form of the work. It will have consisted of one important insertion and a thorough and helpful rearrangement. Can it be regarded as the work of the author himself? Ibn Shaprut had possibly, as noted above, enlarged what began as a twelve-book work by adding books XIII and XIV of the first recension. He clearly relates how he came to add a fifteenth book to these fourteen. Steinschneider allowed it as possible, and Marx assumed, that the revision applied to these fifteen books is once again from Ibn Shaprut's own hand.[33] This revision, as outlined above, is a notable improvement. It may therefore plausibly be credited to an author who is known to have been ready to revise his work, even though ascription to another hand cannot be ruled out.

IV

Before resuming the conclusions which these observations point we may comment further on Marx's treatment of the second-recension citations from the old book XV. These citations form an integral part of the revision as outlined above, whereas Marx, presupposing a seventeen-book revision with the old book XV at the end, regards them (p. 268) as 'repetitions from book XV, Shemtob's refutations of Alfonso, in the early part of the work'. He considers them accordingly together with the sixteenth-century scribal additions of extracts from commentators found in some MSS.[34]

Marx writes, p. 268: 'It seems hardly possible to ascribe such repetitions to the author himself, but if they were due to the above-mentioned copyist of the sixteenth century, one does not understand their occurrence in MS. Oxford 2151 (Mich. 137) and Breslau which do not contain his other additions. Neither Neubauer nor Loeb, who is troubled by these references to Alfonso in the early part of the book, noticed that they occur twice.'

It will be noticed that Marx, even though he was unaware of the

---

[33]Steinschneider, *Catalogus ... Lugduno-Batavae*, 119. In his annotation to J. Benjacob *Ozar ha-Sepharim* (Wilna, 1880), p. 2 n.° 54, Steinschneider says that the revision appears to be the author's own.

[34]De Rossi, loc. cit. n. 29 supra, had mentioned the citations and the scribal reference to commentators together in the same sentence, although of course he did not elaborate a view like Marx's.

identity of the new book XIV, here recognized some difficulty in his own solution. He goes no further in indicating a possible hand to which the citations may be ascribed. It should also be observed, however, that the two MSS. mentioned belong to different recensions. Only the Oxford MS., representing the second recension, could be expected to contain the citations from the old book XV which are under discussion. The Breslau MS. studied by Loeb belongs to the first recension. The only references to Alphonsus in the early part of the work noted by Loeb in this MS. are, as we should expect, those mentioned above to the *Mostrador de Justicia* in book I (Loeb, 221).[35] These of course are entirely distinct from the references in book XV (on the reply to Jacob b. Reuben) and relate to a different work of Alphonsus. They are thus not connected with the passages in question, which as we have seen are readily explicable as resulting from the logical rearrangement and revision embodied in the sixteen-book copies.

The relation of the MSS. to the course of the *Touchstone's* composition and revision may then be reconstructed as follows. The ten MSS. of the fifteen-book first recension witness to the work as it stood after book XV had been added in 1400. Three MSS. of this recension – Casanata, Vat. ebr. 523, and, less completely, the Laurentian copy – append to the *Touchstone* the treatise on the articles of Christian belief. These three first-recension texts already contain the whole of the material which was to be rearranged in the revised version.

The revision consisted of the rearrangement of the books, the incorporation of the treatise on the Christian articles, and the division and redistribution of the old book XV. The seven MSS. of the sixteen-book second recension, exemplified by ULC Add. 1175 (quoted in the appendix below), witness to the work as it stood after this revision. They possess particular value, if, as is probable but not certain, the revision was made by the author himself.

The seventeen-book text, in Jewish Theological Seminary of America MS. 2234, attains this length because, at the end of the sixteen books of the second recension, it adds the old book XV of the first recension in undistributed form. It is likely to represent a copyist's conflation of the two recensions.

The student of Ibn Shaprut's apologetic is therefore provided with textual witness arising from two recensions only. The two differ less considerably than Marx suggested, and neither is defective in the manner he supposed. The first recension only requires the addition of the treatise on the articles of the Christian faith, and the

---

[35]See n. 15 above.

rearrangement of the answer to Alphonsus, to become the work attested in the second recension: and the MSS. of this second recension, which in Marx's view lacked an entire book, in fact bear witness to the complete work in its revised form.

What is here proposed, as will have been observed, is a return to the view of Marx's master Steinschneider, which the fuller evidence now available seems clearly to endorse. It is only possible to make this proposal, however, because of the attention which Marx himself was prepared to give, and to encourage others to give,[36] to the disproportionately neglected *Touchstone*.

---

[36]A. Marx, 'What Our Library Offers to Our Students', *Jewish Theological Seminary Students' Annual* (New York, 1914), 225.

APPENDIX

To show the identity of XV.vi–viii in the first recension with XIV.i–iii in the second the titles, beginnings and endings of the three chapters are given below from book XV of the Laurentian text (first recension) and book XIV of the Cambridge text (second recension).

MS. Laur. Plut. II 17	MS. ULC Add. 1175
f. 180a השער החמשה עשר	f. 244a השער הי'ד
f. 194a פרק ששי באונגיליוש	f. 244a פרק א'
f. 194a *Inc.* אמר המשלש הנה הזכיר ביחוסי ישו נשים הפגומות	f. 244a *Inc.* אמר המשלש הנה הזכיר ביחוס ישו הנשים הפגומות
f. 197a *Expl.* ויכלתו לא יחסר מרצונו ית ישתבח האל אשר נצחנו שלימותו	f. 247a *Expl.*: the same, with the first word spelt *plene* and the last five words omitted.
f. 197a פרק שביעי בתחיית המתים	f. 247a פרק ב' בתחיית המתים
f. 197a *Inc.* אמר המשלש עם היות שאין מחלוקת בין היהודים ובנינו בתחיית המתים	f.247a *Inc.*: the same.
f. 198a *Expl.* ויפח באפיו נשמת חיים	f. 247b *Expl.*: the same.
f. 198a פרק שמיני בראיות שהמשיח לא בא	f. 247b פרק ג' בראיות שהמשיח לא בא
f. 198a *Inc.* אמר המשלש מאד תמהני על הגאון	f. 247b *Inc.*: the same
f. 203b *Expl* וישכימו בבקר והנה כולם פגרים	f. 254b line 10: the same, spelling כלם. 70 lines follow to the end of the chapter, f. 255b: לא הראנו נפלאות מחודשות אין להחזיקו במשיח כל שכן באלוה תם
(lacuna follows).	

12

JUDAH BRIEL AND SEVENTEENTH-CENTURY JEWISH ANTI-CHRISTIAN POLEMIC IN ITALY

His anti-Christian controversy was 'still typical of Jewish–Christian polemic of the Middle Ages'.[1] This is one of S. Simonsohn's remarks on Judah Briel or Leone Brielli (c. 1643–1722), chief rabbi of Mantua from 1697.[2] Simonsohn is implicitly contrasting work such as Briel's with attempts to answer the economic and social charges, typical of modern anti-Semitism, which gained currency in eighteenth-century Italy; and indeed, more than fifty years earlier, such topics had already begun to be prominent in Italian apologetic such as Simone Luzzatto's *Discorso circa il stato de gl'Hebrei* of 1638. Yet, to concentrate present-day study solely on the economic and social questions in the controversy would be to miss those biblical and doctrinal subjects of debate which, at the time, seemed at least equally important. Why was biblically-based controversy so important, in the case of Briel? And why, within discussion which was inevitably mainly on prophecy, was he led to give miracle also an important place? Fairly obvious answers to these questions may quickly suggest themselves, but simply to ask the questions with reference to one particular polemist of some note may bring the voluminous controversial literature of Italy in his time into clearer focus (see p. 41, above).

On biblical and doctrinal themes almost all writers of Jewish-Christian controversy in the seventeenth and eighteenth centuries, whether Jewish or Christian, show a marked degree of continuity with their mediaeval predecessors, just as the mediaeval writers themselves take up a great deal from this controversy in the ancient world. Briel's writings, not least *because* they are sometimes mediaeval in form and content, well exemplify the rich and somewhat neglected controversial literature of the Italian Jews in the period between the Renaissance and the Enlightenment.

---

[1] S. Simonsohn, *History of the Jews in the Duchy of Mantua*, E.T. (Jerusalem, 1977), 84.
[2] Biography in G. B. De Rossi, *Bibliotheca Judaica Antichristiana* (Parma, 1800), 21–3; G. Nepi and M. S. Ghirondi, *Toledoth Gedole Israel u-Geone Italia* (Trieste, 1853), 127, 129 (no. 7); M. Mortara, 'Leone Brielli', *Il Corriere Israelitico i* (Trieste, 1862), 161–6, and id., *Indice alfabetico dei rabbini e scrittori israeliti di cose giudaiche in Italia* (Padua, 1886), 8; H. Graetz, *Geschichte der Juden*, x (Leipzig, 1868), 322–3, xcvi–xcvii; I. Levi, 'Bariel Leone', *Il Vessillo Israelitico* lii (1904), 481–2; U. Cassuto, 'Briel, Jehuda ben Elieser', *EJ* iv (Berlin, 1929), 1074 (bibliography); Simonsohn, *History*, 698–9 (bibliography).

This is a period judged to be one of literary decline among Italian Jews,[3] but their polemical work shows how much energy and talent went into writings which of their nature could not be printed. In the seventeenth and eighteenth centuries the literary deposit of Jewish anti-Christian polemic was greater in Italy than in any other European country; Holland was the nearest competitor.[4] Both sides contributed to a voluminous controversial literature in Latin and Italian; Jews also read and wrote polemic in Hebrew, and a few Christian Hebraists and Jews who had accepted baptism took a strong interest in these writings too.[5] This literature sometimes shows striking knowledge of writings from the opposite camp, and it builds on the intensive disputation of pre-expulsion Spain; the Spanish influence on the Italian church of this period is balanced in the Jewish communities by the presence of Marrano exiles from Spain, by frequent copying of MSS. of the Spanish Hebrew apologies, and by occasional translations from Spanish into Italian or Hebrew. Jews in Italy who pursued the biblical and doctrinal controversies which engaged Briel include his famous Venetian predecessor in apologetic, Leone Modena (especially in a Hebrew polemic on Christian doctrinal topics), his senior contemporary the Marrano Isaac Cardoso (in parts of a Spanish work which is also concerned with anti-Semitic charges), and his pupil Joshua Segre (in biblically oriented Hebrew work building on Briel's polemic, as noted below).[6]

I

Briel's writings open a window into the polemical literature; but to ask why he continued the old debate on the scriptures means asking

---

[3]This is the view of A. Milano, *Storia degli ebrei in Italia* (Turin, 1963), 673–9.

[4]In the bibliography by Judah Rosenthal, 'Anti-Christian Polemics from its Beginnings to the End of the Eighteenth Century', *Aresheth* ii (1960), 130–79, iii (1961), 433–9, Hebrew, Latin and vernacular works from Italy in these centuries amount to 36 items, from Holland to 18.

[5]The Christian writings are studied by M. Steinschneider, 'Letteratura antigiudaica in lingua italiana', *Il Vessillo Israelitico* xxix (1881), 165–7, 201–3, 229–32, 269–71; [on the seventeenth century] xxx (1882), 206–8, 244–6, 371–3; [on the eighteenth century] xxxi (1883), 246–8, 275–7, 313–5 [supplement and index] 380–1, and by F. Parente, 'Il confronto ideologico tra l'Ebraismo e la Chiesa in Italia', in [R. Bonfil and others,] *Italia Judaica*, i (Rome, 1983), 303–81.

[6]See S. Simonsohn (ed.), Leone Modena, *Magen wa-Hereb* (Jerusalem, 1960); and Isaac Cardoso, *Las excelencias de los Hebreos* (Amsterdam, 1679) (written in Verona), discussed by Y. H. Yerushalmi, *From Spanish Court to Italian Ghetto, Isaac Cardoso: a Study in Seventeenth-Century Marranism and Jewish Apologetics* (New York, 1971, repr. Seattle, 1981), 350–472.

also about his background and standpoint as a polemist. He was a man of wide culture and interests, as his writings attest. They touch many subjects other than polemic. His Hebrew work in print includes responsa, verses, and a text-book on grammar; he gave his patronage to the Mantua edition of the *Shulḥan Arukh* (1723). Writings by him which are unpublished, so far as I know, include commentaries on the Minor Prophets and on Daniel, sermons, and – notably for his concern with the classics and morality – a Hebrew version of letters of Seneca (MS. Kaufmann 466).[7]

The range of interests represented here, from the halakhah to biblical exegesis, the Hebrew language, Hebrew verse and the classics, is confirmed by the list of Briel's pupils. Among them were Isaac Lampronti the Talmudist, author of the *Pahad Yitzhaq*; Samson Cohen Modon, who wrote a Hebrew elegy on Briel's death and was well known as a poet;[8] and Abiad Archipace (Sar Shalom) Basilea, a cabbalist who was also versed in the classics and philosophy. A pupil who is not so well known, but has already been mentioned, is Joshua Segre. Jewish apologetic and polemic came not only from Segre (in Hebrew prose and verse) but also from Modon (in Hebrew verse) and Basilea (in Italian prose, to defend the Passover).[9]

Briel's polemic had as part of its background in current Jewish opinion the uneasy coexistence of mysticism and rationalism. Thus the Marrano brothers Isaac and Abraham Cardoso, on their return to Judaism in the mid-seventeenth century, took up respectively a rationalizing and a strongly mystical position; Abraham became a leading supporter of Sabbatai Sevi. In Mantua, the famous cabbalist Moses Zacuto was Briel's predecessor as chief rabbi, moving from Venice to take up this post in 1673. It was during his time that Briel received from Venice his letter conferring the title *Moreh* (1677), a

---

[7] Is a treatise by Briel on questions of *Terefah*, copied in MS. BL Add. 26,966, f. 129b onwards (G. Margoliouth and J. Leveen, *Catalogue of the Hebrew and Samaritan Manuscripts in the British Museum* (4 vols., London, 1899, 1905, 1915, 1935), no. 1071, II) and summarized in MS. Montefiore 142, formerly MS. Halberstam 95 (H. Hirschfeld, *Descriptive Catalogue of the Hebrew MSS. of the Montefiore Library* (London, 1904), p. 490, no. 142.5), identical with Briel's discussion of this subject printed in the responsa Zera' Emeth, according to Ghirondi, *Toledoth*, p. 127?

[8] His other interests are shown by MSS. surviving from his collection of books; they include biblical commentaries (S. M. Schiller-Szinessy, *Catalogue of the Hebrew Manuscripts preserved in the University Library, Cambridge*, i (Cambridge, 1876), nos. 27, 30, 65, 72), the Arba'ah Turim, and Maimonides' *Guide* (Margoliouth nos. 544–5, 911).

[9] Simonsohn, *History*, 639 (Modon and Basilea); A. Marx, 'The Polemical Manuscripts in the Library of the Jewish Theological Seminary of America', in *Studies in Jewish Bibliography and Related Subjects in Memory of Abraham Solomon Freidus* (New York, 1929), nos. 32, 42–4 (Segre and Modon); n. 18, below (Modon's elegy).

promotion that was confirmed in Mantua when he was ordained there, with Zacuto's approval, in 1685.[10]

In the Mantuan community an ardent mysticism led by Zacuto, and represented among Briel's pupils by the messianically-named Basilea, flourished side by side with a spirit of moderation and rational inquiry, somewhat as Quietism co-existed with Jansenism in the contemporary Italian church. Devotional societies of early risers were important in communal piety, learning, and money-raising. Zacuto's own group of the 'New Every Morning', Hadashim Labeqarim, studied the Zohar each morning and the Bible each evening, and were still in existence in Mantua two hundred years later.[11] The tension between the mystical tendency and secular learning is epitomized in the story that Zacuto in his youth fasted for forty days to forget his knowledge of Latin, like a second Jerome;[12] It was a group of members of the Hadashim Labeqarim who posthumously published his Dantesque vision of hell, *Tofteh Arukh* (1715).[13]

In the Mantua where mystical circles were ready to welcome Zacuto the Sabbatian movement had received some support and more sympathy, and its opponent Jacob Frances, who detested the cabbalah, was driven from the city; but Zacuto, by the time he came to Mantua in 1673, had declared his opposition to Sabbatianism. Briel himself is not recorded to have written anything mystical, his works are notable for free rational argument, and it seems fully in character that, notwithstanding his friendly relations with senior and junior Mantuan cabbalists, he emerged in 1713 as one of the weightiest authorities to condemn Nehemiah Hayon of Bosnia, then active in Amsterdam, who interpreted the cabbalah in favour of Sabbatianism.[14]

To Hayon's reply we owe our knowledge of Briel's personal

---

[10]A photograph of the illuminated Adler MS. of the Venice letter, granting the title *ma'alath morenu ha-rab*, is reproduced in M. Zobel, 'Ehrentitel und Amtsbezeichnungen', *EJ* vi (Berlin, 1930), cols. 277–98 (293–4); the 1685 ordination is documented from Mantuan archives by Simonsohn, *History*, 698, n. 32; on the significance of the title, R. Bonfil, *Rabbis and Jewish Communities in Renaissance Italy* (E.T. Oxford, 1990), 85–6.

[11]M. Mortara, *Catalogo dei manoscritti ebraici della Biblioteca della Comunita Israelitica di Mantova* (Livorno, 1878), pp. 65–6, on MS. lxxxiv.

[12]Quoted from Nepi by Graetz, *Geschichte*, x, 169, n. 2; Zacuto 'used to say that [Latin] was the language of the *Kelipah*' – the 'bark' or 'shell' representing evil in the cabbalah – 'and that it would not stand together with the mysteries of Torah'.

[13]Simonsohn, *History*, 555–6.

[14]Another authority to declare himself against Hayon was David Nieto of London, whose polemic is discussed by R. Loewe, 'The Spanish Supplement to Nieto's *'Esh Dath'*, *PAAJR* xlviii (1981), 267–96. On Briel's rôle see Carlebach, *Pursuit*, 128–32.

appearance.[15] The principal rabbi of Mantua was as unlike a respectable eastern European rabbi as could be. He had no beard. Still worse, he had no wife. As Hayon put it, 'They ban him in heaven every day because some seventy years have passed over him, and he has not taken a wife and has not come beneath the marriage canopy, to fulfil the commandment to increase and multiply'.[16] He would have looked, one may surmise, not altogether unlike the more learned of his opponents among the celibate Italian clergy of his time – a body which included the Cistercian Hebrew bibliophiles G. Bartolocci and C. G. Imbonati. Hayon also sketches Briel's intellectual outlook. His view of the Zohar is described in terms which are no doubt calculated to make him as unpopular as possible with friends of the cabbalah, but still carry conviction. 'He is the rabbi of Mantua who has no knowledge in the *Shi'ur Qomah*, but only in the Torah of Latin and philosophy ... He denies the words of the Zohar and says that it is not by Simeon ben Johai, or that as an abortion it should not exist ...'[17]

It seems likely, then, that there was a change of atmosphere in the rabbinate of Mantua when Zacuto died and Briel took his place. There was a contrast in outward conditions. Zacuto, from Amsterdam, had studied in eastern Europe and became famous in Venice, whence he was lured to Mantua with a handsome stipend; he was succeeded in 1697 by a native Mantuan, a rabbi already resident who was ready to be non-stipendiary – a point which made a deep impression,[18] particularly no doubt as at the end of the seventeenth century the community was pressed hard financially by Duke Ferdinando Carlo, in his vain attempt to stave off the annexation of his duchy by the Austrian empire.[19] There was also a momentous change in outlook; a cabbalist was succeeded by a Latinist. One may suspect that not only Briel's seniority, but also his lack of involvement in the Zohar, was a factor when others were appointed to lead the influential society of the Hadashim Labeqarim. The ageing Zacuto made David ben Azriel Finzi his own successor as head, and the Society itself, which purchased Zacuto's Beth Midrash after his death, did not choose Briel as one of their own guides in study.[20] Yet

---

[15] A portrait is mentioned, but not described, by Mortara, 'Brielli', 165.

[16] Hayon, *Ha-Zad Zebi*, f. 6b, quoted by Graetz, *Geschichte*, x, p. xcvi.

[17] Hayon, as cited in the previous note.

[18] It is not mentioned by Simonsohn, but is stated in Briel's 1705 exemption from communal taxation (printed by Mortara, 'Brielli', 165); Samson Cohen Modon's elegy on Briel stresses that he despised wealth (strophe 10, quoted by Graetz, *Geschichte*, x, p. xcvi).

[19] Simonsohn, *History*, 68–9.

[20] Simonsohn, *History*, 555–6.

cabbalist and rationalist had common ground in the concern with preaching and halakhah, and Briel's distance from the cabbalah did not preclude his practising an earnest piety including messianic hope for return and restoration, as appears from the Hebrew verses – a lament for exile and a prayer for the restoration of Israel – which he put up in his room in 1696.[21]

From all this the standpoint from which Briel defended Judaism and criticized Christianity can be at least provisionally identified. He cannot have been so sharply outspoken a critic of the Zohar as Hayon suggested, or he could not have retained as he did the patronage of Moses Zacuto, and the loyalty of his pupil Basilea. Yet there will have been something in Hayon's allegation. Briel appears to have given himself to the Bible, the halakhah, the Hebrew and Latin languages, and secular learning, and not to have been found where the Zohar was studied. He was ready to commit himself to condemning a Sabbatian mystic publicly. Basilea's *Emunath Hakha-mim*, a book which justifies a mystical Judaism on philosophical grounds, can perhaps be regarded as an attempt to hold together the mysticism of Zacuto and the rationalism of Briel, both of whom are named in the author's foreword as his teachers, Briel with special warmth.[22] However that may be, Briel will have had a strong strain of philosophical rationalism, conjoined with an earnest piety. This conjunction sometimes seems evident in his critique of Christianity, and it is not far from the spirit of contemporary reform movements in the Italian church, as exemplified in the rational devotion of Briel's younger contemporary, the Ambrosian librarian L. A. Muratori.[23]

Briel's particular standpoint thus naturally suggested opposition to Christianity, with its important mystical element; but such opposition was shared by all schools of thought, for it appeared in the light of an ancestral duty reinforced by circumstances. Mantua was of course affected by the ecclesiastical pressure for the baptism of Jews and the segregation of Jews from Christians which had been strengthened by the Counter-Reformation. A Casa dei Catecumeni had been instituted in the sixteenth century, a ghetto in 1610; Briel described himself as 'Rabbino nel Ghetto di Mantova'.[24] The establishment of a ghetto was not necessarily viewed negatively by Italian Jews, but the accompanying regulations could only too

---

[21]Two sextets, printed by Mortara, 'Brielli', 165.

[22]Abiad Sar Shalom Basilea, *Emunath Hakhamim* (Mantua, 1730), f. 2b.

[23]On Muratori and his influence see O. Chadwick, *The Popes and European Revolution* (Oxford, 1981), 395–405.

[24]In the MS. of his *Discorso* on the seventy weeks of Daniel, quoted by Mortara, 'Brielli', 161.

readily be used against them. Thus Briel's crowded funeral brought complaints because it looked like a torchlight procession by Jews through the city outside the ghetto,[25] and his pupil Basilea ended his days in 1743 under a harsh sentence of confinement to the ghetto.[26] Notwithstanding ecclesiastical pressure, which was in any case lighter in Mantua than in the Papal States, conversions to Christianity appear to have been few; they were not increased by the contact with Christians on all intellectual and social levels which continued despite the ghetto.[27] Such contact meant, however, that a Jewish apologetic literature was needed.

Why did it take a 'mediaeval' form in the case of Briel? His personal standpoint would have led him to criticize what may broadly be called the mystical element in historic Christianity and the contemporary church, but he might have expressed himself in a philosophically or doctrinally oriented treatise, like Leone Modena. Instead, he chose a predominantly biblical critique, which included Hebrew answers to New Testament texts on the time-honoured mediaeval pattern. Reasons for his choice can be conjectured on the basis of the intellectual background, both classical and rabbinic, which has just been sketched. His academic instincts would have led him *ad fontes*, and his biblical interpretation was closely knit with rational argument. On both grounds he would have been at home in the inherited literary form, in which Hebrew scripture acts as a touchstone for the questionable Christian writings. It would have been similarly natural to him to take up specifically biblical problems posed by the other side.

As this point suggests, however, his personal outlook will not have been the only factor in his choice. There were communal needs for polemic based on the Hebrew scriptures and the Christian New Testament. First, given the pervasive Jewish–Christian contact, biblical answers were needed just as much as defences against economic or social charges. For the good of the community internally, Judaism must be seen to be intellectually respectable. The scriptures were at the basis of the Italian Jewish educational curriculum, and Jews must be convinced that they did indeed have a good case for diverging from the majority Christian community's interpretation of the same scriptures, and from some of the tenets accepted by most educated Italians. Secondly, as far as the outside world was concerned, it had to be made plain to non-Jews that there was an answer to the incessant Christian invitations and attacks,

[25]Simonsohn, *History*, 160, n. 179.
[26]Simonsohn, *History*, 158.
[27]This point is stressed by Simonsohn, *History*, 524–5.

and it was well to show, if possible, that the Jewish No was reasonable rather than obstinate; but the Christian writings to be answered were themselves very largely biblical and doctrinal. There was even what may be called, with due caution, a missionary motive; Jews might sometimes be baptized, but this was also a society in which Marranos and baptized Jews, amid doubts of both Christian and Jewish claims, might come back from Christianity to their Jewish allegiance.[28] Thirdly, this subject-matter was traditional on both sides, and therefore had a certain impetus. Probably, however, this impetus would have been lost if the Jewish communal needs just outlined had ceased to be pressing.[29]

The internal audience will have been very much in the view of a communal rabbi like Briel. The mystical and rational strands in Judaism had their analogues in the contemporary church. Christianity need not have seemed wholly alien. The strength of mystical Jewish piety suggests that there would have been aspects of the counter-Reformation Italian church which could in principle attract Italian Jews. At the same time educated non-cabbalistic Jews might become aware of the church movements towards a more rational and biblical piety, labelled by enemies as Jansenist but influential in northern Italy. What may be called the mediaeval element in Briel's apologetic, to follow Simonsohn, namely its concentration on the Bible and Christian doctrine, was perhaps particularly contemporary as a preservative against any attraction felt by the more mystical in the Jewish community, or against the growth of a sense that a rational case could be made for Christianity. The biblical arguments sought to quench any emotional disturbance or intellectual wavering with a douche of rational cold water. The danger of losses from the Jewish community was keenly felt; in the recent past it had been feared with some justice, for example by Moses Zacuto, that disillusionment with Sabbatianism might lead to acceptance of Christianity.[30] The pressure of force majeure, as felt in the Mantuan ghetto in the

---

[28]Genuine doubt concerning Jewish as well as Christian claims is detected among Marranos and Jews baptized in Italy by Yerushalmi, *Isaac Cardoso*, 197–206 (on Marranos, especially Abraham Cardoso) and B. Pullan, *The Jews of Europe and the Inquisition of Venice*, 1150–1670 (Oxford, 1983), 206–10, 249–51 (on both categories).

[29]The primacy of internal needs is stressed in the analysis of mediaeval Jewish polemic, by H. Trautner-Kromann, *Shield and Sword* (Tübingen, 1993); the present writer accepts their importance, but thinks that external aims should often also be considered, as here.

[30]Moses Zacuto's letter of 1668, summarized by G. Scholem, *Sabbatai Sevi* (E.T., London, 1973), 769; the Mantuan rabbinate took very seriously what proved to be an unfounded rumour that Pelatiah Jagel Monselice, rabbi in Ferrara, was seeking baptism as a result of Sabbatian leanings, according to a narrative in G. Bartolocci and C. G. Imbonati, *Bibliotheca Magna Rabbinica* (4 vols., Rome, 1675–93), iv. 112–3.

seventeenth and eighteenth centuries, could be despised; but the subtler pressures of the non-Jewish majority, including the not-so-subtle pressure of propaganda literature, were more insidious.

In these circumstances Briel replied to Latin or Italian controversy in Italian, thereby securing the widest possible Jewish readership, as noted below, and also, despite the ban on publication, making non-Jews aware that Jewish answers were not lacking. This vernacular work was mainly defensive, though often outspoken. Briel also, however, continued the traditional Hebrew polemic against the New Testament. Here the rabbinically educated sector of the Jewish community will have been in view, and the campaign was offensive rather than defensive, to echo a distinction between vernacular and Hebrew apologetic drawn by Cecil Roth.[31] This traditional form of polemic was probably congenial to Briel as a writer, but it was also well adapted to contemporary Jewish needs. In the vernacular and in Hebrew, therefore, Briel, like a number of other Italian Jews at this time, criticized the New Testament and Christian doctrines and customs with satirical sharpness and an unremittingly rational appeal to scripture.

II

This literary programme meant that Briel's apologetic consisted, like that of his predecessors, mainly in the argument from prophecy, and particularly in rebuttal of those attempts to demonstrate Christian faith from the Jewish scriptures which are so important in the New Testament and later Christianity. Thus far, it has been possible to suggest reasons why Briel should have chosen this apparently mediaeval genre of biblically based polemic. Within it, however, he emphasized the theme of miracle. Debate on miracle is of course already found in the Hebrew Bible, notably in the Pentateuchal passages on Moses's miracles as proof of his divine legation (Exod. iv), on culpable lack of faith despite miracles (Num. xiv), and, by contrast, on the false prophet who produces a sign or a wonder (Deut. xiii; verse 1 in printed Hebrew Bibles, with its warning not to add to or diminish the commandments, is xii 32 in the Vulgate). The debate recurs in the New Testament, especially in the gospels, and is developed in subsequent controversy, but it gains a particular prominence in Briel's writings. Why did he give so much space to rebutting the argument from miracle? This second question can at least be raised in a brief treatment, and it identifies another

---

[31]C. Roth, *History of the Jews in Italy* (Philadelphia, 1946, repr. Farnborough, 1969), 402.

important thread linking Briel's own work with the Jewish and Christian apologetic of his time.

Briel's apologetic and polemical work must now be noted in more detail.[32] He is known to have composed at least six writings of this kind, in Hebrew and in Italian. Of the three Hebrew works, the only one to have been printed is a sonnet addressed to Judah d'Ancona, who had accepted baptism, apparently at the time of his marriage; mordant polemic here subserves an elegant and mournful appeal for return.[33] Briel also wrote a substantial critique of the New Testament, *Hassagoth 'al sippure ha-sheluhim, Criticisms of the Writings of the Apostles*.[34] This work continues a genre of answers to the New Testament which is exemplified in Hebrew polemic from the early mediaeval period onwards. Briel's *hassagoth* extend from Matthew to the Epistle of Jude; the one remaining book, Revelation, is omitted with a characteristically rationalizing and anti-mystical comment: 'The book of the Apocalypse consists of dreams and vanities which need no answer. And Solomon said about it, For in the multitude of dreams are also many vanities; fear God [Eccles. v 6].'[35] After Briel's death these criticisms circulated as a separate work but were also copied with considerable additions by his pupil Joshua Segre, to form the second part of Segre's own polemical work *Asham Talui, Suspended Trespass-Offering* or *Trespass of the Crucified*. Lastly, Segre mentions a set of criticisms by Briel, probably in Hebrew, on a work by Aquinas; conceivably this was the *Summa contra Gentiles*, part of which had been translated into Hebrew and published (1657) by G. M. Ciantes, sometime Jews' Preacher in Rome.[36] These criticisms appear to be unknown apart from the reference to them by Joshua Segre.[37]

[32]The fullest bibliography is in M. Steinschneider, 'Letteratura giudaica italiana: Opere inedite del secolo XVIII', *Il Vessillo Israelitico* xxviii (1879), 270–2, 304–6, briefly summarized in his 'Die italienische Literatur der Juden', *MGWJ* xliv (1900), 88–9.

[33]The poem was edited by J. Schirmann, *Anthologie der hebräischen Dichtung in Italien* (Berlin, 1934), 347.

[34]On the contents see De Rossi, *Bibliotheca*, pp. 22–3 (no. 24), 121–2 (no. 163). The work was printed, but not published, by I. Broydé, according to Marx, 'The Polemical Manuscripts', p. 258, no. 41; notes used here have been taken from the incomplete copies in MSS. Parm. 2253 (De Rossi, 1202) (up to Matt. xix), 2252 (De Rossi, 1268) (on Acts, and Romans i–ix) and from the copies of Joshua Segre, *Asham Talui*, Part II in MS. Bodleian Library, Oxford, Opp. Add. 4° 145 (Neubauer no. 2407) and MS. Jewish National & University Library, Jerusalem, 8° 102 (from a microfilm kindly supplied by the Library).

[35]MS. Jerusalem 8° 102, f. 65b.

[36]Parente, 'Confronto', 346–7.

[37]MS. Jerusalem 8° 102, f. 1a (from the unpublished portion of Segre's introduction to *Asham Talui*, Part II): *mi yitten ve-yabo'u le-yaday hassagoth rabbi asher pa'al ve-'asah 'al teybat no'ah asher hibberah Tommaso me-Aquino*, 'If only I might obtain my master's criticisms which he made on the "Noah's Ark" which Thomas Aquinas composed'.

The three remaining works are in Italian. This was the language in most widespread Jewish use, as Italian versions of Bible and prayers vividly attest; Joshua Segre was one of those who produced a translation of the liturgy.[38] The need for translations can be illustrated from other fields. Thus in Mantua a widely read mediaeval cabbalistic work, the *Berith Menuhah* of Abraham b. Isaac of Granada, was translated into Italian in 1687 by Joseph Rava.[39] Similarly, there was an Italian translation of one of the most famous Hebrew polemical works – as 'mediaeval' as any of Briel's writings – Isaac Troki's *Hizzuq Emunah*, against the New Testament.[40] Hebrew, and especially Latin, were for the better educated. Jews of course wrote Latin verse and composed Latin treatises.[41] Briel himself was lamented with verses in Hebrew and Latin as well as Italian.[42] Nevertheless, most Jews were more at ease with the vernacular. In a work published in 1621 the Jews' Preacher in Rome apologizes despairingly for writing against the Jews in Latin rather than in the Italian which might seem more suitable; when a sure faith is being expounded, he says, 'Jewish depravity' leads a Jewish audience, which does not know Latin, simply to ignore what is set forth in the vernacular – so he might just as well write in Latin, and Christians at least will be able to benefit.[43] At the end of the eighteenth century G. B. De Rossi described the situation similarly: 'Latin works are understood by very few of them, and read by none.'[44]

The choice of Italian would accordingly ensure as wide a Jewish readership as possible, and give the apologetic a good chance of reaching the ears of non-Jews. Two of the Italian compositions are replies to particular Christian works. Both are dated by the author, and both turn out to belong to his period of office as chief rabbi. The first, written in 1700, answers a critique of Manasseh ben Israel, *De Termino Vitae* (1639), by Vincenzo of Ragusa, the court

---

[38]Steinschneider, 'Die italienische Literatur', *MGWJ* xlii (1898), 315–22. Segre's translation is MS. Roth 31, described by C. Roth, 'Catalogue of manuscripts in the Roth Collection', reprinted from the *Alexander Marx Jubilee Volume* (New York, 1950) in C. Roth, *Studies in Books and Booklore* (Farnborough, 1972), 255–87 (259–60); in the preface (f. 1a) Segre notes the ignorance of Hebrew among 'gran parte di noi'.

[39]Steinschneider, 'Die italienische Literatur', *MGWJ* xliii (1899), 515.

[40]De Rossi, *Bibliotheca*, p. 19.

[41]Steinschneider, 'Die italienische Literatur', *MGWJ* xlii (1898), 261–4.

[42]Simonsohn, *History*, 617; n. 18 above.

[43]'Eorum pravitas ... sanae doctrinae nescia, cum de certa fide agitur, ut latina ignorat, ita vernacula negligit' (P. Pichi, *De Partu Virginis Deiparae Adversus Iudaeos* (Rome, 1621), unpaginated preface 'Ad lectores').

[44]G. B. De Rossi, *Della vana aspettazione degli ebrei del loro rè messia* (Parma, 1773), p. xiii.

theologian of Duke Ferdinando Carlo of Mantua. Vincenzo's special subject is the seventy weeks of Daniel ix 24–7. This passage, including the words 'after sixty-two weeks shall an anointed one be cut off', was regarded as a particularly difficult prophecy to explain in favour of Judaism. Samuel Nahmias, who took the name Giulio Morosini when he accepted Christianity in Venice in 1649, wrote that he was finally converted over the interpretation of the seventy weeks, a prophecy which (he says) was admitted by Simone Luzzatto to show that the messiah had already come.[45] Briel's answer to this problem is notable, as M. Mortara pointed out, for sweet but forceful reasonableness in enunciating general principles of biblical interpretation. For example, if a passage is expounded in two ways, and both present difficulties, either one should accept the less difficult, or classify the passage with those that will only be understood when the messiah *indisputably* comes; in this case the unprejudiced reader will either accept the Jewish interpretation, or admit that the prophecy is one of those which cannot yet be understood.[46]

It is also of interest that Vincenzo and Briel attached themselves to one of a new style of Jewish apologists, those who defended Jewish biblical interpretations and national customs not in Hebrew, but in solid Latin works available to any educated person internationally. Manasseh ben Israel was followed in this Latin apologetic in Italy by Isaac Cardoso of Verona (*Philosophia libera*, Venice, 1673) and Isaac Vita Cantarini of Padua (*Vindex Sanguinis*, Amsterdam, 1681). The very existence of this genre must have encouraged educated Jews and intrigued Christian readers. Hence, perhaps, the Duke's theologian took notice of Manasseh's book so long after publication.[47]

The second Italian work (with some Hebrew headings) is a large-scale answer to a perilously compact Italian critique of Judaism, *La sinagoga disingannata, The Synagogue Released from Enchantment*, by the Jesuit Pietro Pinamonti (Bologna, 1694). The author, a tireless missioner and a prolific writer, worked closely in both

---

[45]G. Morosini, *Via della fede* (three continuously paginated parts in four vols., Rome, 1683), i, unpaginated preface, section 2; Luzzatto can hardly have expressed himself exactly in this way, as is stressed by Steinschneider, 'Letteratura antigiudaica', *Il Vessillo Israelitico* xxx (1882), 372–3 and 'Die italienische Literatur', *MGWJ* xliii (1899), 418–19. He must at least have had more to say.

[46]Mortara, 'Brielli', 162–4. An argument for classifying Danielic prophecies as not to be understood 'till the time of the end' can appeal to Dan. xii 9.

[47]An English translation of *De termino vitae* appeared as late as 1699, as noted by Steinschneider, 'Letteratura giudaica', *Vessillo* xxvii (1879), 271, n. 2.

capacities with the great Jesuit preacher Paolo Segneri the elder.[48] Not unfairly, but perhaps unfortunately, Pinamonti has been widely known for his devotional tract current in English as *Hell Opened to Christians*;[49] it was censured in the free-thinker G. J. Holyoake's influential pamphlet *Catholicism the Religion of Fear* (London, 1850).[50] Pinamonti's book on the synagogue, however, is a reasoned treatise which displays his gifts as a catechist, although he states clearly that his account of Talmudic literature is derived from Christian writers.[51] (Its attack on Talmudic 'legend' follows Sixtus Senensis.) Lucidly ordered in twenty-four chapters and 248 paragraphs, anti-Jewish but on the whole in the style of a missioner rather than a prosecutor, the book was printed in a little duodecimo which could accompany young laymen in their hours of polite attendance on patrons, or ladies into their own apartments. Briel's reply, finished on 12th June 1702, is extant in a number of inevitably larger but still attractively produced MS. copies.[52]

The third Italian work, and the only one to have been printed, is an undated booklet entitled *Breve Ragionamento sopra i Miracoli, A Brief Discourse on Miracles*, giving the essentials of an answer to

---

[48]*Enciclopedia Cattolica*, ix (1952), col. 1482, s. 'Pinamonti'. He is termed 'apostate', it seems mistakenly, in Simonsohn, *History*, 84, n. 270.

[49]*Hell opened to Christians; or, Considerations on the Infernal Pains, for Every Day in the Week. Illustrated by Plates emblematic of the infernal agonies.* Translated from the Italian of the Rev. F. Pinamonti, S.J. (London, 1807).

[50]See J. McCabe, *Life and Letters of George Jacob Holyoake* (2 vols., London, 1908), i, 217. The pamphlet is part of Holyoake's characteristic polemic against religion, but its appearance at this time may also be not unconnected with the active support which he was giving to Mazzini and Garibaldi.

[51]The book is discussed by Parente, 'Confronto', 357–8 (saying, perhaps too sweepingly, that its fame is unaccompanied by intrinsic merit) and by Levi, as cited in the following note. Pinamonti, *Sinagoga*, 55–9 describes the origins of the Talmud 'come hanno ricavato dagli Ebrei i nostri Scrittori', mentioning Hadrianus Finus and Sixtus Senensis, and for Talmudic teachings he appeals again to Sixtus, 'che di proprio mano trascrisse il tutto' from originals in Cremona, and to Hieronymus de S. Fide and Petrus Alphonsi. This passage gives an inflated impression of Sixtus's copying, which was simply of a full table of contents (Sixtus Senensis, *Bibliotheca Sancta*, ii, s. 'Traditiones seniorum'), but Pinamonti makes it plain that his own Talmudic knowledge is second-hand.

[52]The contents are discussed by De Rossi, *Bibliotheca*, p. 22, Steinschneider, 'Letteratura giudaica', *Il Vessillo Israelitico* xxvii (1879), 271–2 and I. Levi, 'Confutazione della *Sinagoga Disingannata*', *Il Vessillo Israelitico* lii (1904), 530–3, 581–3; liii (1905), 4–6. Notes taken from the copies of the work in MSS. Parm. 2335 (= Derossiani italiani 12), Roth 415, and Bodleian Library, Oxford, Reggio 50 (Neubauer no. 2480) have been used here; for other MSS. see Marx, 'Polemical Manuscripts', p. 264, no. 70 and Simonsohn, *History*, p. 84, n. 270.

Christian argument from miracle.[53] The proof from miracle is the sole subject of the *Breve Ragionamento*, is important in the answer to Pinamonti, and has its place in Briel's criticism of the New Testament. Why is it so prominent in Briel's works?

Biblical and later deployment and questioning of this argument have been noted already. The *Breve Ragionamento* underlines its continuing use. The last paragraph of the treatise begins as follows.[54] 'This is in brief what I have several times had occasion to maintain in reply to persons of learning who wished to prove the truth of religion from miracles. They found themselves embarrassed to answer reasons of such substance and force.' The arguments Briel has offered are threefold. The first is from the universality of miracles. The treatise begins: 'Miracles are wholly inadmissible as proofs of true religion; for all nations parade their own miracles and mock those of others. Christians laugh at pagan miracles, Turks at those of the Christians, and Christians at those of the Turks. All of them make the same objections against one another, claiming that reputed miracles are the effect of chance, contrived by magic, or ratified by superstition.' Pagan miracles are then exemplified at length, in a passage which takes up most of the booklet, beginning with Apollonius of Tyana, Pharaoh's magicians, and the Vestal Claudia who drew a ship with her girdle to prove her chastity. The rest is very brief. The second argument is from the Torah. Miracles claimed as the attestation of new laws and the abrogation of laws given by Moses are not to be given credence, as shown by Deut. xiii 1–12 on the miracles of the false prophet. (The verse-numbers given here in the booklet indicate that the Hebrew, not the Vulgate, is in mind; verse 1 is therefore the prohibition of any alteration in the law.) The third and last argument is from the general agreement that the law of Moses is of divine origin; Christians, Mahometans and the sects into which they are divided are all at one in recognizing its claims, but it does not recognize the corresponding claims of any other laws. The last two arguments are silently directed against Christianity.

Briel claims that the booklet sums up all his own habitual replies to the 'learned' who try to prove the truth of religion from the argument

---

[53]Edited and translated by N. Patruno and S. T. Lachs, 'A Brief Treatise on Miracles of R. Judah Brieli', *Gratz College Annual of Jewish Studies* iii (1974), 77–82, from the single known MS., Parm. 2149; add to the information given by the editors that this copy (= Derossiani italiani 13; twelve octavo pages) was made by De Rossi himself from a text belonging to a Jew, as noted by De Rossi, *Bibliotheca* (n. 2, above), p. 22.

[54]English translations from the treatise quoted here are by the present writer.

from miracle. There is no reason to doubt its connection with his own way of arguing, for the answers in the booklet are widely attested among Jewish and Christian contemporaries.[55] Most of the composition, however, tallies almost word for word with a passage from Isaac Cardoso's *Excelencias de los Hebreos* (n. 6, above). Cardoso sent Briel a copy of his work, and the younger man replied with a Hebrew poem.[56] The big overlap between the Italian booklet and the Spanish text seems not to have been pointed out, but, so far as I can see, the new material added by Briel is restricted to his final paragraph in which he says that he used these arguments, and the short passage expressly citing Deut. xiii.[57] This chapter supplied (verse 1 in the Hebrew) the text for the ninth of Maimonides' Thirteen Principles, on the immutability of the Torah, and had been used since very early times to combat claims based on the miracles of Christ. (Briel would probably have had in view the interpretations of Deut. xiii in Mishnah, Sanh. vii 4, 10, x 4–6, on the execution of those who lead one or many astray, and Babylonian Talmud, Sanh. 43a, on Jesus as charged with these offences.) This would mean that Briel took over from Cardoso a passage which is carefully written in general terms about true religion, and slightly adapted it so as to sharpen and make more obvious its application to Christianity in particular.

In its earlier context in Cardoso's work it is indeed part of a reply

---

[55]On the three arguments compare, for example, with (i), M. de Elizalde, S.J. (nn. 56–7, below), and Orobio de Castro in Philip Limborch, *De veritate religionis christianae amica Collatio cum erudito Judaeo* (Gouda, 1687), 136 (iii 4, 4: heathen, and notably Muslims, could question the revelation and miracles of both Jews and Christians, and uphold their own); with (i) and (iii) Solomon de Marini of Padua, *Tiqqun 'Olam* (Verona, 1652), in Ad. Neubauer, S. R. Driver, E. B. Pusey, *The Fifty-Third Chapter of Isaiah according to the Jewish Interpreters* (2 vols., Oxford, 1876, 1877, reprinted with Prolegomenon by R. Loewe, New York, 1969), i, 291–2, ii, 333 (on Isa. liii 6; the nations and their religions are divided; each denies the others, but all admit that Israel's religion is divine) (Loewe, Prolegomenon, 26 points to the Thirty Years' War in the background of this argument); with (ii) and (iii), Orobio de Castro in Limborch, 115 (iii 3, 9: Deut. xiii warns against accepting falsehood apparently backed by miracle), 130 (Jews of Christ's time, following Deut. xiii, could not believe him despite miracles), 143 (iii 4, 2–3); with (iii), L. A. Muratori (n. 23, above) under the pseudonym Lamindus Pritanius, *De ingeniorum moderatione in religionis negotio* (Venice, 1727; preface dated 1712), 17 (i 3) (Muslims and Christians unite in accepting the Jews' law as divine).

[56]Yerushalmi, *Isaac Cardoso*, 365, 471–2. This presentation by the author suggests that Briel might already have been known as an apologist.

[57]The Italian text (Patruno and Lachs, 'Treatise', 77–79), from the beginning (77) to 79, line 20, corresponds to *Excelencias* (1679) (n. 6, above), 277a–278b line 11. The surprising Italian 'Ezechiele', where 'Ezechia' would have been expected (Patruno and Lachs, 79 and n. 9, 82 and n, 33), is a slavish reproduction of *Excelencias*, 278b, 'Ezequiel'. Then Patruno and Lachs 79, lines 27–34 (the penultimate paragraph) follow *Excelencias*, 279a line 29–279b line 4.

to an argument from miracle in a Latin apologetic for Christianity, including attacks on Judaism, by the Spanish Jesuit Miguel de Elizalde (Naples, 1662). Elizalde himself had taken the universality of miracles to be the most obvious objection to his line of argument.[58] There is a certain poetic justice in the plundering of Cardoso by Briel, for Cardoso himself sometimes proceeded by silent quotation of his adversary. Thus the sentences by Cardoso quoted above from the beginning of Briel's booklet are not more than a slight expansion of Elizalde's admission: '... all in turn claim miracles; pagans, Turks, Jews, Christian and others, we all laugh at one another, and attribute the miracles claimed by others to chance, superstition, or magic.'[59] Similarly, from the long list of miracles, the group of three beginning with the story of Claudia appears in Elizalde.[60] Behind the Mantuan rabbi's booklet, therefore, is a controversy between two Spaniards, a Jesuit and a Marrano, writing in southern and northern Italy respectively. The subject matter was of equal interest to all three.

This fragment of literary history underlines the importance which the argument from miracle had retained in contemporary Jewish–Christian polemic. What Briel seems particularly to have valued in Cardoso's work is the long series of instances of pagan miracles, a list ending with a sequence which Cardoso himself had used before.[61] The complete list is partly indebted, through Elizalde, to Augustine (n. 60, above), who developed the rebuttals of pagan miracle in earlier Christian apologists such as Lactantius (*Divine Institutes*, ii 8).[62] Its explicit appeal, however, is to an imposing list of classical authors: Plutarch, Suetonius, Livy, Xiphilinus (epitomator of Cassius Dio), Appian; then, on revival and resuscitation (n. 61, above), Philostratus (on Apollonius of Tyana), Hegesippus (on Simon Magus), Apuleius, Pliny, Plato, and the modern writers Sigismund (on Muscovy) and Olaus Magnus (on the northern

---

[58]M. de Elizalde, *Forma verae religionis quaerendae et inveniendae* (Naples, 1662), 299–300.

[59]'... omnes vicissim allegant miracula, et Gentiles, et Turcae, et Iudaei, et Christiani et alii alios vicissim deridemus, et casui, vel superstitioni, vel magicis artibus aliena attribuimus' (Elizalde, *Forma*, 299).

[60]Elizalde, *Forma*, 307; the first two of these are in Augustine, *C.D.* x 16.

[61]The section on resurrection in Cardoso, *Philosophia Libera* (2 vols., Venice, 1673), 720a (vi 108) includes the list beginning with Apollonius of Tyana and ending with Olaus on the Lapps, found again in *Excelencias*, 278a and in *Breve Regionamento*, Patruno and Lachs, 78 foot–79.

[62]On the sources of Lactantius's list (mainly Valerius Maximus) see R. M. Ogilvie, *The Library of Lactantius* (Oxford, 1978), 44–5.

peoples). Christian writers regularly considered and dismissed some part of this pagan material,[63] and its potentially disquieting character for educated Christians is clear from Briel's use of it. An appeal to the classics shows that writers who were otherwise deeply respected were commonly doubted on the subject of miracle. An analogous attitude to the gospels could be suggested with some force. It was the pagan miracles, at any rate, that Briel cited again in his reply to Pinamonti, who had argued that Christianity, by contrast with what he calls the 'modern law' of the Jews, was truly attested by miracle. 'The miracles of Christ', Briel wrote in reply, 'are denied by us; the gospels are not given greater credence than Valerius Maximus, and very many other ancient Roman historians.'[64]

Briel's reply to Pinamonti also exemplifies a Jewish approach to the material on and from post-biblical Jews which Christians regularly used in this argument. Pinamonti had sought to show overall that the Christian gospel is attested by miracles, as would be expected of a truly divine law (his paragraphs 123–48); in outline the argument corresponds to that set out for general use as a defence of Christianity by Segneri (n. 63, above). Miracles, in Pinamonti's view, are part of the 'testimony' mentioned in Ps. xix 8 (paragraph 33, taken up in 123), a verse taken by both Christians and Jews in the Middle Ages to enumerate the attributes of divine law.[65] Pinamonti first (paragraph 124) attacks the view that modern Judaism could claim the support of miracles, a piece of scepticism with which he can hope to carry readers along; he picks out from the fifteenth-century Jewish *converso* Paul of Burgos (Paulus de Sancta Maria) the story of crosses miraculously appearing on the clothes of Jews in 1295, to show that the only kind of miracle modern Jews can claim argues *against* their own Judaism.[66] Only then does he try to show that the miracles of Christ deserve more respect, and that

---

[63]For example, H. Grotius, *De veritate religionis christianae*, iv 8 (Oxford, 1827, reprinting the text issued in Paris, 1640, pp. 207–10); P. Segneri, *L'Incredulo senza scusa* (Venice, 1733), 120–1 (ii 4). Neither approaches the fulness of Cardoso's catalogue.

[64]Paragraph 126, cited from MS. Roth 415, f. 55b; the section 'de miraculis' in Valerius Maximus (i 8) includes four of the miracles listed by Cardoso.

[65]Aquinas, *S.T.*, ia iiae, 91, 4; Albo, *Ikkarim*, iii 25 takes this verse as showing the perfection of the Torah, against Christian polemic and by contrast, in his own view, with the imperfect gospel.

[66]Pinamonti, *Sinagoga*, 223–5, citing Paulus de S. Maria, *Scrutinium Scripturarum*, ii 6, 10; the story is given from the contemporary narrative of Abner of Burgos (Alphonsus of Valladolid) in Y. Baer, *A History of the Jews in Christian Spain*, i (E.T., Philadelphia, 1966), 280, 328.

Christians are not inclined to fabricate miracles, despite the criticisms levelled at hagiography. His treatment of the miracles of Christ includes attempts (paragraphs 133, 136) to show that they are universally attested, whereas those of Moses are upheld only by the Jews, two assertions which lay themselves open to damaging ripostes by Briel (compare the claims for universal assent to Moses, n. 55, above). The second paragraph is part of a defence of Christ's miracles against rabbinic attack (paragraphs 135–9), ending (139) with a summary of Nicolas de Lyra on the Jewish story that Christ worked his miracles by means of the tetragram, copied from the stone in the temple on which the ark once rested.[67] Pinamonti urges that the assertion that miracles were performed with God's name attests belief in their truth. Briel replies that the story is a fable, invented by de Lyra or some other ill-affected person, and not to be found in any book of the Jews.[68] Yet Briel is likely to have known the Toledoth Jeshu in Hebrew, and his sweeping disclaimer seems more readily defensible in the restricted form it takes in the Hebrew section-heading in his response: 'The sages did not say that Jesus took Names from the temple, and did not make the other similar allegations'.[69] His reaction is comparable, however, with Leone Modena's denunciation of the account of Jesus which he has seen circulating among some Jews as a deceitful polemic.[70] The difference is that Modena, admittedly in a Hebrew apology, allows that the work in question (again, the Toledoth Jeshu) is read by Jews.

Pinamonti's argument overall shows how necessary miracles were felt to be, if the teaching of Moses or Jesus was to be commended as true divine law. At this point, as Pinamonti's convergence with Segneri showed, the argument from miracles belonged not only to Jewish–Christian debate, but also to the general arguments in favour of the truth of revealed religion, Mosaic or Christian. This consideration may help to account for the continued prominence of the subject, among both Jews and Christians. Nevertheless, the pitfalls of the argument from miracle, as just illustrated, were notorious.

Christian apologists, from the New Testament onwards, had

---

[67]For this narrative from the Toledoth Jeshu De Lyra probably depends mainly on Raymund Martini, *Pugio Fidei*, ii 8, 6; Raymund argues that the story shows that Christ's miracles could neither be ignored, nor ascribed to demons.

[68]MS. Parm. 2335, ff. 53b–54a.

[69]MS. Parm. 2335, f. 53b.

[70]Leone Modena, *Magen* (ed. Simonsohn, cited in n. 6, above), 43 (iii 9).

consequently tended towards the position that the gospel miracles were worthy of respect principally because they tallied with prophecy.[71] This view, already adumbrated in the Pauline confession of resurrection 'according to the scriptures', is met in Augustine and Dante and Briel's contemporaries such as Samuel Nahmias.[72] Yet there was a strong seventeenth-century impulse for Christians to use the argument from miracle in reasoned apologetic both generally and *adversus Iudaeos*. This impulse is evident in Protestant as well as Roman Catholic writings; they differ on the miracles of the saints (Briel notes with relish that modern western miracles are doubted by the Greek Orthodox and Lutherans),[73] but agree in defending and arguing from the gospel miracles. Similarly, in part of Jewish tradition any argument from miracle was heavily qualified, notably when Maimonides distanced both Moses and the messiah from the argument. 'Israel did not believe in Moses our teacher on account of the miracles which he did' (*Hilekhoth Yesodey Torah* viii 1); 'Let it not enter your thoughts that King Messiah must do signs and wonders' (*Hilekhoth Melakhim* xi 3). Yet the continuing importance of miracles as proof of the divine calling is evident in Abravenel on the messiah,[74] Solomon de Marini on Israel,[75] and Orobio de Castro (iii 4, 3) on Moses. Miracles were still the expected support for any claim that law or gospel was truly divine. It could hardly be otherwise in communities where many looked earnestly for the restoration of Israel, quite apart from any specifically Sabbatian leanings. Isaac Vita Cantarini, in his book *'Eth Qez* (Venice, 1710), reckoned the year of redemption as 1740; Briel himself, not given to such calculations, could still express himself, as an individual and on behalf of the community, in terms of longing for the temple and the

---

[71]Early patristic material is discussed by G. W. H. Lampe, 'Miracles and Early Christian Apologetic' and M. F. Wiles, 'Miracles in the Early Church', in C. F. D. Moule (ed.), *Miracles* (London, 1965), 205–18, 221–34.

[72]I Cor. xv 4, claiming to give pre-Pauline tradition; Luke xxiv 44–7, interpreted in Augustine, *Epistula ad Catholicos contra Donatistas*, 50 (xix) (Christ shown to be risen not by the resurrection appearances, but by the concordance of crucifixion followed by resurrection with canonical prophecy); Dante, *Paradiso* xxiv 97–111 (miracles attested by scripture, both attested by the rise of Christianity); Morosini, *Via della Fede*, Preface (almost all the 'gran cose' said of Christ's birth, life, death and resurrection, Morosini seemed already to have seen in the prophets).

[73]MS. Parm. 2335, ff. 49b–50a.

[74]L. Strauss, 'On Abravanel's Philosophical Tendency and Political Teaching', in J. B. Trend and H. M. J. Loewe (edd.), *Isaac Abravenel* (Cambridge, 1937), 95–129 (107–9); Neubauer, Driver and Pusey, *Fifty-Third Chapter*, i, 154–6; ii, 165–8.

[75]Neubauer, Driver and Pusey, *Fifty-Third Chapter*, i, 289, ii, 329, on liii 3 (while Israel remained in the land, miracles obtained recognition for them from the nations).

redeemer.[76] Both Jews and Christians at this period, therefore, felt the need to appeal to miracles in rational argument for the fundamental truth of their religion, despite the well-known difficulties.

A consideration specific to Christian controversy against Jews was brought forward early in the seventeenth century by the Socinian Valentin Schmalz. He knew that the Jews had a story that Jesus worked his miracles by means of the tetragram. He urged that they could never be persuaded by arguments from scripture, for how would a Christian make the mystical sense seem probable to a Jew? Would a Jew submit to be taught the law by a gentile? Instead, they would be convinced by miracles; the objections they might base on Deut. xiii do not apply.[77] Theodore Hackspan, who edited the biblically based anti-Christian Nizzahon of Lipmann Mühlhausen, strongly denied this argument; miracles would not always convince (here he quoted Maimonides), and scripture was not to be given up.[78] A somewhat similar tendency to appeal to the miraculous because of the inconclusive nature of the usual arguments has been noted in another seventeenth-century controversy which used much of the same material, the argument concerning atheism.[79] Moves of this kind towards the argument from miracle perhaps attest an instinct that, despite rational difficulties, the unusual or startling has value in debate.

Reasons for Briel's special concern with miracles suggest themselves against this background. Most obviously, he was anxious to rebut the standard Christian arguments, as the *Breve Ragionamento* indicates. As a polemist, he must be well-versed in a topic which ramified into many areas of Jewish–Christian controversy. Christians connected the argument from miracle with criticism of post-biblical Jewish life and literature, as in Pinamonti's book, and some of them regarded it as a particularly promising approach to Jews. As a preacher and exponent of Judaism, Briel would have shared, with the kind of reservation he sponsored in his *Breve Ragionamento*, the current interest in miracles as evidence for the truth of religion. In

---

[76]Cantarini's book is judged a possible instance of strong interest in messianic restoration (as opposed to merely homiletic emphasis on the near approach of the day) by G. Scholem, *The Messianic Idea in Judaism* (London, 1971), 184 and n. 12; below Briel's inscribed poem (n. 21, above) was a sentence beginning 'these are the words of Judah Briel, on his own behalf and on behalf of all the congregation of Israel' and concluding with prayer for a rebuilt temple and the coming of a redeemer to Zion.

[77]V. Schmalz, *De divinitate Jesu Christi* (Rakow, 1608), 48–52.

[78]T. Hackspan, *Liber Nizachon Rabbi Lipmanni* (Nuremberg, 1644), 382–96.

[79]H.-M. Barth, *Atheismus und Orthodoxie: Analysen und Modelle christlicher Apologetik im 17. Jahrhundert* (Göttingen, 1971), 299.

any case, the subject was bound up closely with the biblically based controversy so characteristic of Briel and his environment.

Briel's own treatment of miracles, in his adaptation of Isaac Cardoso and in his answer to Pinamonti, betrays his characteristic exegetical and classical interests. In conclusion, therefore, it can be tentatively related to his personal outlook. From the non-mystical standpoint outlined in the previous section, he probably regarded the Christians as over-inclined to argue from miracle. He no doubt sympathized with the restriction of this argument which follows the critique of miracles in the section of *Excelencias* from which his material came; Cardoso there says that the original Mosaic miracles sufficed to credit the Torah, which is confirmed primarily by the tradition of the fathers and natural reason.[80] Briel, like Cardoso, was anti-Sabbatian in his Jewish loyalty. The Sabbatian movement will have been a factor in his concern with miracles and his generally biblical and rationalizing position;[81] but it is unlikely to have been the sole factor. The literary connections of his work with other Jewish-Christian polemic, and the importance of such polemic overall in his writings, suggest that his treatment of miracles primarily belongs in the context of externally directed controversy. Biblical debate with Christianity, of a 'mediaeval' kind, had a genuine actuality for him and his community. One may therefore venture to connect the strongly rational and biblically based piety which he developed with his reaction to the external Christian culture as well as to the internal Jewish conflict between mysticism and rationalism. His intellectual position seems not unlike some that were taken up in contemporary Christian Italy. He was the reverse of what is usually understood by the term 'assimilated', but he was unmistakably a seventeenth-century Italian.

---

[80]Isaac Cardoso, *Excelencias*, 279b–280a.

[81]His negative attitude to the cabbalah is connected with his anti-Sabbatianism in the unsigned article 'Briel, Yehudah', *EH* ix (1958), col. 695.

BIBLIOGRAPHY

This bibliography comprises books and articles bearing on the topics discussed, including works cited by short title, but it does not include all works cited in the volume. For further literature see Krauss & Horbury, *Controversy* and Schreckenberg, *Die christlichen Adversus-Iudaeos-Texte*.

Anna Sapir Abulafia, *Christians and Jews in the Twelfth-Century Renaissance* (London & New York, 1995)

P. S. Alexander, '"The Parting of the Ways" from the Perspective of Rabbinic Judaism', in Dunn (ed.), *Jews and Christians*, 1–25

S. Almog (ed.), *Antisemitism through the Ages* (E.T. Oxford, 1988)

J. van Amersfoort & J. van Oort (edd.), *Juden und Christen in der Antike* (Kampen, 1990)

V. Aptowitzer, 'Bemerkungen zur Liturgie und Geschichte der Liturgie', *MGWJ* lxxiv (1930), 104–26

C. Aziza, *Tertullien et le judaïsme* (Paris, 1977)

C. P. Bammel, 'Law and Temple in Origen', in W. Horbury (ed.), *Templum Amicitiae: Essays on the Second Temple presented to E. Bammel* (Sheffield, 1991), 464–76

———, 'Die erste lateinische Rede gegen die Christen', *ZKG* 104 (1993), 295–311

E. Bammel, 'Christian Origins in Jewish Tradition', reprinted from *NTS* xiii (1967), 317–35 in E. Bammel, *Judaica*

———, *Judaica: Kleine Schriften*, I (Tübingen, 1986)

———, 'Die Zeugen des Christentums', in H. Frohnhofen (ed.), *Christlicher Antijudaismus und jüdischer Antipaganismus* (Hamburg, 1990), 170–80

J. G. M. Barclay, 'Paul among Diaspora Jews: Anomaly or Apostate?', *JSNT* lx (1995), 89–120

———, *Jews in the Mediterranean Diaspora from Alexander to Trajan (323 BCE–117 CE)* (Edinburgh, 1996)

T. D. Barnes, *Tertullian* (Oxford, 1971; reprinted with 'Tertullian Revisited: a Postscript', Oxford, 1985)

———, 'Porphyry *Against the Christians*: Date and the Attribution of Fragments', *JTS* N.S. xxiv (1973), 424–42

C. K. Barrett, *The Gospel of John and Judaism* (E.T. London, 1975)

————, *A Critical and Exegetical Commentary on the Acts of the Apostles*, i (Edinburgh, 1994)

D. Barthélemy, 'L'état de la bible juive depuis le début de notre ère jusqu'à la deuxième révolte contre Rome (131–135)', in Kaestli & Wermelinger, *Canon*, 9–45

J. R. Baskin, 'Rabbinic-Patristic Exegetical Contacts in Late Antiquity: a Bibliographical Reappraisal', in W. S. Green (ed.), *Approaches to Ancient Judaism*, v (Atlanta, 1985), 53–80

R. Bauckham, 'The Parting of the Ways: What Happened and Why', *Studia Theologica* xlvii (1993), 135–51

W. Bauer, *Das Leben Jesu im Zeitalter der neutestamentlichen Apokryphen* (Tübingen, 1909, repr. Darmstadt, 1967)

J. M. Baumgarten, 'Exclusions from the Temple: Proselytes and Agrippa I', *JJS* xxxiii (1982), 215–25

R. T. Beckwith, *The Old Testament Canon of the New Testament Church* (London, 1985)

D. Berger, *The Jewish–Christian Debate in the High Middle Ages: a Critical Edition of the Nizzahon Vetus, with an introduction, translation and commentary* (Philadelphia, 1979)

————, 'Mission to the Jews and Jewish–Christian Contacts in the Polemical Literature of the High Middle Ages', *American Historical Review* xci (1986), 576–91

J. Bergmann, *Jüdische Apologetik im neutestamentlichen Zeitalter* (Berlin, 1908)

E. Best, *A Commentary on the First and Second Epistles to the Thessalonians* (London, 1972)

E. Bickerman, 'The Civic Prayer for Jerusalem', reprinted from *HTR* lv (1962) in E. Bickerman, *Studies in Jewish History*, ii (Leiden, 1980), 290–312

H. Bietenhard, *Caesarea, Origenes, und die Juden* (Stuttgart, 1974)

C. J. Bjerkelund, *Parakalo* (Oslo, 1967)

F. Blanchetière, 'Aux sources de l'antijudaïsme chrétien', *RHPR* 53 (1973), 353–98

————, *Aux sources de l'anti-judaïsme chrétien: IIe–IIIe siècles* (Jerusalem, 1995)

B. Blumenkranz, *Die Judenpredigt Augustins* (Basle, 1946, reprinted Paris, 1973)

————, *Juifs et chrétiens dans le monde occidental 430–1096* (Paris, 1960)

————, *Les auteurs chrétiens latins du moyen âge sur les juifs et le judaïsme* (Paris, 1963)

————, *Le juif médiéval au miroir de l'art chrétien* (Paris, 1966)

———, 'Kirche und Synagoge: Die Entwicklung im Westen zwischen 200 und 1200', reprinted from Rengstorf & Kortzfleisch (edd.), *Kirche und Synagoge*, i, 84–135 in Blumenkranz, *Patristique et Moyen Age*

——— and others, *Histoire des Juifs en France* (Franco-Judaica, 1; Toulouse, 1972)

———, with the collaboration of G. Dahan & S. Kerner, *Auteurs juifs en France mèdiévale* (Toulouse, 1975)

———, *Juifs et Chrétiens: Patristique et Moyen Age* (London, 1977)

G. Boccaccini, *Portraits of Middle Judaism in Scholarship and Arts* (Turin, 1992)

W. Bousset, *Die Religion des Judentums im späthellenistischen Zeitalter* (3rd edn, ed. H. Gressmann, Tübingen, 1926)

P. Bowers, 'Paul and Religious Propaganda', *NT* xxii (1980), 316–23

S. P. Brock, 'The Two Ways and the Palestinian Targum', in P. R. Davies & R. T. White (edd.), *A Tribute to Geza Vermes* (Sheffield, 1990), 139–52

R. Bultmann, *Theologie des Neuen Testaments* (3rd edn, Tübingen, 1958; E.T., 2 vols., London, 1952–5)

F. C. Burkitt, 'The Debt of Christianity to Judaism', in E. R. Bevan & C. Singer (edd.), *The Legacy of Israel* (Oxford, 1927), 69–96

Elisheva Carlebach, *The Pursuit of Heresy: Rabbi Moses Hagiz and the Sabbatian Controversies* (New York, 1990)

J. N. B. Carleton Paget, *The Epistle of Barnabas: Outlook and Background* (WUNT, 2. Reihe, 64, Tübingen, 1994)

———, 'Jewish Proselytism at the Time of Christian Origins: Chimera or Reality?', *JSNT* lxii (1996), 65–103

———, 'Anti-Judaism and Early Christian Identity: a Response to a Recent Work', forthcoming in *Zeitschrift für Antikes Christentum*

M. Casey, *From Jewish Prophet to Gentile God* (Cambridge, 1991)

H. Chadwick, 'Justin Martyr's Defence of Christianity', *BJRL* xlvii (1965), 275–97

B. Chilton & J. Neusner, *Judaism in the New Testament: Practices and Beliefs* (London & New York, 1995)

S. J. D. Cohen, 'Pagan and Christian Evidence on the Ancient Synagogue', in L. I. Levine (ed.), *The Synagogue in Late Antiquity* (Philadelphia, 1987), 159–81

N. A. Dahl, *Das Volk Gottes* (Oslo, 1941)

D. van Damme, *Pseudo-Cyprian Adversus Iudaeos, gegen die Judenchristen: die älteste lateinische Predigt* (Paradosis, 22; Freiburg, Schweiz, 1969)

W. D. Davies, *Paul and Rabbinic Judaism* (London, 1948, 2nd edn 1955, revised edn 1980)

———, *The Setting of the Sermon on the Mount* (Cambridge, 1964)

———, *The Gospel and the Land* (Berkeley, Los Angeles & London, 1974)

———, *Jewish and Pauline Studies* (London, 1984)

N. R. M. de Lange, *Origen and the Jews* (Cambridge, 1976)

———, 'Jews and Christians in the Byzantine Empire: Problems and Prospects', in Diana Wood (ed.), *Christianity and Judaism* (Studies in Church History, 29, Oxford, 1992), 15–32

A.-M. Denis, 'L'Apôtre Paul, prophète "messianique" des Gentils: étude thématique de I Thess., II.1–6', *ETL* xxxiii (1957), 245–318

L. Dequeker, 'L'iconographie de l'arche de la Torah dans les catacombes juives de Rome', *Augustinianum* xxviii (1988), 437–60

F. Dexinger, 'Limits of Tolerance in Judaism: the Samaritan Example', in Sanders, with Baumgarten & Mendelson (edd.), *Self-Definition*, ii, 88–114

E. von Dobschütz, *Die Thessalonicher-Briefe* (Göttingen, 1909)

C. H. Dodd, *According to the Scriptures* (London, 1952)

W. Doskocil, *Der Bann in der Urkirche* (Munich, 1958)

M. Dothan, *Hammath Tiberias* (Jerusalem, 1983)

J. D. G. Dunn, *The Partings of the Ways between Christianity and Judaism and their Significance for the Character of Christianity* (London & Philadelphia, 1991)

——— (ed.), *Jews and Christians: The Parting of the Ways, A.D. 70–135* (Tübingen, 1992)

R. Eisler, ΙΗΣΟΥΣ ΒΑΣΙΛΕΥΣ ΟΥ ΒΑΣΙΛΕΥΣΑΣ (2 vols., Heidelberg, 1929–30); E.T. by A. H. Krappe, *The Messiah Jesus and John the Baptist* (London, 1931)

I. Elbogen, *Der jüdische Gottesdienst in seiner geschichtlichen Entwicklung* (1913), Hebrew translation edited and supplemented by J. Heinemann and others (1972), E.T. from Hebrew and German by R. P. Scheindlin, *Jewish Liturgy: A Comprehensive History* (Philadelphia, New York & Jerusalem, 1993)

D. K. Falk, 'Jewish Prayer Literature and the Jerusalem Church in Acts', in R. Bauckham (ed.), *The Book of Acts in Its Palestinian Setting* (Grand Rapids & Carlisle, 1995), 267–301

P. Figueras, *Decorated Jewish Ossuaries* (Leiden, 1983)

G. Forkman, *The Limits of the Religious Community* (Lund, 1972)

M. Freimann, 'Wie verhielt sich das Judentum zu Jesus und dem entstehenden Christentum?,' *MGWJ* liv (1910), 697–712, lv (1911), 160–76, 296–316

———, 'Die Wortführer des Judentums in den ältesten Kontroversen zwischen Christen und Juden,' *MGWJ* lv (1911) 555–585, lvi (1912) 49–64, 164–80.

W. H. C. Frend, *Martyrdom and Persecution in the Early Church* (Oxford, 1965)

———, 'A Note on Jews and Christians in Third-Century North Africa', *JTS* N.S. xxi (1970), 92–6

J. G. Gager, *The Origins of Anti-Semitism* (New York & Oxford, 1983)

J. E. L. van der Geest, *Le Christ et l'Ancien Testament chez Tertullien* (Nijmegen, 1972)

J. Geffcken, *Zwei griechische Apologeten* (Leipzig & Berlin, 1907)

M. Gil, *A History of Palestine, 634–1099* (E.T. by E. Broido, Cambridge, 1992)

G. Glazov, 'The Invocation of Ps. 51:17 in Jewish and Christian Morning Prayer', *JJS* xlvi (1995), 167–82

M. Goodman, *Mission and Conversion: Proselytizing in the Religious History of the Roman Empire* (Oxford, 1994)

T. Hackspan (ed.), *Liber Nizachon Rabbi Lipmanni* (Nuremberg, 1644)

A. Harnack, *Die Altercatio Simonis et Theophili, nebst Untersuchungen über die antijüdische Polemik in der alten Kirche* (TU i 3, Leipzig, 1883), 1–136

———, 'Zur Schrift Pseudocyprians Adv. Judaeos', in Harnack, *Miscellen* (TU xx 3, Leipzig, 1900), 126–35

———, *Der Vorwurf des Atheismus in den drei ersten Jahrhunderten* (TU xxviii 4, Leipzig, 1905)

———, *Judentum und Judenchristentum in Justins Dialog mit Trypho* (TU xxxix, Leipzig, 1913)

H. St. J. Hart, review of E. R. Goodenough, *Jewish Symbols in the Greco-Roman Period*, i–iv, in *JTS* N.S. vii (1956), 92–7

J. H. A. Hart, 'Philo and the Catholic Judaism of the First Century', *JTS* xi (1910), 25–42

———, *The Hope of Catholick Judaism* (Oxford & London, 1910)

J. Heinemann, *Prayer in the Talmud* (E.T. Berlin, 1977)

M. Hengel, *Nachfolge und Charisma* (Berlin, 1968), E.T. *The*

Charismatic Leader and His Followers (Edinburgh, 1981; reprinted with a new Preface, Edinburgh, 1996)

——, 'Proseuche und Synagoge', in G. Jeremias, H.-W. Kuhn & H. Stegemann (edd.), *Tradition und Glaube ... Festgabe für K. G. Kuhn zum 65. Geburtstag* (Göttingen, 1971), 157–83

——, 'Hadrians Politik gegenüber Juden und Christen', *JAOS* xvi–xvii [1984–5, = *Ancient studies in Memory of Elias Bickerman*] (1987), 153–82

M. Hengel, with R. Deines, 'Die Septuaginta als "christliche Schriftensammlung", ihre Vorgeschichte und das Problem ihres Kanons', in Hengel & Schwemer, *Septuaginta*, 182–284

M. Hengel & A. M. Schwemer (edd.), *Die Septuaginta zwischen Judentum und Christentum* (Tübingen, 1994)

M. Hengel & R. Deines, 'E. P. Sanders' "Common Judaism", Jesus, and the Pharisees', *JTS* N.S. xlvi (1995), 1–70

B. Henneken, *Verkündigung und Prophetie im I. Thessalonicherbrief* (Stuttgart, 1969)

M. Hirshman, 'The Greek Fathers and the Aggada on Ecclesiastes: Formats of Exegesis in Late Antiquity', *HUCA* lix (1988), 137–65

——, 'Polemical Literary Units in the Classical Midrashim and Justin Martyr's *Dialogue with Trypho*', *JQR* N.S. 83 (1992–3), 369–84

G. Hoennicke, *Das Judenchristentum im ersten und zweiten Jahrhundert* (Berlin, 1908)

M. D. Hooker, 'A Further Note on Romans i', *NTS* xiii (1966–7), 181–3

William Horbury, 'The Trial of Jesus in Jewish Tradition', in E. Bammel (ed.), *The Trial of Jesus* (London, 1970), 103–21

——, 'A Critical Examination of the Toledoth Jeshu', Diss. Cambridge, 1970

——, 'Paul and Judaism', *Expository Times* xc (1979), 116–18

——, 'Suffering and Messianism in Yose ben Yose', in Horbury & McNeil (edd.), *Suffering and Martyrdom*, 143–82

——, 'The Aaronic Priesthood in the Epistle to the Hebrews', *JSNT* xix (1983) [= William Horbury & Christopher Rowland (edd.), *Essays in Honour of Ernst Bammel*], 43–71

——, 'Messianism among Jews and Christians in the Second Century', *Augustinianum* xxviii (1988), 71–88

——, 'Old Testament Interpretation in the Writings of the Church Fathers', in M. J. Mulder & H. Sysling (edd.), *Mikra: Text, Translation, Reading and Interpretation of the Hebrew Bible in Ancient Judaism and Early Christianity* (Compendia Rerum Iudaicarum ad Novum Testamentum, Section II, volume i, Assen & Philadelphia, 1988), 727–87

——, 'The Jewish Dimension', in Ian Hazlett (ed.), *Early Christianity: Origins and Evolution to AD 600. In Honour of W. H. C. Frend* (London, 1991), 40–51

——, 'Constitutional Aspects of the Kingdom of God', in R. S. Barbour (ed.), *The Kingdom of God and Human Society* (Edinburgh, 1993), 60–79

——, 'The "Caiaphas" Ossuaries and Joseph Caiaphas', *PEQ* cxxvi (1994), 32–48

——, 'The Wisdom of Solomon in the Muratorian Fragment', *JTS* N.S. xlv (1994), 149–59

——, 'The Christian Use and the Jewish Origins of the Wisdom of Solomon', in J. Day, R. P. Gordon & H. G. M. Williamson (edd.), *Wisdom in Ancient Israel* (Cambridge, 1995), 182–96

——, 'The Hebrew Text of Matthew in Shem Tob Ibn Shaprut's *Eben Bohan*', appendix in W. D. Davies & Dale Allison, *Matthew*, iii (ICC, Edinburgh, 1997), 728–37.

——, 'Land, Sanctuary and Worship', in J. P. M. Sweet & J. M. G. Barclay (edd.), *Early Christian Thought in its Jewish Setting* (Cambridge, 1996), 207–24

——, see also Krauss

—— & B. McNeil (edd.) *Suffering and Martyrdom in the New Testament* (Cambridge, 1981)

P. W. van der Horst, *Hellenism–Judaism–Christianity: Essays on Their Interaction* (Kampen, 1994)

——, 'The Birkat ha-minim in Recent Research', reprinted from *ET* cv (1993–4) in van der Horst, *Hellenism*, 99–111

G. Howard, *Hebrew Gospel of Matthew* (Macon, Georgia, 1995)

R. Hvalvik, *The Struggle for Scripture and Covenant* (Tübingen, 1996)

O. Irshai, 'R. Abbahu Said: "If a Man Should Say to You 'I am God' – He is a Liar"', *Zion* xlvii (1982), 173–7 [in Hebrew]

——, 'Ya'aqov 'ish Kefar Nevurayya – hakham she-nikshal be-minut', *Mehqere Yerushalayim be-mahshevet Yisra'el*, ii (1982), 153–69

——, 'Narcissus of Jerusalem and His Rôle in the Enhancement of the Apostolic Image of the Jerusalem Church', in F. Blanchetière & M. D. Herr (edd.), *Aux origines juives du christianisme* (Jerusalem, 1993), 111–31

——, 'Constantine and the Jews: the Prohibition against Entering Jerusalem – History and Hagiography', *Zion* lx (1995), 129–78 [in Hebrew]

————, 'Cyril of Jerusalem: The Apparition of the Cross and the Jews', in Limor & Stroumsa (edd.), *Contra Iudaeos*, 85–104

R. Jewett, *The Thessalonian Correspondence* (Philadelphia, 1986)

A. H. M. Jones, *The Later Roman Empire, 284–602* (2 vols., Oxford, 1964, repr. 1973)

J. Juster, *Les juifs dans l'empire romain* (2 vols, Paris, 1914)

J. D. Kaestli & O. Wermelinger (edd.), *Le canon de l'Ancien Testament. Sa formation et son histoire* (Geneva, 1984)

A. Kamesar, *Jerome, Greek Scholarship, and the Hebrew Bible* (Oxford, 1993)

————, 'The Evaluation of the Narrative Aggada in Greek and Latin Patristic Literature', *JTS* N.S. xlv (1994), 37–71

————, 'The Narrative Aggada as Seen from the Graeco-Latin Perspective', *JJS* xlv (1994), 52–70

S. Kamin, *Jews and Christians Interpret the Bible* (Jerusalem, 1991)

————, 'The Theological Significance of the *Hebraica Veritas* in Jerome's Thought', reprinted from M. Fishbane & E. Tov (edd.), *Sha'arei Talmon* (Winona Lake, 1991) in Kamin, *Jews and Christians*, 1*–11*

R. Kampling, *Das Blut Christi und die Juden: Mt 27, 25 bei den lateinsprachigen christlichen Autoren bis zu Leo dem Grossen* (Münster, 1984)

J. Katz, *Exclusiveness and Tolerance* (Oxford, 1961)

H. C. Kee, 'The Transformation of the Synagogue after 70 C.E.: its Import for Early Christianity', *NTS* xxxvi (1990), 1–24

————, 'The Changing Meaning of Synagogue: A Response to Richard Oster', *NTS* xl (1994), 281–3

R. Kimelman, '*Birkat Ha-Minim* and the Lack of Evidence for an Anti-Christian Jewish Prayer in Late Antiquity', in Sanders, with Baumgarten & Mendelson (edd.), *Self-Definition*, ii, 226–44

W. Kinzig, *Erbin Kirche: Die Auslegung von Psalm 5,1 in den Psalmenhomilien des Asterius und in der alten Kirche* (Heidelberg, 1990)

————, '"Non-Separation": Closeness and Co-operation between Jews and Christians in the Fourth Century', *VC* xlv (1991), 27–53

W. L. Knox, *St Paul and the Church of the Gentiles* (Cambridge, 1939)

U. Köpf, 'Ferdinand Christian Baur als Begründer einer konsequent historischen Theologie', *ZTK* lxxxix (1992), 440–61

K. Kohler, 'The Origin and Composition of the Eighteen Benedictions', *HUCA* i (1924), 387–425

S. Krauss, 'The Jews in the Works of the Church Fathers', *JQR* v (1892–3), 122–57, vi (1893–4), 82–99, 225–6

———, 'Imprecation against the Minim in the Synagogue', *JQR* ix (1897), 515–17

———, *Das Leben Jesu nach jüdischen Quellen* (Berlin, 1902)

———, *Synagogale Altertümer* (Berlin & Vienna, 1922)

———, 'Zur Literatur der Siddurim: christliche Polemik', in A. Marx & H. Meyer (edd.), *Festschrift für Aron Freimann* (Berlin, 1935), 125–40

———, 'The Christian Legislation on the Synagogue', in S. Löwinger, A. Scheiber & J. Somogyi (edd.), *Ignace Goldziher Memorial Volume*, Part II (Jerusalem, 1958), 14–41

S. Krauss & W. Horbury, *The Jewish–Christian Controversy from the earliest times to 1789*, i, *History* (Tübingen, 1996)

G. Kretschmar, 'Die Kirche aus Juden und Heiden: Forschungsprobleme der ersten christlichen Jahrhunderten', in van Amersfoort & van Oort (edd.), *Juden und Christen in der Antike*, 9–43

G. W. H. Lampe, 'Church Discipline and the Interpretation of the Epistles to the Corinthians', in W. R. Farmer, C. F. D. Moule & R. R. Niebuhr (edd.), *Christian History and Interpretation: Studies presented to John Knox* (Cambridge, 1967), 337–61

———, '"Grievous Wolves" (Acts 20:29)', in B. Lindars & S. S. Smalley (edd.), *Christ and Spirit in the New Testament: Essays in Honour of C. F. D. Moule* (Cambridge, 1973), 253–68

———, *God as Spirit* (Oxford, 1977)

———, 'Martyrdom and Inspiration', in Horbury & McNeil (edd.) *Suffering and Martyrdom*, 118–35

G. I. Langmuir, 'The Faith of Christians and Hostility to Jews', in Diana Wood (ed.), *Christianity and Judaism* (Studies in Church History, 29, Oxford, 1992), 77–92

D. J. Lasker, *Jewish Philosophical Polemics Against Christianity in the Middle Ages* (New York, 1977)

———, 'Jewish Philosophical Polemics in Ashkenaz', in Limor & Stroumsa, *Contra Iudaeos*, 195–213.

L. I. Levine, 'The Second Temple Synagogue: The Formative Years', in Levine, *Synagogue*, 7–31

J. M. Lieu, 'History and Theology in Christian Views of Judaism', in J. Lieu, J. North & T. Rajak (edd.), *The Jews among Pagans and Christians in the Roman Empire* (London, 1992), 79–96

———, *Image and Reality: the Jews in the World of the Christians in the Second Century* (Edinburgh, 1996)

O. Limor & G. G. Stroumsa (edd.), *Contra Iudaeos: Ancient and*

Medieval Polemics between Christians and Jews (Tübingen, 1996)

G. Lindeskog, *Das jüdisch-christliche Problem: Randglossen zu einer Forschungsepoche* (Uppsala, 1986)

R. Loewe, 'Apologetic Motifs in the Targum to the Song of Songs', in A. Altmann (ed.), *Biblical Motifs* (Cambridge, Mass., 1966), 159–96

———, 'Prolegomenon' (1969) (see Neubauer)

J. van der Lof, 'Les liens des chrétiens avec les synagogues locales du temps de saint Cyprien et saint Augustin', *NAK* N.S. lvi (1975–6), 385–95

M. Lowe (ed.), *The New Testament and Christian-Jewish Dialogue: Studies in Honor of David Flusser* (= *Immanuel* xxiv–xxv) (Jerusalem, 1990)

S. Lowy, 'The Confutation of Judaism in the Epistle of Barnabas', *JJS* xi (1960), 1–33

L. Lucas, *Zur Geschichte der Juden im vierten Jahrhundert* (Berlin, 1910), E.T. *The Conflict between Christianity and Judaism: A Contribution to the History of the Jews in the Fourth Century* (Warminster, 1993)

A. C. MacGiffert, *Dialogue between a Christian and a Jew* (Marburg, 1889)

J. Maier, *Jesus von Nazareth in der talmudischen Überlieferung* (Darmstadt, 1978)

———, *Jüdische Auseinandersetzung mit dem Christentum in der Antike* (Darmstadt, 1982)

Z. Malachi, 'Jewish and Christian Liturgical Poetry: Mutual Influences in the First Four Centuries', *Augustinianum* xxviii (1988), 237–48

A. J. Malherbe, 'Gentle as a Nurse', *NT* xii (1970), 203–17

J. Mann, 'Changes in the Divine Service of the Synagogue due to Religious Persecution', *HUCA* iv (1927), 241–310

C. Markschies, 'Hieronymus und die "Hebraica Veritas" – ein Beitrag zur Archäologie des protestantischen Schriftverständnisses?', in Hengel & Schemer, *Septuaginta*, 131–81

A. Marmorstein, 'L'Épître de Barnabé et la polémique juive', *REJ* lx (1910), 213–20

———, 'The Attitude of the Jews towards Early Christianity', *The Expositor* xlix (1923), 383–9

———, *Studies in Jewish Theology* (London, 1950)

B. Mazar, M. Schwabe & B. Lifschitz, & N. Avigad, *Beth She'arim* (Jerusalem, 1957, 1967, 1971)

H. Merkel, 'Israel im lukanischen Werk', *NTS* xl (1994), 371–98

E. M. Meyers & J. F. Strange, *Archaeology, the Rabbis and Early Christianity* (London, 1981)

G. F. Moore, 'Christian Writers on Judaism', *HTR* xiv (1921), 197–254

――――, *Judaism in the First Centuries of the Christian Era: The Age of the Tannaim* (3 vols., Cambridge, Massachusetts, 1927–30)

C. F. D. Moule (ed.), *Miracles* (London, 1965)

C. F. D. Moule, *The Holy Spirit* (London, 1978)

――――, *The Birth of the New Testament* (3rd edn, revised and rewritten, London, 1981)

R. Murray, *Symbols of Church and Kingdom: a Study in Early Syriac Tradition* (Cambridge, 1975)

A. Neubauer, S. R. Driver, & E. B. Pusey, *The Fifty-third Chapter of Isaiah according to the Jewish Interpreters* (2 vols, Oxford, 1876, reprinted with a Prolegomenon by R. Loewe, New York, 1969)

J. Neusner, *Aphrahat and Judaism: The Christian-Jewish Argument in Fourth-Century Iran* (Leiden, 1971)

――――, *Judaism: The Evidence of the Mishnah* (Chicago & London, 1981)

――――, *Judaism and Christianity in the Age of Constantine* (Chicago & London, 1987)

――――, E. S. Frerichs & C. McCracken-Flesher (edd.), *'To See Ourselves as Others See Us': Christians, Jews, 'Others' in Late Antiquity* (Chico, 1985)

――――, W. S. Green & E. S. Frerichs (edd.), *Judaisms and Their Messiahs at the Turn of the Christian Era* (Cambridge, 1987)

――――, see also B. Chilton

G. W. E. Nickelsburg, with R. A. Kraft, 'The Modern Study of Early Judaism', in R. A. Kraft & G. W. E. Nickelsburg (edd.), *Early Judaism and Its Modern Interpreters* (Atlanta, 1986)

B. Nitzan, *Qumran Prayer and Religious Poetry* (E.T. by J. Chipman, Leiden, New York & Cologne, 1994)

David Noy, 'A Jewish Place of Prayer in Roman Egypt', *JTS* N.S. xliii (1992), 118–22

――――, *Jewish Inscriptions of Western Europe*, i, *Italy (excluding the city of Rome), Spain and Gaul*; ii, *The City of Rome* (Cambridge, 1993, 1995)

R. E. Oster, 'Supposed Anachronism in Luke-Acts' Use of συναγωγή: A Rejoinder to H. C. Kee', *NTS* xxxix (1993), 178–208

R. R. Ottley, *The Book of Isaiah according to the Septuagint* (2 vols., Cambridge, 1906)

James Parkes, *The Conflict of the Church and the Synagogue* (London, 1934)

E. Peterson, *Frühkirche, Judentum, und Gnosis* (Rome, 1959)

J. & B. Prijs, *Die Basler hebräischen Drucke* (Olten & Freiburg i. Br., 1964)

B. Reicke, *Diakonie, Festfreude und Zelos in Verbindung mit der altchristlichen Agapenfeier* (Uppsala Universitets Årsskrift 1951: 5, Uppsala, 1951)

S. C. Reif, *Judaism and Hebrew Prayer* (Cambridge, 1993)

——, *Hebrew Manuscripts at Cambridge University Library. A Description and Introduction* (Cambridge, 1997)

J. Reynolds & R. Tannenbaum, *Jews and Godfearers at Aphrodisias* (Cambridge, 1987)

D. Rokeah, *Jews, Pagans and Christians in Conflict* (Jerusalem & Leiden, 1982)

——, 'The Church Fathers and the Jews in Writings Designed for Internal and External Use', in Almog, *Anti-Semitism*, 39–69

B. S. Rosner, *Paul, Scripture & Ethics: A Study of 1 Corinthians 5–7* (AGJU xxii, Leiden, New York & Köln, 1994)

R. R. Ruether, *Faith and Fratricide. The Theological Roots of Anti-Semitism* (New York, 1974)

——, 'Tradition in the Church Fathers: the Exegesis of Christian Anti-Judaism', with comments by J. D. Adams, in P. E. Szarmach, *Aspects of Jewish Culture in the Middle Ages* (Albany, New York, 1979), 27–50, 174–8

L. V. Rutgers, *The Jews in Late Ancient Rome* (Leiden, New York & Köln, 1995)

M. Saebø (ed.), in co-operation with C. Brekelmans & M. Haran, *Hebrew Bible/Old Testament: The History of Its Interpretation*, i, *From the Beginnings to the Middle Ages (Until 1300)*, Part 1, *Antiquity* (Göttingen, 1996)

Z. Safrai, 'Dukhan, Aron and Teva: How was the Ancient Synagogue Furnished?', in R. Hachlili (ed.), *Ancient Synagogues in Israel, Third-Seventh Century C.E.* (BAR International Series 499, Oxford, 1989), 69–84

C. Sainz de la Maza, *Alfonso de Valladolid: edición y estudio del Ms 'Lat. 6423' de la Biblioteca Apostolica Vaticana* (Madrid, 1990)

J. C. Salzmann, *Lehren und Ermahnen: Zur Geschichte des christlichen Wortgottesdienstes in den ersten drei Jahrhunderten* (Tübingen, 1994)

K.-G. Sandelin, *Wisdom as Nourisher* (Åbo, 1986)

E. P. Sanders, *Paul and Palestinian Judaism* (London, 1977)

——, with A. I. Baumgarten & A. Mendelson (edd.), *Jewish and Christian Self-Definition*, ii, *Aspects of Judaism in the Graeco-Roman Period* (London, 1981)

————, *Paul, the Law, and the Jewish People* (Philadelphia, 1983)

————, *Judaism: Practice and Belief, 63 B.C.E.–66 C.E.* (London, 1992)

————, *The Historical Figure of Jesus* (London, 1993)

J. T. Sanders, *Schismatics, Sectarians, Dissidents, Deviants: the First One Hundred Years of Jewish–Christian Relations* (London, 1993)

L. H. Schiffman, 'At the Crossroads: Tannaitic Perspectives on the Jewish–Christian Schism', in Sanders, with Baumgarten & Mendelson (edd.), *Self-Definition*, ii, 115–56

————, *Who Was a Jew?* (Hoboken, 1985)

————, *Reclaiming the Dead Sea Scrolls* (Philadelphia, 1994, repr. New York, 1995)

Carol J. Schlueter, *Filling up the Measure: Polemical Hyperbole in 1 Thessalonians 2.14–16* (Sheffield, 1994)

W. Schmithals, *Paul and the Gnostics* (E.T. Nashville, 1972)

J. Schoon-Janssen, *Umstrittene 'Apologien' in den Paulusbriefen: Studien zur rhetorischen Situation des 1. Thessalonicherbriefes, des Galaterbriefes und des Philipperbriefes* (Göttingen, 1991)

H. Schreckenberg, *Die christlichen Adversus-Judaeos-Texte und ihr literarisches und historisches Umfeld (1.–11. Jh.)* (Europäische Hochschulschriften, Theologie, 172; Frankfurt a.M., 1982, reprinted with Addenda et Corrigenda, 1990)

————, *Die christlichen Adversus-Judaeos-Texte (11.–13. Jh.): Mit einer Ikonographie des Judenthemas bis zum 4. Laterankonzil* (Europäische Hochschulschriften, Theologie, 335; Frankfurt a.M., 1991)

————, *Die christlichen Adversus-Judaeos-Texte und ihr literarisches und historisches Umfeld (13.-20. Jh.)* (Europäische Hochschulschriften, Theologie, 497; Frankfurt a.M., 1994)

E. Schürer, *Geschichte des jüdischen Volkes im Zeitalter Jesu Christi* (3rd-4th edn, Leipzig, 1901–9); E.T. *The History of the Jewish People in the Age of Jesus Christ*, revised by G. Vermes, F. Millar, M. Black, M. Goodman & P. Vermes (Edinburgh, i (1973), ii (1981), iii.1 (1986), iii.2 (1987))

I. L. Seeligmann, *The Septuagint Version of Isaiah* (Leiden, 1948)

E. von Severus, 'Gebet I', *RAC* viii (1972), cols. 1134–256

G. Sgherri, *Chiesa e Sinagoga nelle opere di Origene* (Milan, 1982)

M. Simon, *Verus Israel* (1948; E.T. (Oxford, 1986) of 2nd edn with Post-Scriptum (Paris, 1964))

————, *Recherches d'histoire judéo-chrétienne* (Paris, 1962)

O. Skarsaune, *The Proof from Prophecy, A Study in Justin Martyr's*

Proof-Text Tradition: Text-Type, Provenance, Theological Profile (Supplements to *NT*, 56, Leiden, 1987)

——, 'From Books to Testimonies: Remarks on the Transmission of the Old Testament in the Early Church', in Lowe, *Studies in Honor of David Flusser*, 207–19

——, 'The Neglected Story of Christian Philo-Semitism in Antiquity and the Early Middle Ages', *Mishkan* xxi (Jerusalem, 1994), 40–51

E. M. Smallwood, *Philonis Alexandrini Legatio ad Gaium* (Leiden, 1961)

M. Smith, *Palestinian Parties and Politics that Shaped the Old Testament* (1971, 2nd edn London, 1987)

G. N. Stanton, *A Gospel for a New People: Studies in Matthew* (Edinburgh, 1992)

——, 'Early Objections to the Resurrection of Jesus', in S. Barton & G. N. Stanton (edd.), *Resurrection: Essays in Honour of Leslie Houlden* (London, 1994), 78–93

G. Stemberger, 'Die Patriarchenbilder der Katakombe in der Via Latina im Lichte der jüdischen Tradition', *Kairos* N.F. xvi (1974), 19–78

——, *Juden und Christen im Heiligen Land: Palästina unter Konstantin und Theodosius* (Munich, 1987)

——, 'Exegetical Contacts between Christians and Jews in the Roman Empire', in Saebø (ed.), *Hebrew Bible*, 569–86

——, *Introduction to the Talmud and Midrash* (translated & edited by M. Bockmuehl, 2nd edn, Edinburgh, 1996)

Sacha Stern, *Jewish Identity in Early Rabbinic Writings* (AGJU xxiii, Leiden, New York & Köln, 1994)

H. L. Strack, *Jesus, die Häretiker und die Christen nach den ältesten jüdischen Angaben* (Leipzig, 1910)

G. Stroumsa, 'From Anti-Judaism to Antisemitism in Early Christianity?', in Limor & Stroumsa, *Contra Iudaeos*, 1–26

E. L. Sukenik, *Ancient Synagogues in Palestine and Greece* (London, 1934)

Justin Taylor, S. M., *Les Actes des deux apôtres*, v, *Commentaire historique (Act. 9,1–18, 22)* (Études bibliques N.S. 23, Paris, 1994)

Miriam S. Taylor, *Anti-Judaism and Early Christian Identity: A Critique of the Consensus* (Leiden, 1995)

T. C. G. Thornton, 'The Crucifixion of Haman and the Scandal of the Cross', *JTS* N.S. 37 (1986), 419–26

——, 'Christian Understandings of the *Birkath Ha-Minim* in the Eastern Roman Empire', *JTS* N.S. 38 (1987), 419–31

———, 'Jewish New Moon Festivals, Galatians 4:3–11 and Colossians 2:16', *JTS* N.S. 40 (1989), 97–100

———, 'The Stories of Joseph of Tiberias', *VC* 44 (1990), 54–63

H. Tränkle (ed.), *Q. S. F. Tertulliani Adversus Iudaeos* (Wiesbaden, 1964)

Hanne Trautner-Kromann, *Shield and Sword: Jewish Polemics against Christianity and the Christians in France and Spain 1100–1500* (E.T. Tübingen, 1993)

C. del Valle (ed.), *Polémica Judeo-Cristiana: Estudios* (Madrid, 1992)

G. Veltri, *Eine Tora für den König Talmai* (TSAJ 41, Tübingen, 1994)

———, 'Der griechische Targum Aquilas', in Hengel & Schwemer, *Die Septuaginta*, 92–115

———, 'Die Novelle 146 περὶ Ἑβραίων', in Hengel & Schwemer, *Die Septuaginta*, 116–30

B. L. Visotzky, *Fathers of the World. Essays in Rabbinic and Patristic Literatures* (Tübingen, 1995)

J. S. Vos, 'Legem statuimus: rhetorische Aspekte der Gesetzesdebatte zwischen Juden und Christen', in van Amersfoort & van Oort (edd.), *Juden und Christen in der Antike*, 44–60

J. C. Wagenseil, *Tela Ignea Satanae* (Altdorf, 1681)

B. Wander, *Trennungsprozesse zwischen Frühem Christentum und Judentum im 1. Jahrhundert n. Chr.* (Tübingen, 1994)

F. Watson, *Paul, Judaism and the Gentiles: a Sociological Approach* (Cambridge, 1989)

M. P. Weitzman, 'From Judaism to Christianity: The Syriac Version of the Hebrew Bible', in Lieu, North & Rajak, *The Jews among Pagans and Christians*, 147–73

M. F. Wiles, *The Divine Apostle* (Cambridge, 1967)

R. L. Wilken, *Judaism and the Early Christian Mind: A Study of Cyril of Alexandria's Exegesis and Theology* (New Haven and London, 1971)

———, *John Chrysostom and the Jews: Rhetoric and Reality in the Late 4th Century* (Berkeley, California, 1983)

A. Lukyn Williams, *Justin Martyr, The Dialogue with Trypho: Translation, Introduction and Notes* (London, 1930)

———, *Adversus Judaeos* (Cambridge, 1935)

S. G. Wilson, *Related Strangers: Jews and Christians 70–170 C.E.* (Minneapolis, 1995)

Y. H. Yerushalmi, *From Spanish Court to Italian Ghetto. Isaac Cardoso: A Study in Seventeenth-Century Marranism and Jewish Apologetics* (New York, 1971, reprinted Seattle & London, 1981)

INDEX OF REFERENCES

INDEX OF AUTHORS

INDEX OF SUBJECTS

Excommunication/Exclusion
- at Qumran 43, 45, 47, 53, 61, 66
- connected with cursing 46–7, 50, 51, 56–8, 59, 61–3, 64, 65
- connected with death penalty 7, 46–8, 50, 52, 55–66 *passim*
- during post–exilic period 43, 45, 46–53, 58, 59, 66
- in Christian community 43, 45, 53
- in Jewish community 3, 6–8; 43–66, 99–103, 108, 154
- of Christians from Jewish community 3, 10, 12, 99–103, 108, 154, 160
- relation to concept of covenant in Judaism 6, 7, 46–50, 52, 53, 54, 55, 57–66
- *See also under* 'Associates'; Christian community; Extirpation; Jewish community; Synagogue – ban; Temple – admission to

Extirpation (*kārēt*)
- meaning and relation to excommunication 45–6, 47, 52, 59–62

Fasting, Jewish 136–8, 234, 237

Greek
- Christian use of 26, 216–20 *passim*, 237n.
- Jewish use of 26, 27, 36, 202, 215–20 *passim*, 225, 237n.
Greek translations of the Bible 17, 27, 214, 215–16, 217
- Aquila 34, 35, 220, 222
- Septuagint 27–33, 34–5, 214, 217
  - charges of Jewish alteration of text 151
  - language of in Paul 14
  - use in Christian communities 26, 27–33
  - use in Jewish communities 26, 27, 29–33
- Symmachus 34, 35, 222
- Theodotion 34, 35, 222
- *See also* Greek; New Testament – use of Septuagint; Vernacular

Hammath Tiberias synagogue 216n.
Hebrew, knowledge and use of
- among Christians 33–5, 39, 215, 280, 285
- among Jews 33–5, 39, 40, 41, 206, 215–19, 220, 224, 237n., 277, 278, 281, 284, 285, 286, 287, 290, 293
- *See also* Scriptures – Christian knowledge of in Hebrew
Heretics (*see under* Imprecation – against apostates)

Idolatry 47, 55n., 60, 62, 64, 106, 107, 111, 114–22 *passim*
Imprecation
- against apostates (heretics) 8–9, 10, 57, 68, 70, 71, 82–4, 87, 89, 92–9, 108, 110, 159
- against Christians 3, 8–11, 36–7, 67–111, 157–8, 160, 226, 240–3
- against Gentiles 71, 82, 85, 87–93, 95–7, 99, 108, 109
- against Jesus 10, 67, 72, 75, 94, 95, 102, 154–5, 158, 237–8, 240
- and purpose of 12th Benediction 8–11, 77–96, 158, 241–2
- within Christian community 10
- *See also* Sadducees, cursing of
Invective
- against Christians as criminals 18, 163, 164, 165–6, 170
- against Christians by Jews 14, 18
- against Christians by pagan authors 18
- against Jews by Christians 10, 23
- against Jews by pagan authors 18–19
- against synagogue 10
- within Christian community 14
- *See also* Brigandage; Polemic
Israel
- as a title 182, 187
- biblical, Christian relation to 12–13, 149–50, 186–99
Italian, use of in Jewish community 41, 277, 278, 284, 285, 286–90

Jamnia 69, 80–1, 82, 83, 86, 91, 96, 97, 100–1, 108–9
Jesus 104–7, 117
- Jewish polemic against 1, 3, 16, 17–20, 39, 67, 72–3, 77, 102, 117, 121, 139, 168–74 *passim*, 177–9, 204, 237–8, 248, 255–7, 290, 295
- pagan polemic against 1, 3, 17–19, 162–75
- son of Pantera (Pandera) 20, 95, 105, 107, 177
- teaching of 11–12, 204
- *See also under* Brigandage; Death of Jesus; Imprecation; Magic – charges of; Messiah (messianism); Prophecy, false; Resurrection; Toledoth Jeshu
Jewish Christianity 9, 10, 20, 68–9, 73–7, 98, 99, 109, 149, 182
- *See also* Nazarene, sect
Jewish community
- authority in 6, 159–60
- degree of unity in 1, 3–8, 11, 13n., 43, 44, 97–8, 108, 110, 131, 160
- discipline and punishment in 6, 10, 13, 43–66, 99–102, 108, 110, 153
- influenced by contact with Christianity 19, 201–2, 204, 227, 258, 259